HAZZAN
MORDECAI GUSTAV HEISER

HAZZAN MORDECAI GUSTAV HEISER

An Artist, His Art, and the Cantor Tradition in America

Gilya Gerda Schmidt

The Charles K. Wolfe Music Series
Ted Olson, Series Editor

University of Tennessee Press / Knoxville

The Charles K. Wolfe Music Series was launched in honor of the late Charles K. Wolfe (1943–2006), whose pioneering work in the study of American vernacular music brought a deepened understanding of a wide range of American music to a worldwide audience. In recognition of Dr. Wolfe's approach to music scholarship, the series will include books that investigate genres of folk and popular music as broadly as possible.

Copyright © 2024 by The University of Tennessee Press / Knoxville.
All Rights Reserved. Manufactured in the United States of America.
First Edition.

Library of Congress Cataloging-in-Publication Data

Names: Schmidt, Gilya Gerda, author.
Title: Hazzan Mordecai Gustav Heiser : an artist, his art, and the cantor tradition in America / Gilya Gerda Schmidt.
Description: First edition. | Knoxville : The University of Tennessee Press, 2024. | Series: The Charles K. Wolfe music series | Includes bibliographical references and index. | Summary: "When Gilya Gerda Schmidt met him in 1986, Cantor Heiser had spent forty-six of his eighty-one years as a US citizen. He had assumed the cantorate at Congregation B'nai Israel in the East End of Pittsburgh, Pennsylvania, in 1942. A master of the cantor's art, he was renowned for his style, arrangements, and deeply affecting voice. In this book, Schmidt melds decades of archival research, conservation efforts, family interviews, and trips to Jerusalem and Berlin into a critical reconstruction of the life and vision of Hazzan Mordecai Gustav Heiser in the multiple contexts that shaped him. Coming of age in Berlin in the afterglow of the Second German Empire, young Gustav had tasted European Jewish culture in a rare state of refinement and modernity. But by January 30, 1940, when he reached New York with his wife and two-and-a-half-year-old daughter, Cantor Heiser had lost nearly all of his living family relations to the extermination programs of the German Reich, and narrowly survived incarceration at Sachsenhausen himself. While Cantor Heiser's art was steeped in nineteenth-century tradition, Schmidt contends that Heiser's music was a powerful affirmation of Jewish life in the twentieth century. In a final chapter, Schmidt describes his influence on the American cantorate and American culture and society"— Provided by publisher.
Identifiers: LCCN 2024008495 (print) | LCCN 2024008496 (ebook) | ISBN 9781621908722 (hardcover) | ISBN 9781621908739 (pdf) | ISBN 9781621908906 (kindle edition)
Subjects: LCSH: Heiser, Mordecai Gustav, 1905–1989. | Congregation B'nai Israel (Pittsburgh, Pa.) | Cantors (Judaism)—Pennsylvania—Pittsburgh—Biography. | Synagogue music—Pennsylvania—Pittsburgh—History and criticism. | Jewish chants—History and criticism.
Classification: LCC ML420.H358 S36 2024 (print) | LCC ML420.H358 (ebook) | DDC 296.4/62092 [B]—dc23/eng/20240227
LC record available at https://lccn.loc.gov/2024008495
LC ebook record available at https://lccn.loc.gov/2024008496

To Judith Heiser Stein z"l and Alvin Stein

*Adele Stein Sufrin and Warren Jay Sufrin,
with Rena Anna and Tanner Kennedy with Asher Judah,
Ilana Pearl and Travis Kaufman, Leah Aliza, and Dana Arielle*

*Shari Stein Klafter and Mark Klafter,
with Naomi Ellen and Rebecca*

*Betty Sue Stein Rich and Larry Rich,
with Andrew and Ellie,*

And to the memory of

*Hazzan Mordecai Gustav Heiser
and Elly Hochmann Heiser,*

And to the family members who perished in the Holocaust.

May their memory be for a blessing.

CONTENTS

Foreword	xi
Ted Olson	
Preface. Judith Heiser Stein Remembers	xix
Acknowledgments	xxi
Introduction	1
Chapter 1: European Jewry until the Holocaust: Berlin as the Center of German Jewish Culture and Religion	7
Chapter 2: American Jewry: Pittsburgh Plays an Important Role in the Development of the American Cantorate	43
Chapter 3: Hazzan Mordecai Gustav Heiser—The Sweet Singer of B'nai Israel: One Example of a European-trained Cantor's Contribution to the American Cantorate	133
Conclusion	241
Glossary	245
Notes	249
Bibliography	295
Index	305

ILLUSTRATIONS

Following page 111

Gustav Heiser *Geburtsurkunde*, 1934
Gustav Heiser *Kantorenschule Zeugnis*, 1929
Aron Friedmann *Schir Lischlomo* cover
Neisser letter for Cantor Heiser, 1938
Elly Hochmann birth certificate, 1934
Heiser Hochmann Jewish ceremony, 1935
Judith Heiser Birth Certificate, 1936
Heiser *Hochschule Bescheinigung*, 1937
Hochschule class picture, 1938
Heiser *Lehranstalt* exam Leo Baeck, 1939
Gustav Heiser passport, 1939
Heiser *Sammeltransport*, 1939
Heiser permit to leave Kitchener Camp, 1940
Bnai Israel Synagogue, 2016
Bnai Israel building detail
Hebrew School graduation, 1943
Heiser naturalization front, 1945
Heiser naturalization back, 1945
Heiser Carnegie program, 1949
Heiser Carnegie program, 1949
Confirmation, 1950
Heiser Certificate, 1954
Five Cantors, 1956
Judy Heiser Stein as bride, 1957
Israel Bonds participants with Cantor and Mrs. Heiser, 1972
Heiser 30th anniversary concert, 1970

Cantor Heiser as *mohel*, in *Jewish Chronicle*, Vol. 11, No. 34, October 12, 1972
Cantor Heiser's 40th anniversary, 1980
Betty Sue Stein and Cantor Heiser, 1989
Cantor M. G. Heiser
Heiser Stein family (1975)
Mayor Caliguiri and Cantor Heiser, 1983
Cantor M. G. Heiser in B'nai Israel Sanctuary
Cantor Heiser chanting prayer
Cantor Mordecai G. and Elly Heiser, 1960
Heiser Y'varech'cha notated by Schmidt, 2018
Feidman concert program, 1989
Heiser grave in B'nai Israel cemetery, after 1992
Weissensee Cemetery, Berlin, 1999
Fragment of Heiser family letter
B'nai Israel Sanctuary with *Hazzan* Heiser, Rabbi Marcovitz, and Cantor Haalman, 1980

FOREWORD

IT IS DESTINED

Music as a Spiritual Homecoming

Growing from Gilya Gerda Schmidt's lifelong commitment to deepening personal as well as public understanding of Jewish heritage, *Hazzan Mordecai Gustav Heiser: An Artist, His Art, and the Cantor Tradition in America* is "a spiritual homecoming of sorts." As revealed in the interview with Professor Schmidt, this book is based on research rooted in the author's personal connection to the book's subject; the book is also motivated more generally to exploring of "an element of liminality" in the experience of Jewish immigrants to the U.S. during the twentieth century. A committed Jew as well as a scholar of Judaic Studies, Professor Schmidt wrote this book to document the life and music of Cantor Heiser, an immigrant and Jew "who became a proud American and left his mark on the Jewish community in Pittsburgh, as well as the city and the Tri-States region at large, and beyond." Cantor Heiser lived a difficult yet ultimately triumphant life that had a lasting impact on his own community and that could make a profound impact— Professor Schmidt believes—on other communities today.

"Human beings need spiritual connections to something bigger than themselves," Professor Schmidt asserts in this interview. And how might people today become spiritually connected? Professor Schmidt's book suggests that "Music, and specifically singing, is an excellent vehicle for the journey to the divine." Accordingly, this book offers a detailed and illuminating study of a music tradition associated with Jewish faith as practiced by one charismatic cantor. The following interview with Professor Schmidt was conducted by Ted Olson during February 2024.

An Interview with Professor Gilya Gerda Schmidt

Can you relate why you wrote this book?
Cantor Heiser died in 1989 at age 84. A life well lived, but those of us who were close to him were devastated (see my letter to the editor, p. 108). I decided then that, besides writing that letter, I would collect any tapes that existed of his music to create some sort of memorial. In 1991 I finished my Ph.D. and moved to Tuscaloosa, Alabama, as a post-doc. I had collected a number of cassette tapes that Cantor Heiser's daughter and various congregants had in their possession, and took them with me to Tuscaloosa. Although I decided to help the Jewish students at Hillel with their programming and religious services in addition to teaching, I still had quite a bit of time on my hands, and went through the tapes. Most were nothing usable, but some had snippets of services that someone recorded when Cantor Heiser was singing. I made two memorial cassettes and someone at the University of Alabama was nice enough to make copies of the sets which I gave to my congregation in Pittsburgh, Pennsylvania, for any congregants who wanted a memento from the Heiser era. Coincidentally, while listening to the tapes, I also learned to sing many more prayers than I had known in Pittsburgh.

I always knew that I wanted to write a book eventually, but it's not the kind of book one writes for tenure or promotion. Over the summer, I went back to Pittsburgh and went through all of the papers that Cantor Heiser's daughter had. I copied what she wanted to keep and took everything else with me to Tuscaloosa. That's as far as I got 33 years ago. Two years later, I got a tenure-track position in Knoxville, Tennessee, and that was the end of anything to do with the Heiser project for a while. I put the documents and tapes in my spare room and focused on publish or perish.

After tenure and promotion to associate professor in 1995, and during seven months in Israel in 1996, I started thinking about the Heiser material again. I had in the meantime improved leading services at my synagogue in Knoxville, and the services were all versions of what Cantor Heiser used to sing. While I was no cantor, the congregations I attended both in Birmingham and then in Knoxville, enjoyed my services. Leading services kept me spiritually connected to Cantor Heiser, which in a way kept me grounded while finding my way professionally in a very challenging world.

My research has always had a personal connection as well as an element of liminality. This resulted in books that hovered between two worlds. Martin Buber's world was German and Jewish, at other times Zionist and traditional, or visual art vs. text study. Yehuda Halevi, a Spanish Jew, was experienced through the eyes of Franz Rosenzweig, a German Jewish scholar; Friedrich Schleiermacher, a Christian theologian, chose to dialogue with a Jewish head of household. Roma and Sinti existed in limbo in Austria, the Holocaust cast a long shadow in my hometown in Germany, and this book connects the European cantorate with that in America, and the Eastern European version with that in the West. Interestingly, for this project I was able to draw on all areas of research and teaching that I have explored for the past 35 years. Many of the sources I cite, excluding the Heiser material, are on my bookshelves at home.

Every aspect of writing this book was painstaking. I was fortunate to have excellent and talented assistants during the past two decades, who did a lot of the spade work, such as converting the very fragile cassettes to CDs, sleuthing on the internet to find newspaper articles about Cantor Heiser's activities, and making 38 music clips, 20 of which we put on YouTube and which are the basis for the music in this book. Over years I transcribed the six service fragments that survived, second by second (see Chapter 3). Many of the documents from Germany needed to be translated. I spent one entire summer creating a family tree, and spent many hours in the libraries of Hebrew Union College/Jewish Institute of Religion and Hebrew University in Jerusalem, and Hebrew Union College in Cincinnati, Ohio, and the Heinz Archives in Pittsburgh, looking for the sheet music for Cantor Heiser's services. All the while, I researched, translated, and published other books and articles and wrote papers for professional conferences.

In 2015, I retired with the intention of completing this book. My friend, Cantor Heiser's daughter Judith, by that time had a debilitating chronic illness, and I was hoping to finish the project so she could still enjoy it. Unfortunately, I myself contracted an autoimmune disease, so that I had to shelve the finished manuscript, not being able to shop it to publishers for several years. Fortunately, I recovered somewhat, so that I could make some adjustments to the ms, and here we are. Sadly, my friend Judy succumbed to her illness in 2021.

So why did I write this book? There is a term in Yiddish, it is "beshehrt," it is destined. And so it is.

How might this book contribute to our collective understanding today of the Jewish experience in the twentieth century (and earlier)?
The U.S. Holocaust Memorial Museum in Washington, D.C., admonishes us to collect any life experiences available in connection with the

Holocaust through witness testimony, because the Jewish world consists of a mosaic of experiences. Each life is a window into the wonder that is humanity. The Talmud teaches that "he who saves one life saves an entire universe." This is my intention with this book, to save and preserve the life and art of Cantor Mordecai Gustav Heiser. Jewish existence for the past 4,000 years has been varied, with kingship and slavery, autonomy and homelessness, admiration and hatred. Each life is but one spec in the collectivity that is the Jewish people, yet this instance contributes significantly to the picture of what it is to be a Jew in today's world or over the centuries. What would the world be without Einstein or Bernstein, or Cantor Heiser? I make it clear in this study that Cantor Heiser, immigrant and Jew, became a proud American and left his mark on the Jewish community in Pittsburgh, as well as the city and the Tri-States region at large, and beyond. But from Cantor Heiser's story we will also understand the evil that has and does exist in the world, which robbed him of at least nine family members.

Can you summarize the major contributions of this book to the academic field of Judaic Studies?
As stated above, Judaism values the accounts of individuals for their contribution to Jewish culture, religion and society at large. While Sinti and Roma were reluctant to collect the horrors that they experienced during the Holocaust, Jews were eager to testify to their nightmares. There is a place in the academic field of Judaic Studies for this book, which contributes to our understanding of German Jewish history, antisemitism and the Holocaust, the cantorate in Europe and the United States, American Judaism, Zionism, and Israel. These are all areas that I taught for 23 1/2 years at the University of Tennessee, with visiting lectureships in Germany and China.

Can you summarize the major contributions of this book to the academic field of American Studies?
When I taught about antisemitism, I would also teach about Jim Crow, and when I taught the Holocaust, I would also teach about slavery. While there are differences, there are a number of similarities. Likewise, the early music of the Eastern European cantorate that I describe has more in common with Gregorian chants or Gospel music than with European art music. Abraham Joshua Heschel marched with Dr. Martin Luther King because he recognized that the Black struggle was his and yes, the Jewish people's

struggle. I just saw the Bob Marley film, and the very Jewish Exodus experience became his most acclaimed album. Heschel was ordained as a rabbi by the same teacher in Berlin who taught Cantor Heiser, Alexander Guttmann. Human suffering, joy of music, and the desire for freedom are universally human, but certainly part of the American experience.

Can you summarize the major contributions of this book to music studies generally and to our collective understanding of the musical traditions/styles/repertoires associated with the American cantorate?
Preserving the meager documentation of Cantor Heiser's rich musical treasure was a key goal for this book. Music is a universal language and scholars all over the world are "zamler," collectors of the music of ethnic groups, composers, and performers so that these resources are not lost for posterity. Only since the end of World War II are there effective professional associations for cantors in the United States that offer support and services, such as a placement service and retirement fund. Previous to that, in the U.S. as well as Europe, a cantor was pretty much on his own. Few had annual positions, they would occasionally garner a gig in a community, at a wedding or a bar mitzvah. The pay in general was poor, so that they had to supplement their incomes with regular jobs as butchers, shoemakers, tailors, etc. Training was haphazard, depending on location and opportunity, such as itinerant cantors (see Cantor Samuel Vigoda's story, p. 147 at the top). The texts for specific worship services until the nineteenth century and the advent of the Reform Movement were Orthodox in the Ashkenazi world, based to a great degree on Psalms, but the melodies sprung from a deep well of tradition, retained differently by each individual. For the most part music was not written down, but in the soul of the precentor, and learning consisted of practice as a chorister. The repertoires were highly individualized as well.

What did a young boy hear and see from a perhaps wandering cantor in his childhood? Who were his teachers and what did he learn from them? And what additional sources was he or today also she exposed to as an adult and a professional cantor? There are as many answers as there are stars in the sky. In Chapter 3, this book documents as many of Cantor Heiser's influences as I could locate.

Finally, performance styles likewise differ according to the personality, but also depending on the geographical region. Eastern European cantors sang with great passion, to the brink of what one might term ecstasy, as in the Hasidic *niggunim* (tunes), for example. Their musical modes expressed sadness, sorrow, their prayers longing for freedom and for a homeland, but when praising God, on Shabbat and on religious holidays, their first and foremost mode of expression was joy and glory. Some of these melodies are ancient, though not notated until the nineteenth century, and are figuratively carved in stone, such as the famous Kol Nidre. A number of these types of cantors made it to the U.S. from the 1880s on, and Eastern European *hazzanut* experienced a golden era until the Holocaust. Notice that the large wave of immigration of German Jews in the 1840s did not have the same effect. Cantor Heiser bridged two traditions, the Eastern European, and two specific composers from the German tradition, Louis Lewandowski and Salomon Sulzer, with Eastern roots themselves, who updated cherished traditional Western repertoires for an "enlightened" Jewish community (Jewish Enlightenment in Germany and then Eastern Europe introduced European Jewry to society at large, including opera).

I argue in the book that Cantor Heiser, who lost his father and mother-in-law as well as brother and sister and other in-laws in the Holocaust, lived his life as a memorial service for his lost family by choosing Eastern European composers for his services on the one hand, and Lewandowski and Sulzer, whose compositions were carefully preserved traditional melodies "handed down by God to Moses on Mount Sinai," on the other.

When I first started traveling to Israel for research, my host asked if I could bring him some cassettes with Gregorian chants. I didn't understand then why, but Gregorian chants are very close to traditional Jewish liturgy because they used modes instead of the scales of Western art music. Anyone familiar with a tradition that uses a modal system, such as Arabic, Indian, Persian, would be interested in Cantor Heiser's traditional Jewish liturgy, because of the similarities. (I am not a musicologist, but I can hear the similarities when listening to music from those traditions as well as the Gregorian chants).

Is there anything else you would like to convey to your readers?
Human beings need spiritual connections to something bigger than themselves. Music, and specifically singing, is an excellent vehicle for the journey to the divine. Whether this connection happens, often depends on the opportunity to find a spiritual guide, who has the ability to reach the door to a person's soul, providing the key that opens the door. Chapter 3 in this book guides the reader through the worship services for six major Jewish holidays—Slichot, Rosh Hashanah, Yom Kippur (Kol Nidre and Ne'ilah), Shavuot, and Shabbat—which the reader can listen to simultaneously on

YouTube by simply typing M. G. Heiser in the search bar. Cantor Heiser had a special talent for connecting the words of a particular occasion with the appropriate music which precisely conveyed the sentiments of the words. Since much of the liturgy for the major holidays is quite elaborate, one may ask, what is the difference between an opera singer and a cantor? Many cantors enjoy singing opera, some switch entirely to opera. Others, however, devote themselves to mostly sacred music, and the purpose of their singing is quite different from that of an opera singer. It is not primarily the technical aspect of the art that is most important, but the cantor's ability to lead a person to God. In other words, a cantor's singing is not a performance, but an expression of the soul. Cantorial singing is personal, the cantor knows the individuals for whom he/she sings, and their spiritual needs. Hence he/she is called a "sheliach tsibur," a messenger of the people. An effective cantor is the heart of the community. In the case of B'nai Israel, Cantor Heiser's death eventually also led to the demise of the congregation. Although few of his contemporaries are still alive (I did "meet" a cantor who sang in Cantor Heiser's male choir for *Ne'ilah*), the children are now in their fifties and remember with longing the B'nai Israel services from their childhood. For some of them being able to listen to the music clips and read the book will be a spiritual homecoming of sorts.

Ted Olson
East Tennessee State University

PREFACE

JUDITH HEISER STEIN REMEMBERS

When I visited the Stein family on July 12, 2016 (for the last time, as it turned out), Judy Heiser handed me the following short autobiography. I reproduce it here in its entirety.

> My name is Judith Heiser Stein. My parents were Mordecai and Elly Heiser. All 3 of us were born in Germany before WWII. We were lucky. My mother had cousins in Pittsburgh who sent visas [sic: rather, affidavits for visas] to us to come to the United States.
>
> My father was both a rabbinical and cantorial student in Berlin. During Kristallnacht, his beautiful synagogue was bombed, but not entirely destroyed. It has been only partially restored as a museum.
>
> Some of my father's friends were picked up for violating curfew. While consoling their families, he was arrested twice and sent to Mauthausen [sic] and Sachsenhausen. Luckily, they let him go both times. He was sent to a refugee camp in Kitchener, England. My mom and I stayed to prepare to leave Germany. Our entire German family gave us their precious Judaic possessions to keep safe in the U.S.
>
> A short time later, my mother received a letter from my dad that said 'You know I don't write a letter on Shabbat, but today I am.' That was the sign between the 2 of them which meant we should get out of Berlin FAST.
>
> My mother and I left by train to meet my Dad in Dover, England. While we were passing through Belgium, my family's valuable possessions were confiscated. My first memory is being in a crib behind a window and waving to my Father when we all met up in England. Five days later, WWII began and all borders were closed.

We arrived in NYC in February 1940. Our cousins, Sophie and Joseph Weiss, who had arranged for our visas, met us in Pittsburgh. My dad had an interview with Rabbi Freehof of Rodef Shalom, who arranged a meeting with Rabbi Lichter of B'nai Israel. Rabbi Lichter hired him as an assistant for the cantor. It wasn't long before Mordecai G. Heiser became the cantor of B'nai Israel. He was there through about 5 rabbis over [sic: nearly] 50 years.

My parents tried to save the rest of my family from the Holocaust but it was too late to get them out of Germany. They all died in concentration camps.

My parents spoke very little of their earlier lives in Germany, so not much is known of that time.

My father died in 1989 as a result of being hit by a car crossing the street in front of the Essex House, where my parents lived. My mom lived there until her death in 1992, after she met her first great-grandchildren.

None of my close family survived the Holocaust, other than my parents. I created my own family with the help of my husband, Alvin. We have 3 daughters, Adele Sufrin, Shari Klafter, and Betty Sue Rich. They have given me 7 granddaughters and 1 grandson.

ACKNOWLEDGMENTS

The beauty of Congregation B'nai Israel will forever remain in my mind and my soul. Recording the journey and conserving the music of one of the most enduring members of the congregation, *Hazzan* Mordecai Gustav Heiser, was only possible with the help of a diverse group of individuals.

My dear late friend, Cantor Heiser's daughter Judith Heiser Stein, allowed me to copy and scan many family documents, correspondence, and pictures and to include the recordings of her father. Sadly, Judy succumbed to years of suffering from a chronic illness in July 2021 (13 of Av 5781). May her memory be for a blessing. We shall miss her tremendously. I am especially sad that she will not be able to enjoy the publication of this book which, as a retired teacher, she hoped to give to all of the Pittsburgh libraries. Cantor Heiser's granddaughter Betty Sue Stein Rich gave me permission to use the amateur recordings that include her beautiful voice. Most recently, the genealogical efforts of great-granddaughter Rena Sufrin Kennedy have elucidated relationships, added geographical sites, and discovered additional relatives to add to the family tree. I have also benefited from the help of Michael R. Shaughnessy, Associate Professor of German and Rena's teacher at Washington & Jefferson College, who, more than a decade ago, sent me a link to an electronic archive of Jewish newspapers from the Pittsburgh area. For all of their help, I am deeply grateful.

Equally as important to this project was my teacher and friend Professor Eliyahu Schleifer from Hebrew Union College/Jewish Institute of Religion in Jerusalem, who contributed many hours of his valuable time and his expertise to working with me through the snippets of B'nai Israel services available for analysis. Professor Schleifer is a master of synagogue music and a legend among cantorial students in the Reform Movement who spend their first year of studies at HUC/JIR in Jerusalem and, until his retirement, became his charges and mentees.[1] Although my introduction to Professor Schleifer was not as a student, I became his informal student over more than a decade, whenever I had the opportunity to spend time in Jerusalem. There are no words that can adequately thank Professor

Schleifer for his guidance, for sharing his knowledge, and, above all, for his patience. Without his help I would not dare write about Jewish music at all. At one of our meetings, he presented me with Israel Alter's introduction to the study of Jewish Music and bibliography with these well wishes: "Upon your embarkment on the ship of Jewish musicology, happy sailing." I have certainly taken my studies seriously, but there is so much more to learn.

Additional thanks are due to a group of loyal friends in Jerusalem who supported my work and my well-being when I spent extended periods of time there working on various book projects, including the Jewish art book *The Art and Artists of the Fifth Zionist Congress 1901: Heralds of a New Age* (Syracuse University Press, 2003); adding the final touches to my translation and expansion of Erika Thurner's *National Socialism and Gypsies in Austria* (University of Alabama Press, 1998); and negotiating the Buber Zionism project with his late granddaughter, Judith Buber Agassi (*The First Buber*, Syracuse University Press, 1999), as well as this project. Among these precious friends are the late Dr. David Morrison (ben David) and his dear late wife, Jo Hess; Professor Jo Milgrom and her late husband, Professor Jacob Milgrom; Professor Eliyahu and Aya Schleifer; Carol Caplan; and Rabbi Shaul Feinberg and his wife, Tanya.

Much gratitude goes to the librarians, among them Jackie Singer and Adina Feldstern, at the HUC/JIR library in Jerusalem, where I spent many hours over two decades searching for and finding much of the sheet music Cantor Heiser used in his services. In 2013, the Klau Library at HUC/JIR in Cincinnati and Laurel S. Wolfson and colleagues were especially helpful in locating additional sheet music; Ms. Wolfson has been helpful with additional information since then. At Hebrew University in Jerusalem, in the Music Archives, I owe gratitude to Gila Flam, who assisted me in learning their cataloging system and locating several important pieces for this project. One of Cantor Heiser's admirers was Richard Berlin from Pittsburgh, PA, who studied to become a cantor at JTS in New York, graduating in 2000. For his M.A. thesis, he acquired Cantor Heiser's music library from the family and catalogued it; he also wrote a study about the Partitur, based on one selection that Cantor Heiser had in his collection, "U'vchen Yiskadash." Ina Cohen from the JTS library in New York kindly found the thesis for me, which I much appreciated.

Here at home, I am grateful to the University of Tennessee, to my late department head Charles H. Reynolds, who sadly died on January 25, 2017, and to my colleagues in the Department of Religious Studies, which I headed through much of this research. I owe special thanks to Erika

Magnuson, our work-study student at the time, who digitized all of the very frail cassette tapes from the Heiser-Stein family that contained parts of services. As of 2023, I thank the current administration, Dean Terri Lee, College of Arts and Sciences, and my successor as Head of Religious Studies, Professor Rosalind I. J. Hackett, for leave time in 2010 and 2013 to advance this project. In 2015, Acting Department Head Rachelle Scott negotiated a post-retirement agreement that allowed me to carry out additional research. The current Head of Religious Studies, Professor Christine Shepardson, as well as my successor as Director of the Fern and Manfred Steinfeld Program in Judaic Studies, Associate Professor Helene Sinnreich, continue to support my research beyond the post-retirement agreement, especially in this critical stage of revisions, which I much appreciate. Thanks are also due to Jennifer Ware, one of Professor Sinnreich's student assistants, for proofreading the manuscript and for lending support in other final matters. Not least I am grateful for spade work by my long-time research assistant, Ashley Combest, then a Ph.D. candidate in the Department of English, whose technical and editorial expertise make this work so much more professional. Ashley created all of the clips from Cantor Heiser's services that we put on YouTube as well as additional ones. And most recently, the task of assistant was taken on by Klayton Tietjen, then an M.A. student in the Department of History, who brought an interest in history and a knowledge of music to the task of completing this project. As of July 2016, we created a YouTube channel for twenty of the music clips that are discussed in this book. Much gratitude goes to Klayton for exploring this venue and for creating the account and the YouTube channel as well as uploading the music. In the summer of 2017, Klayton took time before embarking on his Ph.D. program in French here at UT to help with additional research and manuscript corrections. Thank you, Klayton, for going the extra mile! In December 2015, I retired from teaching to focus on finishing this challenging project.

Thanks to the post-retirement agreement, in July 2016 I had the opportunity to visit Pittsburgh and conduct research at the Senator John Heinz History Center Library and Archives. Much gratitude goes to David Schlitt and his staff at the Rauh Jewish Archive, who helped me the week of July 10, 2016. I also was able to visit with the Stein family once again, sharing with them the progress on the project and consulting with them on matters still pending.

Before moving to Tuscaloosa, Alabama, from Pittsburgh, Pennsylvania, in 1991, I decided that I would collect Cantor Heiser's music, as much as that was possible, and create a set of memorial tapes. His daughter, Judy, was kind enough to lend me all of the amateur cassettes she had of his services, and many of the congregants contributed tapes Cantor Heiser had made for them to read Torah, chant the Haftarah, or learn prayers. From these I culled what I thought interesting for a set of memorial tapes for the congregation. With the help of a kind and generous colleague at the University of Alabama in Tuscaloosa who helped with the technology, we created a set of two cassette tapes with a selection of prayers and hymns and a brief biography as well as a print version of a speech Cantor Heiser gave in 1979 on the anniversary of Kristallnacht. I donated the tapes to B'nai Israel for distribution to interested congregants. To all who contributed resources to the tape project, my deepest gratitude.

Over the past decade, I wrote and presented papers on this research at various conferences: the International Humanities and Arts Conference in Honolulu, Hawaii ("A Study in *Hazzanut*—Mordecai Gustav Heiser, the Sweet Singer of B'nai Israel," 2010); Association for Jewish Studies, Washington, D.C. (poster presentation on "Cantor Mordecai Gustav Heiser, B'nai Israel, Pittsburgh, PA," 2011); a works-in-progress session for our Modern Germany and Central Europe research seminar at the University of Tennessee in Knoxville ("Mordecai Gustav Heiser—The Sweet Singer of B'nai Israel," Professor Peter Höyng, Emory University, respondent, 2013); the International Humanities and Arts Conference, Honolulu, Hawaii ("The European Cantor as a Bridge Between European and American Sacred Jewish Music," 2014); Association for Jewish Studies, Boston, MA ("The Class of 1939: The Last Students of the Hochschule für die Wissenschaft des Judentums," 2015); the International Humanities and Arts Conference, Honolulu, Hawaii ("Three Nineteenth-Century Reformers of Jewish Liturgical Music and Their Influence on Twentieth-Century Liturgy," 2017); and the International Humanities and Arts Conference, Honolulu, Hawaii ("Hochschule für die Wissenschaft des Judentums: The Class of 1939—The Teachers," 2019). In January 2020, I presented a paper on the difficulty of escaping from Europe during the Nazi years, entitled "Falling Between the Cracks in Nazi Germany," again for the colleagues of the International Humanities and Arts Conference in Honolulu. This presentation included Cantor Heiser's precarious situation as well as that of several other survivors. It was also the last professional conference I attended in person, as everything shut down on account of the Covid Pandemic.

Recently, I had occasion to correspond with several individuals for permission to use their organizations' materials. Heartfelt thanks to Toby

Tabachnick, editor of the *Pittsburgh Jewish Chronicle*; Eric Lidji, director of the Rauh Jewish Archive at the Heinz History Center; Cantor Stephen Stein, executive director of the Cantors Assembly; and acclaimed Pittsburgh photographer Hans Jonas.

Huge thanks are due to Thomas Wells, associate director for UT Press, who believed in what I had created and shepherded the manuscript with a sure hand through the review process, as well as the very erudite and perceptive readers who contributed crucial and unusual source suggestions, the Press editorial board, Lucy Reynolds, the copy editor for this project, and Stephanie Thompson, designer and typesetter, all of whose support was invaluable for the publication of this book.

Much has changed in the thirty years since I first made the memorial tapes for B'nai Israel, especially my health. I would be remiss if I did not express my deepest gratitude to my doctors, especially Dr. Christy C. Park, my rheumatologist, and the wonderful nurses at the UT Infusion Services, as well as my team of physical therapists under the leadership of Matthew Smith, who, together with my family—Richard, Christina, and Romi—and many loyal friends, keep me alive and mobile.

This book truly did take a village as well as a gigantic mental leap by the author.

@ Gilya G. Schmidt and Rena S. Kennedy
2016/2023

Anna Daniels, Bakersfield
Cousin of Elly via Sophie Weiss

Louis Younger
The Working Man's Store
Bakersfield, CA

Monty Daniels
Fruit of the Loom, New York
Nephew of Anna Daniels,
Cousin of Judith Heiser Stein

Max Birnbaum, Elly Heiser's Uncle
Brother of Eidel Birnbaum Hochmann, and
Father of Sophie Birnbaum in Pittsburgh, PA

Sophie Birnbaum +
Daughter of Max Birnbaum
Sophie married Josef Weiss
in Pittsburgh, PA

Josef Weiss (sponsor), Pittsburgh, PA
Married Sophie Birnbaum,
Max Birnbaum is Adele Birnbaum
Hochmann's brother,
Elly Heiser's uncle

Samuel Weiss (sponsor), Pittsburgh, PA
Cousin of Josef Weiss

Berta (Bayla, Betty, or Betti) Hochmann Lieberson
b. 09/30/1906 Berlin
lived in Berlin
dep. 12/09/1942 to Auschwitz
d. in Holocaust, in Koblenz M. B.

+

Leiser (Leo) Lieberson
b. 03/14/1904 Winnitza, Russia
lived in Berlin
dep. 12/09/1942 to Auschwitz
d. in Holocaust, in Koblenz M. B.

Leo Hochmann,
Brother of Juda Hochmann
b. 1900 in Gemilov, Galicia
d. Holocaust?
NOT in Koblenz M.B.

Salomon (Sally) Hochmann,
b. 02/22/1910
d. 02/14/1928 Berlin
Grave in Weissensee Cemetary, Berlin
Field F, Section V, Row 13, No. 75008,
stone 1931

Gumbert Heuser,
Merchant

(Tovia) Tobias Heuser
b. 02/20/1847
Breitenbach
d. 05/03/1913 Detmold
n. Kassel

Adele[a] (Eidel) Birnbaum Hochmann +
05/20/1877 Gemilov (Grzymalov), Galicia
Married Juda Hochmann 06/07/1915
Mother of Elly Hochmann Heiser
dep. 11/27/1941 to Riga
d. 11/30/1941 Riga
in Koblenz M. B.

Juda Samson Hochmann (Cohen)
b. 10/20/1877
Father of Elly Hochmann Heiser
d. 07/20/1922 Berlin
Grave in Weissensee Cemetary,
Berlin
Section F V, Row 10, No. 62476,
stone 1922

Isaak (Yitzchok) Heiser
b. 01/08/1872 Lohne,
Hessen-Nassau
Father of Mordecai Gustav H.
dep. 08/17/1942 to Theresiens
09/19/1942 to Treblinka acc. t
Koblenz M. B., to Minsk acc.
Till letter
in Koblenz M. B.

Meta Hochmann Heiser
b. 09/20/1905 Berlin
dep. 11/27/1941 to Riga
d. 11/30/1941 Riga
in Koblenz M. B.

Elly (Elke) Hochmann Heiser
b. 10/31/1911 Berlin
Daughter of Juda Hochmann and Eidel
Birnbaum Hochmann
lived in Berlin, then Pittsburgh, PA
married M. G. Heiser 01/08/1935
d. 02/28/1992 Pittsburgh, PA

Mordecai Gustav Heiser, *Hazzan*
b. 05/08/1905 Singhofen,
Germany
son of Itzak Heiser and Selm
Brauer Heiser
lived in Berlin, then
Pittsburgh, PA
d. 10/24/1989 Pittsburgh, PA

Sylvie[a] Heiser
b. 05/05/1934 Amsterdam
dep. 11/27/1941 to Riga
d. 11/30/1941 Riga
in Koblenz M. B.

Judith Heiser
b. 12/28/1936 Berlin
daughter of Mordecai Gustav and Elly
Hochmann Heiser
lived in Pittsburgh, PA
d. 07/22/2021 Pittsburgh, PA

Alvin Joseph Stein
b. 04/27/1935 Pittsburgh,

Larry Rich +
Pittsburgh, PA

Betty Sue Stein Rich
Daughter of Alvin and Judith Heiser Stein
b. 05/09/1968 Pittsburgh, PA

Shari Stein Klafter
Daughter of Alvin and
Judith Heiser Stein
b. 07/14/1964 Pittsburgh, PA
living in Florida

+ **Mark Klafter**
b. 02/28/1964 Smithtown, NY
living in Florida

Andrew Rich
Pittsburgh, PA

Elly Rich
Pittsburgh, PA

Naomi Ellen Klafter
Florida

Rebecca Klafter
Florida

HEISER-HOCHMANN FAMILY TREE

Charles (Karl) Rautenberg, Rabbi
lived in Berlin, then escaped to England

Betty Marcuse Rautenberg
b. 11/05/1874 in Falkenburg, Pommern
lived in Berlin
dep. to Warsaw in 1942
d. in Holocaust

Cilly Ebner, Haifa
Cousin of Judith Heiser Stein in Pittsburgh, PA

+ **Beyer nee Reuter**

+ **Emma Katz Heuser**

Simon Brauer
Brother of Selma Brauer
b. 01/21/1881 in Kovno
lived in Berlin
dep. 12/14/1942 to Auschwitz
in Koblenz M. B.

Albert Brauer
Son of Selma's brother Simon
Lived in England and married Margot
d. 1972 in London

Cilly Brauer Haar
Daughter of Selma's brother Simon
Albert Brauer's sister
Married Alfred Haar
Lives in London, age 101 in 2022

+ **Selma Brauer Heiser**
b. Kovno, Lithuania
married Isaak Heiser
Mother of Mordecai Gustav Heiser
d. 02/28/1931 or 02/18/1931 Berlin
Grave in Weissensee
Section E VI, 5th row, No. 82240, stone 1934

Hugo Naftali Heiser
b. 10/07/1907 Singhofen, Germany
lived in Berlin
married Meta Hochmann in 1934
dep. 11/27/1941 to Riga
d. 11/30/1941 Riga acc. to Till letter,
d. in Minsk acc. to Koblenz M. B.
in Koblenz M.B.

Eleonore (Elli, Elke) Heiser Zellner +
b. 12/31/1903 Singhofen
m. Julius Zellner in 1939 in Aachen
d. in Holocaust? NOT in Koblenz M. B.

Julius Zellner
b. 03/03/1917 Chemnitz
Lived in Aachen, Germany
d. in Holocaust? NOT in Koblenz M. B.

Joel Zellner,
Son of Eleonore and Julius Zellner
b. 1940 or 1941
d. in Holocaust? NOT in Koblenz M. B.

Adele Miriam Stein Sufrin
Daughter of Alvin and Judith Heiser Stein
b. 06/25/1963 Pittsburgh, PA

+ **Warren Jay Sufrin**
b. 08/02/1961 Pittsburgh, PA

anner Kennedy + **Rena Anna Sufrin Kennedy**
Pittsburgh, PA

Ilana Pearl Sufrin
Pittsburgh, PA
+
Travis Kaufman

Dana Arielle Sufrin
Pittsburgh, PA

Leah Aliza Sufrin
Pittsburgh, PA

Asher Judah Kennedy
Pittsburgh, PA

HAZZAN
MORDECAI GUSTAV HEISER

INTRODUCTION

In 1986, for a research project as a graduate student with Visiting Professor Ronald Grimes—from Wilfrid Laurier University in Waterloo, Ontario—at the University of Pittsburgh, I decided to explore and compare different types of synagogues in Pittsburgh, Pennsylvania.[1] During these site visits, I also attended a service at Congregation B'nai Israel in the East End of Pittsburgh. I was drawn to the beautiful Byzantine-design building on a little hill on North Negley Avenue and looked forward to the service. Not knowing what to expect, I sat in the back of the sanctuary to observe. Among the officiants was a little old man whose name I did not know. But no sooner did he begin to sing than a completely new world opened itself to me. I felt transported to a spiritual level that I had never experienced before. From that moment I was certain that this was my synagogue, not just to study, but to attend. Of course, I first had to be Jewish. This happened in due time: In 1988 I became bat mitzvah at Congregation B'nai Israel in the circle of my family, new friends, and colleagues at the university.

Congregation B'nai Israel was my spiritual home from 1986 until 1991 when I moved to Tuscaloosa, Alabama. The man whose voice had so transformed me was Cantor Mordecai Gustav Heiser, known as the sweet singer of B'nai Israel, who in 1986 was eighty-one years old. During his remaining time on this earth—he died in 1989—he became my teacher and my friend. He worked with me at Biblical Hebrew—I was taking Modern Hebrew at the university with Ruth Gelman—and taught me most of the *hazzanut* (Jewish liturgy) that I know today. We started with the *brachot* (blessings) for an *aliyah* (honor) and *birkat hamazon* (blessing after the meal); then I learned to *leyn* (chant Torah) and chant the *Haftarah* (prophetic portion) and most of the weekday and Shabbat services. Although his *Ne'ilah* service was sung by an all-male choir, after his death I adapted that service to my voice and davened something resembling Cantor Heiser's *Ne'ilah* service at my synagogue in Knoxville for nearly three decades.[2]

The Heiser family—Cantor Heiser, his wife, Elly, and their daughter,

Judith—suffered all of their lives from the consequences of their Holocaust experiences. Still, in the 1990s, Elly published a painful article about their precarious situation in Berlin; a traumatized Cantor Heiser likewise related his arrest and incarceration in Sachsenhausen to a close friend and remembered the burning of his synagogue on Kristallnacht in a Pittsburgh speech; and Judith, if nothing else, lived with a fear of Germans. Thanks to the family papers that survived, this study is able to document a number of these experiences and to highlight the traumatic effects especially on Cantor Heiser going forward. The atrocities of the Holocaust, bureaucratic as well as physical and emotional, cast a long shadow over the rest of Cantor Heiser's life. Artistically he chose to dwell in the musical world of the nineteenth-century reformers Louis Lewandowski and Salomon Sulzer as well as Eastern European *hazzanut*, Jewish folk music, Hasidic *niggunim*, and Israeli tunes. He died before the Wall came down and did not have the opportunity to reconnect with the emergent post-Holocaust Jewish world of sacred music in Europe as did some other leaders, such as Professor Eliyahu Schleifer and Rabbi Walter Jacob. But, oh, how thrilled he would have been to experience the Lewandowski revival in Germany during the past decade.

In 1999, ten years after Cantor Heiser's death, and after the death of his wife, Elly, in 1992, their only daughter, Judith Heiser Stein, and two of her three daughters, Betty Sue Stein and Adele Stein Sufrin, planned and went on a trip to rediscover Judy's roots and their family history. They invited me to come along as a guide. We primarily traveled to Berlin, where the family had lived and Judy was born, and we visited some of the addresses that Judy had collected—the former *Hochschule für die Wissenschaft des Judentums* (where her father had attended classes), the Weissensee Jewish cemetery (where we discovered the graves of three family members), places where her mother and father had lived (separately before they were married, and together afterwards, and where she had been born), and addresses where her father and mother had worked.[3] In an article in *The Jewish Chronicle*, August 26, 1999, "You can go home again, family finds," by Iris M. Samson, Judy Stein noted, "I came to the conclusion that Hitler accomplished what he set out to do—to annihilate the Jewish population from Europe. What I saw were mostly old Jewish people and Russians. There are little pockets, but hundreds of thousands of Jews in Berlin are just gone." She concluded, "But, I don't have a fear of the Germans anymore." Judy, Betty Sue, and Adele went on a second trip in 2009 which we planned together but on which I could not accompany them because of family illness. They visited the cemetery in Singhofen, the town where her father was born, and returned to Berlin a second time.

There were two pieces of information that were transmitted by different sources and also published but later turned out to be erroneous or misleading. The first had to do with Cantor Heiser's arrest during the Nazi period. Based on information he provided, I am only able to document his incarceration in Sachsenhausen. Secondly, he himself stated in a brief autobiography that he was from Kovno (Kaunus), Lithuania, and several other sources stated that he was born in Lithuania. This, even though his birth certificate very clearly documents his birth in Singhofen, District Lahn, near Koblenz, Germany. But the mystery can be solved. Kovno was the town of origin for his mother, Selma Brauer. We know this thanks to recent family research by great-granddaughter Rena Sufrin Kennedy.[4] But why would he have wanted to be known as an Eastern European Jew when many Jews from the Baltics, Poland, and Russia clamored to be accepted as Western—and specifically German—Jews?

My premise is that historical events, namely the Holocaust, completely derailed one person's and one family's path in life, in fact an entire community's. Consequently, life had to be reinvented according to new norms—already while still in Berlin, Germany, following the Nazi takeover in 1933; then briefly in England in 1939; and finally, in the United States through Cantor Heiser's work at Congregation B'nai Israel in Pittsburgh starting in 1940. While I am cataloging and conserving whatever service parts survived on amateur tapes—a precious resource for this project and a record of one cantor's contribution to the cantorate—I am also asserting that this particular liturgy was carefully chosen for its ethnic roots mostly in Eastern Europe. Cantor Heiser's comfort zone lay first with nineteenth-century Central European composers such as Louis Lewandowski and Salomon Sulzer, who lived well before the Holocaust and had eastern roots, and then with some of the major Eastern European cantors and music directors of a religious tradition that was destroyed by the Shoah. The scope of Cantor Heiser's *hazzanut* is a living memorial to a way of life that no longer exists.

Mordecai Gustav Heiser was a Holocaust survivor, but he was also so much more—a family man, an observant Jew, a committed Zionist, a musician, a composer, a teacher, a religious leader, and above all, a mentsh. He was a small man who shuffled through the hallways of the synagogue building when I knew him, slightly hunched over, but always with a smile—well, almost always. One day we went to his classroom to practice the *Haftarah* for the upcoming Shabbat when he suddenly stopped in the middle of the hallway, looked at me, and blurted out a story from his imprisonment at Sachsenhausen. He relayed that there was a group of men standing near him, ready to say prayers, when a Nazi came up to the group and shot them. He then broke into tears and resumed walking down the hall. Like other Holocaust victims, Cantor Heiser had his demons from that terrible time period. Did these experiences make him unusually kind? Unusually perceptive? Unusually forgiving? It is hard to say, but he definitely was a very gentle and patient person who would not utter a bad word about anyone. This alone endeared him to those who knew him. The second quality was his gift for music—his choir arrangements and service organization as well as his style of presentation. It was his strong yet soulful voice that made him a star in our eyes, his ability to carry his heart on his sleeve and to allow each of his congregants to discover the hidden emotion within. It is this uniqueness that I hope to convey in the service guides to his music in Chapter 3.

This study brings together in conversation the observations of a number of musicologists, scholars, and cantors such as Idelsohn, Elbogen, Edelman, Slobin, Kalib, Frigyesi, Heschel, Heiser, Glantz, and Schleifer.[5] While Cantor Heiser's music became a life-long memorial for European Jews, East and West, his art became first and foremost a powerful affirmation of Jewish life in the twentieth century, supported by his meaningful inclusion of contemporary American Jewish composers throughout his lifetime.

The organization of this book proceeds from a brief autobiography by Cantor Heiser's late daughter, Judith Heiser Stein, to my connection to Cantor Heiser and the Heiser family; an introduction of Jews into European society and Cantor Heiser's life in Berlin (Chapter 1); his incarceration in Sachsenhausen concentration camp, his journey from Berlin—the center of German Jewish culture and religion—first to a refugee camp in England, then to New York, and from there to Pittsburgh, Pennsylvania, and life in Pittsburgh (Chapter 2), including what is known of the Heiser family history and the role that Cantor Heiser played in the development of the American cantorate. Chapter 3 provides what Judith Vander would call Cantor Heiser's songprint.[6] The chapter contains a catalogue of Cantor Heiser's services, or portions of them, for six holidays. It is not a complete collection by any means, but it will suffice to illustrate the nature of his liturgical art. For these fragments I provide an explanatory guide to the function of each particular service in the liturgical year and the life of the congregation and to Cantor Heiser's art of musical interpretation, as well as a worksheet detailing every prayer or hymn for each raw service that survived. The raw services are not on YouTube, but a selection of twenty clips of Cantor Heiser's *hazzanut* can be accessed on YouTube.com, with M. G. Heiser in the search bar. The final section consists of a brief conclusion, a glossary of terms, endnotes, and a bibliography.

CHAPTER I

EUROPEAN JEWRY UNTIL THE HOLOCAUST

When Charlemagne was crowned emperor of the Holy Roman Empire in 800 CE, many enclaves of Jews already existed in certain areas of Europe. The Jewish people were native to the Middle East, but due to the conquest of their territories by competing civilizations as well as their great wanderlust as traders, they traveled much of the world. Already during Solomon's reign in the First Temple period (960 BCE), they conducted business in Africa. Some may have settled in Europe even before the destruction of the Second Temple in 70 CE, so about 700 years before Charlemagne. The expanse of the Roman Empire offered great business opportunities and after the dispersion also a much needed refuge. With the Islamic conquest in the seventh century CE, some Jews moved to the Iberian Peninsula and settled there. Around 900 CE, Jewish merchants explored the Silk Route that led some of them to settle in China (Kaifeng, primarily), where they thrived for nearly a thousand years. In the early Middle Ages some local nobility, also in German lands, invited Jews to settle in their territories in order to assist with trade, fund their military, provide medical services, and many other matters.

Persecution of European Jews became a major concern with the Crusades in the eleventh and twelfth centuries. While most European Jews until then had lived in the West, in the High and Late Middle Ages they were again and again expelled from some of these countries—German lands during the Crusades, Great Britain in the thirteenth century, Spain in 1492, and Portugal in 1497. During Poland's period of kingship, starting with King Boleslav the Pious in 1264, groups of Jews were invited to live in Poland. In 1343 King Casimir the Great, in Sholom Kalib's words, "expanded the protective conditions offered in the Boleslav charter."[1] From then until the advent of the Polish-Lithuanian Commonwealth that was created in 1569, much of the Jewish population of Europe lived in Poland.

It was only during the Chmielnicki massacres of 1648, a year which also marked the end of the Thirty Years' War and the Peace of Westphalia, that some Jews again gravitated west and settled in, among others, German lands, often in rural areas where they lived side by side with local Christians, making a livelihood by filling the gap in occupations not controlled by the guilds—as traders, cattle dealers, and craftsmen.[2]

Jews and Christians coexisted much of the time. There always were occasions for anti-Semitic incidents, and looking back, one may well see that these occurrences left a troubling trace which would bubble up again and again. Jewish Emancipation in all of Germany following the establishment of the Second German Empire in 1871—an affair that came to realization from the top down, not from the bottom up—left some Germans resentful. In the 1890s there followed a primarily literary backlash that blew up into full-fledged hatred of Jews by the time of World War I. At that time Jews were accused of stabbing the Fatherland in the back, a lie that can be refuted by records of Jewish soldiers who fought and died for Germany.[3] Many right-wing agitators stirred up the muddy waters of hatred. Armed battles between communists and fascists occurred throughout Germany, the short-lived Bavarian Republic in Munich was overthrown, and Jewish Prime Minister Kurt Eisner assassinated. While the Weimar Republic seemed to favor Jewish integration into the nation, Jewish Foreign Minister Walter Rathenau was also assassinated, and Berlin's Jewish population experienced an inkling of things to come with the Holocaust.

While pogroms had always been an ugly possibility in Europe, the Holocaust was an entirely different experience. With the ascent of the Nazis to power in 1933, the 600,000 German Jews especially understood that this phenomenon spelled doom for their lives as Germans. Within three months, a number of worrisome events took place, including the arson attack on the Reichstag in February and the boycott of Jewish businesses on April 1. Later that month the Civil Service was cleansed of Jews and other undesirables, and in May, books were burned in public view in Berlin. In short succession, the concentration camps of Dachau, Sachsenhausen, and Buchenwald were established. The Nuremberg Laws were passed in 1935, and by 1938, Jewish property was confiscated. Kristallnacht on November 9, 1938, made the Nazi intent crystal clear. There was no more German Jew, only a Jew in Germany—and that not for much longer. Of the approximately 180,000 Jews living in Berlin in 1933, only 80,000 remained. By 1939 many Jewish communities in Germany were disbanded, and the struggle for survival became urgent.

Already long before the creation of the Second German Empire in 1871, Jews organized themselves as *kehillot*, or communities, and were by and large autonomous within the larger non-Jewish society. Although restricted in their participation in the host nation, both from without and from within, Jews were recognized as necessary, if pesky, outsiders, lending themselves to abuse whenever society experienced unusual tensions, such as war, disease, or famine. Jews caused the Black Death of 1348, so said the "believers," or they shirked their duty when the nation was in trouble, as claimed by the anti-Semites in the early twentieth century. In between, Jews experienced periods of tolerance that allowed them to live on friendly footing with their neighbors, who were often interested in the culture of their Jewish cohabitants, such as language, food, religion, and customs.

Jewish life revolved around a communal center, namely the synagogue, which served as a place of meeting, study, and prayer, and in whose proximity many Jews lived. On Mondays and Thursdays the square nearby turned into a marketplace. Jews from the provinces would come to town to make a *minyan* (quorum) at the shul and to do business and shmooze. Preparations for Shabbat were quite a public affair, as one needed to clean, shop, cook, and then rest! Christian neighbors visited, sampled the usually parve (neutral, suitable to eat with meat dishes) dessert, and discussed matters of mutual concern, such as new civic regulations and laws, especially those affecting both of them.

Religious life was also of interest to Christians, perhaps not so much on Shabbat, as this service happened every week and was seen as comparable to a Christian Sunday service, but on the festivals of Pesach (Passover) and Sukkot (Feast of Tabernacles) when extraordinary activities took place not paralleled in church, such as the Seder and the Sukkah. The meaning of Easter and Pentecost is far removed from that of the Festival of Freedom and Shavuot, the Jewish Pentecost. Likewise, the High Holy Days—Rosh Hashanah and Yom Kippur—were enshrined in a mysterious aura, and the famous melodies which could be heard outside the building drew attention to an individual not quite equaled in Christianity, the community's *hazzan* or precentor, with his often notable, if not beautiful, voice.[4] It was not unusual for his fame to spread far beyond the prayer house of his hometown.

Music has always been an important part of Jewish life. There is no culture that does not claim its specific songs and dances. Judaism is no exception.[5] As early as the First Temple, nearly 3,000 years ago, we are told, the Levites beautified the prescribed sacrificial rites with their beautiful voices and with instruments. During the Exodus, Moses and the Israelites praised God with the Song at the Sea or *Shirat HaYam* for defeating the Egyptians (Exodus 15:1–18); Miriam not only joined in but also played the timbrel and led the women in dance (Exodus 15:20). King David is said to have played the harp and became known as "the sweet singer of Israel" (II. Samuel 23:1), and Deborah's song after the defeat of Sisera and the Canaanites celebrates victory (Judges 5:2–31). Early in the Bible we are told that God chose Bezalel, the son of Uri, as the master craftsman for the Tabernacle (Exodus 35:30–33), so that beautification of the Torah, *hiddur mitzvah*, became one of the earliest commands.[6] Cantor Leib Glanz, in a powerful book on *hazzanut* edited by his son, Jerry Glantz, *Leib Glantz— The Man Who Spoke to God*, directly derives the Jewish prayer modes from the biblical cantillations,[7] as do Eliyahu Schleifer, Sholom Kalib, Cantor Heiser, and others. Thus, the *hazzan*, through his heartrending prayer, fulfills an important role in realizing the goal of beautification of the Torah.

Following the destruction of the Second Temple in 70 CE, singing, now in synagogues, continued during worship, but there was one big difference. Because Jews were in continual semi-mourning over the loss of their national independence and their sanctuary, musical instruments were forbidden during worship. Only the human male voice was to be heard. As Jewish life reconstituted itself in the aftermath of the dispersion, this rule became enshrined in Talmudic thinking (BT Gittin 7a, 8), along with a prohibition against women's voices (*kol ishah*) in public worship (Brachot 24a, 17), and really only in the twentieth century did instruments and women's voices recover their place in Jewish worship.

The cantorial arts blossomed over the centuries, somewhat differently in Sephardic (Mediterranean) and Ashkenazi (European) Jewish culture.[8] Both Eastern and Western European Jewish liturgy was treasured by congregations, as was the person who presented the prayers to the Almighty— the precentor, or *hazzan*.[9] Until the nineteenth century, the liturgy was primarily handed down from father to son, if the father was knowledgeable in the liturgy, or from cantor to young men not related. Or, as Chayim Ben Shmuel, a Hungarian Chasid, told Judit Frigyesi, "I did not learn this. I have been praying since I was a small child. . . . It had been there since . . . I don't know exactly; but for a very long time." In Eastern Europe, a boy with a nice voice would be apprenticed to a cantor at the local synagogue or somewhere else, literally sitting at the master's feet. Eventually the youngster became an adult and had learned all he could from this master. If he was fortunate, he found a place as a cantor either in his hometown or in some other community, all the while learning more *hazzanut*.

Again, Chayim Ben Shmuel relayed to Judit Frigyesi that he had a special talent for Talmud and a nice voice, which meant that he had "a talent for *chazunes*" (*hazzanut*). "I was taken in by the *tsaddik* . . . and also by the *chazzn*. They taught me for free, which was almost unheard in those days. . . . When I was nine years old, I was already teaching the older boys."[10]

Yet cantors, even those with a good voice, were usually poor. They lived at the beck and call of the community whom they served. Some never had steady employment at a synagogue but only periodic gigs for which they received a fee. Some traveled far and wide for employment, often leaving their families behind for months on end. Yet a mysterious quality attaches itself to the *hazzan*, the *shaliach tzibur*, or messenger of the people, and some lucky cantors, such as the Ukrainian-born Yossele Rosenblatt (1882–1933), were in the right place at the right time and became famous.

The Son of a Prussian Civil Servant

This study follows one German/Lithuanian Jewish family, the Heisers, from their origins in Hesse, which was incorporated into Prussia after 1866, and from Lithuania. By marriage we add Poland to the family. How East and West met is not known, but it is entirely possible that the patriarch and matriarch, Isaak Heiser and Selma Brauer, met in Berlin, an aspiring metropolis with a Jewish population of about 100,000 at the turn of the twentieth century.[11] Although Gustav Heiser, in his musical peregrinations, spent considerable time in the soundscape of Eastern European composers during his lifetime, culturally the family then lived a German Jewish life, far from the Yiddish-speaking environment of the world that brought forth great cantors. Since most German Jews were culturally assimilated, they were often seen as also spiritually distant from the *kavanah* (intent or spiritual energy) so necessary for proper concentration in prayer derived from the mysterious shtiebls of that "foreign" culture of the East, described so hauntingly by Frigyesi. But one did not have to travel to Hungary or Lithuania or Podolia and Volhynia to experience Jewish spirituality, as by the turn of the century (1900) East had begun to come to Berlin, to the displeasure of many of those who considered themselves German Jews.[12]

Mordecai Gustav Heiser (1905–1989) was the sweet singer of Congregation B'nai Israel in the East End of Pittsburgh, Pennsylvania, for nearly fifty years (1940–1989). His path to the cantorate was dramatic and traumatic, but definitely *beshert*. Although he himself later wrote that he was born in Kovno,[13] he was in fact born in Singhofen, district Unterlahn, near

Koblenz, Germany, to Isaak (Yitzchok) Heiser (1872–1942), an itinerant teacher and cantor in the Jewish community, who was born on January 8, 1872, in Lohne, Hessen-Nassau, and to Selma née Brauer who, according to recent family research, came from Kovno, Lithuania.[14]

The Holocaust looms large over the lives of this family, many of whom were not able to escape from its clutches. Isaak Heiser, who became a Prussian civil servant in Berlin, was deported at age seventy with an old people's transport on August 17, 1942, from Berlin, No. 41 Brunnenstrasse, to Theresienstadt, and from there to Minsk, where he perished.[15] Selma Heiser died before the official ascent of Nazism, on February 18, 1931, and is buried in Berlin-Weissensee, Section E VI, 5th Row, No. 82240. The community placed a pauper's headstone on the grave in 1934.[16] Although it is very clear from surviving copies of Gustav Heiser's birth certificate—such as the *Geburtsschein* issued to him by the village of Singhofen in 1933[17]—that he was born in 1905, in the 1930s he desperately tried to make himself younger and attempted to change the date to 1908. He did a poor job but nevertheless managed to get a copy notarized in Pittsburgh as late as 1974.[18] Gustav, as he was known while living in Germany, had an older sister, Eleonore (Elke), born on December 31, 1903, in Singhofen, and a younger brother, Hugo, born on October 7, 1907, also in Singhofen.[19] From a German Jewish source in Koblenz we know that Hugo was deported from Berlin to Riga with the seventh transport on November 27, 1941, and from there to Minsk, where he perished.[20] His wife, Meta née Hochmann, born September 20, 1905, in Berlin, as well as their daughter, Sylvia[e], born on May 5, 1934, in Amsterdam, did not survive the same transport.[21] Forebears include Tobias Heuser and his wife, Emma née Katz, both Jewish. Tobias (Tovia) was born on February 20, 1847, at Breitenbach, District Kassel. He was a teacher by profession, and died at age sixty-six, retired, in Detmold, Germany (May 3, 1913).[22] The names of Tobias' parents were Gumbert Heuser, a merchant, and Beyer née Reuter.[23]

Berlin as the Center of German Jewish Culture and Religion

Gustav Heiser's birthplace of Singhofen was a remote village on a plateau above Koblenz in the Rhineland that belonged to Prussia. Berlin was the capital of Prussia, and by 1871 became the capital of the newly united Second German Empire. Gustav and his siblings grew up in Berlin, east of the Scheunenviertel, which was densely settled by Jewish immigrants from the

East and was known for its "backyard synagogues, Talmud schools, Jewish prayer rooms or guest houses."[24] Exactly when the family moved to Berlin is uncertain, although it could have been as early as 1910, when Gustav was five, after which time the Jewish community of Koblenz can no longer document his whereabouts,[25] but definitely when Gustav was nine [1914], as this is later documented in a record of the places where he had lived in Germany.[26] According to a final report card from the *Königstädtische Oberrealschule* in Berlin 55, No. 44–46 Pasteurstrasse in the Winsviertel, Gustav attended this business high school from 1918 to 1920, so at the end of World War I, when he was thirteen years old.[27]

Berlin had long been a magnet for Jews from the provinces, not only in close proximity to the city, but from as far away as Austria from where they were expelled in 1671[28], and then from all of Eastern Europe. Berlin was the "goldene medine," the hope for a better life via education and employment, and it became the gateway to emigration. By 1847, even before the establishment of the Second German Empire, the Jewish population of Berlin numbered around 8,300.[29] In the 1860s, the community built the fabulous Neue Synagoge at 30 Oranienburger Strasse in the center of Berlin, which was dedicated on September 5, 1866. The edifice seated 3,200 and contained a "majestic" organ. The renowned concert master Louis Lewandowski, by then Royal Music Director—and one of Cantor Heiser's favorite composers—provided suitable modern services for the congregation.[30] On Shabbat and holidays, worshippers approached the house of worship in horse and carriage wearing top hat and tails. Hermann Simon notes, "The Neue Synagoge stood in the center of Jewish Berlin. Within ten minutes' walking time one could find . . . many small prayer rooms, the famous Orthodox synagogue (the Alte Synagoge), the Adass Jisroel Synagogue, the Reform Synagogue, the Hochschule für die Wissenschaft des Judentums, and the Rabbinic Seminary. . . . Close by one could find the Jewish Museum, the community's administrative building, the Kultusverwaltung (Nos. 28/29 Oranienburger Strasse), the Old Age Home at No. 26 Grosse Hamburger Strasse, as well as the first cemetery." He concludes that "all of Jewish religious and cultural life took place in the vicinity of the Neue Synagoge."[31] What a contrast to rural Singhofen, Gustav Heiser's birthplace.

The establishment of the Second German Empire brought with it the most important right of all—Emancipation. While Jewish Berliners had already tasted civil rights as Prussians in 1812, this time it was real for all German Jews. Alas, it would only last for the next sixty years.

In 1920, life in Berlin was harsh for a boy of fifteen who needed to take on the responsibilities of a full-time job. The years following World War I were extremely difficult politically and economically. For decades, Berlin had labored to become a Weltstadt, a cosmopolitan city. But the German defeat in the Great War turned Berlin life, and German life in general, on its head. In *The Pity of It All*, Amos Elon wrote that "The great edifice of the old Reich collapsed almost by itself. Without the firing of a single shot, more than two dozen ancient dynasties—including the Hohenzollern—disappeared overnight, to be replaced by hastily assembled republican governments."[32] Poverty, unemployment, disease, and hunger caused anger and resentment in the German population. Jews were already a scapegoat for the lost war; now it was their fault that the economy nearly collapsed. In his book *Berlin*, David Clay Large writes, " . . . for the Berliners . . . the 1920s were not so much 'golden' as red [communist] in tooth and claw. This was especially true of the first years of the postwar decade, which were marked by coup attempts from left and right, devastating inflation, racially motivated riots, strikes, political assassinations, and a general dog-eat-dog rapaciousness."[33]

It seems fortunate, then, that Gustav Heiser found employment with the haberdashery of Eisenberg & Struck, a Jewish business located in the south of Berlin, at No. 2 Kaiser Wilhelm-Strasse, Berlin C 2. This clothing business belonged to the family of Hermann Struck, a Jewish artist who was simultaneously a religious Zionist and a war artist for the German government during World War I.

After ten years in the textile business, on July 31, 1930, Gustav requested a character reference from his employer. They obliged and wrote, "Herr Gustav Heiser worked for our company from November 15, 1920 to August 1, 1930. Herr Heiser absolved a 3-year apprenticeship and acquired good knowledge of our lines [of clothing]. He supervised the sample room for several years and from 1928 to 1930 he directed all of our shipping. We were always satisfied with Mr. Heiser's work and are happy to highly recommend him as an industrious, diligent, and trustworthy young man."[34]

Hermann Struck (1876–1944), the famous German Jewish etcher and engraver and ardent Zionist, was a member of the German delegation to the 1919 peace negotiations at Versailles. But when the powers did not allow Struck to communicate with Jews from other countries in person,[35] he disappointedly decided not to travel to France but to only participate from Berlin. As a founding member of the Zionist religious organization *Mizrachi* (1902), Struck moved to Eretz Israel when the headquarters of *Mizrachi* were relocated to Jerusalem in 1920. His house on the Hadar HaCarmel in

Haifa was built by the Berlin architect Max Baerwald. Today the building serves as a music school for the city of Haifa.

Gustav Heiser probably knew Hermann Struck personally, perhaps from the business or from the local Jewish community or various Zionist organizations. Zionism was popular in Berlin and Gustav participated in Zionist events. After the Nazis came to power, Mr. Heiser apparently wrote to Struck for advice [letter not extant], for on March 31, 1933, Struck wrote to Gustav, at No. 66 Elbingerstrasse, Berlin N.O. 55.

> Dear Mr. Heiser,
> I am continually overwhelmed with similar queries and unfortunately cannot give you much hope. To find an office job in a commercial business is nearly impossible, even if you can correspond perfectly in Hebrew and English—which I assume you can. Trade with woolen goods hardly exists here at all. You would have to have mastery of bookkeeping as well as typing in the languages mentioned. If you do not have command over all of these things, there is no hope at all. If you do, and you have enough money to hang on for a quarter of a year (6 pounds per month), then you might risk it. The only possibility I see is that you might work illegally in construction, if you are physically strong and can stand the heat in the summer. You have to register with the Palästina-Amt, No. 10 Meinekestrasse [Berlin], no matter what, to obtain an [immigration] certificate. I am sure they will also give you all other information. I am sorry that I cannot write you something more encouraging—but that would be irresponsible of me.
> Sending you best wishes in return,
> Yours,
> Hermann Struck[36]

This correspondence took place even before the German boycott against Jews began on April 1. Gustav clearly understood early that these were not good times for Jews in Germany and was looking for a way to emigrate. At this time, he was still single.

The Cantorate as a Sacred Calling

Although we know that Gustav Heiser worked for Eisenberg & Struck for ten years, from 1920 to 1930, he also furthered his education during this time, but in a very different direction from business. A report card from the *Kultusverwaltung der jüdischen Gemeinde zu Berlin*, 28/30 Oranienburgerstrasse, [January 17, 1929] attests that "Herr Gustav Heiser, living at No. 1 Angermünderstrasse [in the Winsviertel], Berlin N. 4, attended cantorial school between October 1925 and January 1929, with *Oberkantor* Professor Felix Asch and *Musikdirektor* Aron Friedmann."[37] According to Congregation B'nai Israel's fiftieth anniversary booklet, *Oberkantor* Leo Gollanin was another one of Gustav's teachers.[38] Gustav's education consisted of instruction in music theory, voice, Liturgy, theory of synagogue service and musicology, and singing by his teachers. While there were German music conservatories, they were Christian-oriented and until 1871 mostly did not allow Jews. There was one exception: the Stern Conservatory, a private music school which was founded by Julius Stern and others in 1850. Oberkantor Aron Friedmann, one of Mr. Heiser's teachers, was connected to that school of music as well, and Mr. Heiser may have been a student there through his association with Friedmann.[39] Gustav Heiser passed all of his subjects with high grades. The examination commission noted that "His musical talent and cantorial abilities are to be commended." The document was signed by *Oberkantor* Felix Asch, who died in that very year. Despite his obvious prominence in his day, and a thorough search for information on his person, I was only able to find on the internet possible birth and death dates of 1853–1929, that he was a cantor, had a baritone voice, and made an early recording of "Kol Nidre" (1902) to Louis Lewandowski's composition (01:55).[40]

Aron Friedmann (1855–1936) was a well-known composer and director as well as cantor in Berlin until 1924 when he retired. He was a student of renowned choir master Louis Lewandowski. In his autobiography, *50 Jahre in Berlin (1878–1928)*, Friedmann recounts how Lewandowski mentored him from the time Friedmann came to Berlin from Szaki, Lithuania, and how close they were his entire life. For Lewandowski's tenth *yahrzeit* (1904), Friedmann concluded his study, *Der Synagogale Gesang*, published in 1908, with a brief study of Lewandowski, as well as a brief biography of Salomon Sulzer, on his 100th birthday. Friedman also published a three-volume biography of three famous cantors and choir directors, *Lebensbilder berühmter Kantoren*, published in 1929; the second volume is about Louis Lewandowski on the occasion of his 100th birthday.[41]

Leo Gollanin (1872–1948), also a concert singer, was a celebrated cantor of the Berlin community who started to officiate at the Neue Synagoge at Oranienburger Strasse in 1924. He became *Oberkantor* of the Jewish community in 1925 and survived the Holocaust. In 1945, he beseeched Greek Holocaust survivor Estrongo Nachama (1918–2000) to stay in Berlin and help rebuild the Jewish community. Cantor Nachama, who was born in Saloniki, Greece, survived a death march from Auschwitz to Sachsenhausen and another one from Sachsenhausen toward Hamburg on which he was liberated.[42] Having lost his entire family in the Holocaust, he studied the Ashkenazi *nusach* (prayer modes) as well as the popular compositions by Lewandowski and Sulzer with Cantor Gollanin. In a very moving account in Michael Brenner's book *After the Holocaust: Rebuilding Jewish Lives in Postwar Germany*, Cantor Nachama explained, "The head cantor, Leo Gollanin, who had been the cantor on Oranienburger Strasse before the war, was an old man by then. One week later, he let me sing the lead at the service. So I sang a solo.... After the service, Gollanin came to me and asked, 'Herr Nachama, I am old. Don't you want to take my place and help build the community?' I replied, 'Cantor, I can sing *hazzanut* [Jewish liturgical chants], I was trained to do that in Greece, but I would like to go back to Greece.' Every week he tried to persuade me: 'Help us, please.' So I studied with Gollanin for half a year. Then he died."[43]

Cantor Nachama led services at the Pestalozzi Street Synagogue from July 2, 1947, until the end of his life. After the Holocaust, he was the first Jewish clergy person to hold a concert in a Christian house of worship, and beginning in 1948, he and the RIAS Kammerchor broadcast a weekly twenty-minute Shabbat service on the radio.[44]

Another version (II) of the above-mentioned report card/letter from the *Jüdische Gemeinde zu Berlin, Kultusverwaltung*, also dated January 17, 1929, and signed by Elieser Ehrenreich, adds that they "recommend Herrn Heiser in every respect, professionally as well as personally," wishing him much success for the future.[45] The expectation was that Gustav Heiser would find work as a cantor in Germany. His training in the clothing business was not wasted, however. Many officiants in the Jewish community supported their families by supplementing the fees they received for their services with ordinary work.

We only learn from a letter signed by Simon Neisser for the *Israelitische Religionsverein* in Berlin-Lichterfelde-Lankwitz just nine days before Kristallnacht in 1938 that Gustav Heiser actually officiated for a congregation as their First Cantor, from November 1, 1925, to November 1, 1938, some of it while he was studying for the cantorate and worked as a haberdasher.[46] This congregation was the Jewish Old Age Home in Berlin-Lichterfelde-Lankwitz, in the southern part of Berlin, to which a friend of the family, John Rayner, makes reference in a letter to Cantor Heiser's wife, Elly, after his death.[47] He continued this sacred work upon concluding his studies in 1929, at which time he quit his job with Eisenberg & Struck. There is no evidence of any other employment between 1929 and 1938, although there is an announcement of a job talk in 1936. The notice states that, on February 22, 1936, "Herr Kantor Gustav Heiser – Berlin" would give a "Probevortrag" at the Synagogengemeinde Göttingen.[48] The announcement asked for a good turnout for services on Friday evening at 5:45 p.m. and Sabbath morning at 9:00 a.m., when he would recite the Prayer for the New Month and give a sermon. A third service was to take place on Saturday afternoon at 3:00 p.m. [the traditional *mincha* service, perhaps followed by a *seudah shlishit* meal and study, and a *Havdalah* service, as is customary in a traditional synagogue]. However, there is no evidence of further engagement.

Heiser Family Matters

While little changed professionally until Kristallnacht, there was development on two fronts in this time period—politically, and in Gustav's personal life. Enter Elly Hochmann into Gustav's life. According to the family, Elly and Gustav met at Gustav's younger brother Hugo's wedding to Elly's older sister, Meta, in 1934. We also know some additional information about Elly and her family background. On November 6, 1911, birth certificate No. 1884 was issued by the Family Registry official in Berlin to Juda Samson Hochmann, a Jewish tailor, who was born on October 20, 1877, and died on July 30, 1922. Juda, a *cohen* [priest], is buried in Weissensee Cemetery, Section F V, Row 10, No. 62476. A beautiful granite tombstone was placed on the grave in 1922. Juda lived at No. 17 Neue Königstrasse, with his wife, [Adele] Eidel Hochmann née Birnbaum (born May 20, 1877, in Gemilov, Galicia), Jewish, No. 85 Elsässer Strasse [not same address]; they had a daughter, Elly, who was born on October 31, 1911, at "11 in the afternoon." It is obvious that not all of the details in this document make sense. Although there is no explanation for the time of day—it can only be 11:00 a.m., as 11:00 p.m. is 23:00 hours in German usage—there is an explanation for the two separate addresses. This we know from an official note in the margin, which states, "Today there appeared before the official of record tailor Juda Samson Hochmann, Jewish, living at No. 35 Winsstrasse in Berlin. [This is his brother Salomon's address in the Winsviertel.] He presented his marriage certificate No. 49, dated June 7,

1915, Family Registry office Berlin 8, and declared: I recognize the child whose first name is Elly and whose mother I have married as documented by the marriage certificate, as my own." The document is signed by Juda Hochmann and the official.[49]

A different official, on August 14, 1915, entered a second note into the margin of Elly's birth certificate correcting the initial and incorrect report of marriage between Eidel and Juda at the time of Elly's birth. "On order of the Royal Lower Court of Berlin-Mitte, Section 114, dated July 3, 1915, the correction is made that the mother of the child was not married at the time of her birth."[50] As we see in so many ways, "Ordnung muss sein" [There has to be order].

Elly had two sisters. Meta was born September 20, 1905, in Berlin; in 1934 she married Gustav's brother, Hugo, born October 7, 1907, in Singhofen; they had one daughter, Sylvia[e], born May 5, 1934, in Amsterdam. We have an address of No. 26 Stallschreiber Strasse, Berlin SW 68, for Meta and Hugo.[51] Unfortunately all of them were murdered in the Holocaust. Elly's other sister, Berta (Betti or Bayla [also Betty Sue Stein's

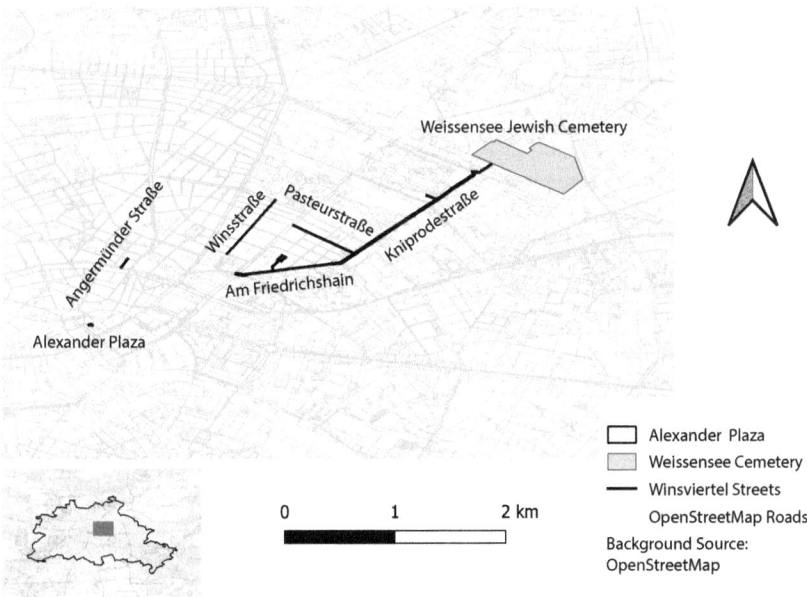

Map of Berlin. Courtesy UT Cartographic Services, 2023.

Hebrew name]), born October 30, 1906, in Berlin, married Leiser (Leo) Lieberson. Lieberson was born March 14, 1904, in Winnitza. In Berlin, we have an address of No. 214 Elsässer Strasse, Berlin W 4.[52] Both Betti and Leo were deported to Auschwitz on December 9, 1942. At some point, Elly's mother, Adela (Eidel) née Birnbaum, lived at No. 10 Alexander Platz, Berlin.[53] The Birnbaum and the Hochmann families both were from Gemilov, Galicia, Poland. Eidel had a brother, Max Birnbaum, whose daughter, Sophie, married Josef Weiss in Pittsburgh, Pennsylvania. This will be of great consequence for Gustav and Elly. Juda Hochmann had two brothers, Salomon and Leo. Salomon was born on February 22, 1910, and died February 14, 1928. He is buried in the Berlin Weissensee Cemetery, No. 75008, Field F, Section V, Row 13.[54] His other brother, Leo (Leiser) Hochmann, was born in Gemilov in 1900 and was deported to his death by the Nazis.[55]

Within the family, Elly Heiser was known as Pucci. We know that she attended a Jewish school at No. 33 Rankestrasse in Berlin. When she got married, she worked as *Stenotypistin*, a shorthand typist, at No. 124 Leipziger Strasse (January 6, 1933-September 30, 1938). Previous to that, from April 1 to July 15, 1927, she had worked for a lawyer, Dr. Jur. H. J. Barwinkel-Leue, No. 159 Uhlandstrasse, Berlin W 15; and thereafter from August 1 to December 27, 1927, she worked at No. 29 Dorotheenstrasse, Berlin NW 7.[56] What she may have done from December 1927 through January 1933—a full five years—is not known.

According to an announcement in the *Jüdische Rundschau*, Elly and Gustav were engaged on Friday, September 7, 1934.[57] The High Holy Days that year began on Sunday evening, September 9. The wedding took place within a few months. On January 8, 1935, we have *Aufgebotsverzeichnis* No. 2044/1934, the record of a civil marriage by

1. Cantor Gustav Heiser, born on May 8, 1905, at Singhofen, District Unterlahn, Birth Register No. 10 of the Family Registry in Singhofen, Living at [No. ?] Am Friedrichshain [in the Winsviertel] in Berlin, and
2. Shorthand Typist (*Stenotypistin*) Elly Hochmann, born on October 31, 1911, at Berlin, Birth Register No. 864 of the Registry in Berlin 9, living at [No. ?] Wiryomstrasse in Berlin.

Witnesses were "3. Isaak Heiser, retired, age 63, living in Berlin, at No. 14 [. . . ?] Wasen," and "4. Tobacco merchant Leiser Lieberson, age 30, living in Berlin, at No. 30 [. . . ?] Wasen."[58]

The official asked the engaged couple "separately and consecutively" whether it was their desire to get married. The couple answered this question in the affirmative, and the official then announced that, according to civil law, they were now man and wife. Their residence was to be Berlin-Charlottenburg, No. 64 Augsburger Strasse, in the Bavarian Quarter (Bayerische Viertel), favored by professional residents of Berlin. The document was signed by Gustav Heiser, Elly Heiser née Hochmann, Isaak Heiser, and Leiser Lieberson.[59]

A Jewish wedding (No. 483) followed on the same day. A fee of twenty-five marks was paid by "Herrn Heiser" to the main cashier of the Jewish community, receipt No. 2101.[60] The papers from the civil marriage were a precondition for the Jewish wedding. Among Cantor Heiser's papers was also a receipt for a bridal bouquet, provided by Blumen-Handlung Franz Wagner, 11 Kniprodestrasse in the Winsviertel, Berlin N.O. 18, a continuation of Am Friedrichshain, where Mr. Heiser lived at the time. The cost for the *Brautstrauss* was five marks.[61]

There probably was little time for a honeymoon, as Cantor Heiser was about to embark on classes at the *Hochschule für die Wissenschaft des*

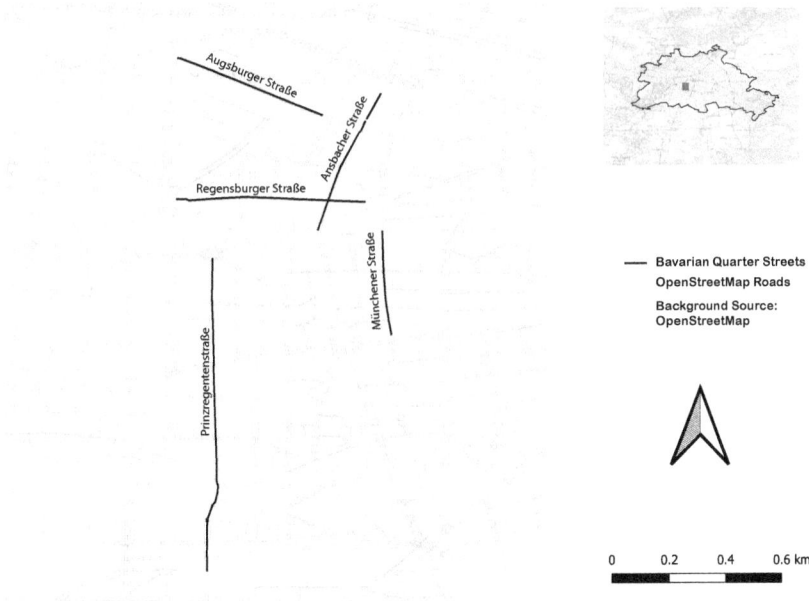

Map of Berlin. Courtesy UT Cartographic Services, 2023.

Judentums (April 1935), in addition to his duties at the Berlin-Lichterfelde-Lankwitz congregation. All of this occurred before the Parteitag in September and the issuance of the Nuremberg Laws.

Germany Is Home No More

Soon after President Paul von Hindenburg's death in 1934, Jews no longer had freedom of movement. The Old Guard had been pushed out and the Nazis made sure that Germany was no longer home to German Jews. They were quickly excluded from participation in the German economy and from receiving benefits citizens were entitled to. Cantor Heiser required a police permit attesting to his German citizenship for purposes of travel within Germany. The permit was issued on November 5, 1934, by Josef Goebbels in the name of the Berlin Police President.[62] In 1933, Goebbels, who had earned a Ph.D. in philology, became Hitler's Propaganda Minister, a position he retained until his suicide in 1945. In September 1935, with the Nuremberg Laws proclaimed at the Parteitag, the political tensions increased even further. The Law of German Blood and Honor and the Reich Citizenship Law effectively excluded German Jews from membership in the German nation.

In 1936, in preparation for the Olympics, Sachsenhausen concentration camp was established in a suburb of Berlin. That same year also brought the birth of Elly and Gustav's only child, daughter Judith. Judith Heiser came into this world on December 28, 1936. She was born at No. 49 Münchener Strasse in Berlin-Schöneberg in the Bavarian Quarter (her parents' residence is still Berlin-Charlottenburg). Her birth certificate No. 762/1936 was issued by the *Standesamt* Berlin-Schöneberg 2.[63] Unfortunately, little Judith entered a world that was not friendly to Jews. Her life was difficult from the beginning, perhaps reflected in the coded telegram that was sent to "Humesyl" with the nonsensical text, "Na sichste ohne Trodelel, alles Gute."[64]

In spite of all the political tumult that surrounded the Heisers, Judy's father passed his interim exam at the *Hochschule* in 1937,[65] and acquired additional duties with his congregation. Yet Judy's parents understood that the dragnet was slowly closing in on them. On January 10, 1937, little Judith received a postcard from Onkel Emil and Tante Mäuschen. "Dear Judith! A new uncle and a new aunt want to introduce themselves. We hope that you are a joy to your parents and that you help your Papa when he cannot figure out a Gemara. We will visit you soon."[66] Papa was known not only as a sacred singer, but as a scholar as well. On October 5, 1937, the family, consisting of Elly, Judy, and Gustav (birthdate altered to 1908), moved from No. 30 Ansbacher Strasse in the Bavarian Quarter, Berlin W 50, to No. 28 Regensburger Strasse, in the same district of Berlin. This appears not to have been a voluntary move, as they had owned the apartment at Ansbacher Strasse, while they were only allowed to rent the new apartment at Regensburger Strasse "from themselves" [*bei sich selbst*].[67]

Search for a Refuge

The year 1938 was heavy with foreboding of things to come politically. Jews were still able to leave Germany, sometimes with their belongings, if they were able to pay a hefty fine and were able to obtain an affidavit for a visa from someone abroad. Elly Heiser wrote a letter in English to a cousin, which one cannot be ascertained, asking for help.[68] The letter has neither date nor signature, but makes clear that current events were at best unpleasant and at most dangerous to anyone who was Jewish. "It is already a long time we have not received from you a sign of life. We had, therefore, charged a good friend in New York, Mr. Hans E. Rosenberg, to call on you; but as he could not come to see you direct, he had asked a Mr. Marcus, as he wrote us, to visit you. You certainly know that the question of emigration has become to us an urgent matter nowadays." In the margin to the left of these words is the date 1. 6. 38, which means June 1, 1938. Elly continues,

> A great many people are now going to the States, having been claimed by relatives of theirs. After all, this is the only possibility to emigrate on basis of an affidavit of a relative. The only address of relatives over there of which we know is yours, and therefore we can only apply to you and entreat you not to refuse this affidavit for us. You need not by all means be afraid that we shall become a burden to you. My husband was assured that he would get a job almost as soon as he has come to your side. He has the best references and Rabbi Dr. Jung in New York has promised to do his best for him. The execution of the affidavit is, therefore, only a matter of formality, nothing else. I enclose herein the exact statement of our personalities. [The confirmation that this is Elly writing the letter comes in the next sentence.] My mother Eidel Hochmann, née Birnbaum, sends you hearty greetings and hands you enclosed

a new photo of herself. She is now 61 years old, but still vigorous and good-looking. We hope that, once arrived there, we shall soon be able to let her come over to us too.

She then returns to her foremost concern, the affidavit. "Mr. Schenkelowsky, New York, and Professor Isaak Asher, your city [Pittsburgh?] will likewise be so kind—by the intermediary of Rabbi Dr. Jung [New York]—as to get into contact with you in this respect, and I trust that we shall hear from you about this matter in the nearest future."

The address, "Dear Cousin," and the concluding salutation, "With kind regards to you and your family, I am, yours sincerely," are in Mr. Heiser's hand, so that we can assume that he was coaching his wife in writing this letter to her cousin. This is followed by the vitals for Gustav, Elly, and Judith. Here it is noteworthy that Gustav gives his correct place of birth, Singhofen, as well as his correct birth year, 1905.

Later on in the year, because of the expulsion of Polish Jews from Germany in October of 1938 and the resultant attack on Ernst vom Rath at the German Embassy in Paris on November 7, 1938, tensions in Germany between Nazis and Jews escalated dramatically. Emigration was a must for those who were able to do so.

To this end, on November 1, 1938, [before Kristallnacht] the *Israelitische Religionsverein* in Berlin-Lichterfelde-Lankwitz wrote a letter of recommendation for Mr. Heiser in which they spoke highly of his years of service from November 1, 1925, to November 1, 1938, as their First Cantor. "During this time Mr. Heiser managed to create solemn and edifying worship services. He has a wonderful tenor voice, which he has mastered technically. His prayer recitation shows absolute mastery of *Chasonus* (*hazzanut*). His deep knowledge of the content of the prayers, paired with his sonorous voice, creates a true worship service. His inner pious attitude [*kavanah*] and his modest demeanor especially endeared Herr Heiser to us. Our community is very unhappy at Herr Heiser's departure. [However,] objective and subjective circumstances make his departure necessary at this time." Congregation and Board wished Herr Heiser the very best for the future and expressed the hope that he might soon succeed in finding a position abroad that would value his great talent and knowledge.[69] At this time there were no longer any illusions about employment in the Jewish community in Germany. It is clear what the "subjective circumstances" mentioned in the letter were, namely his personal safety and, as he had a family by then, that of his family.

A second letter, also dated November 1, 1938, from the same congregation, tells of the objective circumstances that necessitated his dismissal. This letter is also more of a professional recommendation than a character reference, as was the previous letter. It documents more precisely Mr. Heiser's training for the cantorate, even for the rabbinate. There is also a difference of one month in the dates that he served this congregation. This letter states that he served from October 1, 1925, until November 1, 1938. He was initially hired as their First Cantor, and "in the past three years also served as *Prediger* (preacher) and *Seelsorger* (minister)." The latter additional employment resulted from his progress in additional studies at the *Hochschule für die Wissenschaft des Judentums*, studies in rabbinics. "With his sonorous, pleasant tenor voice that he continuously improved to perfection through intensive and continuous training, and through the spiritual depth of his recitation, he is able to create an uplifting and heart-rending service for all members of the congregation."

> In addition to serving as a First Cantor, Herr Heiser also served to our full satisfaction as a Thorah reader and a shofar blower [for the High Holy Days]. When Herr Heiser passed the interim exam at the *Lehranstalt für die Wissenschaft des Judentums*, we partially transferred to him, as our rabbi's delegate, the duties of *Prediger* and *Seelsorger* in our congregation. Herr Heiser also displayed exceptional talent and diligence for this work, his sermons received complete approval from our membership; they were imbued with holy zeal for our teachings and for our faith. Herr Heiser also ministered to our congregation, and he found ways to introduce the youth of our area to the sources of our teachings and our faith through religious instruction, bar mitzvah lessons, Modern Hebrew courses, and religious events, and more. He thereby educated them to become useful members of the Jewish community. He always carried out his work in our congregation with piety and modesty, which earned him love and esteem from our congregants. The dissolution of our congregation forces us to dismiss Herr Heiser from his position. We wish him the very best for his future.[70]

This letter affirms the objective circumstances of Mr. Heiser's dismissal from the congregation—there was no congregation anymore. It had been dissolved by the Nazi regime.

The Hochschule für die Wissenschaft des Judentums.

As the Berlin-Lichterfelde-Lankwitz congregation noted in their letter, Mr. Heiser also attended classes at the *Hochschule für die Wissenschaft des Judentums*, No. 14 Artillerie-Strasse (today No. 9 Tucholskystrasse), the progressive Jewish college in Berlin-Mitte, from April 1935 until April 1937, at which time he passed his interim examination towards the rabbinate.[71] According to the documents available, he actually continued his studies following his release from Sachsenhausen until spring of 1939, when he fled to England.

The *Hochschule für die Wissenschaft des Judentums* arose from the desire for change that overcame some rabbis in the nineteenth century. In 1872, this progressive nondenominational Jewish university was founded in Berlin, with Abraham Geiger, Hermann Steinthal, David Cassel, and Israel Lewy as the first teachers.[72] Says the renowned philosopher Emil Fackenheim, "The institute could be attended by Gentiles as well as Jews, and, among the latter, equally by Orthodox, liberal, secularist, and even atheist Jews. After all, the facts, as well as the objective method required for their study, were the same for them all."[73] Due to "intense anti-Semitism" in 1883, this college was then renamed the *Lehranstalt für die Wissenschaft des Judentums* until 1922, during the Weimar Republic, when the term "Hochschule" was restored. Alas, the Nazis again demoted this institution of higher Jewish learning in 1934.[74] As noted above, until 1933, the *Hochschule* attracted diverse scholars of Judaism, but after 1933 also some of the giants of German Jewry, who had striven for more than a community position but who parted company or were forced to part company with their German universities after Hitler came to power because they were Jewish. Fackenheim observes that "The Berlin of 1935–38 was a place of nearly unbearable distress, for it was Nazi. But insofar as it was Jewish it was also a place of inspiration and of strength.... [W]e at the *Hochschule* studied the Jewish sources with deep intensity, and had much to say to each other."[75]

Emil Fackenheim, who attended the *Hochschule*, was a classmate of Gustav Heiser's. Fackenheim wrote in his autobiography, *An Epitaph for German Judaism: From Halle to Jerusalem*, that the *Hochschule* was "a Jewish center for Jewish spirit in radical question and self-questioning, always under stress, never far from the edge."[76] He entered this body as a student in spring of 1935, just in time to experience and witness all of the horrors that the Nazis would bestow on Germany's Jewish citizens, including arrest and incarceration at Sachsenhausen concentration camp. He reminisced that he did not wish to study at the *Hochschule* to prepare for a job—"I simply wished to become knowledgeable."[77] In a speech in Pittsburgh in 1979, Cantor Heiser acknowledged that "the philosopher Emil Fackenheim" was a classmate of his.[78] Over the years he had lost touch with Fackenheim, and when I started to travel to Israel for research, he asked me to look him up. Unfortunately, I was only able to give him Cantor Heiser's greetings by telephone.

We know nothing from Cantor Heiser firsthand about his educational experience at the *Hochschule*; however, from his credentials we do know who his teachers were. Since he and Emil Fackenheim shared the same cultural environment and the same teachers at the same time, we can discern from Fackenheim's account what it was like to be a student at the *Hochschule* and what the teachers were like.

The dean of Jewish scholarship at the *Hochschule* was Rabbi Leo Baeck (1873–1956) who had been educated, as were so many of the teachers at this institution, at the University of Breslau. He was a rabbi in Berlin from 1912 on. By 1935, he was a giant among German Jews, serving as president of the B'nai B'rith Lodge and as a member of the *Centralverein* as well as the head of the *Reichsvertretung*—all this in addition to his duties as a teacher at the *Hochschule*. Fackenheim comments, "Leo Baeck impressed me as a person. An awe-inspiring figure, he understood better than most others the catastrophe that had befallen German Jewry, yet he stayed with his people to the end. Leo Baeck will remain unforgettable to me. He ought to remain unforgettable."[79] Rabbi Baeck had many opportunities to leave Germany, but he refused to do so. Imprisoned in Theresienstadt, where he lost his four sisters, he moved to London upon his liberation in 1945.[80]

If Leo Baeck was the most important teacher at the *Hochschule*, Professor and Rabbi Max Wiener (1882–1950), also a graduate of the Breslau Seminary, was an important educator in Jewish philosophy. Fackenheim shares his observation of Wiener in his book, *What is Judaism?* "Max Wiener was a philosopher. Of considerable originality, he never received the recognition he deserved, for he did not write much. Moreover, what he did write was on the obscure side, and he was a rather dry lecturer to boot. But he knew how to provoke thought."[81] Wiener was born in Oppeln during Leo Baeck's first rabbinate from 1897 through 1907, so Baeck could possibly have been his rabbi growing up.[82] Before joining the *Hochschule*, Wiener served as Leo Baeck's assistant in Düsseldorf. Following that appointment, and when Leo Baeck moved to Berlin in 1912, Wiener became the rabbi of a liberal Stettin congregation. In 1926 he also moved to Berlin to serve another liberal congregation. After a long association with the *Hochschule*, substituting for colleagues Harry Torczyner and Julius Guttmann, in 1935 he was appointed Professor of Jewish Philosophy of Religion and Ethics. In 1939, he immigrated to the United States where he served as rabbi in West Virginia and later New York, where he died at age sixty-eight.[83]

Another teacher of Mr. Heiser's was Eugen Täubler (1879–1953), a distinguished historian and philologist who, like Leo Baeck, was born in Poznan. In fact, they were childhood friends.[84] Täubler had a distinguished career already before World War I. After studies at the University of Berlin, Täubler founded the *Gesamtarchiv der deutschen Juden* in 1906, which he then directed until 1918, minus his years of military service during World War I. He also taught history at the *Hochschule*, where he had previously been himself a student. Täubler left a full professorship at the University of Heidelberg, where he had taught from 1925 through 1933, in protest against the Nazis, and found refuge at the *Hochschule*. In Fackenheim's opinion, he inspired the crop of upcoming existential refugees with real scholarship— he was "a breath of fresh air" and "a builder of morale."[85] Another *Hochschule* student, Nathan Peter Levinson, attested, "In 1940, when I started studying at the rabbinical seminary, I really didn't want to emigrate. I was nineteen years old, and even though all the horror was going on around us, we at the seminary were on a kind of island. If you can attend lectures by personalities like Rabbi Leo Baeck or the historian Eugen Täubler, you necessarily abstract yourself from everything going on all around. Those were such important, fantastic things, those lectures, so you really did dismiss the other things."[86] After consulting with Leo Baeck, Täubler left Germany for the U.S. in 1941 and joined Hebrew Union College (HUC) in Cincinnati.[87]

Ismar Elbogen (1874–1943) was a prolific scholar of Jewish history, whose writings on Jewish liturgy are still interesting and instructive. Fackenheim calls him "the great scholar and greater Jew."[88] His 1913 study, *Der jüdische Gottesdienst in seiner geschichtlichen Entwicklung*, became an important work in the history of Jewish liturgy and is available in English. He is also famous for his book *A Century of Jewish Life*, published in 1944. Born in Schildberg, Poznan, he immigrated to New York in 1938 and simultaneously joined several institutions of higher learning there.[89]

The written sources initially only revealed one picture of Alexander Guttmann (1904–1994). It is the 1938 class picture from the *Hochschule* in his book in which Fackenheim identifies him as one of his teachers.[90] More recently I discovered a Manuscript Collection, No. 663, in The Jacob Rader Marcus Center of the American Jewish Archives that contains quite a bit of material for those who are interested. Guttmann—not to be confused with Julius Guttmann, who also taught at the Hochschule—was of Hungarian origin. Born in Budapest, he studied at the Budapest Theological Seminary which was led by his father. He then received degrees from the University of Budapest and a Ph.D. in 1924 from the University of Breslau. Alexander Guttmann moved to Berlin, where he taught at the *Hochschule* but did not become a professor until 1935. It was his exclusive privilege to ordain rabbis at the *Hochschule*, among them Emil Fackenheim and Abraham Joshua Heschel. Guttmann left Berlin for America in 1940, where he joined Hebrew Union College as a visiting Talmud professor, a position that was made permanent in 1943. Despite periodic travels to Europe, Guttmann lived out his life in Cincinnati.[91]

Another teacher, of Biblical Hebrew and Tanach, was Moshe Sister (no dates), who took the place of Harry Torczyner (1886–1973) when the latter left the *Hochschule* and Berlin because of the Nazis in 1933 and settled in Palestine.[92] Writes Fackenheim, "Our Tenach professor was Moshe Sister, an outstanding teacher and a temperamental person whom we loved dearly for his sense of humor, his complete lack of professorial pomposity, and above all, for the high philological and critical demands he made on us." Fackenheim characterized Sister as "the hard taskmaster," "a radical critic"[93] and as "a warm person,"[94] one with whom he had theoretical differences because of his use of the documentary hypothesis, a form of biblical criticism that was anathema to Fackenheim. "This is why, though I loved him, I always fought with him."[95]

Sister had come from Poland seeking the "light" of the "modern" German academy, as Fackenheim says in his autobiography, only to be plunged into a deeper darkness than he ever experienced in the ghetto. The Nazis expelled him from the *Hochschule* when they attempted to deport all Polish Jews back to Poland. When the Polish government did not repatriate them, in October 1938 they were stuck in camps at the border between Germany and Poland. As Fackenheim reports, the Nazis "wouldn't let him even take a suitcase. His landlady phoned one of us students. Fischel [a fellow student] and I packed a suitcase and found him at a Berlin railway station." It was the sight of his esteemed professor among the hopeless other Polish refugees that brought Fackenheim to the realization that no one was safe and that it might be time to leave Germany.[96] His fellow classmate Gustav Heiser knew already in 1933 that he needed to leave, as evidenced by his correspondence with Hermann Struck in 1933 and other efforts to establish contact abroad, such as his visit to Amsterdam in 1934.[97] It apparently took Fackenheim and some of his fellow students until Kristallnacht and their subsequent incarceration at Sachsenhausen to realize this fact; some others at the *Hochschule* still didn't grasp this reality, even after Fackenheim warned them when he was released from the concentration camp.[98]

Fackenheim explains that in 1935 there were about a hundred students enrolled at the *Hochschule*, whom he classified somewhat sarcastically in three groups: "the 'boring' old-timers" who wanted an easy and cushy job with their diplomas; those "waiting for Nazism to go away, or just waiting" (eternal students); and those like himself and his classmate Gustav, now driven by their need to make a living. We learn that the normal course of study lasted six years. However, the 1930s were not normal times for German Jews nor for the students at the *Hochschule*. Fackenheim concluded his studies in three and a half years,[99] out of necessity, as did Gustav Heiser. Their subsequent arrest on November 10 and 11, 1938, interrupted both of their studies temporarily, but they were fortunately able to continue them briefly upon their release from Sachsenhausen and to leave Germany with certificates in hand before the beginning of World War II. It was too early to know whether their existence had been saved, but their lives thankfully had.

The committee that examined Gustav Heiser for his interim exam [*Zwischenprüfung*] in April 1937 consisted of Professors [Leo] Baeck, [Moshe] Sister, [Ismar] Elbogen, [Max] Wiener, and [Alexander] Guttmann. All of them are in the previously referenced picture taken of Heiser's and Fackenheim's class in 1938 and also identified by Fackenheim in his book.[100] In this picture, Gustav Heiser is likewise identified by Fackenheim as "Cantor Heiser," testifying to his reputation as a precentor in Jewish Berlin already at that time. This college education was of a more scholarly nature than his cantorial training, testing Gustav's knowledge in Linguistics, Bible Exegesis, Talmud, Midrash, Liturgy, Philosophy of Religion, and in Jewish History and Literature.[101] As had been the case with the business high school, the scientific study of subjects was not Mr. Heiser's strength, while he excelled in those areas that would serve him as Cantor and as *Prediger*—Liturgy, Bible Exegesis, Talmud, and Midrash. Following this interim rabbinic examination, the Berlin-Lichterfelde-Lankwitz congregation entrusted him with the sermons and spiritual care of the congregants in addition to his role as cantor. Whether he received an increase in pay for the extra work we do not know. Fackenheim actually took his exam in rabbinics and received a diploma as "Rabbiner, Prediger und Religionslehrer,"[102] while Mr. Heiser received a certificate for the courses he took, dated May 24, 1937, apparently without later taking the final examination for which the certificate was a prerequisite and that would have entitled him to call himself rabbi.

Kristallnacht and the Terror of the Sachsenhausen Concentration Camp

On October 2, 1938, Mr. Heiser wrote a letter to a student and friend by the name of Hans Sigismund Rahmer (1924–2005). Hans was a Jewish man whom Cantor Heiser knew when he served the Berlin Lichterfelde congregation. He, in fact, prepared him for his Bar Mitzvah at that time. Hans immigrated to England in 1939 and later became a rabbi in London.[103] Gustav wrote,

> Dear Hans,
> I assume that you have received our letter and our Rosh Hashanah greetings by now. Last week we also received the remaining papers from Weiss in Pittsburgh. Now I turned everything over to the Consulate and await what may be. I am told that one has to wait for three quarters of a year for a visa. Since I would prefer to leave the country sooner, I write to you today with the hope that you may also be able to help me this time. Here is the situation. [As you know], I have also been trained as a Prediger [preacher] at the Lehranstalt and have already worked in that field for some years. I understand that ministers are able to receive a visa at once as "non-quota immigrants," if they are able to present a contract from a congregation in the U.S. Mr. J. Balschofsky, 1247 S. Spauldings Avenue, Chicago, Illinois, U.S.A., the uncle of a colleague here, wrote me that a board member of a Jewish congregation in Chicago wants to send such a contract (proforma) to this colleague for $100. Since the colleague here—a preacher—is already planning to leave for the U.S. on an affidavit at the end of this month, he doesn't need this contract and plans to write to his uncle to send such a contract for me. I beg you, dear Hans, to write to me whether such a thing is possible and what you think about it. Perhaps you could write to Mr. Balschofsky and ask him for the man's name who would write a contract for $100 and then write to him and explain that it is impossible for me to send $100 from here and ask him to forego the fee since he is performing a mitzvah. I really have no idea whom in the U.S. I might approach for the money.

I don't want to ask my relatives in Pittsburgh since they provided the affidavit with a sponsorship for me. It doesn't look good if I now want this. And I really can't write to Mr. Schenkolensky since the matter is supposed to be confidential. Dear Hans, please see what you can do in the matter. [. . . .]
Best regards,
Gustav

Elly Heiser also added a few words.

Dear Hans,
I am enclosing a picture of little Judith, who now is 1–3/4 years old. Thank goodness the papers arrived and everything moves forward. I hope so! We have a little more hope again and hope for a reunion soon. Will your brother please write to the Hilfsverein for us regarding the passage? Perhaps we will need it soon? Write us soon, we look forward to hearing from you, also best regards to Arno H. and to your brother. Best, Elly
How do you like our big daughter? You will be surprised how quickly they grow.[104]

Contrary to many other German Jews, including his classmate Emil Fackenheim, Gustav Heiser keenly felt the urgency of emigration. During the night of November 9–10, 1938, Cantor Heiser witnessed the horrendous happenings of Kristallnacht. Seven thousand Jewish businesses all over Germany as well as homes were looted, damaged, or destroyed; ninety-six Jews were killed; 30,000 Jewish men were arrested and sent to concentration camps, including Cantor Heiser and Emil Fackenheim; and about 1,000 synagogues were damaged and burned.[105] In his farewell address on the occasion of the closing of the Friendship Club in Pittsburgh in 1979 he mentioned these horrific events, and his and his friends' dismay as they watched, in silence, as the synagogue at Prinzregentenstrasse in the Bavarian Quarter burned.

Forty-one years and two days ago, I was a young man standing with thousands of other Jews in front of the synagogue in Berlin, Prinzregentenstrasse, and witnessing the synagogue burning without any attempt to extinguish the fire. We were standing silently, the eyes of so many were filled with tears—even those who never had stepped in a synagogue felt that this is the end of our Jewish life, because they felt, as the Nazis did, without a synagogue there cannot be a Jewish life. [106]

This frightening event was followed by Gustav Heiser's arrest and incarceration in Sachsenhausen Concentration Camp. Mr. Heiser only mentions his arrest and stay in Sachsenhausen once, in a letter to his friend Hans when he was already in England (May 30, 1939).

> I am sure you can imagine that I didn't easily leave behind my wife and child to come here. But I was incarcerated for five weeks in concentration camp Sachsenhausen in beautiful Germany, from November 10 to the middle of December 1938. I had to agree to leave Germany as quickly as possible and when I wasn't ready yet in March, I had to report to the police every day at 1 PM, starting on March 1 [1939]. I still wasn't willing to leave my family behind. After two weeks (on March 14) I was ordered to emigrate within four weeks, or else.... Then I decided with a heavy heart to come here to this camp and to try from here to travel to the U.S. with my wife and child.[107]

Cantor Heiser's daughter, granddaughters, and I visited the Sachsenhausen memorial site on our trip to Berlin in 1999. In the back office we were shown the original file cards of the inmates which also contained one filled out in Mr. Heiser's own hand. Recently I contacted the Gedenkstätte und Museum Sachsenhausen and received the response that there indeed are two entries for Gustav Heiser, both concerning Cantor Heiser's release from the concentration camp. The exact date in their files is December 8, 1938.[108]

In 1975 Emil Fackenheim published an article about his experience in Sachsenhausen, "Sachsenhausen 1938: Groundwork for Auschwitz."[109] In this article, and even more so in his autobiography, he makes specific observations about the conditions in the camp. While we cannot know whether the two men experienced the same treatment in Sachsenhausen, Fackenheim's remarks certainly give us a flavor of the inhumanity of this concentration camp. About their transportation to Sachsenhausen he wrote, "For well over two hours we had sat in trucks. There were two of them, one covered, one open. It was November; the night was cold, and—naturally, they were Nazis—they had filled the open one, only putting the overflow in the other. Sitting in the open truck, I was frozen...."[110] In the appendix, Fackenheim again summarized the experience of his arrival at Sachsenhausen. "After we arrived in the camp, we had to stand and run through the night. In the morning came an 'interrogation.' We had to stand in rows, while an SS officer walked back and forth in front, leisurely, at length he stopped in front of someone and asked about his profession. On hearing 'doctor,' he burst into screams and began beating the unfortunate victim.... Then he moved on, still in leisurely fashion, and repeated his question; whatever the answer... again came the beating and the screaming...."[111]

The daily routine was brutal. "Life in camp consisted of work, most of which was at the *Klinkerwerke*,[112] several miles away from the camp, carrying hundred pound bags, shoveling sand into a boat, pushing lorries. In this place much depended on the kapo.... But kapos were a matter of luck. ..."[113] Prisoners themselves, kapos were assigned by the camp administration to supervise the other prisoners. Just how brutal of an existence they led can be seen from Fackenheim's explanation of this activity. "Many a day we spent carrying sand—always on the double!—from place A to place B, only in order to be ordered the next day to carry it back from place B to place A. The senselessness of this labor was so obvious that everyone understood it.... Its only purpose could be torture for torture's sake—to break us down."[114] He was genuinely concerned whether he would leave there alive. "In February 1939, of the original 6,000 prisoners, only 280 were left."[115] Plenty of reason to worry for his survival. But he was one of the lucky ones who survived. As was his classmate Gustav Heiser.

After the shocking events of Kristallnacht and Mr. Heiser's arrest and incarceration, the political pressure and the urgency to leave Germany became a matter of life and death. The activities in that direction were initiated by a Certificate of Admission from the Hebrew University in Jerusalem, dated February 2, 1939, certifying that "Mr. Gustav Heiser has been admitted as a regular student of the Hebrew University."[116] Fackenheim likewise has such a letter in his book.[117] However, if pursued, this effort, too, could have been fraught with great difficulties, as the British government issued the 1939 White Paper in May, severely limiting Jewish immigration into Palestine, leading to total closure in 1944.

As previously mentioned, the *Hochschule für die Wissenschaft des Judentums* had been demoted to a *Lehranstalt* by the Nazis in 1934, and Emil Fackenheim later commented that he would never have used this demeaning term. Still in 1937 the institution used the letterhead with *Hochschule*; thereafter it is blocked out and replaced by *Lehranstalt*. Educational activities and training of students for the rabbinate continued until the closing of the institution in 1942. On February 16, 1939, Gustav Heiser received a certificate from the *Lehranstalt* that he had "participated in a two-semester course on German Literature and a three-semester course in Latin" with Max Israel Wiener and [Hans] Liebeschütz (1893–1978).[118] This document also verified that Mr. Heiser had "the general intellectual maturity of one who had taken the *Abitur (Hochschulreife)*."[119] Thereafter the *Lehranstalt* accepted him as a regular auditor of their courses at the university level.

A variety of activities followed on February 28, 1939, all geared toward emigration—the Heisers had some of their valuables appraised, Mr. Heiser obtained a letter of good conduct from the police, and the *Lehranstalt* issued a certificate attesting to competency in general subjects. Perhaps to facilitate the opportunity to attend the Hebrew University, a certificate was issued jointly by Leo Israel Baeck, Max Israel Wiener, Eugen Israel Täubler, and A.[lexander] Guttmann on February 28, 1939, only twelve days after he was admitted to audit courses at the *Lehranstalt*. These gentlemen attested that "Herr Gustav Heiser has passed an examination on general subjects that he studied in lectures and exercises of our *Lehranstalt*, in which he participated enthusiastically and from which he gained extensive knowledge in various areas of the *Wissenschaft des Judentums*." Accordingly, he studied Jewish History and Literature with Professor Dr. [Ismar] Elbogen; History of Religion, Homiletics, and Pedagogy (Methods of Teaching Religion) with Rabbi Dr. [Leo] Baeck; Philosophy of Religion with Rabbi Dr. [Max] Wiener; Linguistics and Bible with Dr. [Moshe] Sister; and Talmud with Dr. [?] Kahane[120] and Dr. A.[lexander] Guttmann. Based on these studies he was awarded Certification as *Prediger* and *Religionslehrer* [as a Preacher and Teacher of the Jewish Religion].

The luminaries concluded, "Our institution discharges Mr. Heiser with the best wishes and blessings. May he continue to develop the scholarly abilities that he has already proven and contribute to the enrichment of Jewish life."[121] But where? Gustav Heiser had embarked exactly on the same life path as his father, with much more formal education, but with no certainty whatsoever that he would ever be able to practice his art in a Jewish community again.

The Heisers Prepare to Leave Nazi Germany

February 28, 1939, was a busy day for the Heisers. Gustav Israel Heiser and his wife, Elly Sara née Hochmann, living at No. 28 Regensburgerstrasse in the Bavarian Quarter, Berlin W 50, presented some of their valuables to Franz Grosse, appraiser, located at No. 17/18 Wall-Strasse, Berlin C 2. These valuables consisted of two wedding bands worth fourteen RM and one ring worth four RM. The appraiser returned the wedding bands to the couple but kept the ring under lock and key.[122]

A letter of good conduct from the police in Berlin, dated February 28, 1939, was to be used for emigration and was valid for three months from the date it was issued. According to the character reference, Cantor Heiser's police record was confirmed as clean. The *Führungszeugnis* also tells us that he was registered as a resident in Berlin from August 13, 1914, until October 1932, so from age nine until after his employment with Eisenberg & Struck. Then he was again registered from April 25, 1933, until March 4, 1934, and from October 1, 1934, until February 28, 1939, when the letter was issued. Where he lived between October 20, 1932, and April 25, 1933, is not known. Also, while I cannot say for sure that he spent the entire period from March 5, 1934, to October 1, 1934, out of the country, there are several letters to Elly from Amsterdam in 1934.[123] He got engaged to Elly in September of 1934, for which occasion he might have returned to Berlin. We know that Elly's sister, Meta, and Gustav's brother, Hugo, lived in Amsterdam at that time and that Sylvia was born there during that time.[124] So it is reasonable that he scouted the situation for himself and his future wife in the Netherlands or beyond by visiting family in Amsterdam. In a letter dated March 27, he writes to Elly that he applied for two opportunities: 1) Hachscharah at the Haarlem Sea, 40 kilometers from Amsterdam (agricultural training with the goal of immigrating to Eretz Israel), and 2) travel to Brazil.[125]

On March 16, 1939, a passport was issued to Gustav Israel Heiser in Berlin, with the identification number A 449747. The document revealed that he wore glasses and that he had a permanent scar on the back of his left hand (*Handrücken*). A big J for *Jude* was spread across the entire page.[126]

Although Mr. Heiser had been awarded a certificate of graduation by the *Lehranstalt* on April 14, 1939, just three days before leaving Berlin for England, he underwent another battery of tests in the Teachers' College toward fulfillment of the rabbinic requirements. He was examined in History by Professor Eugen Israel Täubler, by Max Israel Wiener in Philosophy of Religion, and by Dr. Arthur Israel Spanier (1889–1944), a lecturer [*Dozent*] in Biblical Studies and in Linguistics since 1935.[127] And, finally, Rabbi Leo Israel Baeck examined him in History of Religion, Pedagogy, and Homiletics.[128] Although he now had the certificate to qualify for the rabbinic examination, he apparently did not take it while in Berlin.

Life in England and the Kitchener Refugee Camp

On April 17, 1939, "Gustav Israel Heiser, married, Cantor and Religion Teacher, born May 8, 1905, at Singhofen, Unterlahnkreis, German citizen, Jewish," left Berlin for good and traveled to England with a group of refugees. Mr. Heiser's departure was reported to the police authorities by his wife, Elly, on April 21, 1939, so after his departure.[129] The fact of Gustav Heiser's emigration to England was confirmed by the *Hilfsverein der Juden in Deutschland e.V.*, Berlin W 35, No. 20 Ludendorffstrasse, on June 6, 1939. "We hereby confirm that on April 16, 1939, Herr Gustav Heiser, Berlin W 50, No. 28 Regensburgerstrasse, left for England transit camp Richborough/Kent with a mass transport (*Sammel-Transport*)."[130]

In England, Cantor Heiser found refuge in the Kitchener Camp in Richborough, Kent. The camp had been opened in 1939 by the Central British Fund for German Jewry at a disused World War I army camp in Sandwich, Kent. We know little about this time period, with the exception of a letter that Gustav Heiser wrote to his friend Hans on May 30, 1939, pouring out his heart to his friend, before Elly and Judy were able to join him. "You cannot imagine what I have gone through since November. Here I am doing pretty well. My stay in this camp is meant as temporary. We work, learn English, and wait, wait . . . "[131]

A final recommendation from the *Jüdische Gemeinde* in Berlin is dated May 2, 1939. The chairman wrote, "We confirm here that Cantor Gustav Heiser repeatedly served as precentor in our synagogues on the Sabbath and on holidays. The service in these traditionally oriented synagogues was accompanied by a choir. Mr. Heiser, who has a good voice, demonstrated that he is able to organize such a service successfully and knows to shape it with solemnity and in a dignified manner. Our best wishes for the future accompany him."[132]

With the Jewish community of Germany mortally wounded and the beginning of World War II on September 1, 1939, in the offing, a new and gruesome stage in the Holocaust was about to begin. After her husband's departure, Elly's—and Judy's—situation continuously deteriorated. Germany to this day has a tracking system for its population. One is registered with the municipal authorities upon birth and death and every time in between when one moves from one place to another within Germany. On April 18, 1939, Elly Sara Heiser notified the authorities that her daughter "Judith Sara Heiser, child, Jewess, born in Berlin on December 28, 1936, German citizen," would move from her residence at No. 28 Regensburger

Strasse, Berlin W 50, to the Baby and Toddler Children's Home at No. 8/9 Moltke Strasse in Berlin Diedernhönhausen,[133] quite a distance away in the west of Berlin. This arrangement, which probably facilitated Elly's forced labor for the Nazis, was fortunately temporary, and a month later, a May 22, 1939, registration informed the authorities in Berlin W 50 that both Elly and Judy took up residence at No. 28 Regensburger Strasse.[134]

Also during this time, Elly made arrangements for emigration. Among the family papers are instructions on how to apply for a visa. On May 2, 1939, she visited Dr. med W. Israel Leszczynski at No. 7 Spichernstrasse in the Bavarian Quarter in Berlin W 50, a Jewish physician who, at this time, was authorized to only treat Jews. He attested that he examined Elly Heiser and that "she is physically and mentally completely healthy, especially free of tuberculosis and other contagious diseases." This was an important element in obtaining a visa to emigrate.[135]

Rumors of impending war got louder during the summer of 1939. Gustav had escaped the clutches of the Nazis, but in spite of Elly's efforts, she and Judy had not. On August 6, 1939, "Elly Sara Heiser, ID No. A. 449740, Berlin," applied to the Foreign Currency Office of the Office of the President of Finance in Berlin for permission to take her valuables with her into emigration. This application had to be made via the Central Office for Jewish Emigration at No. 116 Kurfürstenstrasse, Berlin W 62. According to the application, in Elly's possession were:

A) 1 wedding band
B) 1 silver wristwatch
C)—
D) Silver items weighing no more than 40 grams per item
    Total weight up to 200 grams per person
        1) Children's bracelet
        2) 1 chain with pendant
    Total of approximately 16 grams

Elly also stated that she would have one child emigrating with her.

On the back of the document, dated August 11, 1939, she received permission to take all of the listed items into emigration with her, based on the law on foreign currency management dated December 12, 1938.[136]

A second document lists all of the items Elly and Judy planned to take with them into emigration. From their apartment at No. 28 Regensburgerstrasse, Berlin W 50, Elly and Judy planned to take with them:

1 woman's coat
2 small combs
1 briefcase
1 small album with family photos
1 thermos
1 hairbrush, all acquired in 1937
1 box of children's powder, worth 50 pfennig
1 small first aid kit, worth 2 RM

The Foreign Currency Office permitted items No. 1–98 into emigration. No. 71, whatever it was, was disallowed. There are three pages previous to this list that have been torn off the document. Only a fragment of the pages remains, so we do not know what else they may have wanted to take along into emigration.[137]

In her short autobiography at the beginning of this book, Judy Heiser states that they also were entrusted with relatives' valuables, and that whatever belongings she and her mother took with them to England by train were intercepted in Belgium and confiscated by the War Office. This was a common Nazi practice. A letter from the *Feldkommandantur* 520 in Antwerp, dated June 22, 1942, orders the shipping company of Emile Meerberger, S.A. to hand over "7 Kolli No. G.H.10/15 & 17" to the War Office who, in turn, will reimburse the company for the shipping expenses.[138] On March 27, 1945, the Heisers apparently sent an inquiry about their lost goods [letter not extant] to the company and received a postcard, dated May 7, 1945, addressed to Gustav Heiser Esq. at 830 Mellon Street in Pittsburgh, informing him that "as soon as the postal service between our countries is more safe we will not fail to send you the original receipt delivered by the German authorities."[139] Whether any further action was taken is not known.

On August 18, 1939, a passport was issued to Elly Sara Heiser née Hochmann by the Deutsche Reich in Berlin.[140] In the Stein collection was a booklet with helpful information and guidance for refugees while in England.[141] As early as August 21, 1939, Elly made a down payment to the Hamburg-Amerika Line in Hamburg for two places, tourist class, on the steamer "Hansa" from Southampton to New York. This passage was to take place on February 22, 1940, but did not happen. The good news is that just five days before the outbreak of World War II, Elly Heiser and daughter Judith, age two and a half, were able to leave Berlin for England by train. The notification to the local police of their departure, dated August 23, 1939, is extant.

On August 26, 1939,
1) Heiser, née Hochmann, Elly Sara, married, shorthand typist, born October 31, 1911, in Berlin, German citizen, Jewess,
2) Heiser, Judith Sara, single, child, born December 28, 1936, in Berlin, German citizen, Jewess, will move away, emigration to England. Their last residence was Berlin W 50, No. 28 Regensburger Strasse, rented from themselves (*Mieter bei selbst*).
Signed: Elly Sara Heiser née Hochmann, ID No. 449740, Berlin.[142]

The memory of this traumatic experience weighed on Elly all of her life. In 1989, she submitted an article entitled "A Holocaust remembrance" to *The Jewish Chronicle of Pittsburgh* for publication (February 2). In it she recounted those fateful days before their departure from Berlin.

> Germany had a very strict "postal censorship" concerning mail and telephone. No letter or telegram went through which had the slightest wording of the war, the regime, the situation, etc. How could he let me know that it was dangerous to wait? He pondered and pondered and then I received a note from him. This is what it said: 'Dearest, Today is Shabbat. You know, I do not write on a Shabbat. This letter is written on a Shabbat!' I understood. Dear God, he meant it as an 'S.O.S.' The letter went through, thank the Lord. The next morning my little girl and I left forever from Berlin. . . . We arrived safely in Dover. It was August 25, 1939. Five days later Hitler bombed Warsaw and World War II began; all borders were closed.[143]

From a letter by Mr. Heiser to his friend Hans we know that the Heisers' sponsors were Joseph Weiss, a cousin by marriage (Sophie Birnbaum Weiss) of Elly Hochmann Heiser's, and Joseph's cousin, Samuel Weiss, in Pittsburgh.

> Dear Hans, if you want to help me you can do so by looking after my affidavit business. On July 14, 1939, we submitted an affidavit from Joseph Weiss, Pittsburgh, a cousin of my wife's. This affidavit was sufficient only for one person, and the consul in Berlin agreed (when I was released from Sachsenhausen) to allow me to go ahead (of my Family). I already received my appointment in Berlin for May 25. In the meantime the transfer of my affidavit from

Berlin to London has been initiated. As soon as the papers arrive, I assume I will have my appointment here and will receive the visa in London. My case is thus taken care of, for what a consul in Berlin decides another consul will not change. In order to bring my wife and child to the U.S. I will need an additional affidavit. Three months ago we received a fine additional affidavit from the cousin of Joseph Weiss, Mr. Samuel Weiss, in Pittsburgh. This affidavit had several errors. . . .

Cantor Heiser was hoping that Hans would be able to help straighten out the bureaucratic nightmare, and from two receipts from the American Consulate—one in Berlin W, dated September 28, 1939, and another one in Berlin 4, dated December 8, 1939, as well as later correspondence— we learn that he did.[144] These receipts state that they are for a handling fee of 2.50 RM to the American Consulate, Visa Section, Berlin 4, Hermann-Goering Strasse, for Gustav Heiser as husband. A note on the back states, "For transfer of Gustav Heiser's affidavit, formerly Berlin 4 50, No. 28 Regensburger Strasse, now Richborough. Payment occurred with permission from the Foreign Currency Office (36E 2Pr), Berlin, No. 62 Neue König Strasse, German quota No. 39491 b, c, d. Please transfer files to London."[145] As we saw from Mr. Heiser's letter to Hans, this affidavit was crucial for the family's eventual embarkment for the United States.

The Heisers remained in England until January 30, 1940. This was not always a good experience, as the British were suspicious of German nationals [even though technically Jews had already lost their German citizenship with the Nuremberg Laws of 1935]. On December 19, 1939, Elly S. Heiser, No. 32 Highbury Grove, No. 5, [London], received a letter from the Metropolitan Police which stated,

> Tribunals have been appointed by the Secretary of State to examine the position of all Germans and Austrians over the age of 16 in this country, and to consider which of them can properly be exempted from internment and which of those exempted from internment can be exempted also from the special restrictions which are imposed by the Aliens Order on enemy aliens, etc. . . .
> Your case will be considered by the tribunal sitting at
> Homsey Road L. c. c. Schools,
> Homsey Road, N.Y.
> Friday, December 29, 1939, at 9AM and you should bring with

you your Police Registration Certificate, Passport, Testimonials,
etc.
Signed for the Secretary,
Aliens Tribunal No. 7
Metropolitan Police Area [London][146]

On January 25, 1940, the assistant camp director of the Kitchener Camp wrote a very complimentary recommendation for Cantor Heiser:

Mr. Heiser, formerly of Berlin, acted as First Precentor in this Camp from April 1939 to January 1940. The Camp Congregation consists of some 3,000 men, and his musical and cantorial abilities were appreciated and his thorough knowledge of Judaistics enabled him to recite the prayers correctly and solemnly. Besides his musical qualifications, he proved to be an exceptionally good *Baal Kore* [Torah reader]. He trained from the laymen in the Camp a very fine choir, which greatly enriched the religious ceremonies. Divine Service has been far more a matter of conviction and faith for Mr. Heiser than a matter of profession, and his personal qualities, combined with his professional skills, have gained him many friends. Mr. Heiser is leaving us in order to immigrate, together with his family, to the United States.[147]

A permit was issued to Cantor Heiser so he could leave the Kitchener Camp, Richborough, Kent. This permit, No. 724, was approved by the Home Office on January 24, 1940, and allowed Mr. Heiser to leave camp on January 24, 1940, for good.[148] The January 30 passage for Gustav, Elly, and Judy on the M. V. "Georgie" from Liverpool to New York was facilitated by HIAS (Hebrew Immigrant Aid Society), thanks to the intercession of Hans's brother.[149] The Manifest of Alien Passengers for the United States Immigrant Inspector at Port of Arrival is extant.[150]

CHAPTER 2

AMERICAN JEWRY

Pittsburgh Plays an Important Role in the Development of the American Cantorate

The Heisers as Refugees and Immigrants

Upon arrival in New York, the Heisers lived at 425 Lafayette Street in New York City.[1] On March 15, 1940, they received a letter from Monte Daniels of Wertheimer & Company, Manufacturers of Fruit-of-the-Loom Blouses-Sportswear-Pajamas, at 1350 Broadway, New York, asking whether he could help the Heisers in some way.

> Dear Friends,
> I have just had a letter from my Aunt, Mrs. Anna Daniels, in Bakersfield, California, and she informs me that you are her cousins. She tells me that you probably will be leaving for Pittsburgh soon and asked me to get in touch with you and find out how you are. Will you be good enough to please phone me here at my office at your own convenience so that we may perhaps get to know each other.

Anna Daniels was a cousin to Elly Heiser, Cantor Heiser's wife. While the Heisers were still in Berlin, she wrote to Elly. An envelope from Anna addressed to Elly dated January 27, 1939, in Berlin W 50, No. 28 Regensburger Strasse, is in the Stein Collection. We do not know whether they ever met, but the letter confirms three facts: the Heisers' address in New York, an early visit to Pittsburgh after their arrival in the U.S., and another cousin of Elly's in Bakersfield, California. From the B'nai Israel fiftieth anniversary booklet we learn that on a visit to his wife's cousin [Sophie

Birnbaum Weiss, wife of Josef Weiss] in Pittsburgh, Rabbi Benjamin Lichter of Congregation B'nai Israel invited Cantor Heiser to stay in Pittsburgh. This visit would have taken place between February and March of 1940. The Heisers moved to Pittsburgh soon thereafter and, according to an envelope addressed to them there (dated June 5, 1940), initially received mail c/o cousin Sophie Weiss at 1134 Mellon Street.[2] According to the B'nai Israel files in the Heinz History Center in Pittsburgh, Mordecai Gustav Heiser became a Torah "reader" for Cantor Bloom at $330 annually.[3]

Already the same year that they moved to Pittsburgh, the Heisers lived at 1114 North Euclid Avenue.[4] In subsequent years, Gustav, Elly, and Judy also lived at 830 Mellon Street,[5] at 5565 Wellesley Avenue,[6] and, in their final years, at 702 Essex House on Negley Avenue.[7]

Efforts to Save the Family

With Elly, husband, and child safely in the U.S., the focus now turned to the rescue of other Heiser relatives, especially Mr. Heiser's brother, Hugo, and Meta and Sylvia[e] Heiser in Berlin, and Betti (also spelled Betty) and Leo Lieberson. Dr. George Feldstein in Pittsburgh issued an affidavit for Betty and Leo Lieberson.[8] But sadly the Liebersons were not saved. The reason is unknown. Dr. Feldstein likewise provided an affidavit for Abraham, Feige, and Blanka Kanozuker, whose connection to the Heisers, if any, is unknown.[9] Also in need of help were Elly's mother, Eidel, Gustav's father, Isaac, and Leo Hochmann, Juda Hochmann's brother. Cantor Heiser's sister, Elli, and her husband, Julius Zellner, in Aachen were also hoping for rescue to the U.S. It is heartbreaking to learn, in an undated 1941 letter from Leo Lieberson, that Elli Heiser Zellner gave birth to a son, Joel, sometime in the spring of 1941.[10] There are a number of letters that make it abundantly clear that Julius fervently hoped that Gustav and Elly could help them. Existing correspondence shows that they certainly tried.

In an undated letter from Elli, Julius's wife, to Gustav Heiser, 1114 N. Euclid Ave., Pittsburgh, PA, she advises the Heisers of their new address at No. 21, I Promenadenstrasse, c/o Gottschalk. We know that the letter is from 1940 because Cantor Heiser complied with a request from Elli in a letter of June 8, 1940.

> Dear Gustav, dear Elly,
> We hear about you fairly regularly via Meta, only, we were wondering why you have not one time written directly to us, even though we have written you frequently. Didn't you get our various letters?

Especially the letter we sent you with the confirmation from the community here that Julius has been working as a rabbi already for two years. Couldn't you manage to get a permit for him to come to the U.S. outside the quota system? Today I would like to ask you for a favor, and it would be great if you could take care of this soon: the *Hilfsverein* here requested that we get our sponsorship renewed and our passage booked. The sooner both are taken care of, the more quickly we will be able to leave for the States.

Please contact
Mr. Philip M. Brenner
Counsellor at Law
46 Paterson Street
New Brunswick, N. J.

He is the lawyer for Mr. Leo Rifkin, 402 South First Avenue, Highland Park, New Jersey. Ask him to renew the affidavit with all the supporting documents for two people: Julius Israel Zellner, born March 3, 1917, in Chemnitz, and Eleonore Sara Zellner, née Heiser, born December 31, 1903, in Singhofen/Lahn. Maybe you can also ask him about payment of the passages. I am sure he knows, as you do, that one can only count on receiving an exit permit or rather a visa when the passage has been paid from the United States. Julius also has two friends in the United States who may be able to help him with the money for passage. Please write to them as well and ask them in Julius's name to help him secure the money for passage: Marianne Gunzenhäuser, 643 Wadsworth Terrace, New York City, and Mr. Herbert Kander, 165 French Street, New Brunswick, N.J. We would be most grateful if you would take care of these matters for us. The sooner, the better. I am hoping that you will be able to send us good news very soon, and remain, with best wishes and kisses, for little Judith and for you,

Your
[no signature]

Please make sure that the papers will be sent directly to us by airmail via Lisbon.[11]

On June 8, 1940, Gustav Heiser wrote to Mr. Philipp [*sic!* Philip] M. Brenner, Attorney at Law, 46 Paterson Street, New Brunswick, N.J. on behalf of Julius [English in the original].

Dear Sir,

My brother-in-law Mr. Julius Zellner, living in Aachen, wrote me that Mr. Leo Rifkin, 402 South First Ave, Highland Park, New Jersey, sent him an Affidavit of support by your assistance. This affidavit has to be renewed—so he wrote. He asks me to get in touch with you and to ask you to suggest Mr. Rifkin to send him a new Affidavit as soon as possible by Air-Mail letter. Mr. Julius Zellner is married with my sister. He is Rabbi, Cantor and Teacher in Aachen near the Belgian frontier and you may imagine how dangerous it might be to live there now. Mr. Zellner is a very handsome man and I am quite sure that Mr. Rifkin would have no trouble with him. The Affidavit is only a matter of form. Until he can make a living here, the Federation takes care for him. That was the same thing with me. I am now more than 4 months in this country. In spite of that fact that I have got an affidavit the Committee here takes care for me and my family until I shall have a position. I am Cantor and Hebrew Teacher and was more than 15 years in a very fine position in Berlin. But as I did not succeed in finding out a job for me the Committee in Pittsburgh takes care for me. My relatives here in Pittsburgh has given four Affidavits to my family in Germany and they are unable to give new Affidavits. Therefore I beg you to help my sister and my brother-in-law to leave the dangerous zone as soon as possible by sending them a renewed Affidavit. I thank you very much for your kind assistance and should like to hear from you agreeable news.

    I am, dear Sir,
    Very faithfully yours,
    Gustave [sic] Heiser
    1114 Euclid Ave.
    Pittsburgh, Pa.[12]

On July 15, 1940, a frustrated and somewhat dejected Julius wrote to Elly and Gustav.

Dear Family,

I have been in Berlin for about a week, and since I am at Meta's just now, I am using the opportunity to write to you.—We are really surprised not to hear from you for such a long time. We have been expecting a reply to our letter.—Today I read your most recent letter and learned that you are doing well. I only wish that we would already have the opportunity to emigrate. Unfortunately it doesn't look like such an opportunity will occur soon. We'll just have to wait.—We are still doing fine in Aachen and can't complain. But it doesn't help if one does not know what the future holds. Although I haven't been directly asked to send you greetings, I am doing so anyhow. I hope that you will write us sometime soon (51 I Seilgraben). We'll write back a detailed letter. Continued good wishes.

With best wishes, also from Elli, Julius
A special hello to little Judith.[13]

Whether there was any further correspondence on this matter from this side of the ocean to Aachen or Berlin is not known, but on September 27, 1940, Gustav, Elly, and Judy received another letter from Gustav's sister, Elli, in Aachen. From her voice we also can hear the urgency and the frustration that they are still waiting, even envy that Gustav managed to find a suitable position in such short order. The reason can be ascertained from an undated letter from Leo and Betty Lieberson with an addition from Meta which tells the Heisers that Elli and Julius are expecting "something little"—a way of saying that Elli is expecting a baby. Betty writes, "We can imagine that Judith is a sweet doll. She is now already more than four years old. Soon she will be joined by a little cousin. Dear Gustav, Elli [Zellner] is expecting something little, it [he] will arrive in a few months." This is confirmed by Meta.[14] Elli writes to the Heisers:

Dear Family,
For the New Year [October 3 and 4] best wishes. You should have only good things happening in your new homeland, may luck continue to be with you. We wish with all our heart to be able to present our good wishes to you in person very soon. It is especially nice that you, dear Gustav, adjusted so well to your position; after all, everything happened so quickly. Let's hope that Julius will also be lucky soon. We are attaching the confirmation of the community here that he serves as teacher and substitute rabbi. Please try to use this to further our cause. Our American number will probably come up in the course of the next year, but one cannot be sure, of course. Dear Gustav, if you could manage to get a job for Julius, that would be great and finally a ray of light for our emigration. We are, thank G-d [in the original], fine, and we hear from

Meta that Mama and Papa are also well. We enjoyed receiving the picture. Judithlein is already a big girl! May G-d protect her and give her good health so that she will continue to bring joy to her parents and grandparents. Perhaps we will be able to celebrate her birthday together. That would be wonderful. In closing once more, and with all my heart, also from Julius, all good wishes for the New Year to you, and to us.
    Your Sister, Sister-in-Law, and Aunt Elli

To this letter, Julius adds:

Dear Family,
I would also like to add my good wishes for the New Year. We are very happy that you were so lucky and adapted to your new situation so well. Best wishes,
    Yours, Julius
    Allow me to thank you in advance for your efforts on my behalf.[15]

While there is additional often undated or fragmentary or illegible correspondence extant in the year between September 1940 and September 1941, the next letter in the collection is from Louis Younger, proprietor of The Working Man's Store in Bakersfield, California. He must have been related to or a friend or employee of Anna Daniels, 2200 D Street, a relative of Elly Heiser's in Bakersfield. On February 21, 1941, months before deportations started in Germany, Louis Younger wrote to Elly Heiser at 1114 North Euclid Avenue in Pittsburgh:

Dear Folks,
I am enclosing herewith all documents complete and trust this will meet with the approval of all concerned. I am glad to have been of some service and trust this will be the means of bringing about a happy reunion in the near future. With kindest regards from my family and Sophy [Birnbaum Weiss?], I remain,
    Sincerely,
    Louis Younger[16]

These documents may have been for Julius and Elli or for any of the other relatives requiring rescue. But a happy end did not occur. In his prayer book, Cantor Heiser listed as perished his father, Isaak (Yitzchok) Heiser; his brother, Hugo (Naftali) Heiser, with wife, Meta Hochmann Heiser, and daughter, Sylvia; Elly Heiser's mother, Adele (Eidel) Birnbaum Hochmann, and sister, Berta (Betti) Hochmann Lieberson, and husband, Leo (Leiser) Lieberson, as well as Elly's uncle Leo Hochmann. All but Leo are listed in the Koblenz Memor Book. Eleonore (Elke) Heiser is also on the list, for a total of nine, but her husband and small son are not. Neither are the three of them in the Koblenz Memor Book. Cantor Heiser's uncle, his mother Selma's brother Simon, is listed in the Koblenz Memor Book but is not on Cantor Heiser's list. From this one may conclude that at least nine immediate relatives were deported and murdered by the Nazis, but perhaps as many as twelve.

Being the time of the High Holy Days, Mr. Heiser wrote a letter to his former classmate at the Hochschule, Charles, dated September 21, 1941. Charles's last name was Rautenberg; he was Karl Rautenberg, Rabbi Karl Rautenberg, also a friend of Emil Fackenheim's.[17] He may have been married or related to someone named Betti Sara Marcuse Rautenberg who lived at No. 7 Trendelenburgstrasse in Charlottenburg [see letter addressed to Gustav Heiser at 1114 N. Euclid Avenue in Pittsburgh, dated July 20, 1940]. Charles was now living in England. The returned envelope c/o Mr. F. Rautenberg, 116 Adelaide Road, London NW 3, is extant. The letter is written in English and Hebrew and is for the Jewish New Year. Elly added a postscript in German.

> Dear Charles,
> Today is the eve of Rosh Hashono and we are ready to welcome another new year. It is only natural that I write to you today for I know how often you will think of our cooperation just during these days and you shall learn by this letter that I, too, did not forget the past few years of our work. I do hope that you will have nice and relatively beautiful and peaceful holy days over there [in England], that you have nice services. To the changing year I wish you from the depth of my heart *L'Shanah Tovah Tikatevu* [in Hebrew] and *Gmar Chatimah Tovah* [in Hebrew]. May this coming year bring us the peace and the victory. The festival season and the preparations for it kept and will keep me pretty busy. You certainly know that a lot of work is to do until this can be brought to some effect and especially in a strange country with strange customs and songs, etc. But as I already have some experience I

hope to overcome the difficulties. This new year brings me a lot of new tasks. Beside my teaching in Hebrew School every day 4 hours, I have to teach in the Sunday School every Sunday 2–1/2 hours. I have there a class of 45 pupils to instruct in history, Religion, customs, etc. and then a lot of little things beside this. Cemetery, synagogue, choir rehearsals, etc. Going to meetings and special occasions and my original duties, chasonus and reading of the Thora. You see that my time is filled and that I am a hard working man. But we make the best of it. But although I am busy enough, I always think of you and of the just past year and I hope that we both will be united again in our work. I still think that some day you will be a rabbi in America. When I see the kind of rabbis around me I still know that you will not be a bad figure amongst them. So, dear Charles, I hope to hear from you as soon as possible and that you write me about your work. Now I wish you again that you will have a good and prosperous new year and that you will remain strong and healthy.

 Yours,
 M. G. Heiser

Dear Charles!
For Rosh Hashanah my best wishes for health and especially a happy reunion with us. We can only report the absolute best about our own situation. Gustav has a good position, and after all of our adventurous wanderings we feel like this is our home. America is a wonderful country and we only wish that you will be able to live here after the war. Little Judithlein has now outgrown the baby stage and we enjoy her very much. The way she speaks is funny—fairly mixed. Strangers say that one cannot tell that she isn't born here. The American slang is pretty hard for us adults. May the New Year bring peace to the world.

 With best wishes,
 Your
 Elly Heiser

December 6. Unfortunately, the letter came back, it went to the old address. [116 Adelaide Road, London NW 3. Envelope is extant.]
We hope that you have been well in the meantime. We are not happy about the news from home. We will try to at least send my

mother to Cuba, but that costs $1,500 which we unfortunately do not yet have raised. What did your brother do for Betty?[18]

Deportations of Jews from Berlin began in November 1941. In the end, Elly and Gustav's efforts were not sufficient. They never saw their loved ones again.

Although travel across the Atlantic Ocean was dangerous after the beginning of World War II on September 1, 1939, it was still possible, but any chance to escape across the big water ceased altogether following the entry of the U.S. into the war on December 7, 1941. American involvement in the hostilities also interrupted written communications between the Old World and the New, so that the correspondence between loved ones ended.

Coming to America

Refugees and immigrants are two sides of the same coin, although not all immigrants are refugees and not all refugees become immigrants. While refugees need to deal primarily with their losses—of home, family, property, employment, culture, community, and citizenship, and mental anguish such as fear and despair, immigrants are full of hope for the future, a new life with often a new family, home, employment, education, assets, culture, and above all, a new community and country.

The United States is called a nation of immigrants.[19] We as a country were built by the hard work of individuals who often were the less fortunate among humanity. Until 1924, access to the United States was open to almost anyone, one exception being Chinese people. This opportunity was a boon to Jews and non-Jews from Eastern and Western Europe as well as many other places in the world. The many Eastern European Jews who tried to flee the *pogroms* (persecutions) in their homeland and who wanted to make a better life for themselves were especially grateful for access to the land that Emma Lazarus celebrated in "The New Colossus" written in 1883.[20] But this ended with the new immigration laws that restricted not only the number of new immigrants who were allowed to enter the country but also the types of individuals who were welcome. Jews from the East were among those who were mostly excluded, exactly at a time when they desperately needed a refuge. Western Europeans were preferred over Eastern Europeans, so that German Jews were somewhat more fortunate because they were included in the German quota. But once the Nazis came to power and their intentions towards Jews were clear, all quotas reached their limits quickly. In 1938, the international community tried to grapple with the dilemma of European refugees. Thirty-two nations convened the Evian Conference in France to discuss and find a solution to this problem. Alas, only the Dominican Republic was willing to take in a sizeable number of Jews (100,000); other countries, including the United States, shied away from helping in a significant way.[21]

For the refugee who advanced to immigrant status, it surely wasn't easy to make the transition from being persecuted, restricted, even hunted, to being free. The emotional stress of harassment and abuse by the Nazis haunted new Americans for a long time, sometimes for their entire life. Recovery was difficult and lengthy. How does one learn to trust again and to plan for the future? Upon arrival, there were no counseling services for the survivors and refugees, and it was up to them to figure out how to fit in and how to resume a normal life.

Gustav Heiser needed to recover from the trauma of the Nazi experience as much as that was possible and figure out how to live again as a free man. He likewise had to care for his wife's and child's emotional and material well-being. As we learn from his earlier correspondence with his family, a good job was not immediately forthcoming, so that he was dependent on financial support from the local Jewish community. Things were done differently than in Germany, and it was not easy for him to familiarize himself with the new ways.

While fitting into Jewish life was a challenge for a new immigrant, it was not the only challenge. Cantor Heiser also had to acclimatize himself to a new language and a new culture as well as the duties and rights of being an American. The ultimate privilege of any new immigrant is, of course, citizenship. Four years after their arrival, on June 14, 1944, Rabbi Herman Hailperin, Ph.D., a colleague in the Conservative Movement and spiritual head of Tree of Life Congregation, Craft Avenue, Pittsburgh, Pennsylvania, wrote a letter in support of Cantor Heiser's citizenship.

> This is to certify that I have known Cantor Mordecai G. Heiser, 830 Mellon Street, Pittsburgh, PA, for almost five years. Cantor Heiser has added much toward the enrichment of the religious and civic life of our city. He is a person of sterling personal character, very loyal to the institutions of the United States, and highly appreciative of the blessings that American citizenship confers upon those who hold citizenship. I have no doubt that he will become a highly respected and valuable citizen of our land.[22]

In 1945, both Gustav and Elly Heiser became naturalized American citizens. Although he had already used his Hebrew name Mordecai rather than Gustav previous to becoming a citizen, on the back of his naturalization document, Mr. Heiser legally changed his name to Mordecai Gustav Heiser. The date was November 16, 1945.[23]

Becoming an American also meant integration into the larger American society. This Cantor Heiser did fairly quickly by participating in the cultural life of Pittsburgh and even of the nation. From reports in the Jewish and Pittsburgh press we can ascertain that Cantor Heiser did not have time to rest on the laurels of his rescue. Life had taken on new meaning and urgency, keeping him very busy.

The American Cantorate

The cantorate in America is not nearly as old as the cantorate in Europe.[24] Jews have been living in America for less than 400 years, compared to 2,000 years in Europe. The first twenty-three Jews came to New Amsterdam not from Europe, but from Recife, Brazil, in 1654, and were of Sephardic (Mediterranean) background. They had originated in Portugal and were connected to the Jews of Amsterdam who had settled there after the Expulsion from Spain in 1492 and then from Portugal in 1497. The Dutch governor of New Amsterdam, Peter Stuyvesant (1592–1672), was not a friend of the Jews and wanted to expel them, but with the help of their brothers in the Netherlands, the Portuguese Jews prevailed. They settled in Manhattan and managed to hold on until the Revolution of 1776, albeit in small numbers.[25]

The role of the cantor was not well defined in colonial American synagogue life, with the meaning of "cantor" changing from generation to generation. Early American cantors were seen as "jacks of all trades," who could do anything that was needed in the synagogue.[26] The cantor could lead services, give a sermon, serve as a beadle in the synagogue, be a ritual slaughterer, serve as a *mohel* (circumciser), write amulets to ward off evil spirits, teach and tutor, but also earn a living by doing regular work—whatever helped him to earn his keep for himself and his family. The training was similar to Europe, one-on-one tutoring with an experienced precentor or knowledgeable community member.[27]

American Jewish life only changed in the mid-nineteenth century when many German Reform Jews came to the United States because the process of Emancipation in Germany did not progress quickly enough

(1871). In the United States, every citizen had been guaranteed civic and religious freedom nearly a hundred years earlier. Sephardic Jewry did not ordain rabbis, as such; any learned member of the community was a *chacham*, a wise person, and could be a prayer leader.[28] The German wave of immigration in the 1840s brought a large number of Ashkenazi Jews, who were mostly Reform and practiced their Judaism differently from the Sephardic Jews living here. They founded their own synagogues, continued the German rites, as my friend Marga Randall stated, and valued their learned rabbis with an academic education and a Ph.D., something the German states had required. Interesting sermons were more important than drawn-out recitatives. They preferred Lutheran-style chorales, which is one reason why Sulzer and Lewandowski survived in America. With the rabbi being the recognized congregational leader, this period deemphasized the importance of the cantor.

A European style cantorate did not really take off until the 1880s, when the Eastern European Jews came to the United States. The Russian cantors' reputations often preceded them, and Ashkenazi American synagogues invited European cantors to become their prayer leaders. Recordings were new at the turn of the century, and the so-called star cantors recorded their popular pieces. Some tried their fortunes in the world of opera. From approximately 1890 through 1940, the American Jewish community experienced what is known as the Golden Age of Cantors.[29] While this was good for the community, it was not always good for the cantor. Although he was an employee of the congregation, he had no economic safety net. If a cantor's novelty wore off, he might be let go. Some might return to the Old World, or find work with another congregation, but others became indigent. Likewise, if a cantor got sick or just old, who would support him? An initial attempt, in 1897, at organizing cantors in a professional organization in New York, the *Hazzanim Farband*, also known as the Jewish Ministers Cantors Association, did little to advance fair treatment of cantors within the synagogue system.[30] Yet this exchange of musical talent across the ocean—and it wasn't always one-sided either—continued until the Nazis cut off the supply line with the Holocaust.

Jewish Pittsburgh

Between 1840 and 1880, approximately 200,000 Jewish immigrants settled in various areas of the U.S. Another two and a half million joined them between 1880 and 1924, so that the Jewish population in the United States by then neared three million. Although it is not exactly known when Jews started to settle in the Pittsburgh area, the consensus seems to be that serious Jewish settlement of Western Pennsylvania began at the time of German immigration in the middle of the nineteenth century. Because of the abundant natural resources such as coal and wood and the two rivers that merge in Pittsburgh, the Monongahala and the Allegheny, to create the Ohio River, and therewith easy transportation to some parts of the area, Pittsburgh developed as an industrial center. In Württemberg and Bavaria, families had sustained themselves through peddling, cattle dealing, farming, and the manufacture of textiles. This did not change very much now. A good number of them spent some amount of time in small towns, "operating retail establishments, usually opened after peddling in the hinterlands." Grunberger tells the story of Joseph Seligman from Bavaria, "the oldest son of a weaver and itinerant woolen merchant." Immigrating in 1837, "he peddled in and around western Pennsylvania, selling to the miners and farmers." To make a long story short, we are told that he ended up "one of America's wealthiest and most powerful individuals."[31] A charming feature of the region that may have attracted some of these immigrants was the similarity of the Western Pennsylvania landscape to Württemberg and Bavaria with its rolling hills and inviting rivers and lakes. First dubbed "Iron City", as still today in Iron City beer, by 1870 the availability of bituminous coal led to the sustained production of steel, giving Pittsburgh its name of "Steel City."[32]

There are records of small numbers of German Jews settling in and around Pittsburgh between 1838 and 1844.[33] Barbara S. Burstin, Ph.D., teacher on the American Jewish experience at both the University of Pittsburgh and Carnegie Mellon University in Pittsburgh, wrote a fascinating study of the "Steel City Jews" from 1840 to 1915, with a myriad of interesting details.

While Pittsburgh provided a variety of military products and other supplies during the civil war, Burstin points out that Pittsburgh was not so favorably situated for commerce, because there was in 1843 "no direct connection from Ohio to Philadelphia." She writes: "It was just too hard to get over the Allegheny Mountains from the East both for settlers and for goods." And when the interior was developed, Burstin points out, Pittsburgh did not become the gateway to the West either, despite its location at the head of the Ohio River, but rather Wheeling, West Virginia, and the newly built Erie Canal (1827) in northern Pennsylvania.[34]

In the late 1840s, "improvements in river transportation, steamboats," and the demand for goods of many kinds attracted more settlers, including Jews. By the 1860s, Burstin reports fifty to sixty Jewish families, most of whom still eked out a living as peddlers in the surrounding areas.[35] But not for long. Soon not only the Carnegies, Fricks, and Mellons made a name for themselves, but so did the Kaufmanns and the Hornes, who established successful department stores. We know that "Jakob Kaufmann, son of a horse and cattle dealer in Bavaria also began in the United States as a peddler. His first actual store on the outskirts of Pittsburgh measured no more than 17 by 28 feet." I still shopped at Kaufmann's, not at the outskirts of the city, but downtown, when I lived near Pittsburgh in the 1970s and 80s. Grunberger concludes that "an impressive number of these immigrants experienced in their lifetimes a rapid rise from being humble peddlers, to solid shopkeepers, to 'merchant princes'."[36]

The famous Rodef Shalom Reform congregation was founded in 1853, even before the Civil War.[37] In 1885, a national convention of rabbis took place at Rodef Shalom and the Concordia Club, resulting in the famous Pittsburgh Platform that influenced the Reform Movement into the 1930s, but also highlighted the relaxed customs of Reform, especially concerning *kashrut*. In the twentieth century, both of Rodef Shalom's Rabbi Solomon Freehof (1892–1990) and Rabbi Walter Jacob (1930–) became important leaders in the Reform Movement.[38]

Starting around 1885, the poor immigrant Jews of Eastern Europe settled in the Lower Hill District or the ghetto.[39] A place of crowding and squalor, many immigrants worked in the factories and sweat shops and were not able to rise above their poverty, remaining mired in this depressing area. Burstin notes that once Pittsburgh's industry took off, however, some of the poor Jews of the Lower Hill district also were able to advance economically and socially, and therefore move out of this neighborhood. Some decided to live in East Liberty, the area in which Congregation B'nai Israel would eventually be located.

Around the time that the Burstin study ends, in the Teens and Twenties, Jews from the Lower Hill District no longer moved to the East End but to Squirrel Hill, the Jerusalem of the Pittsburgh Jews. Over the next century, more than a dozen other synagogues such as Tree of Life, Beth Shalom, Temple Sinai, New Light Synagogue, and Beth El and Temple Emanuel in the South Hills were also founded. Today Jewish Pittsburgh is a thriving community of about 50,000 Jews (in 2018), synagogues, cultural institutions, restaurants, and a very active Federation and Community Center.[40] The soot and smog of steel mills such as Jones & Laughlin have long been replaced by the sparkle of one of the greenest cities in the nation. The University of Pittsburgh features an Israel Heritage Room among its thirty-one Nationality Rooms, which had just been dedicated when I started to write my dissertation on Martin Buber, and in 1988 I was awarded one of the first scholarships to conduct research at the Buber Archives of the Jewish National and University Library at Hebrew University in Jerusalem (Givat Ram campus).

Congregation B'nai Israel

Among Cantor Heiser's priorities upon being awarded the position of cantor at B'nai Israel was to learn American Jewish religious practices and synagogue life, as such. As we saw from his letter to Charles, the new customs were different, hence strange, as were the hymns, whose melodies were often composed by contemporary American cantors and composers. B'nai Israel, although Conservative, was still fairly traditional and changed only gradually and in small ways over the years. As is often the case, a Jewish congregation is not born as a full-blown institution but as a *minyan* of at least ten [men traditionally] that gradually increases in number and resources and eventually organizes into a corporate body. Congregation B'nai Israel was no different. In 1904, the Jewish residents of the crowded Lower Hill District who moved to the East End were in need of their own services.[41] They organized several *minyanim* in people's homes. As the number of Jews in the East End grew, especially in the World War I era, these newcomers rented space in a number of buildings in the area, among them the Masonic Building on Collins Avenue.[42]

In 1920, the congregation, which named itself B'nai Israel, hired a rabbi—Rabbi Benjamin A. Lichter, who was originally from Pittsburgh but had been ministering at the famous Touro Synagogue in Rhode Island. This was a most fortunate choice for the congregation, as Rabbi Lichter had a kind and forward-looking attitude and was a fine match for the members of this congregation. He served them for thirty-seven years until his retirement. Rabbi Lichter brought new ideas to this traditional congregation, specifically a late Friday night service, at 8:00 p.m., which became popular with the businessmen who had to work late and could not make it to the traditional Kabbalat Shabbat service at sundown. Other innovations included the singing of Sabbath hymns in English, a "mixed choir of male and female voices," and the establishment of a Sisterhood under the able leadership of Mrs. Barnett Davis, for whom the social hall was later named. A forerunner to the Men's Club, the LaTovah Society, also formed. The congregation held services at a number of different locations over the years. Jewish education was a challenge, and from 1923 to 1929 the Religious School affiliated with the Hebrew Institute for economic reasons. Thereafter, Jewish education as well as the Hebrew language were again taught in-house.[43]

One cannot help but admire the vision and energy of this young congregation which acquired the site for the future synagogue building on North Negley Avenue as early as 1921, breaking ground for their *shul* on October 22, 1922.[44] "The new Synagogue ... was built by H. Miller & Sons Company, contractors. The building was completed according to schedule. It is Byzantine in design, circular and contains the Sanctuary of the Congregation. It has a seating capacity of fifteen hundred."[45] In her *Pittsburgh Post-Gazette* article of December 9, 1997, Patricia Lowry described the synagogue building.

> On the outside, the synagogue is simple and austere, a great stone drum occupying a rise in the land that gives it even greater presence. The architect was Henry Hornbostel with Sharoove and Friedman, presumably with the renowned Hornbostel providing the design concept. By 1923, his portfolio included many landmarks, among them the Carnegie Tech campus, Soldiers and Sailors Memorial Hall and Shadyside's Rodef Shalom temple. While the latter is a cheery confection of pastel terra cotta ornaments, B'nai Israel's exterior is faced in random stone separated by belt courses or bands of limestone. The top layer of this sober cake is rubble within a blind arcade of bricks, the whole thing topped with limestone six-pointed stars and what look to be terra cotta grapes and leaves—all best seen with binoculars. While the drum and its dome are Byzantine, the arcaded porch is Classical. Pittsburgh History and Landmarks Foundation architectural historian Walter Kidney, who is writing a book on Hornbostel, thinks the latter was inspired by Brunelleschi's Pazzi Chapel in Florence.[46]

Ambitious indeed! In April 1929, the congregation celebrated its Silver Jubilee with a week-long celebration; it had grown up and "took its place among the leading religious institutions of Western Pennsylvanian Jewry."[47] I. A. Melnick, who penned and edited B'nai Israel's Silver Jubilee Volume, wrote:

Such an occasion could not be permitted to pass unnoticed or with an ordinary program. Elaborate preparations accordingly were made for an entire week of celebration to commemorate this historic event.... Appropriately, the program of commemoration began with religious services on the Sabbath eve, Friday, April 12, 1929, under the direction of Rabbi Lichter, assisted by Cantor Julius Bloom and a fully augmented choir.... At divine services Sabbath morning, Rabbi [Charles I.] Hoffman [of Newark, N.J.] spoke again and, at a Sabbath Tea of which the Sisterhood was hostess, following Z'miros, addresses were delivered by Rabbi Herman Hailperin of Tree of Life Congregation and by the late Rabbi Goodman A. Rose of Beth Shalom Congregation. The gala event of the celebration was the Silver Anniversary Banquet held on Sunday evening at the Hotel Schenley.... Other events of the week included Sisterhood Night at the Synagogue on Tuesday. ... The Chevra Shas also celebrated with a Melave Malke.... Alumni Night in the Synagogue, Children's Day at the Enright Theater and Community Night in the Synagogue rounded out the program of a crowded week of memorable events which are still fondly remembered by the older members to this day.[48]

Just reading about the events is exhilarating! But seriously, putting together such a series of events—major events—within such a short timespan demands an enormous volunteer workforce. At that time, B'nai Israel was moving toward its prime and had enough volunteers in the Sisterhood, the Men's Club, the Young Adult Congregation, and the membership at large. Each of these events took planning, fund raising, organizing, publicity, speakers, music, hosting, cooking, and cleanup, by unpaid members who were proud to participate in these positive and joyful festivities.

The second twenty-five years brought more growth and more changes in religious services, such as family pews, responsive readings by the rabbi and congregation, and new *Machzorim* for the High Holy Days. In the years when the congregation expanded and Rabbi Lichter got older, B'nai Israel hired an assistant to the rabbi—beginning with Seymour J. Cohen in 1951.[49] Cantor Heiser served with five rabbis—beginning with Rabbi Benjamin Lichter, a single man, known as "the marrying rabbi," who spent nearly four decades at B'nai Israel (1920–1957). The three subsequent rabbis—Seymour J. Cohen (1957–61), Mordecai S. Chertoff (1961–66), and Jack Schechter (1966–76)—served the congregation for shorter terms, and

Rabbi Richard Marcovitz had been the rabbi for twenty years (since 1976) when B'nai Israel closed its doors in 1996.[50]

Already much earlier, before the arrival of Cantor Heiser in 1940, the synagogue also hired "sextons," or *shamashim*, to support the work of the congregation. They were Hyman Lippman, Rev. Hyman Perlmutter, and the most recent Rev. Mordechai (Max) Haalman.[51] Max Haalman—whom I remember personally—was also a Holocaust survivor like Cantor Heiser.

Max, who was Dutch, had a sad story, having lost his family in the Holocaust. After the Holocaust, he remarried and raised four more children. He was a large, strapping man with a heart of gold, a solid and pleasant baritone vice, who took his work very seriously. When reading Torah, he was a perfectionist. He once told me that no matter how often he had *leyned* a particular *parshah*, he would practice it again and again, to be sure he did not make a mistake. Only when I learned to read Torah myself did I appreciate the care which he took in carrying out this sacred duty. Max was our beloved beadle, but Mordecai was the soul of B'nai Israel.

The division of labor between Cantor Heiser and Reverend Haalman was fixed by their contracts and was updated from time to time. Cantor Heiser officiated on Shabbat and on festivals as well as on the High Holy Days; he also read Torah and chanted the Haftarah, instructed *b'nei mitzvah* students, and officiated at weddings, funerals, and unveilings. He visited the sick and served as a *mohel* in the community. Contract negotiations in 1953 detailed Cantor Heiser's teaching in the Hebrew School and his cantorial duties for 1953–1954. "Assume all cantorial duties for High Holidays, minor holidays, and Saturdays. Read Torah on Saturday A.M. and P.M.; Monday A.M; Thursday A.M. Train all B'nai Israel choirs."[52] In 1960, the executive committee reported, "After the High Holiday season of 1961 the Congregation will procure the services of a Scroll Reader for Saturday mornings. *Hazzan* Heiser will continue to read the Torah on Monday and Thursday mornings, Rosh Chodesh and minor festivals which come on a weekday, as well as on Saturday afternoon."[53]

The congregation tried to be even-handed in the assignment of duties, if hierarchical. Each year during the High Holy Days, B'nai Israel ran two sets of services: one in the main sanctuary, the other in the Mrs. Barnett Davis Social Hall. For 1962 we learn that "Cantor Haalman and choir will again officiate [at the parallel service]. The second day of Rosh Hashonah the Rabbi, Cantor and choir from the main synagogue will be at the Parallel services and Cantor Haalman and choir will be in the main sanctuary."[54] In 1966, the board noted that "Cantor Heiser will begin with the Shacharis service on Sabbath morning [with] Mr. Haalman to lead the prayers from the beginning of the Sabbath service up to Shacharis."[55]

Reverend Haalman also read Torah, led weekday services [B'nai Israel had daily morning and evening *minyanim* as well as a Kabbalat Shabbat service on Friday], and took care of other duties in the shul, including some religious instruction. From the board minutes of June 3, 1969, we learn of a contract renewal for three years, starting September 1. "Duties would include teaching, *mashgiach* [kitchen supervisor], and Saturday services."[56] In *B'nai Israel's 75th Anniversary* booklet we read, "The sexton reads the Torah, leads the daily minyan, sends Yahrzeit notices and tends the vestments and prayerbooks."[57]

Religious School grew both "in curriculum and in numbers," requiring "new texts and new modes of instruction."[58] When Rabbi Cohen began serving the congregation in 1951, the board meeting minutes record an astounding 141 children in the Hebrew School and 419 in the Sunday School.[59] In 1952, the Hebrew School recorded 159 children and the Religious School 488.[60] These are impressive numbers! All of these challenges were weathered by the congregation thanks to the able and inspired leadership of Rabbi Benjamin Lichter and Chazen Julius Bloom, who had come from the Lower Hill District to join the congregation in 1924.

When Cantor Heiser came to Pittsburgh in 1940, he was fortunate to find a well-organized and *menshlich* group of Jews who welcomed him and his family with kindness and grace. American entry into World War II mobilized not only the Men's Club to sell war bonds but also the Sisterhood to provide a variety of services. In 1942, the Sisterhood presented a service flag to the congregation honoring 135 members of the congregation serving in the Armed Forces.[61]

Although the post-war years were tough economic times, with the development of the Stanton Heights Neighborhood in the 1950s, which was in close proximity to the synagogue, B'nai Israel continued to grow in membership. This expansion and the congregation's tough pay-as-you go policy permitted additional construction of needed classrooms, social hall, and rabbi's office with groundbreaking on June 21, 1950. A tremendous expression of thanks was due to an industrious Sisterhood and active Men's Club, who contributed $60,000 and $20,000 respectively. A library followed somewhat later. When the money ran out, "[T]there were more appeals and members again dug deep into their pockets." On May 15, 16, and 17, 1953, just in time for the fiftieth anniversary of the congregation, the dedication services of the "magnificent structure" were held. I. A. Melnick wrote, "B'nai Israel now is truly fulfilling its three-fold function as a 'Beth Ha'T'filoh, a Beth Ha'Midrash and a Beth Ha'Knesset."[62]

While the congregation was still growing at fifty, this was no longer true at seventy-five. A number of significant changes were still occurring in the intervening twenty-five years, such as the introduction of a Bat Mitzvah for girls at the Friday evening service in 1955, then a permanent switch to Saturday morning in 1972; changes in the Shabbat service and Torah reading cycle, transitioning from Ashkenazi Hebrew pronunciation for services to Sephardic pronunciation in school as well as services in 1966; participation of women on the *bimah* with Sisterhood Shabbat, and the full participation of women in the service by granting them *aliyot* (honors) in 1979, just in time for the seventy-fifth anniversary. Harold Grinberg, the author of the text for the anniversary brochure, noted, "Though nothing like the period of growth in the early '50s was achieved from 1953 to 1979, B'nai Israel continued to improve its facilities."[63] This was achieved primarily through the dedication of the Scheinman Library in 1961, refurbishing of the synagogue in 1965, and the addition of nine stained-glass windows, designed by Jean-Jacques Duval (1930–2021). Duval was an American artist who lived in the Adirondacks. He was born in Strassbourg, France, and was famous for his glass art and especially his stained-glass windows. In 2005, he received the Lifetime Achievement Award by the Stained-Glass Association of America.[64]

In 1967, "the sanctuary was rededicated in memory of Rabbi Lichter," who had died in 1963.[65] But in the 1970s, the growth of B'nai Israel had "leveled off, mostly because Stanton Heights has lost some of its Jewish population." On October 22, 1978—declared Congregation B'nai Israel Day by Pittsburgh Mayor Richard Caliguiri—the congregation initiated a year-long celebration with another lovely brochure to remember their diamond jubilee under the leadership of Rabbi Richard M. E. Marcovitz, who had been installed in 1977. Alas, the writer's hope that "we can expect this to continue for another 75 years" was not to come true.[66] Just a decade later, the heart and soul of the synagogue would go to his eternal rest and the congregation would struggle to survive.

The Transition from Cantor Julius Bloom to the Heiser Era

Even before Cantor Bloom's unexpected death in 1942, Cantor Heiser participated in events in the larger Jewish community, such as Hadassah's

Chanukkah party on December 10, 1940, less than a year after his arrival, when he illustrated a lecture by Rabbi Lichter, "The History of Jewish Music," with Jewish folk songs.[67] He performed a Purim sketch on March 9, 1941,[68] and chanted the Purim Megillah on March 1, 1942.[69]

Julius Bloom served as B'nai Israel's *hazzan* from 1924 until 1942, when he died suddenly on April 6. At his memorial service, Cantor Heiser led a mournful congregation and community with the "El Male Rachamim" memorial prayer.

> The general public is invited to attend the memorial services in memory of the late Cantor Julius Bloom, who officiated at the B'nai Israel for the past 18 years. The services will be held at the B'nai Israel Synagogue, 327 N. Negley Avenue on Sunday evening, March 15 at 8:30 o'clock, at which time there will be a musical prelude by Joseph C. Derdeyn and Jerome Tagress; an invocation by Rabbi Herman Hailperin of the Tree of Life Congregation; remarks and tributes by Benjamin Chait, Saul Schein, Morris Neaman, Judge Lencher and Rabbi Benjamin Lichter; music by the B'nai Israel Women's choir, with a special arrangement of the Twenty-third Psalm made by Cantor Bloom; Memorial Prayer by Rev. G. Mordecai Heiser and Benediction by Rabbi Goodman Rose.[70]

Following Cantor Bloom's death, the executive committee of B'nai Israel met to discuss the congregation's options. Mr. Saul Schein reported that "the Executive Committee interviewed Mr. Heiser with reference to taking on additional duties, and as a result of these deliberations, came to some terms as to compensation."[71]

So far, Cantor Heiser—who would for quite some time be known as Reverend Heiser—carried out certain regular congregational duties which consisted of "teaching in Hebrew School every day four hours, teach[ing] in the Sunday School every Sunday two and a half hours, cemetery, synagogue, choir rehearsal, meetings, special occasions, and chasonus and reading of the Thora."[72] In 1941–1942, his salary for these duties was $1,235,[73] an increase over the amount he received as a "reader" in his first year. At the April 6, 1942, board meeting immediately following Cantor Bloom's death, Mr. Saul Schein recommended that "(h)is duties would be the same as heretofore with the exception, he will take on additional ones that become necessary on the account of the passing away of Rev. Julius Bloom. It was the recommendation of the Executive Committee that the proper officers enter into a contract with Rev. Heiser from March 1."[74] After full deliberations regarding Rev. Heiser, Mr. Schein moved, "That we continue employment of Rev. Heiser to perform the same duties as he has been performing with the exception of the Schacharis for the High Holidays, and that in addition to that, he should officiate at Kol Nidre, Musafim and Ne'ilah services during the Yomim Neroim, and Musaf services on Saturday, and the various holidays, and train the choir at the salary of $2,000 per annum effective as of March 1, 1942, payable monthly." This motion was passed.[75]

The congregation seems to have been pleased with the new arrangement, as on August 3, 1943, Mr. Saul Schein, Esq., again made a motion, seconded by Mrs. Barnett Davis, "to the effect that the former motion of fixing the salary of Cantor M. G. Heiser in the amount of $2,600 as of July 1, 1943, be amended to apply retroactively to January 1, 1943." The amendment was adopted.[76] In addition, "A motion made by Mrs. Barnett Davis, seconded by Mrs. I. L. Giffen, Esq., to make a gift to Cantor M. G. Heiser in the amount of $200 in order to assist him in straightening out his financial affairs, was likewise adopted."[77] The salary increases kept coming in small increments, to $2,900, and by May 1, 1945, "$400 per year, increasing his compensation from $2,900 to $3,300 per year."[78] While the congregation appreciated Cantor Heiser's efforts on their behalf, there is plenty of evidence concerning contract negotiations, choir demands, school needs, and other weighty matters through the years. A good bit of juggling took place to cover all of the different services offered—children's services, youth services, a second and parallel High Holy Day service led by Rev. Haalman, and later, in the 1990s, Sisterhood events with female participation.

Beyond Congregation B'nai Israel

Other refugees settled in the Pittsburgh area as well. On May 31, 1942, Cantor Heiser participated in a concert by the B'nai Israel Hebrew School with Jewish and Hebrew selections. The event featured Hans Bassermann, former concertmaster of the Berlin Philharmonic Orchestra, who was a fellow refugee and now a member of the Pittsburgh Symphony Orchestra, in a violin recital.[79] On October 16, B'nai Israel hosted a service for the B'nai B'rith Council of Pittsburgh's centennial celebration with a service; Cantor Heiser led the women's choir with vocal selections.[80]

For Armistice Day, on November 7, 1943, B'nai B'rith presented a program at the Y.M.&W.H.A. Here Cantor Heiser again chanted the memorial prayer, "El [Male] Rachamim".[81] Likewise, at the Annual Luncheon of the Conference of the United Jewish Appeal in the Tri-State area, which was held at the William Penn Hotel, Cantor Heiser chanted "an unusually impressive memorial service for the Jewish victims in Europe."[82] No surprise there, since at least nine and perhaps as many as twelve members of his own family had been murdered by Hitler's henchmen, including his own father and his mother-in-law. The Holocaust was a very personal matter throughout his life. On December 9, 1945, a special memorial service was held at B'nai Israel Synagogue for "the 131 men of Jewish faith who died in the war just ended." Reverend Mordecai Heiser again chanted the El Male Rachamim prayer.[83] B'nai Israel's cemetery is located at Blackadore Street in Penn Township. On September 22, 1946, the first veterans' plots in a Jewish Cemetery in Allegheny County were dedicated there. Cantor Heiser and the male choir of the congregation as well as the Jewish veterans participated in the program.[84]

Cantor Heiser was well accepted and appreciated beyond his own synagogue and across denominations in the greater Pittsburgh Jewish community and participated in many events over the years. As early as 1943, Cantor Heiser was elected to office. The [Pittsburgh] Cantors Association, "under the leaderships of Rev. Zaludkowski," Cantor of the Beth Shalom Congregation in Pittsburgh, which spread "musical and liturgical culture among the public at large," elected him to be their secretary.[85] Rev. Zaludkowsky died that very same year, and the Ministers and Cantors Association of Pittsburgh and Vicinity took out a large memorial ad in *The Jewish Criterion*, signed by Rev. Mordecai G. Heiser, Secretary, and Rev. Benjamin M. Kimel, Treasurer.[86]

On April 27, 1945, the Ladies Aid Society for the Slabodka Yeshiva celebrated its thirteenth anniversary with participation from Rev. Bernard Poupko [Orthodox] and "Reverend Mordecai G. Heiser," who sang Palestinian and [Jewish] folk songs.[87] We know that Cantor Heiser was a committed Zionist already in Germany, and it is no surprise that he later became a strong supporter of the newly created State of Israel (1948). Cantor Heiser participated in many events to benefit Israel over the years. He and Elly visited Israel at least five times. In October 1948, he contributed "Palestinian and folk songs" to an Israel Night that included the showing of the movie *Freedom Bound*.[88] Israel's first birthday was celebrated on May 11, 1949, with a program organized by the Labor Zionist Movement of Pittsburgh at the Y. Speaker was "Israel hero, Captain Yaakov Wayland," who related "the epic battles in the kibbutz of Negba in the Negev desert, where he served as Commander." Cantor Heiser along with colleague David Messeroff presented the musical program.[89] On November 6, 1949, the Labor Zionist Organization Poale Zion and the Jewish National Workers Alliance organized a program titled "No Israel without Jerusalem—No Jerusalem without Israel" at the Y, to which Cantor Heiser contributed a musical program.[90]

Over the years, Cantor Heiser's service to the larger Jewish community was unstinting. From at least 1948 on, he served on the Third Seder Committee of the United Jewish Fund.[91] In 1949, he served on the renamed After the Seder committee and participated in the April 24 kick-off program of the annual campaign at the Syria Mosque, a popular event venue. The Pittsburgh Youth Symphony and the Taylor Allderdice [High School] A Capella Choir, as well as Cantor Heiser along with his B'nai Israel Choir, participated in "a moving cantata depicting Jewish history," called 'What is Torah?'"[92] The musical program of the community-wide Chanukkah program at the Y on December 18, 1949, was entirely in Cantor Heiser's hands—from "the traditional blessings for the Chanukkah lights, to a group of Chanukkah songs, and the singing of traditional Chanukkah melodies."[93]

The Hebrew Institute Parent-Teachers Association organized a Music Festival in honor of Purim for March 26, 1949. Cantor Heiser had the distinct honor of being featured as a member of the Pittsburgh Opera Company, singing excerpts from "Samson and Delilah" to the accompaniment of Harry Franklin, official pianist of the Pittsburgh Symphony, alongside Pittsburgh Opera Company members Vivian John and Phyllis Sidney, and "outstanding Pittsburgh musician" Lorin Maazel [Maestro Maazel died as I was writing this on July 13, 2014], playing the violin with the Fine Arts String Quartet of the Pittsburgh Symphony Orchestra.[94] The *American Jewish Outlook* reported, "Mordecai G. Heiser, Cantor of the B'nai Israel Synagogue, is a graduate of the Rabbinical Seminary in Berlin. He attended the College of Music in Berlin. He studied with Bernard Ulrich and Bachner in Berlin and with Byron D. Blumenthal in Pittsburgh and was elected to his first cantorial position at the age of 20. Cantor Heiser has given recitals and lectures on Jewish music both abroad and in this country. He has also appeared in recitals of classical songs and lieder. Only a few weeks ago he was presented at the Stephen Collins Foster Memorial Hall by the Pittsburgh Concert Society. He is scheduled to give a full length recital in New York City at Carnegie Recital Hall on March 22."[95] If Cantor Heiser ever was to become a concert singer, now would have been the time. But although he enjoyed concertizing all of his life, that was not his calling.

Congregation B'nai Israel was affiliated with the United Synagogue and supported the Jewish Theological Seminary (JTS), the seminary of the Conservative Movement in New York. Activities in connection with the third annual dinner for the seminary by the Pittsburgh Friends of the Jewish Theological Seminary of America were organized by each of the four Conservative synagogues in Pittsburgh separately as well as together. On Friday, November 25, 1949, B'nai Israel contributed a late Friday night service, by now one of their specialties, with Cantor Heiser and the choir participating.[96] The community-wide dinner for the seminary was held at the William Penn Hotel on December 4 and Cantor Heiser led "Birkat Hamazon."[97] *The American Jewish Outlook* of December 2, 1949, noted that "The Program . . . traditionally emphasizes classical Jewish music and dramatic presentations from the famous Eternal Light radio program."[98] From 1944 through 1989, The Eternal Light program was a nationally famous radio series on NBC, sponsored by JTS. Milton E. Krents (1912–2000) produced the radio program for 44 years, and received a Lifetime Achievement Award from the National Academy of Television Arts and Sciences. The series was edited by Dr. Moshe Davis and enjoyed the participation of Cantor Robert H. Segal. It aired on Sundays at noon as part of NBC's religious programming, with a weekly audience of more than six million. Overall, the program won two Emmy Awards plus several more nominations and three Peabody Awards. In 1952 it expanded to television as well.

Beyond the Jewish Community

As we have already learned, Cantor Heiser's world of music was not restricted to the Jewish realm. On January 8, 1949, the Pittsburgh Concert Society featured Mordecai Heiser, Tenor, and Helen Hougham, Soprano, in a New Year's concert at the Stephen Collins Foster Memorial Hall.[99] An article in the *Jewish Criterion* stated that "Cantor Heiser has studied music and voice abroad and in this country. He is the only male vocalist selected by the Pittsburgh Concert Society for a concert appearance this season. A Graduate of College of Music and Rabbinical College in Berlin, Cantor Heiser has been with B'nai Israel Congregation since summer 1940. His program at the Recital will include selections from opera, oratorio, classical songs and lieder. He will be accompanied at the piano by Mrs. Julia Golomb."[100]

The actual program stated that "Mordecai Heiser, Tenor, is Cantor and musical director of B'nai Israel Congregation. He was born in Lithuania [sic!], but spent most of his life, prior to coming to this country in 1940, in Berlin, where he graduated from the Rabbinical College."[101] This local event provided a "Vorspeise" for music lovers. On March 22, 1949, Cantor Heiser made his national concert debut with a recital at Carnegie Recital Hall in New York City. The event was managed by an agent, Henry Colbert, 15 West 44th Street, New York 18, NY. *The American Jewish Outlook* reported, "Cantor Mordecai G. Heiser of the B'nai Israel Congregation will be presented by Henry Colbert of New York in a full length recital at Carnegie Recital Hall in New York on Tuesday, March 22. His program will include Hebrew songs and operatic arias. Mr. Otto Herz will assist at the piano. Cantor Heiser who studied voice and music abroad and in this country has been connected with the B'nai Israel Congregation for the past 9 years."[102]

As the program is extant, we know exactly what Cantor Heiser sang at Carnegie Recital Hall. The offering consisted of eight separate sections. As the publicity stated, most of the selections were classical music, with the exception of two Hebrew songs and a few modern compositions. The first part of the program included [Georg Friedrich] Händel's "Where'r You Walk," [Felix] Mendelssohn's "Ye People Rend Your Hearts," and two selections each from [Richard] Strauss ("Zueignung" and "Allerseelen") and [Robert] Schumann ("Die Lotosblume" and "Ich grolle nicht"). These were followed by the *Preislied* from "Die Meistersinger" by [Richard] Wagner; "Who is Sylvia?" and "Der Doppelgänger" by [Franz] Schubert, "Rachel, Quand du Seigneur" by [Jacques] Halevy and "O Paradiso" by [Giacomo] Meyerbeer. Both Halevy and Meyerbeer were Jewish and enjoyed great popularity in the cultural environment that Cantor Heiser had frequented in Germany.

The second part was less culturally German and more Jewish and international. Israel had just come into being and was celebrated with "Chazak veemats."[103] The text was set to music by [?] Weinberg. A second selection was a song of the *chalutzim*, "Bagalil" by [Julius] Chajes [spelled 'Chayes' in program]. These were followed by several songs in English, "When I Have Sung My Songs to You," by [Ernest] Charles, "Daisies" and "Sure on the Shining Night" by [Samuel] Barber, "Velvet Shoes" by [Randall] Thompson, and "In the Silence of the Night" by [Sergei] Rachmaninoff. Mr. Heiser concluded his presentation with two Italian selections, "Una Furtiva Lagrima" by [Gaetano] Donizetti and "Vesti la Giuba [sic! Giubba]" from *Il Pagliacci* by [Ruggero] Leoncavallo.[104]

What was Cantor Heiser trying to show with this program? Clearly, he demonstrated his vast repertoire of musical knowledge that he had acquired mostly in Germany and that he felt comfortable with. He heavily favored operatic selections and lieder, and he tried to show the diversity of his concert repertoire. Did he hope to become an opera singer like some of the other famous *hazzanim*, such as Richard Tucker and Jan Peerce? Probably not, as he, like Greek Cantor Estrongo Nechama and Yossele Rosenblatt, had made a commitment to *hazzanut*. But he perhaps hoped to periodically offer up a concert to the wider society—which he did amply in Pittsburgh and in the region, all for the benefit of his congregation, JTS, the Cantors Assembly, or the Zionist organization and Israel.

The artist's performance at Carnegie Recital Hall was reviewed by R.P. from the *New York Times* in a brief article, "Mordecai Heiser, Tenor, Bows," on March 23. "Mordecai Heiser, Pittsburgh tenor, made his New York debut last night at Carnegie Recital Hall. Otto Herz was the accompanist and the program included the Prize Song from "Meistersinger," Meyerbeer's "O Paradiso," Donizetti's "Una Furtiva Lagrima" and "Vesti la Giubba " from "Pagliacci." The singer had a big voice that was naturally pleasant in quality. But he sang with little flexibility or variety of approach and there was a tendency to sing too loud at the climaxes."[105]

While complimentary, one would not exactly call this a rave review. Recently, Cantor Heiser's great-granddaughter sent me three samples of concert pieces that Cantor Heiser performed—we do not know where or when—but probably early in his career. Two of them, "O Paradiso" by Meyerbeer and "Rachel, Quand du Seigneur" by Halevy, were in the Carnegie Hall concert. Halevy's and Meyerbeer's works were in much demand for performances. The third selection, "Rachamono Deone," Cantor Heiser performed in a 1954 concert in Pittsburgh. When one listens to these musical selections, one is inclined to agree with the above critic of the Carnegie Recital Hall concert. The steady, strong delivery of the music lacks the nuancing that contributes so much to the meaning of a piece.

One cannot say this about Cantor Heiser's *hazzanut*, which exhibits a wide range of styles such as solos, choir accompaniment, duets with his granddaughter, and confident modulations between modes, word repetition, and falsetto in the delivery. Although his voice mellowed with age, giving it the soulfulness that made his prayers so meaningful to his congregation, this kind of praise was already heaped on him in his very earliest renditions in Berlin and then in England. The *Israelitische Religionsverein* praised his "resounding, pleasant tenor voice" which allowed him to present a "soulful" worship service (November 1, 1938). A second letter on the same date praises his "wonderful tenor voice" which, "paired with his deep knowledge of the prayer contents" creates a true worship service

(November 1, 1938). The Assistant Camp Director of the Kitchener Camp in England wrote in appreciation of Cantor Heiser's "musical and cantorial abilities" and his "thorough knowledge of Judaistics" that "enabled him to recite the prayers right and solemnly" (January 25, 1940). Cantor Heiser was clearly more of a sacred singer than a concert performer.

The Evolution of the American Cantorate and Cantor Heiser's Contribution

It is only after the European source dried up that American congregations seriously tried to figure out where their liturgical specialists would come from and established cantorial institutes. Although there had been the early version of a cantors' organization previously mentioned—the *Hazzanim Farband*—the denominational institutes did not develop until after World War II: Reform in 1947, Conservative in 1951, and Orthodox in 1954.[106] These cantors' institutes offered classes to cantors already in the profession with the goal of achieving a common base. They created a certificate, then a curriculum, held an annual convention, created a pension plan and a placement service, and arbitrated between synagogue and cantor when needed. This helped European cantors to become American cantors and produced new cantors who had grown up in this country. Together they created what would become American synagogue music, often blending the old and the new. The establishment of these institutes led to the professionalization of the cantorate, a development to which Cantor Heiser contributed and from which he benefitted for his own career.[107]

The Cantors Assembly

What better way to connect with a new country than to associate with other cantors and like-minded individuals? On February 26, 1947, a conference on Jewish Music in the Synagogue was held at The Jewish Theological Seminary of America at Broadway and 122nd Street in New York City. The conference "was attended by 168 representatives of congregational and other groups and organizations throughout the United States and Canada. Of these, 87 represented congregations directly affiliated with the United Synagogue of America."[108] The contributors were a Who's Who of famous cantors: David J. Putterman, Gershon Ephros, Isadore Freed, Israel Goldfarb, Max Wohlberg, Max Helfman, and others. Rabbi Israel Goldfarb noted that "As far back as 1924, the United Synagogue of America ... adopted a resolution at its convention, calling upon the Seminary to establish a school for Cantors."[109] Why did this not happen? Says Rabbi Goldfarb, "It was the lack of funds which delayed the plan and prevented its execution."[110] This was a problem that would haunt the Cantors Assembly into the Sixties—competition for funding between the cantors and the rabbis. During the conference, three committees were formed to consider the following issues: 1. Organization of a Cantors Assembly of America; 2. Standards and Qualifications for the Cantor; and 3. Establishment of a Cantors' Seminary in the Jewish Theological Seminary.[111]

We know from the proceedings of the conference that Cantor Heiser attended this first meeting of the American Cantors Institute.[112] *The Jewish Criterion* of February 28, 1947, reported that "Cantor Mordecai G. Heiser of B'nai Israel Congregation returned from New York, where he attended the Conference of the Cantors of the United Synagogue of America."[113]

Cantor Heiser not only took his responsibilities to his congregation and to his new country seriously, but also his obligations to the newly created Cantors Assembly. For a decade after his legitimation, he held several offices and participated in the life of this professional organization. Thanks to the diligence of the Cantors Assembly, we have all of the proceedings of the annual CA conferences on a wonderful and easy-to-access website, the Internet Archive. These reports provide us with a record of the business dealings, the offices held, liturgical music, and the developments in the world of the American cantorate.

The Cantors Assembly of the United Synagogue of America was officially established on April 1, 1947. Abraham J. Rose served as President, Martin Adolf as Vice-President, Gershon Ephros as Treasurer, Morris Shore as Recording Secretary, and David J. Putterman as Corresponding Secretary.[114] There was no meeting in 1948, the year in which the new state of Israel came into being. The second Annual Conference-Convention took place on February 21, 22, and 23, 1949, again at JTS. Cantors were asked to raise funds in their congregations for The School for Cantors Fund of the JTSA. In 1950 Cantor Heiser raised $125, a good first effort from B'nai Israel. Other cantors' collections ranged from $15 to $1,000. The total that year netted the fund nearly $20,000.[115] This was also the year of Cantor Heiser's debut at Carnegie Hall [March]. Cantor and Mrs. Heiser and Judith now lived at 5565 Wellesley Avenue in Pittsburgh.

Although established in 1947, the Cantors Assembly did not actually get off the ground until the summer of 1952, receiving a generous competitive push by the founding of a School of Sacred Music at Hebrew Union College in 1951. That same year, the Cantors Conventions of the CA started to convene at resorts such as the Concord Hotel at Kiamesha Lake, New York. The board of B'nai Israel allotted Cantor Heiser "$75 for expenses to attend the Cantors' Convention."[116] That year, Cantor Heiser attended by himself. The following year, 1952, both Cantor and Mrs. Heiser attended the Fifth Annual Conference-Convention, again at the Concord Hotel, from May 4 through 7. During the summer, he also attended courses at the newly created Cantors Institute in New York. On August 21 of that year, Max J. Routtenberg, Director of the Cantors Institute, responded to a query Cantor Heiser had sent him. "I am happy to inform you that you have received four (4) credits for the courses you took in the Summer Sessions of the Cantors Institute. If you are interested in your exact grades you may write in asking for them."[117] This Cantor Heiser did, for on October 21, 1952, Routtenberg again wrote to him.

> Dear Cantor Heiser:
> In reply to your request, I am happy to submit your grades.
>
> | | | |
> |---|---|---|
> | Liturgy | B | Dr. Leon J. Lebreich |
> | Choral Repertoire | A | Mr. Siegfried Landau |
> | Comparative Nushaot | B | Cantor Max Wohlberg[118] |

From 1953 on, Cantor Heiser became more deeply involved in the workings of the organization. He was now enrolled in the Retirement and Insurance Plan, which was established in 1949 and of which he would remain a member until his death in 1989. On August 5, 1952, the congregation voted to support Cantor Heiser's retirement contributions.[119]

In the conference proceedings, he was included in a group picture taken of the Officers and Members of the Executive and National Councils. His representation on the National Council was due to his new duties as the chairman of the newly formed Tri-State Regional Branch. The minutes reflect:

> TRI-STATE REGIONAL BRANCH – Rev. Mordecai Heiser
> The youngest branch of the Cantors Assembly was officially established at a meeting held in Pittsburgh on May 6th, 1953. This branch will consist of the colleagues living in Eastern and Northern Ohio, Western Pennsylvania and West Virginia, an area known as the Tri State Region. At the initial meeting it was dedicated to hold bi-monthly meetings in connection with work-

shops, lectures, concerts and social gatherings. The first of such meetings will be called for August. We all are looking forward to a very fruitful beginning since the colleagues in our Region never had any contact with each other except at the annual conventions. The meetings will be held in different places throughout the Tri State. By doing so we hope to bring the work of the Cantors Assembly close to the home of every colleague.[120]

He also raised $50 for the Cantors Institute through personal solicitation and contributed $25 of his own to the cause.

Now that the Cantors Institute existed, different factions of the United Synagogue of America vied for the available funds. In 1953, "a very heated and lengthy discussion ensued wherein it was learned that many of our members were meeting with a great deal of opposition from the lay leaders and Rabbis of their Congregations, whenever the Cantor suggested a Concert or any other medium by which he could raise funds for support of The Cantors Institute."[121] Rev. David Putterman, Executive Vice President, pleaded for additional solicitations. Cantor Heiser was one of 17 cantors who responded with another $100.

The final and very important certification that he was indeed accepted into the Conservative Movement's Cantors Assembly as a *Hazzan* and *Sheliach Tsibbur* was issued on 1 Cheshvan 5715 (1954), the first year that the certification was available. "The Cantors Assembly of America does hereby certify that Mordecai ben Itzhak Heiser, Hazzan Mordecai G. Heiser, has by virtue of his training, dedicated service and exemplary character met the standards of a Hazzan and Sheliach Tsibbur as prescribed by our tradition, and having complied with the standards and requirements of our Assembly is hereby designated as a member for 5715 (1954–55) and is authorized to exercise all sacred and religious functions of a Hazzan and Sheliach Tsibbur. In testimony whereof we have hereunto set our hand, Cheshvan 1 5715."

The certificate was signed by Samuel Rosenbaum, Vice President; Charles Sudock, President; David J. Putterman, Executive Vice President; Henry Fried, Secretary; and Moshe Nathanson, Treasurer.[122] *Hazzan* Heiser was now legitimized as a precentor in the Conservative tradition. Since this was the first time the certificate was awarded, a discussion ensued during the 1955 convention concerning both the wording of the certificate and the qualifications for the cantorate. The final wording would be ratified at the 1956 convention.

Fourteen years had passed since Mr. Heiser and family arrived on the shores of these United States as refugees from Hitler's Europe. Over time Cantor Heiser became a spiritual and political force within Congregation B'nai Israel, within the Cantors Assembly (especially in the Tri-State Region), within the Zionist movement, and within the cultural life of Western Pennsylvania, to all four of which he devoted his time and energies until that fateful day in 1989 when he was struck by an automobile while crossing the street. Despite later illness, his wife, Elly, faithfully supported her husband's efforts, becoming a powerful partner in his life's work. With her humor and gift for gab, she enlivened parties and contributed glamour to congregational as well as general social events.

The Golden Year of B'nai Israel and Beyond

The year 1954 was a banner year in Cantor Heiser's life, because in 1953–1954 B'nai Israel celebrated its Golden Anniversary with a year-long series of events. The congregation's *Golden Anniversary Book* proudly lauded *Hazzan* Heiser's service to B'nai Israel as "unstinting" and stressed that this "has not gone unappreciated by a grateful congregation."[123]

As usual, Jewish Music Month occurred in March. Cantor Heiser worked very hard to promote the event that would raise funds for the new Cantors Institute. He was fortunate that he was supported in his efforts for Jewish music by both Rabbi Lichter and then Associate Rabbi Cohen, with whom he produced at least seven cantatas until 1961. The *Congregation B'nai Israel Bulletin* of January 22, 1954, announced, "Throughout the country Jewish Music Month is being observed, dedicated to the theme of 'A People that Lives Sings and a People that Sings Lives.' Attention is being drawn to the musical dimension in Jewish life. Our Cantor, together with his colleagues in the Tri-State Region, is planning a gala Jewish Music Festival on Tuesday, March 9. This evening will be an outstanding one in the synagogue calendar."[124]

The participants in this benefit concert included Cantor Saul Meisels of the Cleveland Heights Temple, Cleveland, Ohio; Cantor William W. Lipson of Beth El Congregation, Akron, Ohio; and Cantor Mordecai G. Heiser. The concert, consisting of "traditional synagogue chants, modern Israeli music and Jewish folk songs," was to benefit the brand new Cantors School of the Jewish Theological Seminary of America.[125]

A letter to congregants for patronage or sponsorship and dated January 20, 1954, was signed by Rabbis Lichter and Cohen and Benjamin Shanblatt, the treasurer of B'nai Israel, as well as Cantor Heiser. It basically has the same text as the letter below but invites "a number of our friends to be Patrons, the donation for which is $5.00, or Sponsors for a donation of $10.00."[126]

On January 19, 1954, another letter was sent by Cantor Heiser on CA Tri-State Branch stationery to congregants and friends.

> Jewish communities all over the nation are now celebrating Jewish Music Month. This year, for the first time, the Cantors of this region are commemorating this event with an outstanding concert to be held at the B'nai Israel Synagogue on Tuesday, March 9, 1954, at 8:30 P.M. . . . The entire proceeds will be donated to the School for Cantors at the Jewish Theological Seminary of America. This School, now in existence for two years, is presently training a number of young men to be able to assume the leadership at synagogue services. The Jewish Theological Seminary, realizing the dire need for competently trained cantors, has opened this school on condition that members of the Cantors Assembly of America shall raise the necessary funds for the maintenance and support of this school. . . . [127]

And, finally, a follow-up letter in the name of the Cantors Concert Committee and Rabbi Lichter was sent out on February 23, 1954, to a broad audience, reminding them that "Our Cantor, who is vitally interested in this project, joins me and the other members of the committee in appealing to you to sponsor the forthcoming benefit concert on Tuesday, March 9th at the B'nai Israel Synagogue."[128]

The actual concert ticket is extant:[129]

> Tri-State Branch of Cantors Assembly of America
> Presents Jewish Music Festival in a Concert of Cantorial, Jewish and Hebrew Music at the B'nai Israel Synagogue
> 327 N. Negley Avenue
> Tuesday, March 9, 1954—8:30 P.M.
> The Entire Proceeds Will Go Towards the Cantors School of the Jewish Theological Seminary
> Donation $1.50 per Person $2.50 per Couple

We likewise are in possession of the Concert Program.[130]

"The Cantors Assembly" of the United Synagogue of America
Tri-State Region presents
Cantors Mordecai G. Heiser, William W. Lipson
and
Saul Meisels
in
Jewish Music Festival
Tuesday, March 9, 1954—8:30 P.M.
B'nai Israel Synagogue

Program

V'haarev no (Morning Prayer)	Yassinovsky
Rachamono deoney (Have mercy upon us)	Leow

Cantor Heiser

Retse (Prayer for the Restoration of the Holy Temple)	Schlossberg
Ani maamin (I Believe)	Alter

Cantor Lipson

Haben yakir li: (Reb Yitschoks Story)	Traditional
Sadot Sh'baemek (The Fields of the Emek)	Ben-Hayim
Fin Jan	Israeli Folksong
Hassidic Rhapsody (Song without words)	Folk Themes Meisels

Cantor Meisels

Intermission

Greetings	Dr. Seymour J. Cohen
Shir haemek (Song of the Emek)	Lavri
Yerushalayim (in commemoration of the 3000th Anniversary of the Holy City)	

Cantor Heiser

Sochrenu LeHayim (He May Remember Us For Life)	Singer

Cantor Lipson

Yankele	Gebirtig-Meisels
My Mother's Sabbath Candles	Yellen
Drei Techter (The Three Daughters)	Schnaer
Der Batchen (Wedding Scene)	Kon
Motele	Gebirtig-Kon

Cantors Meisels and Heiser

Cantors Heiser and Lipson will be accompanied at the piano by Ilse Karp.
Cantor Meisels will be accompanied by Ida Ruth Meisels.

This March 9 concert was the highlight of B'nai Israel's fiftieth anniversary year. The congregation, under the leadership of Cantor Heiser, not only celebrated the importance of this institution, but also the glory of Jewish music and the success of the Cantors Assembly.

The Cantors Assembly changed the venue for the Seventh Annual Conference-Convention from June 28 to July 1, 1954, to the Grand Hotel in Highmount, New York. The group picture from here on only included members of the Executive Council, no longer the National Council, on which Cantor Heiser continued to serve by virtue of his chairmanship of the Tri-State Region. For the region, he submitted the following lengthy report [English in the original] which he signed with his new title of *Hazzan*.

> The Region now in its second year has had some activities. Several meetings were held in Pittsburgh, Akron and Youngstown. Members of the Region participated in concerts held in Pittsburgh, Akron and Steubenville. Our region is working under some difficulties. To attend the meetings or to participate at the concerts our colleagues have to travel from 40 to 120 miles one way. On account of this we could not meet as frequently as we wanted. The meetings were attended well. Our concerts showed a splendid spirit of comradeship and cooperation. Since in our area the Cantors Institute is unknown we had to spend a large amount for posters, printing and mailing to bring close to the people the existence of a Cantors School. This of course affected the net income. In the following years I am sure we can save us a lot of these expenses. Cantor Grossman did a splendid job of alarming the community himself and although small in numbers he netted as much as we in the big cities. Our plans for the coming year are to continue the activities by meeting as often as possible. We shall try to organize several concerts for the benefit of the Cantors Institute and shall try to include small but substantial communities where there are no professional cantors employed. A word of thanks to Cantor Rev. Lipson, Akron, for his fine job as Secretary of the Region and for his participation at all three concerts. Thanks also to Cantors Edelstein, Meisels and Schindler. Cantor Schindler participated at two of our Concerts and traveled to Steubenville 90 miles one way and to Akron 40 miles one way. Thanks also to Cantor Putterman for his help and advice he has given to us during the past year.[131]

During this year, Cantor Heiser raised a respectable $267 for the Cantors Institute.

In 1955, Cantor Heiser was listed as "Hazzan" in the Conference Proceedings, according to his new standing in the organization. On his work for the Tri-State Regional Branch he reported, "The work of our Regional Branch has been progressing during the past year. Two colleagues have joined our Region: Hazzan Ashery of Pittsburgh and Hazzan Wahrman of Dayton. Our sessions have been fruitful and inspirational. We discuss matters pertaining to Hazzanut, we listened to and evaluated recordings, we discussed problems with which we are confronted in our Congregations and communities. These meetings are always very pleasant and we enjoy the fellowship of our colleagues. In the past year the colleagues Lipson, Akron; Edelstein, Youngstown; and Bermanis, Cleveland have been hosts and we express our gratitude to them and their facilities for the sessions."[132]

For the Cantors Institute, Cantor Heiser raised $60. He wrote:

In our deliberations we have stressed the importance of supporting the program of our Assembly especially as far as the raising of funds for the Cantors School of the Seminary is concerned. Cantor Wahrman of Dayton, Ohio and Cantor Lipson of Akron, Ohio have held concerts which were successful both artistically and financially. Most of the other colleagues have raised funds otherwise. During the coming year concerts in other parts of the region are planned.

He further reported very matter-of-factly that "the Region is comprised of 13 members from Pittsburgh, Cleveland, Akron, Youngstown, Johnstown, Steubenville, Dayton and Altoona."[133] This was quite an achievement in a very short time.

The year 1956 brought an ambitious program for the Ninth Annual Conference-Convention which took place at Grossingers in the Catskills. Cantor Heiser continued his duties as chairman of the Tri-State Region and on the National Council. He raised $261.60 for the Cantors Institute, but he also pointed out a new challenge and competitive cause for community funds. This new challenge was Israel. "In Pittsburgh as well as in Youngstown and Cleveland it was impossible to hold Concerts of local Hazzanim since they are giving concerts at times during the year for the Synagogue and National Organizations, without charge."[134] Just as an example, on April 19, 1956, five Pittsburgh cantors came together for a concert at the Y.M.&W.H.A, in honor of Israel's Eighth Anniversary Celebration. They were Uri Frenkel of Poale Zedeck and Mordecai Heiser, of B'nai Israel, William Hofstadter of Shaare Torah, Irving Ashery of Tree of Life, and David Gold of Adath Jeshurun. The concert was free of charge. Not only did the seminary compete for resources, the ZOA did as well.

To alleviate the continued shortage of funds for the Cantors Institute, Cantor Heiser suggested that "the Seminary give us the permission to participate actively in the Seminary campaign and to allocate a certain percentage for the Cantors Institute."[135] At this convention also a Late Friday Evening Service based on the Silverman *siddur* was discussed as an example of a service that could be adapted to special occasions. Thanks to Cantor Bloom, the congregation had offered a Late Friday Evening Service since the 1920s, which Cantor Heiser cleverly used as a showcase for the cantatas that he and Rabbi Seymour Cohen created during the latter's tenure at B'nai Israel. In 1957, Cantor Heiser raised $255 for the Cantors Institute and chaired the Tri-State Regional Branch. Because of this office he was again appointed to the National Council.

Cantatas for the Nation

In the 1950s Cantor Heiser collaborated with Rabbi Dr. Seymour J. Cohen —who was associate rabbi of B'nai Israel from 1951 to 1957 and became the rabbi upon Rabbi Lichter's retirement and until his departure in 1961—in the creation of several cantatas.

Although it is hard to know how many cantatas were created by the Cohen-Heiser team, there are at least seven, starting in 1952 with one entitled "Sabbath in Song," premiered on March 14 during Jewish Music Month. "The cantata is built around the theme of the role of Jewish Music and the observance of the Sabbath at home and in the synagogue. Beginning with the candle lighting ceremony, through which the mother of the house inaugurates the Sabbath, the cantata takes the listener through the full day of rest, accompanies him to the synagogue and leaves him at the end of the Sabbath, spiritually refreshed and emotionally renewed. The closing musical portion of the cantata is the rendition of Zavel Zilbert's Havdalah."[136]

In 1953, the cantata "The Psalms, the Jew's Life Companion" was presented on March 20, again during Jewish Music Month. "The cantata deals with the role that the Psalms have played in the life of the Jew as a source of morale and hope, accompanying him through the sublimest moments of human existence. The music of the cantata is based upon the compositions of such outstanding modern Jewish composers as Levandowsky, Zilberts, Secunda, Jasinowsky, Schalit and Graumann."[137] Thus, this was an occasion not only to showcase B'nai Israel's musical talents, but also to update the music for Jewish occasions.

We could not find a cantata for 1954, but the 1955 offering, "Our Festive Days," was performed on March 25. According to B'nai Israel president Max Pearlstein, the "series [of cantatas] have been presented annually by the Rabbi and Hazzan . . . in observance of Jewish Music Month" in March.[138]

The 1956 cantata was entitled "The Sabbath in a Chassidic Home" and performed on March 9.[139]

In 1957, the fifth, "Like Unto Them That Dream," was premiered during B'nai Israel's late evening service on April 5. Samuel Schreiber, who was acting president at the time, noted that "the original works have been warmly received in the past and have been reproduced in other cities, on radio and TV [perhaps on "The Eternal Lights" program?]. The music relates to [the people] Israel's love for Zion," expressing "the hope and yearning of the Jewish people."[140]

In 1958, the tenth anniversary of the State of Israel, the offering consisted of "The Greatness and the Glory" on April 18 and on April 25, as well as "Our Glorious Years" on May 25. According to an article in the *American Jewish Outlook*, "The cantata ['The Greatness and the Glory'] relives the last 16 years in the life of the Jewish people and ['Our Glorious Years'] the confirmation class [of B'nai Israel]."[141]

The seventh cantata, "The Sabbath at Home" was presented during the afternoon session of a two-day Sisterhood conference on May 10, 1959, and again at the B'nai Israel late evening service of that day. The same cantata was also presented a year later, on April 15, 1960, during another United Synagogue event.[142]

The cantatas did not end with the departure of Rabbi Cohen in 1961. Beginning in 1962 with Rabbi Mordecai S. Chertoff, a concert—"A Sabbath at Home"—was performed, perhaps a variation on the 1959/1960 cantata.

The Heinz History Center archives revealed an eighth cantata, "The Living Word," composed by Rabbi Mordecai S. Chertoff in 1966, with music by Hazzan Mordecai G. Heiser.[143]

Unfortunately, no recordings of these cantatas seem to be extant. A testimony to Cantor Heiser's creative and collaborative spirit, they also served to modernize the B'nai Israel services—a constant demand from the board throughout the years.

Cantor and Mrs. Heiser as Empty-Nesters

In 1955, Cantor and Mrs. Heiser's daughter, Judith, had gotten engaged to Alvin Stein. An unidentified article in the Stein Collection reads, "Cantor and Mrs. Mordecai G. Heiser of Congregation B'nai Israel announce the engagement of their daughter, Judith, to Alvin Joseph Stein, son of Mr. and Mrs. Sam L. Stein of Morningside Avenue. The bride elect is a junior at the University of Pittsburgh School of Education and member of Phi Sigma Sigma sorority. Mr. Stein will graduate in February [1957] from Pitt's School of Engineering. He is a member of Kappa Nu fraternity and Sigma [Tau]."[144] Preceding the wedding was a Tea on Saturday, May 4 [1957], from 3:00 to 5:00 p.m. at B'nai Israel. And it wasn't a small affair. According to an article, "To Be Honored," in the *Squirrel Hill News*, "Some 700 women are expected to attend the tea...."[145]

For the wedding, which took place on Sunday, June 2, 1957, at B'nai Israel, with Cantor Heiser and Rabbis Cohen and Lichter officiating, the bride wore a "gown of white Chantilly lace with a high neckline in appliques fitted botice, the bride had a full bouffant skirt ending in a chapel train. She wore a fingertip veil of imported illusion attached to a three petal Chantilly lace half hat with pearls. The bride also carried a white Bible with white Cymbrum orchids with Stepnoits...."[146]

A June 7, 1957, article in *The Jewish Criterion* reported that the marriage had taken place.

> Cantor and Mrs. Mordecai G. Heiser of B'nai Israel Congregation announce the marriage of their daughter, Judith, to Alvin J. Stein, son of Mr. and Mrs. Sam L. Stein of Morningside Avenue. The ceremony took place June 2 at the B'nai Israel Synagogue with Rabbis Benjamin A. Lichter and Seymour J. Cohen and the father of the bride, Cantor Mordecai G. Heiser, officiating. The Cantor escorted the bride down the aisle and then performed at the ceremony. A private dinner followed the ceremony which was held in the Mrs. Barnett Davis Assembly Hall....
>
> Following a trip to the Nevele [New York] and to Niagara Falls, the couple will make their home in Akron, Ohio, after September 1.
>
> The bride will graduate in August from the University of

Pittsburgh School of Education. She will teach in the Akron Public Schools. Her husband graduated in February "cum laude" from the University of Pittsburgh, School of Engineering. He is presently connected with the Good Year Aircraft in Akron.[147]

With their only child on her own, life for the empty nesters continued with many exciting activities. In 1958, Cantor Heiser served on the National Council of the CA and chaired the Tri-State Region. He announced that the next meeting of the Tri-State Region "will be held in May with the election of regional officers on the agenda."[148] This is the last year that he appears as an officer of the CA. It is in this year that the CA recognized 111 cantors who had been awarded Certificates, Cantor Heiser among them. The qualifications now seem to have been established to everyone's satisfaction. They consist of three points:
1. Membership in The Cantors Assembly for a period of five years;
2. Service to Congregation exclusively on a full-time basis for a period of eight years; and
3. Approval of Executive Council.

These qualifications had been passed by the Convention in 1956.[149]

In 1959, Cantor Heiser attended the Convention, continued in the Retirement Fund, and raised $286 for the Cantors Institute, but did not chair any committees. Between July 1, 1959, and June 30, 1960, he continued to raise funds for the Cantors Institute, collecting $414.[150] The 1960 Convention was held at Grossinger's from April 25 through 28. The Proceedings list Cantor Heiser as a member of the Convention Management Committee. He was also designated an "Honorary Fellow" of the Cantors Institute of JTS, which was a great honor. An article in *The Jewish Criterion* announced that "Hazzan Mordecai G. Heiser of B'nai Israel congregation was honored by the 'Cantors Institute' of the Jewish Theological Seminary of America with an appointment as an 'Honorary Fellow' of the Institute, according to a letter he received from Dr. Louis Finkelstein, Chancellor of the Seminary."[151] Thus, 1960 was the twentieth anniversary of Cantor Heiser's arrival in the U.S. and his affiliation with B'nai Israel. It was also the year of the Heisers' twenty-fifth wedding anniversary, which was celebrated with the community's participation.[152] The January 12, 1960, minutes of B'nai Israel recorded a vote to hold "special services honoring Cantor and Mrs. Heiser...."[153]

Toward the end of the twentieth-anniversary year, on March 24, 1961, Jewish Music Month was celebrated, and Cantor Heiser was honored with a Festival of Music, followed by a reception for him and his wife, Elly. On this occasion, Hazzan Samuel Rosenbaum, Executive Vice President of the Cantors Assembly, wrote to the President of B'nai Israel.

> My dear Sir:
>
> I am writing you to express the delight of the entire membership of the Cantors Assembly of America at the forthcoming testimonial which your congregation is planning to tender to our colleague, Hazzan Mordecai Heiser.
>
> The completion of 20 years of service to a congregation is, of course, a noteworthy achievement for Hazzan Heiser. However, it is even more significant to the members of our Assembly. It points up a new and most welcome trend in American synagogue life. It indicates that congregations are becoming increasingly aware of the benefit to be derived from long association with those men who serve their spiritual needs.
>
> We deem this celebration to have even more meaning, for the honor you extend to your Hazzan will also underline the importance of one of the loftiest callings that man can have on earth: to lead his fellow man in prayer and to direct him in the search for eternal truths. In the pursuit of this calling, Mordecai Heiser has given it dignity, respect and stature.
>
> [. . .]
>
> I pray with all of you for the continued health and vigor of your <u>sheliah tzibbur</u>. May he continue to guide you and to serve our Maker for many years to come and may he enjoy a full share of all the good things that are his due.
>
> Faithfully yours,
> Samuel Rosenbaum
> Hazzan[154]

The Festival of Music, held on Friday evening, March 24, 1961, at 8:15 p.m. in the main sanctuary of the B'nai Israel Synagogue, consisted of Kabbalat Shabbat with music by Sholom Secunda, presented by *Hazzan* Mordecai G. Heiser and choir. Mildred Rubenstein, Arthur Steinberg, Herman Weisberg, and Claryne Karsh participated, as well as organist Thornton Wilcox. The program was followed by a reception for Cantor and Mrs. Heiser in the Mrs. Barnett Davis Assembly Hall.[155]

Subsequently, Cantor Heiser graciously thanked the President of B'nai Israel Congregation, Mr. Samuel Schreiber, for the honor.

Dear Mr. Schreiber:

My wife joins me in expressing our sincere gratitude for honoring me upon the occasion of twenty years of service to the Congregation.

My association with you, the officers, and the members of B'nai Israel has always been a pleasant one. May we be privileged to share each other's friendship for many years to come.

With my prayerful wishes for health and happiness to you and your associates in the leadership of our Congregation, I remain

Sincerely yours,

Mordecai G. Heiser [hand signed][156]

The fourteenth Annual Convention of the CA in 1961 took place at Grossinger's. As a member of the Convention Management Team, Cantor Heiser was being honored through participation in the Cantors Assembly conference program by officiating at a 6:30 p.m. Ma'ariv (evening) Service on Wednesday, April 19, 1961.[157]

On Sunday, April 1, 1962, "A Grand Concert of Jewish Music" took place at B'nai Israel with Cantor Saul Meisels and Music Director Sholom Secunda and, of course, Cantor Heiser. In the program, both Meisels' and Secunda's most recent musical works for the Friday Evening Service and Shabbat at Home are highlighted. Meisels, cantor of the Temple on the Heights, Cleveland, Ohio, and Secunda, musical director of the Concord Hotel in Kiamesha Lake, New York, were about to release new recordings. This is in contrast to Cantor Heiser, who did not record professionally. The star-studded program, featuring songs for the Sabbath in the first part and Song Hits of the Yiddish Theatre in the second, is extant.[158]

Also in 1962, during that year's CA Convention, on Wednesday, May 16, at 10:00 p.m., Cantor Heiser participated in a concert of the Cantors Assembly Convention on "Music for the Synagogue: From the European Tradition." The selection was the recitative "R'tze Vimnuchosenu" (Accept our rest), from the repetition of the Shabbat Amidah by contemporary Sholom Secunda, with Lazar Weiner at the piano.[159] Cantor Heiser enjoyed collaborating with Secunda throughout his career.

The Zionist Organization of America and the State of Israel

In the 1950s, Cantor Heiser had been incredibly busy with the Cantors Assembly. In the 1960s, the *Hazzan* shifted most of his leadership activities from the Cantors Assembly to the support of Israel and the Zionist Organization of America, where he joined the leadership team to head the local ZOA Membership Campaign.[160] Starting in 1961, he led a "Sing Along with Cantor Heiser."[161] Events like these served to introduce the community to and educate them about new Israeli tunes and Jewish folk tunes in general.[162] Cantor Heiser thoroughly enjoyed the music of the *chalutzim* (pioneers), saying about their songs, "the old tunes [from Eastern Europe] . . . became groundwork for a new musical language. . . . Gradually new songs arose, which bore witness to the fusion of the two strains."[163] From then on, he actively participated in ZOA events and motivated Pittsburgh Jews across the community to support Israel by buying Israel Bonds.

In 1961–62, Cantor Heiser served as chairman of the local ZOA's Membership Campaign. The following year, 1962–63, he continued to serve on a spirited leadership team which began its efforts for that year with a rally.[164] The 1962 Israel Bonds Chanukkah concert took place at the Y.M.&W.H.A. on December 23. The three great artists participating were Cantor Mordecai G. Heiser; Milt Moss, a popular American entertainer; and Israeli Rakhel Hadass, founder of the Haifa Oranim Folk Group. The biographical blurb for Cantor Heiser states, "Since his debut in Carnegie Recital Hall in New York, Cantor Heiser has been featured in numerous recitals and concerts, as well as on radio and television [through the cantatas or the Eternal Light radio program?]. A dramatic tenor, his extensive repertoire includes Hebrew, Cantorial, Jewish, operatic and classical songs, arias and modern melodies of Israel. He has been Cantor of B'nai Israel Synagogue since 1940 and was a winner of the Pittsburgh Concert Society auditions."[165]

On June 13, 1965, on the occasion of Cantor Heiser's silver anniversary with B'nai Israel, the congregation presented him with a beautifully crafted brass candelabra which is in his family's possession. Perhaps as an anniversary trip to themselves, perhaps as a more visible leader for the ZOA, or even in preparation for a congregational trip in 1969,[166] that same year Cantor and Mrs. Heiser traveled to Israel. While there, they befriended a Christian family who were searching for their son's grave. William Edmundson had fought as a paratrooper in the War of Independence and was buried in Haifa. With the help of the Arab caretaker, they found the grave. Cantor Heiser chanted the "El Male Rachamim" prayer for the fallen soldier. Elly comments in a newspaper article in *The Jewish Chronicle*, "It was a moment of great dignity and oh, so very touching."[167]

An unidentified Pittsburgh newspaper lists Cantor Heiser among the Leadership of the 1966–67 Membership Campaign of the Pittsburgh Zionist District. "The PZD was cited for top honors in enrollment of new members in 1965–66." Cantor Heiser is listed as the coordinator of the campaign.[168]

The 1970s: Thirty Years in the United States

By 1970, Cantor Heiser had become a fixture and indispensable leader mostly in Jewish Pittsburgh. The congregation was well into its adult phase and had weathered growth in membership, students, and structures. The 1970s brought long-term maintenance of the real estate, the membership, and an aging cantor. Cantor and Mrs. Heiser celebrated their thirty-fifth wedding anniversary on January 8, 1970, for which the congregation honored them with a special service and a bouquet of flowers.[169]

On April 12 of that year Cantor Heiser also celebrated his thirtieth anniversary as B'nai Israel's *hazzan* with a Music Festival. This event was approved by the Board at the February 3 meeting.[170] An article in *The Jewish Chronicle*, "Cantor Heiser to Sing of 30 B'nai Israel Years" announced the landmark celebration to the wider community. "Cantor Mordecai G. Heiser will celebrate 30 years with Congregation B'nai Israel of East End on April 12 by leading a Music Festival program. . . . " According to the article, "The Music Festival will feature a blend of various music trends—rock and roll, traditional, Yiddish, Israeli, and contemporary—and a sing-a-long utilizing the combined choirs of adults, youths and juniors from the congregation." Dr. Mervin L. Binstock, congregational president, announced that "The Cantor requested this unique way of observing his anniversary and asked that the proceeds from this function be allocated to the B'nai Israel Summer Camp Scholarship Fund."[171]

The *Congregation B'nai Israel Bulletin* of March 27 announced: "Music Festival honoring Hazzan Heiser's 30th Anniversary with B'nai Israel. Proceeds from this function will be allocated to the B'nai Israel Summer Camp Scholarship Fund. Tickets can be purchased at the door. Festival starts at 8:00 p.m."[172] The actual ticket reads,

Music Festival
honoring
Hazzan Mordecai G. Heiser's
30 Years as Cantor of Congregation B'nai Israel
Sunday, April 12, 1970—8:00 p.m.
at Barnett Davis Social Hall
Proceeds for Summer Camp Scholarship Fund
Donation: $2.75[173]

One of the first to congratulate him on his achievement was Morton Siegel, Director of the United Synagogue of America, Department of Education, 218 East 70th Street, New York, NY 10021.

> April 1, 1970
> Hazzan Mordecai G. Heiser, B'nai Israel,
> 327 North Negley Avenue, Pittsburgh, Pa. 15206
> Dear Hazzan Heiser:
> I was delighted to learn, from the March 27th issue of B'nai Israel Bulletin that, in a very few days, you will celebrate three decades with the Congregation. I hope that you will permit me to be one among many to extend to you every good wish on this happy occasion to which is wedded the hope that you will provide the same kind of dignified and meaningful religious service to the Congregation for many, many more years to come. Mazel Tov![174]

Other laudations arrived, from the Executive Vice President of the Cantors Assembly, Samuel Rosenbaum, from colleague Cantor Raymond Smolover of the Jewish Community Center in White Plains, and from his local colleague Rabbi Mordecai L. Glatstein, who served the Jewish Home for the Aged.

> My Dear Colleague and Friend:
> It is my privilege and my honor to join the countless segments of our population in paying tribute to you for the thirty years of musical service and excellence in interpreting our rich liturgy to thousands of people. I personally am expressing admiration for you, not only for your gifted cantorial abilities, but also for your beautiful qualities of refinement, kindness, and friendship. My family joins me in wishing you and your loved ones many happy years of good health, family bliss, and peace of mind. Special expressions of best wishes and sincere felicitations come from our distinguished leadership of the Home, residents, and friends, for your warm relationship to our great institution. With kindest personal regards, best wishes, and warm friendship.
> Sincerely yours,
> Rabbi Mordecai L. Glatstein[175]

A very special congratulatory telegram was sent to Cantor Heiser from B'nai Israel's Young Adult Congregation. "Mazeltov on your 30 years at B'nai

Israel Synagogue may you have many more happy and healthy ones."[176] The message was signed by Presidents Judy and Al Stein, Cantor Heiser's daughter and son-in-law, who had been elected to office on April 28, 1969.[177]

On April 16, 1970, Milton K. Susman, columnist for *The Jewish Chronicle*, wrote in his column, "As I See It," "By any reckoning, 30 years are not just a weekend. And when a cantor can serve a congregation for that span, he must have more than just a voice. For well into two generations Mordecai Heiser has enriched B'nai Israel with his spiritual leadership and Jewish content as well as his broad musical talents. In fact, Cantor Heiser has known no other affiliation during his professional career in America for he came to the East End Congregation directly from his cantorial duties in Berlin in 1940 [sic: via the Kitchener Refugee Camp in England]. And it was not unfitting that the Congregation marked this signal anniversary last Sunday night with a musical pastiche arranged and directed by Mr. Heiser running the full gamut of styles and traditions to which he has devoted himself."[178]

Cantor Heiser was deeply grateful for the community-wide wishes and wrote a letter of thanks.

> "Expression of Thanks"
>
> The many good wishes I received on the occasion of my 30th Anniversary with our Congregation have touched me deeply. I am grateful for the many donations that were made in my honor to the Scholarship Fund of our Congregation. My sincere thanks to all those who helped make this affair successful: Mr. Max Stone, Dr. Robert Ruben, and Bertram Katz for their excellent leadership in the campaign: to the Rabbi and the President of the Congregation for their help and their kind words at the Concert, and especially to the many who attended the Concert. May we all be privileged to celebrate many happy occasions together, and may the good Lord bless you.
> —Mordecai G. Heiser, Hazzan[179]

Israeli Independence Day was always celebrated big in Pittsburgh, and by the entire community. On April 28, 1971, Cantor Heiser chaired the Pittsburgh Zionist Federation's Twenty-Third Annual Anniversary Celebration, held at Congregation Beth Shalom. The theme for that year was right down Cantor Heiser's alley—a cantata—"Israel Sings," featuring the cantors, choirs, and artists from the Pittsburgh community, plus Israeli artist Noah Marcel. The program featured Cantors Murray Gold of Temple Emanuel, Mordecai G. Heiser of B'nai Israel, Harry Silversmith of Tree of Life, and Moshe Taube of Beth Shalom, who had begun his tenure as Beth Shalom's cantor in 1965.[180] Also participating were the choirs of Beth Shalom Congregation and B'nai Israel Congregation, as well as the Youth Choir of Hillel Academy and the Youth Choir of Temple Rodef Shalom directed by Mrs. Betty Levine.[181]

On October 25, 1972, the Jewish social service organization B'nai Brith celebrated a century of existence as a national and international organization.[182] In honor of the occasion, B'nai Israel presented a concert, "Judaism Reflected In Its Liturgy," at the Sacred Heart Church in Pittsburgh with Rabbi Jack Schechter, Cantor Heiser, Wayne Galbraith, Organist and Choir Director, and the B'nai Israel Choir participating in "The Lord of All," by Isadore Freed [Hartt Musical Foundation, Hartford, Connecticut]. Choir selections were Lewandowski's "Ma Tovu," and Dunajewsky's version of "Enosh" by Lewandowski for the Memorial Service, and together they sang Dunajewsky's "Od'cho," and Hast's "Tal," the prayer for dew recited on Passover.[183]

The selection is interesting not only for its diversity of participation, but also for its range of composers, from Solomon Rossi, an Italian Jewish composer and probably the first Jewish choral director, who is very popular in our day again, to Leopold Edelstein, a contemporary of Cantor Heiser's. And of course, hymns such as "Kol Nidre" are not only popular among Jews, but, thanks perhaps to the movie *The Jazz Singer* (primarily Al Jolson's version), also among Gentiles.

Israel's twenty-fifth anniversary tribute dinner on October 29, 1972, was a double celebration, honoring Cantor Heiser for thirty-two years of distinguished service to Congregation B'nai Israel and celebrating twenty-five years of existence of the State of Israel.

Preceding the dinner was a reception at the home of Dr. and Mrs. Mervin L. Binstock [no date given], featuring best-selling author and attorney Eleazar Lipsky, who wrote the book *Malpractice* and was the chairman of the Jewish Telegraphic Agency (JTA).[184]

The officers and board of directors of B'nai Israel Congregation extended a cordial invitation to attend the tribute dinner to those who love B'nai Israel, the State of Israel, and Cantor Heiser—a winning combination.

Tribute Dinner
for

Hazzan Mordecai G. Heiser
in recognition of distinguished service to Israel and our
congregation
at the Mrs. Barnett Davis Assembly Hall
Sunday Evening, October 29, 1972
highlighting the Congregation's Campaign for State of Israel
Bonds.[185]

The blurb in the program reads, "Our Hazzan for 32 years, Mordecai Heiser is a dedicated Zionist and a distinguished Cantor and leader of our Congregation. We are proud to honor him on this occasion. It is significant that we will do so by aiding Israel through our purchases of Israel Bonds."[186] A picture in *The Jewish Chronicle* shows Cantor and Mrs. Heiser; the key speaker Robert Mayer Evans, a foreign correspondent; Jules Silberg, the dinner chairman; Rabbi Jack Schechter, and Edward A. Perlow, then president of B'nai Israel. The caption states that "The occasion produced $409,000 of Israel Bonds, a new record for the congregation."[187]

B'nai Israel was not only a place of employment for Cantor Heiser, but his and his family's spiritual home. Again and again, congregational *simchas* include Cantor Heiser's own family. In fact, this is the reason we have amateur recordings of services at all—family *simchas* and Cantor Heiser's granddaughter's participation in services. On Shavuot, June 26, 1976, Adele Miriam Stein, named for her murdered maternal great-grandmother, celebrated her Bat Mitzvah in the circle of her family, friends, and congregation. Unfortunately, no recording of this service has survived.[188]

The Twilight Years

The year 1978–79 was a weighty time in the history of B'nai Israel and in the life of Cantor Heiser. On the weekend of September 15–17, 1978, under the presidency of Meyer Gisser, the congregation kicked off a year-long celebration of seventy-five years of existence with a visit by Rabbi David Wolf Silverman, Associate Professor of Philosophies of Judaism at the Jewish Theological Seminary of America in New York. Additional events included an open house for the Pittsburgh Community on October 22, 1978, at which Mayor Caliguiri presented a proclamation that declared Sunday, October 22, "B'nai Israel Day" in honor of the Congregation's seventy-fifth anniversary celebration.[189] Additional festivities consisted of "the dedication of special Torah mantels, reunion of Confirmation Classes and appearances of other guest speakers," culminating with a dinner-dance in May 1979. In *The Jewish Chronicle*, President Gisser explained,

> B'nai Israel has been a leading force in the shaping of the Jewish Community of Pittsburgh. We take pride in the achievements of the past with the full knowledge that the past is prologue. The vibrancy and excitement that is continually being generated within our congregation as we enter into the last quarter of our first century of existence demonstrates clearly that we are still very young in outlook; that we will continue to pioneer in new and exciting frontiers in the Jewish world.[190]

Alas, the congregation would not be able to hold out to celebrate its centennial, which would have occurred in 2003–04.

The Demise of the Friendship Club

The same year, 1979, an organization that Cantor Heiser had been very involved in closed its doors. Already before World War II [in 1936], Jewish Pittsburgh created a social club for the support of newly arriving refugees. The Friendship Club served those Jews who were new to Pittsburgh and to the country. An ad in the *Aufbau* from December 22, 1944, in German, announced that the Friendship Club, 5824 Forbes Street, would celebrate Chanukah in the Club building on Sunday, December 21, at 8:00 p.m. Rabbi Benjamin Lichter would be the speaker, Rev. Mordecai Heiser would light the candles, and a program under the musical direction of Leon Kusheroff would follow. Net profits would go "to our boys in the Army." Admission was three packages of cigarettes or equal value. In addition, the ad stated that the Club building would be closed on December 23, and the citizenship class was cancelled.

> The Friendship Club
> 5824 Forbes Street
> President Ernest Nachman; Vice President Erwin Pollitzer und Herman Eckstein; Secretary Lotte Dicker; Treasurer Leopold Strauss; Social Chairman Leon Kusheroff.
> Sonntag, 21. Dezember, 8 p.m., Chanukka-Feier im Clubheim.
> Ansprache: Rabbi Benjamin Lichter,
> Anzünder der Kerzen: Rev. Mordecai Heiser;

anschliessend Darbietungen; musikalische Leitung: Leon Kusheroff.
Reingewinn für "Unsere Boys in der Armee."
Eintritt: drei Pakete Zigaretten oder Gegenwert.—
Am 23. Dezember bleibt unser Klubheim geschlossen.
Der Citizenship-Kurs entfällt.[191]

My late friend Marga Silbermann Randall from the South Hills, who had come from Nazi Germany with her mother and sister, used to tell that she and her mother cooked for the dinners of the group. In a little book, *How Beautiful We Once Were*, she gave more details. "Over the years in Pittsburgh, Jews from Germany and Austria formed the Friendship Club and, during the High Holidays, we held our own services according to German tradition. Originally we organized to help one another as needed, but that quickly grew into casual get-togethers every Saturday night to play cards and socialize. I can remember making potato salad and wieners with my mother and serving coffee and macaroon cake for dessert. How strange it was that just a few years ago our life could be so fraught with turmoil and now we were having tasty meals in the quiet comfort of our own home."[192] Cantor Heiser officiated at the marriage of Marga Silbermann and Jordan Randall, both deceased.

On November 11, 1979, The Friendship Club held its final event, at which Cantor Heiser spoke. It is obvious that this was a group that understood the dark side of life in Germany and appreciated the hospitality and freedom of their new homeland.

> When I was invited to speak at this banquet which marks the end of the Friendship Club here in Pittsburgh, I was not quite sure whether this is a happy or a sad occasion. In a sense, I think it's both. First of all, we are grateful that we are privileged to be here, to live and experience the integration of our brothers and sisters into the American and the Jewish community, a goal that the Friendship Club has pursued all through the years since its inception more than forty years ago. But we are also a bit sad, as parents are seeing their children mature, leaving their home and going their own way. I am sure that every one of us will remember the wonderful and meaningful hours having spent together in happy fellowship, especially at the time when we all came here as strangers, and besides everything else, the language was a bit strange to

us.... There are many of us who worked and helped and organized the activities of the Friendship Club.... As we are gathered here, we express our gratitude to all for the warmth and meaningful comradeship and for the kind and gracious help and assistance. ... But we also and foremost express our grateful thanks to this beloved country for giving us shelter and giving us the opportunity to start a new life after having been made homeless and bereaved of our families and friends.[193]

In his column, "As I See It," in *The Jewish Chronicle*, Milton K. Susman lamented, "Regretful note: a notice in *The Chronicle* announces the dissolution of The Friendship Club as a non-profit corporation. Which apparently means that this group of early refugees from the Hitler scourge (which this writer helped to organize) is gradually disappearing from the scene. Death and departures to other settings have corroded its membership. In its prime the Friendship Club was, as its name suggests, a well of Comradeship and hope in a new land."[194]

In a slightly later column, Susman announced, "The recently dissolved Friendship Club, a group of German emigres who fled their Hitlerized country in the late 30's and early 40's, has donated its entire assets to the newly organized Club Shalom, comprised of Russian immigrants, which meets regularly at the Jewish Community Center in Squirrel Hill. Here is not only an instance of history coming full circle but also an example of sympathetic understanding at its noblest."[195]

Reaping Personal and Professional Rewards

Forty years of life in Pittsburgh had brought many joys to the Heiser family. Daughter Judith was married and had three daughters, two of whom had become bat mitzvah, with one yet to go. The Heisers' oldest granddaughter, Shari Stein, celebrated her confirmation in her grandparents' shul. Again, we are fortunate to have an amateur recording of some of the Shavuot service. Cantor and Mrs. Heiser had brought tremendous culture and soul to B'nai Israel and to Pittsburgh at large; Cantor Heiser had thrown himself fully into the support of our new spiritual homeland of Israel; and he had played a founding role in the creation of the Cantors Assembly and the Cantors Institute and lent support to the Jewish Theological Seminary, the heart of the Conservative Movement. The 1980s were the decade to reap the rewards for all of the *hazzan's* hard work over four decades.

The celebrations began with a breakfast on December 14, 1980, on behalf of the Jewish Theological Seminary of America, honoring *Hazzan* Mordecai G. Heiser for his forty years of dedication and service to Congregation B'nai Israel and the Conservative Movement. Rabbi Richard M. E. Marcovitz was honorary chairman and Doris D. Binstock served as chairman. This is one of the articles which erroneously states that Cantor Heiser was born in Kovno, Lithuania.[196] The anonymous text of a speech honoring Hazzan Mordecai G. Heiser is in the Stein Collection. Fortunately, the program for the event is extant and the guest speaker was Rabbi Sanford D. Shanblatt of Temple Israel, Swampscott, Massachusetts.[197] A December 4, 1980, article in *The Jewish Chronicle* notes that Rabbi Shanblatt had himself grown up at B'nai Israel and returned because he was asked to do so for this celebration. He considered himself a disciple of *Hazzan* Mordecai G. Heiser.[198] No one who reads the following words would disagree.

> It is always a joy to return. I am deeply flattered that you have asked me to come here today, and when I received the call from Mr. Heller, and he told me that Cantor Heiser is to be honored, I told him immediately I am coming, and my plane reservations were made in a matter of minutes. I wanted to come very much because Cantor Heiser is very dear to me, and when I heard that it has been forty years of service, I was overwhelmed with memories. Sentimental fellow that I am, I think back forty years ago, when I was nine years old and witnessed the transition from Hazzan Bloom to Hazzan Heiser [in 1942]. Yes, I really do remember.
> . . . For forty years, Mordecai Heiser has blessed us with song. For forty years he has inspired the hearts of those who came here to worship. For forty years he has warmed the souls of all those who listened to the sweetness of his voice, the quality of his song, the lyric tone of tenderness that has always marked his musicianship. I can honestly tell you that as the years passed, and I left Pittsburgh, and attended other synagogues, and became a rabbi, I always heard his voice. I always compared other cantors to him, I always measured other synagogue melodies to his, because he was my standard, and he was always the best in my eyes. I confess that I still use his melodies, I have taught the cantors of my synagogues some of his melodies, and for me he will always be the sweet singer of Israel. . . . The enormous respect I have for a hazzan, the great love I have for a hazzan, the admiration I have for the very posi-

tion of a hazzan—a position which I have always honored—was engendered in me, fostered in me, nourished and nurtured within me because of Hazzan Mordecai G. Heiser. He was my inspiration and he was my teacher, and he was my symbol and my standard for what synagogue music should be like. Because of the honor I have for a cantor, I have had no troubles in that regard, and I learned it all here at B'nai Israel. I learned it from him, and I credit him with that. . . . Hazzan, may you continue serving B'nai Israel in your usual very special way, in good health, for many years to come, and may you and your dear wife always enjoy 'naches' from your children and grandchildren. . . .[199]

Rabbi Shanblatt was one of many who felt this way about Cantor Heiser's music. During this very exciting time for the Heiser family, on May 2, 1981, Betty Sue Stein, Cantor and Mrs. Heiser's third and final granddaughter, celebrated her bat mitzvah at B'nai Israel—more than six years after she had sung her first solo with her grandfather. It was a gala event for the congregation, and the entire clan participated in the happy occasion. We are fortunate to have a fairly extensive recording of this particular service, including remarks by Elly Heiser and Betty Sue's bat mitzvah speech.

Music was B'nai Israel's ultimate trump card in congregational and communal programming. Few other synagogues held as many concerts and festival-related music programs as B'nai Israel, all because of Cantor Heiser's dedication and great community relations within the Jewish as well as greater Pittsburgh community. On May 23, 1982, "a star-studded performance" took place at B'nai Israel with three outstanding artists in concert. First was *Hazzan* Leon Lissek of B'nai Amoona, St. Louis. He was billed as a "rising tenor who has concertized internationally. He recently sang with [opera singer] Roberta Peters." The second performer was Mimi Lerner, "Star of Pittsburgh and New York City Opera. Alumna of B'nai Israel." And, of course, *Hazzan* Mordecai G. Heiser, "B'nai Israel's Beloved Hazzan." They were accompanied by B'nai Israel organist Wayne Galbraith. An "extra added attraction" was Betty Sue Stein, *Hazzan* Heiser's granddaughter, who was all of fourteen years old at the time. According to the elaborate advertisement, the concert was "to inaugurate and benefit the Mordecai and Elly Heiser Music Fund of B'nai Israel Congregation," which from then on benefited the entire Western Pennsylvania region. Event chairman was Meyer Gisser, past president of the congregation, supported by reservation chairman Erwin Glick.[200]

One Jewish community program in which Cantor Heiser always participated was Yom HaShoah (Holocaust Remembrance Day). In 1983 the observance commemorated the fortieth anniversary of the Warsaw Ghetto Uprising, featuring Dr. Michael Berenbaum, later at the U.S. Holocaust Memorial Museum in Washington, D.C., as the keynote speaker. Cantor Heiser was joined by his colleague Cantor Moshe Taube from Beth Shalom Congregation and the other program participants.[201] He sang the "El Mohle Rachamim" prayer by Hugo Adler, which he sang numerous times over the years, so that it became something of a signature prayer for him.

At the thirty-sixth annual convention that year, the Cantors Assembly awarded Cantor Heiser the Yuval Award—forty years after he had received his certification as *hazzan* with the first group to receive such a diploma. He also was a *mohel* for thirty-five years; there are many ads in editions of *The Jewish Chronicle* over the years. On June 29, 1983, the Pittsburgh Zionist District of the ZOA honored Cantor Heiser on behalf of Israel Bonds. Israeli television producer-director Israel Amitai was the guest speaker.[202]

Hanukkah was celebrated in the congregation and in the community. The program of another joint concert at Congregation B'nai Israel for Hanukkah on December 4, 1983, 8 p.m., with the support of the Elly and Mordecai Heiser Music Fund, is also extant.[203] A Candle Lighting Ceremony and Torch Relay organized by the ZOA involved several of the Jewish institutions in Pittsburgh. Mayor Caliguiri participated in the lighting of the candles, along with Cantor Heiser and Rabbi Eliezer Ben Yehuda.[204] The community-wide Hanukkah celebration was an annual event organized by the ZOA. The 1984 ceremony took place on December 19, and Mayor Caliguiri again lit the Hanukkah candles, for the fifth time in a row as *The Jewish Chronicle* reported. Cantor Heiser conducted brief services.[205]

On December 16, 1984, the Ramah Chanukkah Concert with the Wilkinsburg Civic Symphony took place at Congregation B'nai Israel. In addition to Cantor Heiser and Betty Sue Stein, participants were Eugene Reichenfeld, Musical Director and Conductor; Charlotte Day, pianist; Catherine Bomstein, soprano; Robert Borman, violin, and Shannon Osborn and Eugene Reichenfeld, viola. Rabbi Richard Marcovitz welcomed the audience. This event was another benefit for the Camp Ramah Scholarship Fund, which sends Conservative youngsters to a Jewish summer camp every year. The program is extant.[206]

Consistently throughout the years, those who were privileged to hear Cantor Heiser sing were moved by his renditions of Jewish music. On January 28, 1985, Shannon Osborn of the Wilkinsburg Symphony, who had been playing in the orchestra when Cantor Heiser sang, expressed a sentiment that many people, Jewish and non-Jewish, shared. She wrote Cantor Heiser to express her gratitude for his voice.

> Dear Cantor Heiser,
> I am a member of the Wilkinsburg Symphony, and I have been wanting to write to you ever since December 1983 when the Wilkinsburg Symphony was part of the Hanukkah concert at B'nai Israel Synagogue. At the 1983 [sic], the orchestra members were seated near to where you were singing. I am a viola player, so I was just a few feet away from you. Mr. Heiser, that evening was one of the most wonderful of my life. It was thrilling and inspiring to be near to someone as gifted as you are. My entire family came to the December 1984 concert, and they also said what I have said—that it is a wonderful privilege to hear you sing.
> Best wishes to you and thank you,
> Shannon Osborn
>
> P.s. I also enjoy it when your granddaughter [Betty Sue Stein] sings.[207]

On January 5, 1985, just three days before their actual anniversary on January 8 [1935], Elly and Mordecai Heiser celebrated their Golden Wedding Anniversary with their friends. Hy and Lucille Kimel were some of the many friends who wished the Heisers well.

> January 3, 1985
> Dear Mordecai and Eli [sic!]:
> We are looking forward to share with you and your host of friends and admirers the glorious occasion of the 50th Anniversary Celebration. As we look back at the many years of our friendship and your impact on our Jewish community, it is easy to understand the love and affection that you enjoy in B'nai Israel and our Jewish community at large. Mordecai and Eli [sic] Heiser are symbolic of all the good things and positive values that is [sic!] symbolic in Jewish life.
> Lucille and I wish for you many more years of joy and contentment together with all members of your beloved family.
> Needless to say that we cherish your friendship.[208]

B'nai Israel honored *Hazzan* Mordecai and Elly Heiser on this occasion with a special service in which the family participated, and a festive Kiddush afterwards.[209] Their children and grandchildren honored the Heisers with the inscription of a leaf on B'nai Israel's Simcha Tree.[210] Sidney L. Singer, President of B'nai Israel, also notified Cantor and Mrs. Heiser that "the congregation which you have served so valiantly for lo these many years is inscribing a leaf on our Simcha Tree as an everlasting reminder of this date."[211] The Simcha Tree went to Congregation Adat Shalom in Fox Chapel when B'nai Israel closed its doors. They were very kind to take a picture for me. There are two leaves for Cantor and Mrs. Heiser's Fiftieth Anniversary—one from the family, the other from the congregation. Thank you!

Following the celebrations, Elly and Mordecai Heiser placed this thank you in the congregational bulletin of April 1985. "In honor of our 50th Wedding Anniversary, our friends and members of our Congregation made contributions to different organizations and we received so many letters and congratulations that it is impossible to thank each and every one as we would have liked to do. We appreciate and we thank all of you, hoping and praying that we shall be privileged to share many more happy occasions with you."[212]

Over the years, the board of directors liberally expressed their views—in spite of all the adoration for Cantor Heiser, not always in a complimentary way. For the January 7, 1964, board of directors meeting, the religious services committee reported, "Rabbi Chertoff and Cantor Heiser felt that the [High Holy Day] services this year were very effective, very moving, and were conducted with great dignity.... It was agreed that more emphasis must be placed on congregational participation both by the Rabbi and Cantor. More emphasis should be given to responsive reading both in English and Hebrew, more explanation of the prayers should be given, and more congregational singing of traditional High Holiday Prayers should be encouraged."[213]

Whatever changes were made did not altogether please. Five years later, after the 1969 High Holy Days, at the September 9 meeting, "It was commented that the Slichot service was too long."[214] This was reiterated on November 4, 1969, when the religious services committee made detailed comments especially about the Slichot and Rosh Hashanah services. Concerning Slichot, "The Committee agreed this service was too long. There was too much singing by the Cantor alone and not enough audience participation.... The service is to begin at midnight and conclude no later than 1:15 a.m." As far as Rosh Hashanah was concerned, "The evening Family Service was very good. . . . While the quality of the [morning] Rosh Hashonah services was considered excellent, they were too long. A recommendation was passed to conclude the [morning] Rosh Hashonah services next year at 12:15 p.m. Suggested guidelines to achieve this were: 1. Cantor to limit certain cantorial singing and encourage more audience participation. 2. Less repetition of prayers. 3. Shorten explanations of prayers by Rabbi. 4. Rabbi to limit sermon to 20 or 25 minutes. 5. Faster pace in reading and chanting. 6. Delete prayers where possible."[215] Enough progress was made over time to let some criticisms rest for a while, only to introduce others. Nevertheless, there also was appreciation of the hard work of Rabbi, Cantor, and others. A November 2, 1971, religious services committee report notes:

[1. . . .]
2. Selichot Service was beautiful.
3. Rosh Hashonah [morning] Services should be timed to a 12:15 p.m. conclusion.
[. . .]
10. It was agreed that future Yom Kippur Services would blend more traditional liturgy with the modern.
11. The joint Ne'ilah Service was considered successful except for the excessive heat and the misunderstanding about seating arrangements.
12. Certain Sabbath services pulpit arrangements were discussed and the experimental period to continue as to choir and Hazzan position.
13. The committee recognized the time and effort spent by the clergical staff in planning, preparing, and conducting our beautiful and impressive High Holiday Services.[216]

Shabbat services, too, did not escape the critical eye of the religious services committee. On January 7, 1969, the committee commented on Shabbat services, "In essence the services have been modified to make them more orderly and attractive to what is believed the majority of our members would like. The Saturday service starts later and at a fixed time and ends at a fixed time. More prayers are in English, more Torah and pulpit honors are given, and revisions have been made in the length of the Torah section covered."[217] Furthermore, at the February 4, 1969, meeting, the religious services committee evaluated the Shabbat service. "The Committee agreed that we should continue to hold the preliminary service in the Deaktor Chapel. In addition, it was recommended that the choir open all Shabbat services in the main Sanctuary with the singing of "Mah Tovu" [the hymn "How good it is for siblings to dwell together" to the Lewandowski melody].[218]

As we shall see in our journey through Cantor Heiser's cantorial repertoire in Chapter 3, he was not averse to modern music, and he courageously mixed the old and the new in his services, to differing effects.

The Joy of Family and Friends

B'nai Israel's membership consisted of outstanding individuals—they were genuinely kind and generous human beings. I will always fondly remember Rose Caplan, her daughter Joelle, and her sisters Molly and Selma; Mervin and Doris Binstock, Karl Adler, Abe and Betty Ainsman, Harry and Irene Louik, Meyer Parker, Helen Gisser and her sister Irene, and many others too numerous to mention. Among the stellar members was Charlotte Finkelstein, who celebrated her seventy-fifth birthday in 1985. Elly Heiser enjoyed writing poetry for family and friends. In one of her many poems, she captured the essence of our friend Charlotte.

> There is a lovely lady named
> "Charlotte Finkelstein"
> They threw away the mold, there are not
> Many as talented and fine
> Today we pray—and for this great
> Moment, that "He," the Lord
> Will be tender to you and reward
> The splendor of his everlasting Bounty.
> Charlotte loves to read, believes
> In the "Book"
> That's why she spends time in
> The "Library" so much as it took
> May I mention Charlotte's
> Artistry in "Embroidery"
> Unbelievable neat and in
> Fine taste, and talented "she"
> The tablecloths she made for me
> Are precious and beautiful as

Can "be," I will cherish them
To 100 degree[s].
We wish you well—good luck
And "happiness,"
No matter what is in the future,—
"God Bless."
Be happy, be healthy, with Sunshine
Contented we pray, and Skies of "Blue"
From Elly, Mordy,
Judy, Al, Adele, Shari, and of course
"Betty Sue"
Be well—for many years.
Charlotte, hopefully, because I
Am psychic and "wiser"
And oh, am I glad, our
Name is Mordecai and
Elly "Heiser"
On her "75th Birthday"
December 14, 1985.[219]

Elly Heiser was able to enrich any occasion with her sense of humor. Quick to capture the essence with her pen, on July 5, 1987, she blessed Adele and Warren's upcoming nuptials with her special stamp of approval.

A Bocher, a schener, so handsome and pale,
Met a nice Jewish girl with the name of Adele
They met at the Oakland Y Recreation Hall
Busily playing ball,
They were relaxed, not hurried
They fell in love, and now they are getting married,
. . . So ring the Bells,
Turn the Greggors,
Blow the Shofar,
Warren and Adele are going to the Altar
"Love is sweet, like sweet old wine"
So say Alvin and Judith Stein,
No more Headaches with Aspirin, Tylenol and Bufferin
Declare Jo and Judith Sufrin
Be fruitful and multiply, have many kids,

Advises Rabbi and Mrs. Markovitz (*sic!*),
Love is the greatest, we know, we are older
And hopefully wiser,
So say Mordecai and Elly Heiser.[220]

The Aufruf took place on July 4, 1987, at Beth El Congregation in the South Hills. Future in-laws Joe and Judy Sufrin sponsored the Kiddush luncheon following services.[221] Then, "Adele Miriam Stein and Warren J. Sufrin exchanged wedding vows . . . in B'nai Israel Congregation, East End. Parents of the couple are Mr. and Mrs. Alvin J. Stein of Squirrel Hill and Mr. and Mrs. Joseph Sufrin of Mt. Lebanon. After a wedding trip to Jamaica, the couple live in Bethel Park."[222]

A Friend to the State of Israel

Cantor Heiser's exemplary dedication to the State of Israel was recognized with the First Annual Classical Zionist Award by the ZOA (Zionist Organization of America) at the Tri-State Annual Region Conference of the ZOA which took place at the Greentree Marriott on July 19, 1987. Louis Zeiden, chairman of the conference, stated in a *Pittsburgh Press* article of June 24, 1987, "Cantor Heiser was selected for this honor for his outstanding contributions to the cause of Zionism and for his long-standing tenure as an active, contributing member of the ZOA."[223] At this point, Cantor Heiser had been a member of the Zionist Organization for nearly fifty years. He was also serving as a member of the board of directors of the Tri-State Region and was an honorary board member of the Pittsburgh Zionist District.[224] The Director of the ZOA, Hyman H. Kimel, wrote to Cantor Heiser following the event, thanking him for his participation in the Regional Conference. "You have acquired scores of friends only because you are a friend to so many people who respect and admire you. Please accept my thanks for your part in our program and many years of involvement in ZOA."[225]

Within a month of the honor from the ZOA, Cantor Heiser "created a ZOA foundation for a Masada Scholarship Program for needy and deserving students at Kfar Silver in Israel. The foundation will be known as the Mordecai and Elly Heiser ZOA Masada Foundation Fund."[226]

Cantor Heiser continued his close involvement with the ZOA until his death. In 1988 he was elected honorary vice chairman of the Board of the Tri-State Region of the ZOA.[227] The very year in which he died he was nominated for a position on the Tri-State Region Board of the organization, but he was no longer able to participate.[228]

A Life Well Lived

Many years after the Holocaust, on January 18, 1988, Cilly Brauer Haar [thank you, Rena!], the daughter of Cantor Heiser's mother Selma's brother Simon, who lived in England, contacted him [same age as Judy].

> Dear Gustav,
> I have just received a letter from our mutual cousin Sophie [Birnbaum-Weiss], in which she gave me your address, but please let me re-introduce myself to you, I am your cousin Cilly Brauer from Berlin. When Sophie's letter came this morning it took me back many years when we used to visit the whole family and the little dog Tiffy. It seems like a different life. Now we are all scattered all over the globe. I don't know if you know that I live in England, trained and qualified as a nurse, married an English Jewish man, we have three married sons and 2 grandchildren and are both retired now, but we keep busy and are very active with various social and cultural activities. Do you know what happened to your sister Elli [Eleonore Heiser, married to Julius Zellner with infant Joel], and Hugo and Meta and family. Have you ever been back to Berlin? I have been back several times, I have seen the rebuilding of the Jewish community East and West, even survivors from Auschwitz had returned to Berlin, it's sad, but I suppose that's where their roots are. Well Gustav, I don't want to make this a too lengthy letter, but would be very happy if you would write and tell me all your news. Hoping you and your family are well.
> I remain with best wishes,
> Cilly [Haar]
>
> Are you in touch with Cilly [Ebner] in Israel?[229] We do write to each other and have seen each other several times when she came to Europe. I don't know if you know that my brother Albert has died in 1972. It was very tragic, but he just could not cope with life anymore. I miss him terribly we could have had such happy times together but it was not to be.
> Lots of love, Cilly[230]

The original family left after the Holocaust was pitiful in number. Over the years, the Heisers slowly built a new family through the marriage of daughter, Judy, to Al Stein and subsequently the marriages of their three daughters.

In matters of the heart, Shari Stein was not far behind her sister Adele, getting engaged to Mark Klafter from Smithtown, New York, even before Adele's wedding in 1987. Mark, a medical student at the University of Pittsburgh, was also an athlete who had the distinction of being chosen for the American gymnastics team at the 1985 Maccabiah Games in Israel where he won a silver medal for his floor exercise routine.[231] These were the very games at which another Mark, Mark Spitz, the American gold-medal-winning swimmer, carried the Maccabiah torch into the Tel Aviv stadium.[232] Clearly, the family was proud of Mark's accomplishments in gymnastics. Within a year of Adele's wedding, on June 26, 1988, Shari and Mark married at B'nai Israel. "Parents of the couple are Mr. and Mrs. Alvin J. Stein of Squirrel Hill and Mr. and Mrs. Gerald L. Klafter of Smithtown, N.Y. The couple are residing in Chicago, Ill."[233] Pucci did not miss the occasion and penned the following:

> Many greetings from house to house
> Much love from me and my spouse
> From his home in the east,
> Way east, like Long Island
> Came a boy—strong and stark
> He wants to be a doctor
> And his name is Mark
> Mark met our Shari
> He had chosen our city
> Our Cathedral of Learning—Pitt
> He wants to study about all the bones in
> Feet and hip
> In hopes to be a "hit" whenever
> Comes in his ship
> Mark is very agile
> And he is a gymnast—one of the best
> Pitt sent him to Israel to be one of the cast
> At the Maccabee with all the rest
> Well, Mark won the silver medal
> As a gymnast he won good reviews

In the press—no less
When Mark met at Pitt
Our Shari
Both heard violins
Like a "Stradavarius"
When they met, on the spot
They liked each other a lot
What can we say to such a lovely pair
I have to think and see
I remind myself of President Kennedy
Mark, "Do not think what Shari can do for you
But see what you can do for her"
"Your full name is Mark Jeffrey Klafter
Now you have Shari for a lifetime to look after"
So, Shalom to your family, friends and all your peers
From us all to Shari and Mark—Cheers.[234]

An Era Comes to an End

At some point in 1988 I had agreed to chair an event for B'nai Israel's eighty-fifth anniversary in the spring of 1989. Cantor Heiser wanted to invite the Israeli clarinetist Giora Feidman, the "King of Klezmer," and his trio. We established a committee, set the date, raised the funds, and went ahead with the gala event which took place at the synagogue on June 6. To this day, the huge poster that Larry Resnick, a gifted member of the congregation, created for the occasion, is hanging in my home.

B'nai Israel's
85th Anniversary Concert
Featuring the
Giora Feidman Trio
The art of the Klezmer
Tuesday, June 6, 8 p.m.
Tickets: Adults $10, Students $5
This program is in arrangement with the J.W.B. Lecture Bureau.[235]

We placed several well-directed publicity articles about the event in *The Jewish Chronicle*, the first one on May 18, announcing the concert as one of the eighty-fifth anniversary events.[236] The second article, entitled,

"Klezmorizing at B'nai Israel," proudly states, "He stands alone. Those who hear him play quickly become his loyal fans; and once entranced by his music, they often remain lifelong followers who will go to great lengths to hear him perform.... In fact, Giora Feidman is a one-man United Nations. He was born in Argentina into a Bessarabian family, was educated in South America, became an Israeli citizen as a young adult, and now makes a home both in the U.S. and Israel."[237]

Greeting Feidman at the Pittsburgh airport with his colleagues Jeff Israel and Peter Weitzner was indeed a pleasure; squeezing them, their luggage, and instruments in my little Rabbit car an adventure, and the event was the success we expected it to be. The president of the congregation, Maxine Horn, stated, "We are most privileged and delighted to present an artist of the caliber of Giora Feidman to the Pittsburgh community. We are confident that this concert will not only prove to be a memorable event in the annals of B'nai Israel, but that it will be recalled with pleasure by members of the greater Jewish community as well."[238] Indeed it was. The program of the event is extant.

Alas, a few months before the concert, Cantor Heiser was hit by a car while crossing the street in front of his apartment building. He was not immediately unconscious, and we all hoped that he would recover from his injuries. Instead, he slipped into a coma that lasted for several months until his death in October. As a result, a tremendous dark cloud hung over the eighty-fifth anniversary concert to which he had so much looked forward.

On July 20, 1989, Florence Rosner, staff writer for *The Jewish Chronicle* in Pittsburgh wrote and published an article that she entitled, "Singing team at B'nai Israel." Whether it was inspired by the tragic accident is hard to say, but the article focused on perhaps the greatest joy in the Cantor's life—his granddaughter Betty Sue Stein.

> They are an institution at B'nai Israel Synagogue—the team of Mordecai Heiser and his granddaughter, Betty Sue Stein, have been singing together since she was just a child.... Her mother, Judy Stein, Cantor Heiser's daughter, remembers when Betty Sue was about two and liked singing along with the radio. When Cantor Heiser noticed Betty Sue's singing, he was amazed at how well she sang for a toddler, that she seemed to have perfect pitch. 'That child is going to have a voice,' he correctly predicted. Betty Sue recalls singing little solos at first for the High Holidays. 'Then,' she remembers, 'he and I sang together. We would sing back and

forth to each other.' Cantor Heiser says that as far back as he can recall, Betty Sue had a beautiful soprano voice, and that by the age of five she was singing with him. At 16, she became a full-fledged member of the synagogue choir she had sung with unofficially for many years. Today, at 21, she is still with the choir.[239]

Sadly, with the accident—and although we all hoped it would not be true—Cantor Heiser's voice had been silenced . . . as it turned out, for good. Betty Sue never sang in the synagogue again after her beloved Papa's death.

When Cantor Heiser died on 25 Tishrei 5740 (October 24, 1989), one day after Simchat Torah, B'nai Israel and the Pittsburgh Jewish Community suffered a shattering loss. His obituary in the *Pittsburgh Post-Gazette*, compiled by Michael A. Fuoco, reads as follows:

> Mordecai G. Heiser, who was in his 50th year as cantor and musical director of B'nai Israel Congregation, East End, died of a brain tumor Tuesday in Heritage-Shadyside nursing center, Squirrel Hill. Mr. Heiser, 81 [not correct, 84], of Shadyside, also directed the congregation choir, which included his youngest granddaughter. He graduated from the Hoch Schule Des [*sic:* Hochschule für die Wissenschaft des Judentums] in Berlin, the school of higher learning for Jews before the rise of Adolf Hitler. He fled during the Nazi purge, ministering to Jewish refugees in England before coming to the United States in 1940. In 1949, he gave a recital at the Carnegie Music Hall in New York and has presented numerous cantorial concerts in and around the [*sic!*] Pittsburgh. He has received numerous honors, including being made an honorary fellow of the Cantors Assembly in 1960. In 1983, he received the group's Jubilee Award, celebrating the assembly's 36th anniversary. The State of Israel Bonds honored him with its Independence Award in 1972 and its Negev Award in 1983. In 1962 and 1983, the Zionist Organization of America honored him for "leadership and dedication" and presented him with its first Classical Zionist Award in 1987. The Jewish Theological Seminary in New York honored him in 1980 on his 40th year of service to his synagogue. On his 39th anniversary at the synagogue, a special work of art was commissioned in his honor by the congregation. Survivors include his wife, Elly; a daughter, Judy Stein of Squirrel Hill; and three granddaughters. Services will be held at 1 p.m. today in the

main sanctuary of B'nai Israel Congregation, 327 N. Negley Ave. There will be no visitation before the service. Interment will be in B'nai Israel Cemetery, Penn Hills.[240]

There was an outpouring of grief and of sympathy for the family—and for ourselves. Services would never be the same again. Life as we had known it at B'nai Israel had been immensely impoverished by Cantor Heiser's passing. I expressed this in a tribute in *The Jewish Chronicle* of November 16, 1989, entitled "Remembering Cantor Heiser."

To the Editor:

Some of you knew him better, many of you much longer, some as a colleague or as a musician, some as a teacher or advisor, and others as a friend or family member. Mordecai G. Heiser, cantor of Congregation B'nai Israel for nearly 50 years, has been laid to his final rest after prolonged illness. There are few lives in Jewish Pittsburgh that he did not touch in some way, and the Heiser legacy will live on in this community through vivid memories of weddings, bar and bat mitzvas, births, baby-namings, funerals, birthday parties, and other occasions in which he participated. We shall sorely miss his powerful presence in many ways—his rich and melodious voice, his dry sense of humor, the twinkle in his eyes, the gentle touch of his hands. We shall miss a master teacher, who patiently instructed young and adult; we shall miss his comforting the sick and the bereft, and his uplifting the down-trodden, as well as his rejoicing in our simchas, the wisdom of his age and the certainty of his decisions. And we shall miss his footsteps entering the chapel for the daily minyan, his pacing back and forth while davening, his powerful "Amen" during the Kaddish. And although our sorrow overshadows all else at the moment, may the loving memory of his long and productive life outshine our grief. Perhaps we may in our loss also be comforted by words which he liked to share with those who experienced the loss of a loved one.

In his Rabbi's Manual, I found the anonymous poem below, written in his own hand. Since it is so fitting, I decided to include it with the letter.

> Let none of you weep for me,
> Especially you with whom I've smiled.

Nor bow down your head in utter grief.
Put on no mourning, as if the pall
Induces forgetfulness and conceals all
We've done together. We have lived:
Remember!
Say not that I have died, that this is death.
Say that I lived, enjoying each mortal breath.
We have learned and labored and wrought.
What our hands found to do we sought
In quest to raise to nobler height.
My life was blessed in the living,
My death hallowed because of giving.
Life to me was a challenge. I was happy so to live. . . .

Gerda Schmidt
Pittsburgh[241]

Among the many letters of condolence that Mrs. Heiser received was one from England, from Cantor Heiser's longtime friend Hans Rahmer, now John D. Rayner—Rabbi Rayner, who had succeeded in building a solid career in England in the half century since their parting in Berlin. The letter expressed, as did so many over the Cantor's lifetime, the impact that he had made on congregants and those in the larger community who encountered his singing and his person. On June 21, 1990, nearly six months after Cantor Heiser's death, John wrote,

> Dear Mrs. Heiser,
> I am deeply distressed to learn—from Abu (Arthur) Wolff—that your husband died some while ago, and that the sad news did not reach me earlier. As you may remember, I was a regular attendee at Sabbath Eve and Sabbath Morning Services at the Old People's Home in Lichterfelde, where I became enthralled by your husband's magnificent singing (which played a large part in drawing me to Judaism and ultimately to the Rabbinate) and where he also taught me for my Bar Mitzvah—or, rather, I used to come to your home for my lessons. It has always been a matter of great regret to me that—apart from a brief visit to Pittsburgh in 1963 [while John Rayner was at HUC in Cincinnati]—I have not seen you or your husband since our Berlin days, and that my hope that one day he would visit England and sing in my synagogue,

remained unfulfilled. But let me assure you that I have thought of him countless times over the years, and that some of his renderings of Lewandowski are regularly sung in my synagogue, as I dictated them to our late choirmaster many years ago. Therefore his influence endures in more ways than you may realize, and I will certainly hold him in admiring and affectionate memory for the rest of my days on this earth. Please accept this belated but sincerely felt expression of my deep sympathy.

Yours sincerely,
John Rayner[242]

Indeed, this is also a major purpose of this study—to preserve and perpetuate Cantor Heiser's *hazzanut* for posterity.

To try to mitigate the tremendous loss somewhat, a wonderful portrait of Cantor Heiser by Pittsburgh photographer Hans Jonas was dedicated during the service on May 19, 1990. That Shabbat, the Heiser family dedicated the flowers on the bimah in Cantor Heiser's memory.[243] Today, the portrait is in the possession of Cantor Heiser's family.

Despite hiring another cantor, B'nai Israel did not recover from Cantor Heiser's death. On April 8, 1996, Gary Rotstein, staff writer for the *Pittsburgh Post-Gazette*, highlighted the plight of this unique institution in an article entitled "A Final Shalom at B'nai Israel." Rotstein noted that "12 Saturdays from now, the B'nai Israel Congregation will conduct its last Sabbath service at the well-recognized, cylindrical synagogue it has used on North Negley Avenue since 1924."[244] In July, the congregation closed its doors for good—an era had come to an end. B'nai Israel organizationally merged with a Conservative congregation in New Kensington (Beth Jacob) which reinvented itself as Congregation Adat Shalom (B'nai Israel-Beth Jacob) located in Fox Chapel. Rotstein, along with Jan Ackerman of the *Pittsburgh Post-Gazette*, captured the situation accurately with an article the week before the final Shabbat service took place that they entitled, "A Jewish beacon goes out."

> 'Bittersweet.' It was a word used again and again yesterday by current and former members of the B'nai Israel congregation in East Liberty. They snapped photographs, looked for their deceased loved ones' names on lighted [yahrzeit] plaques and remembered how the magnificent synagogue—which is closing—has been a

beacon of Conservative Jewish life for more than seven decades.[245]

Closing the synagogue to services was the hardest part; having the membership torn apart and dispersed to several other congregations was perhaps the saddest; but facing the possibility that the building might be torn down if the congregation could not find a buyer for it was the most heart-wrenching.

In 1997, the Eastside Alliance, a coalition of groups from various Pittsburgh neighborhoods, was interested in using the building as a multi-purpose community building but could not afford to buy it for $3.25 million, or even for the discount price of $2.9 million. Patricia Lowry, staff writer for the *Pittsburgh Post-Gazette*, publicized the plight of this expensive, yet architecturally intriguing building with an article, "Looking for an Angel."[246] Although the building was designated a historic landmark by the Pittsburgh History and Landmarks Foundation already in 1979, this does not ensure that it will continue to grace "the little hill" in the East End of Pittsburgh.

A discouraging article of July 7, 2016, welcomed me to Pittsburgh on July 10, 2016. Toby Tabachnick, then senior staff writer for *The Jewish Chronicle*, continued the building's sad saga. She wrote, "On the block again, former synagogue building might disappear." The writer explained that the building, "purchased by the Urban League in 2001 for $670,000, [. . .] no longer fills the needs of the growing charter school that it housed."[247] The future of the building is indeed dim. During my 2016 visit to Pittsburgh, I couldn't help but drive to my former synagogue one afternoon and was saddened by the sight of the orphaned building—plastic bags and papers drifting across the portico floor, the door of the empty bulletin board gently clanging open and shut in the afternoon breeze. Only the grape vines below the roof were intact. Where was the spirit that used to inspire us so?

Geburtsurkunde.

Nr. 10.

Singhofen am 10 Mai 19 05.

Vor dem unterzeichneten Standesbeamten erschien heute, der Persönlichkeit nach _____ er kannt,

der Lehrer Frank Heiser

wohnhaft in Singhofen israelitischer Religion und zeigte an, daß von der Selma Heiser geborene Brauer seiner Ehefrau israelitischer Religion wohnhaft bei ihm

zu Singhofen in seiner Wohnung am ach ten Mai des Jahres tausend neunhundert fünf haupts mittags um zwölf Uhr ein Knabe geboren worden sei und daß das Kind den Vornamen Gustav erhalten habe. Vorstehend ein Druckwort gestrichen.

Vorgelesen, genehmigt und unterschrieben
Frank Heiser

Der Standesbeamte.
Winter

Daß vorstehender Auszug mit dem Geburts-Hauptregister des Standesamts zu Singhofen gleichlautend ist, wird hiermit bestätigt.

Singhofen am 12 September 1934.

Der Standesbeamte.
Winter

Geburtsurkunde Gustav Heiser (copy) 1934, Stein Collection.

Heiser Kantorenschule Zeugnis 1929, Stein Collection.

Aron Friedmann, Schir Lisch'lomo, Chasonus *für das ganze liturgische Jahr,* 1901, HUC-JIR Library, Jerusalem.

Jsraelitische Religionsgemeinde Berlin-Lichterfelde-Lankwitz E.V.

Z e u g n i s !

Herr Gustav H e i s e r aus Berlin war in unserer Gemeinde vom 1.Oktober 1925 bis 1. November 1938 zunächst als I.Kantor und in den letzten 3 Jahren als Prediger und Seelsorger angestellt.

Mit einer sehr wohltönenden, angenehmen Tenorstimme versehen, hat er es verstanden, durch Innigkeit seines Vortrages den Gottesdienst für alle Gemeindemitglieder zu einem erhebenden und zu Herzen gehenden zu gestalten.

Neben der Funktion eines I.Kantors hat Herr Heiser auch noch die eines Thoravorlesers und eines Schoffarbläsers zu unserer vollsten Zufriedenheit ausgeführt.

Als Herr Heiser das Zwischen-Examen bei der Lehranstalt für die Wissenschaft des Judentums ablegte, übertrugen wir ihm teilweise das Amt eines Predigers und Seelsorgers an unserer Gemeinde. Auch für diese Tätigkeit brachte Herr Heiser ausserordentliche Begabung und Fleiss mit, seine Predigten fanden den vollsten Beifall unserer Gemeindemitglieder und waren durchdrungen von heiligem Eifer für unsere Lehre und unseren Glauben.

Herr Heiser betätigte sich in unserer Gemeinde auch seelsorgerisch und hat es verstanden, die Jugend unseres Bezirkes durch Abhaltung von Religions-und Barmizwoh-Unterricht, neuhebräischen Kursen, religiösen Veranstaltungen, usw. an die Quellen unserer Lehre und unseres Glaubens heranzuführen und sie zu nützlichen Mitgliedern der jüdischen Gemeinschaft zu erziehen.

Sein Wirken in unserer Gemeinde war stets begleitet vonseinem frommen und bescheidenen Wesen, wodurch er sich Liebe und Hochachtung bei unseren Gemeindemitgliedern erworben hat.

Durch die Auflösung unserer Gemeinde müssen wir Herrn Heiser aus seinen Diensten entlassen. Wir wünschen ihm das Allerbeste für seine fernere Zukunft.

Jsraelitische Religionsgemeinde
Lichterfelde-Lankwitz E.V.

Berlin, den 1.November 1938.   Der Vorstand:

Simon Neisser letter for Cantor Heiser from Israelitische Religionsverein B-L-L 1938, Stein Collection.

Elly Hochmann Geburtsurkunde (copy) 1934, Stein Collection.

Receipt for Heiser marriage fee 1935, Stein Collection.

Judith Heiser birth certificate 1936, Stein Collection.

Heiser Zwischenprüfung at the Hochschule in Berlin 1937, Stein Collection.

Hochschule class picture 1938, Cantor Heiser second row, center, with bowtie, Stein Collection.

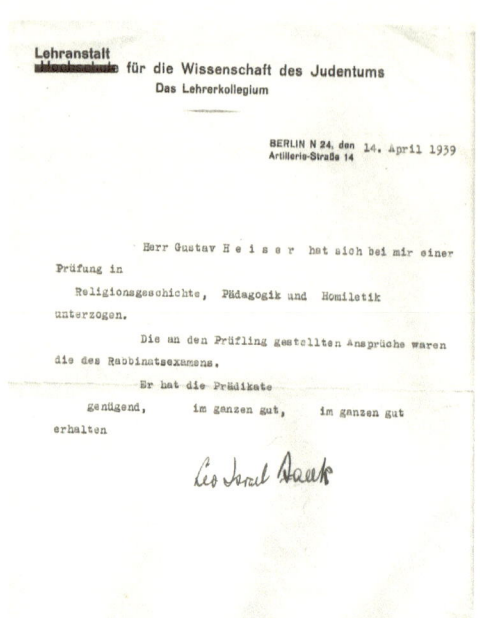

Heiser Lehranstalt examination Leo Baeck 1939, Stein Collection.

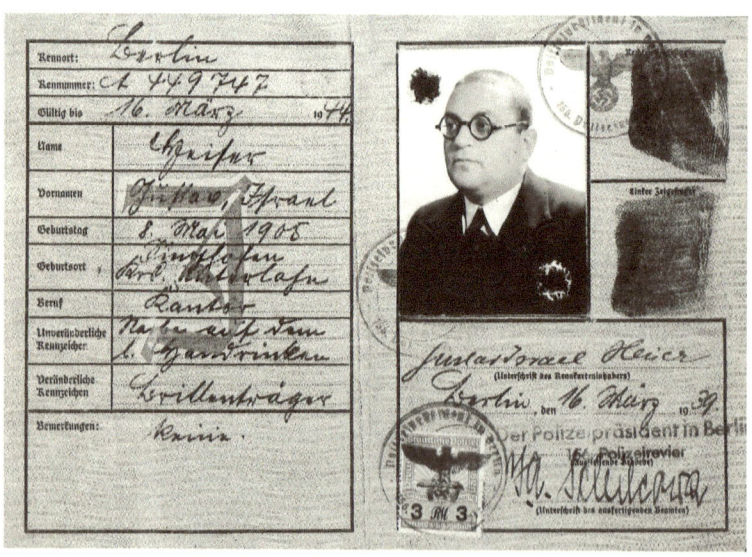

Gustav Heiser Passport 1939, Stein family.

Sammel-Transport by Hilfsverein der Juden für Deutschland, 1939 Stein Collection.

Permit for Gustav Heiser to leave Kitchener Camp 1940, Stein Collection.

B'nai Israel exterior 2016, Schmidt.

B'nai Israel detail 2016, Schmidt.

B'nai Israel Hebrew School Class Graduation 1943, Cantor Heiser back row standing, second from left, Rabbi Lichter, back row standing, third from right, Heinz Archive.

Gustav Heiser naturalization (front) 1945, Stein Collection.

Gustav Heiser naturalization (back) 1945, Stein Collection.

Heiser Carnegie Recital Hall concert
1949, Stein Collection.

Heiser Carnegie Recital Hall concert program
1949, Stein Collection.

B'nai Israel Confirmation picture 1950, Cantor Heiser back row standing, eighth from right, Heinz Archive.

Heiser Cantors Assembly Certificate 1954, Stein Collection.

Five Cantors concert 1956, newspaper clipping, Stein Collection.

Judy Heiser as bride 1957, Stein Collection. Photo by Jonas.

Israel Bonds participants with Cantor and Ms. Heiser, 1972. CMU Libraries Digital Collection.

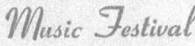

Cantor's 30th Anniversary Concert 1970, Stein Collection.

Cantor Heiser as mohel, 1972. CMU Libraries Digital Collection.

Certificate of appreciation on occasion of 40th anniversary, Cantor Heiser and Rabbi Marcovitz, 1980. Heinz Archive.

Cantor Heiser and Betty Sue Stein 1989, newspaper clipping, Jewish Newspaper Collection, CMU Libraries Digital Collection.

Cantor Heiser with siddur (no date), Stein Collection. Photo by Jonas.

Six Heiser/Steins c. 1975. Stein Collection.

Mayor Caliguiri lights Hanukkah Candles, 1983, newspaper clipping, Stein Collection.

Cantor Heiser in B'nai Israel sanctuary 1980, Photo by Jonas.

Cantor Heiser chanting prayer (no date), Stein Collection.

Mordecai and Elly Heiser 1960. Photo by Jonas.

Heiser "Y'varech'cha" notated by Schmidt.

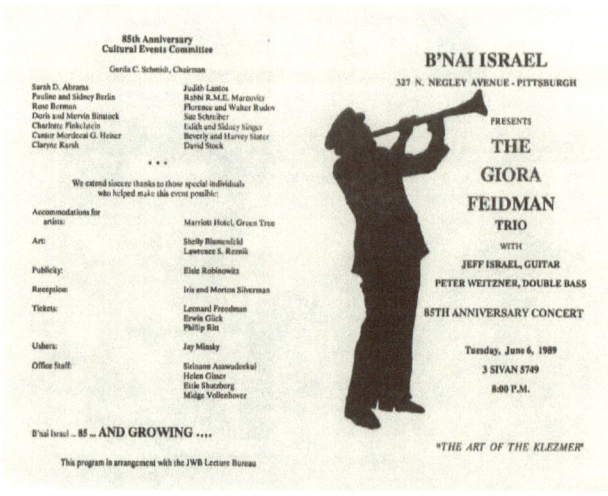

Giora Feidman concert program 1989, B'nai Israel, Schmidt.

Heiser grave, B'nai Israel cemetery after 1992, Schmidt.

Weissensee Cemetery, Judith Stein, Betty Sue Stein, and Adele Stein Sufrin, Berlin 1999, Schmidt.

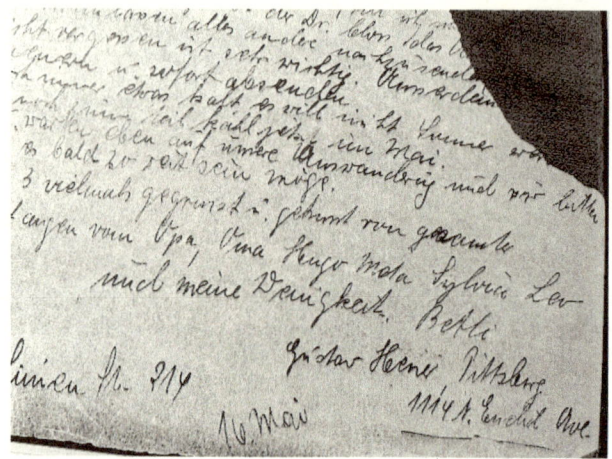

Fragment of Heiser family letter. Stein Collection.

B'nai Israel Sanctuary, 1980. Left Hazzan Mordecai Gustav Heiser, Rabbi Richard M. E. Marcovitz, and Cantor Mordechai Max Haalman. Photo by Jonas.

CHAPTER 3

HAZZAN MORDECAI GUSTAV HEISER—THE SWEET SINGER OF B'NAI ISRAEL

One Example of a European-trained Cantor's Contribution to the American Cantorate

The Choral Synagogue

B'nai Israel was a *Khorshul* (choral synagogue) on the models of those in Riga, Vilna, Kovno, Odessa, and others before the Holocaust, a type of synagogue that developed in nineteenth-century Eastern Europe out of the traditional liturgical pattern where choristers or a loosely organized male choir supported the prayers of the cantor. Cantors and others who traveled to the West, like Vienna, during the time period of Salomon Sulzer, brought back to their home synagogues the innovations practiced there, such as an organized and trained male choir, new arrangements for the hymns, and some updating of the decorum during the service. Even prayers and sermons in the vernacular caught on, as did the organ. Hence, the relationship between congregation and *hazzan* evolved during this time (and not to everyone's liking). Cantor and four-part choir exchanged musical phrases, almost like call and response in a church service, pretty much to the exclusion of congregational participation. Marsha Bryan Edelman notes that in the United States eventually "many congregations rejected this type of service as paternalistic and indulgent on the part of professional musicians and an affront to congregants eager to take an active role in the service."[1] Yet the opposite view also exists, namely that "congregational singing . . . constituted a threat to the continuance of the synagogue choir."[2]

B'nai Israel was also aware of the periodic inadequacy of their efforts when it came to congregational participation and struggled with the problem off and on. Spiritually these exchanges between cantor and choir are the most powerful service parts in Cantor Heiser's worship services and the congregation enjoyed them—certainly during the years that I attended the services. And we know from both the Berlin-Lichterfelde-Lankwitz congregation and from the Kitchener Camp in England that the choir was one of Cantor Heiser's great strengths already in Berlin and in England. At B'nai Israel, in addition to the mixed choir, he also formed either a men's choir or a woman's choir—even a children's choir if the occasion or the congregation demanded it.

For many years, Claryne Bernstein Karsh was the director for the mixed choir that beautified festival, High Holy Day, and some Shabbat services, especially for *simchas* (celebrations) and for *Birchat HaChodesh* (Prayer for the New Month). Even though B'nai Israel already used a choir under Cantor Bloom, the existence of a choir was not self-evident. When the congregation suffered from a financial shortfall, the choir was the first budgetary item to be questioned. At times combined with poor worship attendance, the board did not hesitate to either cut or entirely eliminate the choir, whose members were paid. Apparently, the use of a choir experienced an interruption in the 1940s; why is not known. It could have been due to Cantor Bloom's death or to World War II. The board meeting minutes of June 1, 1948, report that "a decision had been reached to recommend the engagement of a choir on an annual basis, at a cost not to exceed the amount of $3,000." A motion to that effect was introduced and passed with a split vote of 12–10.[3] Poor attendance of the Slichot service in 1949 caused Cantor Heiser to reconsider the use of a choir in 1950. The Ritual Committee reported to the June 6, 1950, board meeting that "Cantor Heiser suggested that we do not use the choir for Selichos services as there is not enough of an attendance. The choir last year [1949] consisted of 10 singers at a cost of $1,775. This year it was proposed to have 8 singers at an approximate cost of $1,700." A motion was made and passed that "the choir be dispensed with for the Selichos services and that the Cantor chant the services."[4] The question of the choir resurfaces in 1951 when the Ritual Committee decides "to engage a choir consisting of 8 people at a compensation of $1,775, which is $100 more than we paid last year. This is for the High Holidays only."[5]

The Ritual Committee "also decided to engage the services of the organist and 4 singers for the Late Friday Night services—4 days of Passover, 4 days Succos, and 2 days Shevuos. The cost entailed for these services will be $580 for the organist, which includes children's services and $875 for Friday Night. The total cost will be . . . $1,455 for Friday Night services and Minor Festivals."[6] In 1963, Dr. Mervin Binstock reported that "The Religious Service Committee recommends the modification of the congregational choir effective the first Sabbath, September 1963, with a maximum number of 11 members including the choir director."[7] By 1970, B'nai Israel's financial situation was no longer so rosy. The Religious Service Committee met on March 17 "mainly to consider the size of the Sabbath Choir for the next fiscal year in view of our present and potential budget problems."[8] Earlier that year "the projected expense for the choir and organist for the Sabbath and the three festivals was $11,500." Cantor Heiser and Mrs. Karsh eliminated two singers and the use of the choir on 4 Shabbosim, reducing the cost to about $9,500. They agreed "they could perform adequately with 7 choir members including the leader. It was further agreed upon that the cost for the choir and organist would be a maximum of $9,000 for the aforementioned days and that the choir would also sing when there are no Bar Mitzvahs."[9]

To have an organ in a synagogue or not is a question that synagogues, especially outside the Reform movement, struggled with since the nineteenth century. The first organ in a synagogue was introduced in Seesen in Northern Germany in 1810. Before then, only the human male voice was heard during services. With Jewish acceptance into society at large, Christian worship services presented a challenge to Jewish congregations. B'nai Israel was no exception. At the January 4, 1949, board meeting, "Rabbi Lichter advised that a meeting will be held on Sunday morning. The question of having an organ in the synagogue is again being discussed. A member of the synagogue has promised to pay the full cost of an organ if it will be permitted by the Board." Apparently, this subject had come up before. The member alluded to was the family of the late Harry Schreiber, and the organ was to be donated in his memory.[10] Other board members weighed in on the matter, going on record "as being glad and grateful for the presentation of an organ." But there was still considerable unease about the use of an organ during certain services, and one board member made an amendment "that the organ is not used for Friday Night Services, Saturday morning, or High Holiday services at the present time." However, after some discussion, the amendment was withdrawn and "the original motion was then passed."[11]

Upon approval, this instrument served to accompany the singing, especially at weddings, but also on the Festivals, and on one Shabbat a month that was led by the Religious School.[12] The board minutes of January 3, 1950, record that "the organ was used last Friday night and it was very well received. Rabbi Lichter reported that on Friday night the attendance looked as though it were the High Holidays. There were quite a few people from other synagogues in attendance. The Rabbi suggested that the organ be used once a month on Saturday morning for the children's service and asked that this be considered for the February services."[13] Likewise, later board minutes note that "the organ was played at the services on the second day of Passover, and that the services were very beautiful." Another board member added "that it was the most beautiful service ever held at B'nai Israel."[14] Yet concerns led to a "request for the elimination of the playing of the organ on Saturday" in 1952.[15]

Beginning in 1974 or 1975, the real star of festive occasions was Cantor Heiser's youngest granddaughter, Betty Sue Stein, who started singing duets with her grandfather as well as solo parts when she was barely six years old and had to stand on a box to reach the microphone, as she noted in her Bat Mitzvah speech.[16] The choir's place upstairs in the balcony with the organ during the later years was also not a given. That placement dates to the 1970s, while Cantor Heiser continued to sing from the *bimah* downstairs in the front of the sanctuary. This is the reason why the volume on some of our tapes is uneven, especially when Cantor Heiser walked around the sanctuary in the Torah procession—no lapel mikes were used then.

Over the years the location of cantor and/or choir was much in dispute and moved around the synagogue for better effect and better audience participation. Still, in April 1970, the board decided that "Cantor Heiser will experiment with the choir in various locations [to increase audience involvement]."[17] This they did, and the November 2, 1971, board meeting minutes record that "the experimental period [is] to continue as to choir and Hazzan positions."[18] We learn from the December minutes what was transpiring during this experimental period. "The position of the Cantor facing the Ark along with the choir on the Bimah during Sabbath Services is continuing in order to recapture the spiritual beauty of prayer."[19] Similarly, this is mentioned again in October 1972.[20] Finally, in July 1973, "A recommendation was passed after lengthy discussion to have the choir relocated in the balcony for all religious services."[21] It certainly was located there during the time that I attended B'nai Israel, until Cantor Heiser's death in 1989.

In his office, Cantor Heiser had both a shelf of books as well as a music library. He also had a small Stradolin electric cord organ on which he practiced both melodies and harmonies. This instrument, missing a number of buttons now, found a home in my living room upon his death. From the files of sheet music Cantor Heiser chose what he and the choir director would practice with his beloved choir for a given service. After Cantor Heiser's death, the sheet music and a Partitur book went to Richard Berlin for his M.A. thesis at JTS.[22] Sadly, Cantor Berlin, who was my contemporary at B'nai Israel, died on May 1, 2019. May his memory be for a blessing.

Thanks to great-granddaughter Rena Sufrin Kennedy, we have three examples of Cantor Heiser's recorded concert singing. When Judith Heiser Stein contemplated what to do with her father's cantorial record collection, she was guided to the Judaica Sound Archives at Florida Atlantic University which started as a small project in 2002.[23] From an article, "Pittsburgh Music Preserved," by Hilary Daninhirsch in *The Jewish Chronicle* from November 14, 2013, we learn that the collection seems to be mainly of other cantors' recordings, not her dad's. In fact, by putting an ad in the *Chronicle* for a few years, Judy became what Daninhirsch calls a "zamler" of other people's Jewish recordings for the FAU Judaica Sound Archive.[24]

Hazzan Mordecai Gustav Heiser's Hazzanut

In 1988, Judith Vander, an ethnomusicologist, analyzed the work of five Shoshone women in whose work of music and dance she was a participant observer. She called their song repertoire, which she described as "distinctive" to their "culture, age, and personality," their songprint.[25] Later in this chapter we will accompany Cantor Heiser word for word—and almost note for note—through the service fragments at our disposal, but first we shall take a look into his philosophy of liturgy, the different types of influences from his childhood to early adulthood to maturity, the repertoire he assembled over a lifetime, as well as his style of presentation.

Heiser Philosophy of Liturgy

It is a cantor's privilege and burden to decide which music is right for his particular congregation. For Jewish Music Month in March 1985 (only four years before his death), Cantor Heiser wrote an article in the *Congregation B'nai Israel Bulletin* entitled "Jewish Music Month," expressing his view on the "right" music for B'nai Israel.

The famous composer Verdi once advised a young aspiring composer: "You are looking for something new? Look back into the past; you will find much that is new." Today there is a trend in our conservative Synagogue to bring new Synagogue music into our services and to do away with the "old-fashioned" melodies. Should we bring new "modern" melodies into our services which are strange to the regular worshippers? Or do we want to go on with the development of our own national culture and not break away from our traditional tunes? In some conservative Synagogues the new more modern Service is supposed to attract the younger element to join the regular worshippers at services. It has been proven that this is not the case. In our B'nai Israel Synagogue we have held on to the traditional tunes in the cantorial recitals as well as in the congregation singing. Looking for something new in our Synagogue music? Let us look in the past and we shall find what we are looking for.

—Hazzan Mordecai G. Heiser[26]

Cantor Heiser was a simple and straightforward individual and he thought about his music in simple terms. One does not have to guess what he is saying in the above essay: Hold on to tradition, hold on to Jewish culture, and look inside to create something new. In the Talmud, Chapter V:24 of *Pirke Avot*, R. Ben Bag-Bag teaches about the Torah, "Turn it and turn it again, for everything is contained in it."[27] Innovation needs to come from within; nothing strange from outside the culture needs to be added for the musical offerings to be contemporary (although fragments of marches and dances may be added to spice up the tune). This message set the scene for B'nai Israel's liturgy for nearly half a century.

In an article entitled "His Ministry Is More Than Music. Cantor Interprets the Prayers of Jewish People in Worship," subtitled "Hazzan's Responsibility Carries a Sacred Trust for Tenor Here," in honor of Passover 1967, Robert Schwartz, the *Pittsburgh Press* religion editor, made an effort to shed light on Cantor Heiser's *hazzanut*. "One of the veteran cantors in the Pittsburgh area is Cantor Mordecai G. Heiser of B'nai Israel Congregation in East Liberty. . . . It is his responsibility to interpret the prayers in worship services and to interpret prayers in song."[28] The article transmits to us Cantor Heiser's philosophy of liturgy pretty much in his own words, also confirmed in Cantor Heiser's third-person and undated autobiography, "Hazzan Heiser believes in the sacredness of the cantorial profession, communicating the traditional style of the Hebrew chant; the Cantor must be the student of the ancient sources and must be qualified in diverse areas such as attitude to God, relationship to his people, liturgy, nussach (the traditional modes), music and voice. He should have a strong desire to pray and he must stand before his congregation in humility and piety as a sheliach tsibur—a messenger of the congregation—to bring the prayers of his fellow-worshippers before the throne of the Almighty. To lead the congregation in prayer is a challenge to the Cantor and he must be aware of it at all times."[29]

This is a tall order. The great Jewish sage, Abraham Joshua Heschel, who was raised in a Hasidic family, noted in a critical article about the cantorate entitled "The Vocation of the Cantor" that "the cantorial voice is a door."[30] To open this door bears with it great responsibility. Music is often called a universal language, and song is one branch of music that lends itself very well to the unlocking of the human psyche, our heart and our soul. While all the aspects Cantor Heiser mentions above are necessary—knowledge of the sources, the right attitude to God, a good relationship to his people ("I have come to know each of them well," says Chayim ben Shmuel in Frigyesi), liturgy, *nusach*, music, and voice, one crucial component that cannot be learned is *kavanah* or intent/spiritual energy "to pray from the heart." What does it mean to pray with *kavanah*? Chayim ben Shmuel in Frigyesi states, "What matters is the intensity with which you live through the words. . . . What is difficult, indeed terribly difficult, is *concentration*: to live through, with all your might, the meaning of every word."[31] Heschel agrees with this perspective when he declares "A word has a soul" and "Music is the soul of language." But prayer is not a one-way street. In Heschel's words, "Song, and particularly liturgical song, is not only an act of expression but also a way of bringing down the spirit from heaven to earth. . . . Prayer is song."[32]

To be clear, Cantor Heiser, a Conservative American *hazzan* from an enlightened German Jewish environment, did not align himself with Hasidism, but he warmly embraced the spiritual intensity of Hasidic prayer. A number of the composers he enjoyed came from Hasidic families and communities. In his anonymous lecture he stated, "They fashioned their melodies out of synagogue modes, and out of street songs. They blended them into a new form, beginning with contemplation [*devekut*], concentration [*kavanah*], proceeding to the shedding of the physical world, to identification and ecstasy. They moved as they sang, slowly at first, but in the end with the abandon of complete joy."[33] Cantor Heiser confirmed the value of

Hasidic inspiration in prayer in an article in the New Year edition of the *B'nai Israel Bulletin* of September 1973. (The congregation had invited a group of Hasidim to the synagogue the previous year and were planning to do so again.)

> The present search of the young people for a soulful expression and a meaningful approach to religion and to God paved the way for the Hassidic Niggun in our worship service. In the eyes of the Hassidim, worship must be cheerful. Joy was a necessary ingredient for devotional prayer. God must be served, as it is said in the Psalms, with gladness and thanksgiving. According to Hasidic tradition, prayer alone was not considered to bring about unity with God. Physical ecstasy, a rapturous state of mind, was necessary. . . . We here at B'nai Israel had the opportunity last year during a Hassidic weekend to come under the spell of the Hassidic tune. We shall have another chance to see, to hear, to sing, to dance and to clap with our Hassidic friends at another weekend this year.[34]

In the end, the message is clear—no matter in how many ways the cantor's calling is stated: *hazzanut* is a sacred task which requires *kavanah*; the *hazzan* has a responsibility to God and to his congregation. And no one took this task more seriously than Cantor Heiser.

Childhood Influences

As some scholars observe, cantors are first influenced by the cantors they encounter during their childhood, then by those during their schooling, and finally by contemporaries. This seems to have been true of Cantor Heiser as well. In an interview he recalled that his father took him to the synagogue when he was a child, where he was able to hear great cantors and where he developed an appreciation for *hazzanut*. "Ever since I was a little boy and my father took me to the synagogue I listened to renditions of great cantors. It was my ambition one day to be able to stand before a congregation and lead in the prayer service."[35] In the Schwartz interview Cantor Heiser explained, "Music in Jewish life and especially in our worship service is not something tacked onto it. It is a sacred part, and has been transmitted to us from generation to generation." He remarked, "The cantorate is indeed a sacred calling" and, one might add, a desire of his soul. He also explained how he saw his own role in the service. "When I stand before the congregation, I must be constantly aware that my chief task is that of interpretation. I must be able to weave the music and sacred word into a prayer that will stir the senses and open the heart of my fellow worshipers."[36] Heschel's point exactly.

Influences through Education

Gustav Heiser began his cantorial studies the same year in which Leo Gollanin (1872–1948) became *Oberkantor* of Berlin and Gustav's teacher, in 1925. Gustav was then twenty years old. Gollanin was born in Schlagory[37] and survived the Holocaust; he died in Berlin and is buried in the Weissensee Jewish Cemetery, Honor Row Feld G 1.[38] Gollanin was also a concert singer and a Zionist who began to officiate at the majestic Oranienburger Strasse synagogue in 1924 and had a reputation as an excellent teacher.[39]

Another one of Gustav's teachers was the just-retired *Oberkantor* of the Jewish community of Berlin, Aron Friedmann (1855–1936), a student and disciple of Louis Lewandowski's, who concluded his book, *Der synagogale Gesang*, with an account of the choir master's life and career as well as that of Sulzer. This work as well as Volume II of three volumes of *Lebensbilder berühmter Kantoren* and his own autobiography, *50 Jahre in Berlin (1878–1928)*, give us great insight into Jewish Berlin and the world of Jewish liturgy in the nineteenth century. Friedmann's autobiography is especially instructive as to the fancy footwork in diplomacy that was necessary to survive and thrive in that environment. The musicologist Artur Holde thinks that it is "his literary work in the field of synagogue music . . . these publications . . . that have kept the name of Aron Friedmann before the public."[40] Friedmann's publications on Jewish liturgy certainly were among the earliest in the field of Jewish liturgy, and his 1901 publication, *Schir Lisch'laumau*, contains a fascinating detail—the appropriate mode for singing a particular prayer or hymn is written above many of the liturgical pieces. Correct *nusach* was taken seriously in the world of German *hazzanut!*

Oberkantor Felix Asch, a baritone, was a third teacher who not only influenced Cantor Heiser but also served as his mentor. He oversaw Mr. Heiser's course of study at the "Kantorenschule," which probably was individual instruction under the auspices of the *Kultusgemeinde*. It is therefore peculiar that there is nothing in print on Asch and only minimal information on the internet, such as that he made an early recording of Kol

Nidre—before 1902! Cantor Jerry Glantz seems to have been aware of him but does not add any personal information.[41]

As one can see, Gustav Heiser was serious about his studies in *hazzanut*. He chose three ranking cantors in the community—one retiring, one ascending, and Asch, who outranked them both, especially in age.

According to Cantor Heiser's third-person autobiography, "On the recommendation of his teachers, while still a young man, he was elected by the Kultus-Gemeinde in Berlin as Cantor of one of the oldest and well-known Synagogues."[42] That was the Berlin-Lichterfelde-Lankwitz congregation in the south of Berlin, which he began to serve in 1925 and only left when they were shut down in 1939 and he had to flee Germany.

Through Friedmann, Gollanin, and Asch, Mr. Heiser was most certainly exposed to, if not trained in, the compositions of Louis Lewandowski (1821–1894)[43] and Salomon Sulzer (1804–1890),[44] both of whom were giants in Berlin and Vienna congregational life. Lewandowski so respected the elder Sulzer, with whom he studied in Vienna, that he honored him by including certain traditional prayers the way Sulzer had written them down, merely restating them in his own sets of compositions—for example "Mi chamochah," "Malchutecha," "Adonai Imloch," and V'ne'emar" for Festivals. Sulzer and Lewandowski were known as reformers in their day, as was Samuel Naumbourg (1817–1880),[45] who, though German-born, made his mark in France as the chief cantor of the Paris synagogue. Musicologist Irene Heskes characterizes their influence in the United States in this way: Salomon Sulzer "became the role model for the American cantorate in terms of musicianship and religious outlook." As a dedicated and highly skillful choirmaster and liturgical coach, Louis Lewandowski became "the ideal prototype for American synagogue music directors," and Samuel Naumbourg was a "broadly educated musician of serious intellectual bent, qualities that became the hallmarks of cantorial education as it was later formalized at American Jewish theological institutions." She notes that "these three liturgists had inaugurated dynamic changes in Jewish sacred music, which proved appealing to observant Jewry, because their ideas of reformation did not entail displacement of traditional devotional melodies nor time-honored prayers. This was to be an evolutionary development whose objectives were liturgical continuity, preservation, and enrichment."[46] Continuity was provided by such powerhouses as Sulzer and Lewandowski, who preserved the *nusach* with traditional melodies and prayers and enriched the service with compositions as well as new arrangements with a four-part choir and perhaps an organ.

The Tools of the Cantor

What musical choices does a cantor have at his disposal for service building?

The congregation only has a prayer book (*siddur*) with the texts of all the prayers and hymns for services. There are no musical notations. The *siddur* contains the structure for weekday, Shabbat, and Festival services. It incorporates biblical phrases and passages from the Psalms into the prayers. According to one of Idelsohn's sources, "over two hundred and fifty passages [from Psalms] are worked into the prayers."[47] There are prayers for major festivals (*haggim*) and inserts for minor ones (Purim, Hanukkah, etc.). There are also separate weekday prayer books available. What to do with these texts depends on the geographic location, the movement in Judaism, the congregation, and the cantor and the rabbi. It is the cantor's responsibility to build a meaningful service.[48] It is up to the cantor and the choir director or, if there isn't a cantor, the rabbi (and also the religious services or ritual committee), as to which music is most suitable for a particular service and congregation. The congregation isn't necessarily aware of the origin of a particular melody. Often the music, especially cantorial improvisations, are instantaneous, and since there traditionally was no recording of the service, they were one-time events and there is no record for posterity.

Today, music for most of the prayers can be found in notation; there are complete services by a single composer and anthologies with several compositions for each service by a variety of composers, such as Gershon Ephros' *Cantorial Anthology of Traditional and Modern Synagogue Music*, which was used by Cantor Heiser. Ephros explained, "My main object is to give the modern American synagogue a well-ordered and systematic compilation, containing complete musical services for all occasions during the year."[49] What cannot be found in the notations is the *ruach*, the spirit, of the delivery. To be sure, there are instructions about how to sing a particular part, but it is up to the precentor to carry out faithfully the intent of the composer or the Traditional melody. This can only be achieved through *kavanah* or inner concentration.

1a. *Nusach*. Each service has a specific singsong, not necessarily a chant, not quite a melody, but what is called *nusach* or prayer mode. *Nusach* consists of short phrases or patterns that have existed for a very long time and tell the worshipper, anywhere in the world, what day in the Jewish calendar it is: a weekday (morning, afternoon, or evening), Shabbat (morning, afternoon or evening), a festival, or the High Holy Days (Rosh Hashanah and Yom Kippur). Writes Edelman, "The proper utilization of nusach guarantees that a Jewish 'Rip van Winkle' could sleep for 20 years and identify the service to which he had awakened just by its musical motifs."[50] This was likely to be true in Cantor Heiser's synagogue but, in discussing Debbie Friedman,[51] who was considered by many an outsider to the cantorate during her lifetime, Judah Cohen notes that, by the time of her death, her music was already considered "traditional" by some, something that those who consider themselves true Traditionalists would not accept.[52]

Nusach is the constant in a particular service, and the cantor builds his service on the *nusach*, following the textual order that the prayerbook provides.[53] Cantor Heiser, in his lecture on Jewish music, explained *nusach* this way, "These melodies are more free than the biblical chants, more subject to improvised variation and elaboration. A Nussach is a series of melodic patterns. The cantor may use the tone group in any order he wishes and may take them as a mere outline for his own flights of musical fancy."[54] Cantor Leib Glantz describes *nusach* as "a short musical line, a musical group, or a musical phrase, which was the basis of their [the Jews'] melodies. Once the performer knew these short musical lines, he was left to himself to improvise and elaborate upon that basic line." Later, Glantz once more reiterates, "The cantors use these Nus'cha'ot [plural of nusach] as a basis for their recitatives, improvisations or compositions."[55] Frigyesi understands this intuitively: "The nusach is the traditional path on the map [of prayer] and the prayer leader is the wanderer who follows it." She struggles mightily with what *nusach* is, but concludes, "If he knows the path and the map and has fantasy and courage, he can take you to wondrous and magical places."[56] Indeed "he"—and today also "she"—certainly can.

Simply put, the oldest structure for Jewish composition is modal—as in mood, not tonal, in the sense of major and minor keys.[57] This musical system consists of at least three basic musical modes (scales), also called *shtayger*,[58] from which a cantor chooses for the various prayers. Named after specific parts of the worship service, these Jewish modes are known as "Ahavah Rabah" (d, e flat, f sharp, g, a, b flat, c, d), "Magen Avot" (d, e, f, g, a, b flat, c, d), and "Adonai Malach" (c, c sharp, d, e flat, f, g, b flat, c).[59] "The basic musical idea or modal pattern consists of not more than one or two tetra-chords (four-tone rows); this framework is filled, in actual singing, with melodic curves, step patterns, and ornaments of every kind."[60] There are many sub-modes which we will not deal with here. The modes are often mentioned in the same breath with medieval Christian Gregorian chants that are sometimes credited with direct descent from the ancient

Jewish modes, or is it the other way around? Or perhaps they are not so ancient after all? Cantor Heiser thought that "Some of the [Jewish] chants may have had their origin in a day even before the Gregorian chant was written down," and that "such chants as these were the first music of the Christian Church."[61] Not only are old Christian Church modes connected to the Jewish modes, but the Jewish modes have something in common with Greek, Arabic, Hindu, and Persian musical systems as well.

What is Eastern European *nusach*? It is sacred song based on the traditional Jewish modes, expressing deep feelings of longing for the ancient homeland and a life of freedom from oppression. Earlier in history, Polish and other Eastern European Jews did not have the same opportunities that Western Jews experienced in connection with non-Jewish society. It is often said that culture and civilization passed them by, that they were backward. When Western Jews moved to the East, they took their liturgy and other musical conventions with them and some of their melodies blended with the Eastern European sounds, without fully displacing the quality of Eastern European *nusach*, the emotional delivery of the *hazzan*, and the dark sounds of the ghetto. The Jewish Haskalah dates from 1770 to 1881, the year that Czar Alexander II was assassinated. During this time many different ways of being Jewish developed. In Berlin, Moses Mendelssohn translated the Hebrew Bible into German and had it written in Hebrew characters, so that German Jews could learn proper German while studying Jewish content. In the East, Jews continued to speak Yiddish; they valued the Kabbalah and texts like the *Zohar*, and the Baal Shem Tov inspired the great movement of Hasidism. But soon after the Baal Shem Tov's death, Salomon Sulzer in Vienna revolutionized Jewish worship, and the changes found their way to the East where they were received with a good bit of enthusiasm. Consequently, even new synagogues were built in Odessa and Brody and other places, so-called choral *shuls*, to house the cantor and the choir, whom the population clamored to hear. Their worship services became known for "choral interludes and responses" and a "fixed cantorial line, supported harmonically by the choir,"[62] very Western characteristics.

Eastern European *nusach* is word repetition and "emotional, extensively embellished" song "with cantorial improvisation and reflective of the folk styles of the region, including Klezmer," and I might add, Hasidic *niggunim*. Writes Kalib, "As a rule, it [Eastern European *nusach*] projected a mood of awe and devotion, piety and reverence, as well as impassioned appeal, and in texts of laudation or exaltation, dignity and majesty."[63] Traditionally, it had been "singerl" or choristers, *meshorerim* in Hebrew, who interacted with the cantor, created bridges between recitatives (cantorial solos) that were perhaps in different modes, and sang introductions. They "improvise[d] an accompaniment of hummed chords, drones, or short figures." They also sang solos, "extended coloraturas," to give the cantor a chance to catch his breath.[64] All of these features remained, and the more Western, more modern, more orderly, and *less* emotional way became integrated into the emotional, improvisational, and amateurish but "authentic" way to pray. The Hasidic *niggun*, the Eastern European folk song—Jewish and not—and the Sulzerian chorale influenced the soundscape of the Jewish community from the Baltics to Odessa.

Of course, the Eastern European cultural world from which these descriptions are taken no longer exists. Most of the Jews who produced such powerful music were among the six million who were murdered by the Nazis between 1939 and 1945. Says Cantor Heiser, "They [Eastern European Jewry] had—awake and palpitating in their consciousness—a vast hoard of melodic fragments, each fraught with its own warm and profound association." It is often stated that the Eastern European Jewish music is expressed more by dark, melancholy colors in minor keys that reflect the destruction of the Temple and the misery of Jewish life in the *shtetl*. But these are not the only feelings to express in prayer. Enthusiasm and passion as well as joy likewise have a place in Eastern European prayer. In fact, Cantor Heiser argued, "Who says that Jews always sing in the minor mode? Here we have what is probably the most important fragment of Jewish music, and how far is it from weeping and wailing, or minor modes!"[65] The reference is to the music of Shabbat, which avails itself of many examples from major modes, if with a nod to the tragedies of Jewish history by a periodic peregrination into a minor key—like a teardrop. Originally the music was not written down, but improvised, and taught from teacher to student, individually. Or, as Chayim ben Shmuel mused, one did not have to learn it, per se, because one grew up with it. In Hasidic circles, "Everybody had been singing it [the melody] before. It had been there since.... I don't know exactly, but for a very long time."[66]

One might think that studying with a master was a glorious arrangement, but it was not necessarily so, as a boy who had a good voice might have to leave home at a young age to study with a well-known cantor somewhere far away. If he was lucky, the cantor would board and feed him for the duration of his apprenticeship. Slobin quotes Cantor Samuel Vigoda (1892–1990) on how he came to live with Cantor Yossele Rosenblatt, one of the star cantors of the early twentieth century. "One day Yosele came to town [Dobrzin, for a wedding]. Yosele sang at the . . . 'banquet' and my father sang something and we assisted. So Yosele says to my father, 'give me the two boys' to sing in my choir, I'll take them to Pressburg. I was about seven years old. . . . My father says, 'you should promise me you'll keep them in your home, they'll eat at your table, they'll sleep at your bed, and you'll enroll them in the Talmud Torah [school], they wouldn't be just loafing around and you'll take good care of them, I'll give them to you.' So we lived in the home of Yosele Rosenblatt. Yosele stayed in Pressburg another two and a half years, then he went to Hamburg, so then we went home."[67] This was a difficult and haphazard way to obtain an education, but in the nineteenth century and earlier, it was the only way.

1b. <u>Service-building</u> is the most important job of a cantor. He, and in today's Jewish world she, builds the service based on a knowledge of themselves—what they like, what skills they have musically, what sources they can access, both in musical notation and in choir members and instruments . . . and, not unimportant, what the congregation wants. Some congregations are quite outspoken about their likes and dislikes—they "regulate the musical taste by giving or denying their emotional approval to the precentor"—and if the cantor is smart, he or she will at least in part please the hand that feeds them.[68] Chayim ben Shmuel explained, "A good cantor composes his service; he shapes it according to the custom, with taste, and with his own ideas and feeling."[69]

Cantor Heiser was very good at service-building. He was a gentle and humble human being. This disposition was informed by a deep religiosity, by a fear of God (*yirat shamayim*) that uplifted him in his prayers beyond his self to a level where he was truly a *shaliach tzibur*, a messenger of the people. Recently a rabbi friend asked, "Did he really do that, *interpret* the prayers?" Yes, he did, in an original and genuine way, down to the last word. One could say of Cantor Heiser what was said of Cantor David Roitman (1884–1943), that "he was able to sing the liturgy with the clarity of a spoken sentence."[70] While Cantor Heiser clearly stood on the shoulders of those who came before him, using existing *hazzanut* as his foundation, he hardly ever completely stuck to the music as transmitted. More often than not, he would take a few identifiable musical phrases from the *nusach* and improvise on them. Improvisation enriches *nusach*, and composition is incorporated into *nusach*, mostly seamlessly, so that one has to have a quick ear to hear what has changed. Professor Eliyahu Schleifer, in the introductory remarks to a musical program honoring him recently in Jerusalem, spoke of himself as a melodist.[71] One could describe Cantor Heiser as a melodist as well. In addition to *nusach*, his musical choices were at times grounded in folk melodies, Hasidic *niggunim*, and the melodies of the *chalutzim* (pioneers). This was especially true for his sing-along programs over the years.

2. <u>Mi Sinai Nusach.</u> Some *nusach* is very old; we don't quite know when and where it originated. Sometimes it is just "part of the tradition." These tunes are called *mi Sinai*—from Sinai, implying something ancient, like Mount Sinai. They are often glorious, heart-rending—they move the congregation—and they are mostly employed in important, even crucial parts of the service, such as when the Torah is taken out of the Holy Ark on Shabbat, during a particular service such as "Kol Nidre" on Yom Kippur, for the "Prayer for Rain (*Geshem*)" on *Shmini Atzeret* at the end of Sukkot, or in a prayer thanking or praising God. Cantor Glantz's explanation is most enlightening. He divides *nusach* into two groups: those that can be altered [1a. above] and those that are fixed. The second group "consists of . . . *fixed prayer melodies* that have been associated with certain texts from time immemorial. These fixed melodies are not subject to improvisation, elaboration or any kind of change. . . . They include some of the most beloved and important prayers of the liturgy" [such as "Akdamut" or "Kol Nidre"]. He adds, "Poetic legend has it that God himself sang these melodies to Moses on Mt. Sinai, when He gave him the To'rah."[72] These *mi Sinai* tunes are often seasonal. When we hear them, we know where we are in the liturgical year.[73]

3. <u>Composition.</u> *Nusach* and especially on the High Holy Days *mi Sinai* tunes take up a good part of a particular service, but if there was no variation, the service would become static and congregations would get bored. Although Judaism emphasizes the old over the new, musical composition has always existed. "All music was once new," we hear on the local public radio station. According to Idelsohn, "the liturgy was complete in its main parts" already "at the time of the redaction of the Babylonian Talmud."[74] From the time the worship pattern was set, around 600 CE, Jewish poets penned poems that were set to music composed especially for that particular poem to be sung by the cantor on a specific occasion. These poems are known as *piyyutim*, and the poets who created them are *payyetanim*.[75] For most of Jewish history, *piyyutim* filled out the service with creative enhancement, and cantors took liberties with their renditions of these hymns, making services often very long. One *piyyut* still popular is "Akdamut" for the festival of Shavuot [see the service discussion for Shavuot], though we seldom sing all 90 verses. In the modern period, congregations have done

away with most of the *piyyutim* because they were seen as outdated or too time-consuming. However, contemporary hymns and prayers—or hymns just new to a congregation—are constantly incorporated into the service [see "Sim Shalom" in the Shabbat discussion]. Innovation is an important creative aspect that keeps a service fresh and current and the cantor and choir engaged.

Cantor Heiser also composed music, some of which the Cantors Assembly included in their publications for congregations.[76] He did not usually include his own compositions in his services, although he used his own tune for "Hu Eloheinu" in one of the Shabbat services that was recorded (November 5, 1988).

4. <u>Recitative and Improvisation:</u> One of the most powerful creative acts of the worship service is the recitative by the cantor—a paragraph, a sentence, a musical phrase in a longer prayer, or just a word—that is improvised on by the cantor and sometimes repeated, perhaps in a different key, perhaps in and out of the *nusach*, so long as the vocal artist returns to the *nusach* at the end of their liturgical peregrinations. Neil W. Levin says about Israel Alter, "Whether you repeat or not depends on how you repeat. . . . A repeated word must be invested with some fresh nuance, some different shade of meaning, some emphasis—just as an orator would do."[77] Cantor Heiser's impressive mastery of the recitative was recognized early on by the Cantors Assembly who, in 1962, invited him to participate in the convention program with a rendition of the recitative "R'tze Vimnuchosenu" (Accept our rest) by Sholom Secunda, an American composer, with Lazar Weiner at the piano.[78] Unfortunately we do not have a recording of this section of the Shabbat Amidah. Eliyahu Schleifer says about the recitative, "The synagogue chant repertoire . . . serves . . . as the mere basis for the liturgical recitative of the professional Cantor. It makes use of the traditional melodic patterns—some of them fixed [*mi Sinai*], others flexible or modular—in order to create an artistic musical expression of the form or content of the prayer." He cautions, however, that "Liturgical recitative involves some improvisation and artistic freedom; yet at its best, it is firmly bound to the traditional melodic formulas that in turn are connected to the liturgical function of the prayer and its calendrical setting."[79]

I'd like to intersperse here one example of a selection that I hold dear and a recent discovery of one of its peregrinations. Cantor Heiser occasionally sang the Priestly Blessing, "May the Lord bless you and keep you. May the Lord shine God's Countenance upon you and be gracious unto you. May the Lord turn God's Countenance unto you and give you peace," to a very sweet melody, usually for a special occasion such as a wedding or confirmation.[80] On January 14, 2023, I tuned into Zoom for our contemporary Shabbat service at my Conservative synagogue led by Rabbi Shoshana Carson. I nearly jumped into the laptop when she sang the Benediction (Priestly Blessing) to Cantor Heiser's melody, albeit in a more compressed fashion and without the congregational response. I had never been able to trace it and was delighted that it was "out there." After Shabbat I spoke with her and asked how she knows this melody. She said, "from my rabbi," then in California. When she contacted Rabbi Jonathan Slater, he responded, "I can't quite remember learning this melody" [which was correct]. She asked him to send the clip she had made to some colleagues—which he did, and sure enough, the answer came back from Cantor Richard Cohn in the Reform Movement that it is "Y'vorech'cho" No. 1 in Gershon Ephros' *Cantorial Anthology of Traditional and Modern Synagogue Music*, Volume 5 Y'mot Hachol (Week Day Services and Special Occasions, page 275), with a screen shot of the sheet music. The arrangement is for four-part choir and Ephros bases the melody on a Yemenite Motif. Cantor Cohn commented, "I have sung the melody as shown in Ephros at weddings a cappella for a very long time now!" But this is not the end of the story. It bothered Rabbi Shush that she couldn't remember how she learned the melody, and she contacted another colleague, Rabbi Elisheva Salamo, who had been a Sabbatical replacement for Rabbi Slater. Indeed, it was Rabbi Salamo who taught Shush the melody. How did *she* know it? She explained that it was taught at the Reconstructionist Rabbinic College in Philadelphia because it was part of the Philadelphia community music. This is how we often pass on and adapt traditional melodies over time and space.[81] I am including my notation of Cantor Heiser's rendition for our perusal.

These four aspects of music form the artistic structure of the Jewish worship service—*nusach*, *mi Sinai nusach*, composition, and recitative/improvisation.[82] There is, of course, no limit to the ways in which these types of music can be combined, so that the modern cantor is not much different from his earlier colleague, with one big exception—most cantors today have been trained not only at cantorial institutes in rabbinic seminaries, but also at conservatories. Thus, today's cantors are quite sophisticated: they know music theory, read music, compose, and notate music like any other professional in the discipline of music—and they continue to teach the next generation, in the U.S. since around 1950, in an institutional setting.

Heiser Repertoire

Although the catalogue of Cantor Heiser's repertoire available for this study is far from complete, we nevertheless can document many hymns and prayers that recurred on an annual (High Holy Days and Festivals), monthly (Prayer for the New Month), or even weekly (Shabbat) basis.

Cantor Heiser used and adapted many of Louis Lewandowski's compositions, among them:

> "Mah tovu," in *Todah W'simrah, Part I: Shabbat*, Out-of-Print Classics Series of Synagogue Music No. 10, Sacred Music Press, New York, 1954, 3; also, in Gershon Ephros, ed., *Cantorial Anthology of Traditional and Modern Synagogue Music*, Volume 1 Rosh Hashonoh, Bloch Publishing Company, New York, 1972, 7.
>
> "Shema Israel" for festivals in *Todah W'simrah Part II: Festgesänge*, Volume 1, Out-of-Print Classics Series of Synagogue Music No. 11, Sacred Music Press, New York, (no year), 57–58; also, in Gershon Ephros, ed., *Cantorial Anthology of Traditional and Modern Synagogue Music*, Volume III Sholosh R'golim, Bloch Publishing Company, New York (no year), 266.
>
> "Bor'chu," Traditional, arranged by L. Lewandowski, in Gershon Ephros, ed., *Cantorial Anthology of Traditional and Modern Synagogue Music*, Volume I Rosh Hashonoh, Sacred Music Press, New York, 1972, 11.
>
> Parts of the Festival Musaf Amidah, "Somech noflim" in *Todah W'simrah Part I: Shabbat*, Out-of-Print Classics Series of Synagogue Music No. 10, Sacred Music Press, New York, 1954, 142.
>
> "Vayihi binsoa" for festival in *Todah W'simrah Part II: Festgesänge*, Volume 1, Out-of-Print Classics Series of Synagogue Music No. 11, Sacred Music Press, New York, (no year), 24.
>
> "Kol Nidre" in *Kol Rinnah U'T'fillah*, Out-of-Print Classics Series of Synagogue Music No. 9, Sacred Music Press, New York, (no year), 79.
>
> "Hashivenu" in *Todah W'simrah Part I: Shabbat*, Out-of-Print Classics Series of Synagogue Music No. 10, Sacred Music Press, New York, 1954, 129.
>
> "Ki lekach tov" in *Todah W'simrah Part I: Shabbat*, Out-of-Print Classics Series of Synagogue Music No. 10, Sacred Music Press, New York, 1954, 128.
>
> "L'cha Adonai Hag'dulah," in *Todah W'simrah Part I: Shabbat*,

Out-of-Print Classics Series of Synagogue Music No. 10, Sacred Music Press, New York, 1954, 288–289.

"Kakatuv" for festivals, in *Todah W'simrah Part II: Festgesänge*, Volume 1, Out-of-Print Classics Series of Synagogue Music No. 12, Sacred Music Press, New York, (no year), 179.

"V'hagen ba'adenu," No. 85 in *Todah W'simrah Part II: Festgesänge*, Volume 1, Out-of-Print Classics Series of Synagogue Music No. 12, Sacred Music Press, New York, (no year), 127; also, in Gershon Ephros, ed., *Cantorial Anthology of Traditional and Modern Synagogue Music,* Volume I Rosh Hashonoh, Bloch Publishing Company, New York, 1972, 22–23.

"Uv'zel k'nafecha tas'tirenu" No. 86 in *Todah W'simrah Part II: Festgesänge*, Out-of-Print Classics Series of Synagogue Music No. 12, Sacred Music Press, New York, (no year), 128; also, in Gershon Ephros, ed., *Cantorial Anthology of Traditional and Modern Synagogue Music*, Volume I Rosh Hashonoh, Bloch Publishing Company, New York, 1972, 23.

"Y'chadeshehu" for *Birchat HaChodesh*, in *Todah W'simrah, Part I: Shabbat*, Out-of-Print Classics Series of Synagogue Music No. 10, Sacred Music Press, New York, (no year), 121; also, in *Liturgisches Liederbuch für den Gebrauch der Religionsschulen*, herausgegeben vom Vorstand der jüdischen Gemeinde zu Berlin. Verlag von M. Poppelauer, Berlin, 1912, 14.

Cantor Heiser respected Salomon Sulzer equally and featured much of his music:

"Shema Israel," for Friday night in *Schir Zion, Gesänge für den israelitischen Gottesdienst*, 150th Jubilee Issue, Joseph Sulzer, ed., Out-of-Print Classics Series of Synagogue Music No. 6, Sacred Music Press, New York, 1953, 45; also in *Union Hymnal, Songs and Prayers for Worship*, CCAR, New York, 1949, 291, and in *Shir U'Tefilah Songs and Prayers for Jewish Youth*, Central Conference of American Rabbis, New York, 1960, 320.

"Bar'chu" in Moshe Nathanson, ed., *Zamru Lo, Congregational Melodies for the Shalosh R'galim and the High Holidays,* Volume III, Cantors Assembly, New York, 1974, 110.

"Kedushah for Shabbat: Kadosh, kadosh, kadosh" in Moshe Nathanson, ed., *Zamru Lo, Congregational Melodies and Z'mirot for the Entire Sabbath Day*, Volume II, Cantors Assembly, New York, 1974, 114; and *Schir Zion, Gesänge für den israelitischen Gottesdienst*, 150th Jubilee Issue, Joseph Sulzer, ed., Out-of-Print Classics Series of Synagogue Music No. 6, Sacred Music Press, New York, 1953, 85.

"Adon Olam" for Shabbat and Festivals in *Schir Zion, Gesänge für den israelitischen Gottesdienst*, 150th Jubilee Issue, Joseph Sulzer, ed., Out-of-Print Classics Series of Synagogue Music No. 6, Sacred Music Press, New York, 1953, 57.

"Mi chamochah," Traditional, in *Schir Zion, Gesänge für den israelitischen Gottesdienst*, Joseph Sulzer, ed., Out-of-Print Classics Series of Synagogue Music No. 7, Sacred Music Press, New York, 231; also, Gershon Ephros, ed., *Cantorial Anthology of Traditional and Modern Synagogue Music*, Volume I Rosh Hashonoh, 1972, 14; and Moshe Nathanson, ed., *Zamru Lo, Congregational Melodies for the Shalosh R'galim and the High Holidays*, Volume III 1974, Cantors Assembly, New York, 110.

"Hapores sukkat shalom" in *Schir Zion, Gesänge für den israelitischen Gottesdienst*, Joseph Sulzer, ed., Out-of-Print Classics Series of Synagogue Music No. 7, Sacred Music Press, New York, 231; also in Moshe Nathanson, ed., *Zamru Lo, Congregational Melodies for the Shalosh R'galim and the High Holidays*, Volume III, Cantors Assembly, New York, 111.

"Imloch Adonai l'olam" for Shabbat and Holidays in Moshe Nathanson, ed., *Zamru Lo, Congregational Melodies and Z'mirot for the Entire Sabbath Day*, Volume II, Cantors Assembly, New York, 1974, 115; also, in *Shir U'Tefilah Union Songster: Songs and Prayers for Jewish Youth*, CCAR, 1960, 314.

"Ein kamocha ba Elohim Adonai" for Shabbat in Moshe Nathanson, ed., *Zamru Lo, Congregational Melodies and Z'mirot for the Entire Sabbath Day*, Volume II, Cantors Assembly, New York, 1974, 75.

"Baruch shenatan Torah" for Shabbat, arranged by Harry Coppersmith, in *Shir U'Tefilah Union Songster: Songs and Prayers for Jewish Youth*, CCAR, 1960, 318.

"Ki mi Zion," arranged by Harry Coppersmith, in *Shir U'Tefilah Union Songster: Songs and Prayers for Jewish Youth*, CCAR, 1960, 377.

"Hodo al eretz" for Shabbat in *Schir Zion, Gesänge für den israelitischen Gottesdienst*, 150th Jubilee Issue, Joseph Sulzer, ed., Out-of-Print Classics Series of Synagogue Music No. 6, Sacred Music Press, New York, 1953, 104; also, in Gershon Ephros, ed.,

Cantorial Anthology of Traditional and Modern Synagogue Music, Volume III, Sholosh R'golim, Cantors Assembly, New York, 1974, p. 275.

There was no festival service on the Shalosh Regalim (Pilgrim Festivals) at B'nai Israel without Samuel Naumbourg's "Adonai, Adonai" before taking out the Torah scrolls [in Gershon Ephros, ed., *Cantorial Anthology of Traditional and Modern Synagogue Music*, Volume I Rosh Hashonoh, Bloch Publishing Company, New York, (no year), 12–13], or "S'u shearim" before returning the Torah scrolls to the Ark [in *Z'mirot Israel. Chants Religieux des Israelites*, Out-of-Print Classics Series of Synagogue Music No. 14, Sacred Music Press, New York, 1954, 195; also, in G. Ephros, ed., *Cantorial Anthology of Traditional and Modern Synagogue Music*, Volume III Sholosh R'golim, Bloch Publishing Company, New York, (no year), 276–281].

Other cantorial influences included mostly Eastern European composers and arrangers:

- Jacob Beimel's (1875 Parichi, Belarus–1944 New York) "Ki anu amecha" No. 2 in Nathanson, ed., *Zamru Lo* III, Congregational Melodies for the Shalosh R'galim and the High Holidays, 197.[83]
- Abraham Dunajewsky's (1843 Russia–1911) Torah service for Shalosh Regalim in Ephros, ed., *Cantorial Anthology of Traditional and Modern Synagogue Music*, Volume III Sholosh R'golim, 243–246.[84]
- Baruch Schorr's "N'ilo" in Ephros, ed., *Cantorial Anthology of Traditional and Modern Synagogue Music*, Volume II Yom Kippur.[85]
- Israel Schorr's (1886 Galicia–1935 New York) "Petach Lanu" and "HaYom Yifneh" for *Ne'ilah* in Ephros, ed., *Cantorial Anthology of Traditional and Modern Synagogue Music*, Volume II Yom Kippur.[86]
- David Nowakowsky's (1848 Malin, Province of Kiev, Ukraine–1921 Odessa) "Adonai, Adonai" in *Ephros II Yom Kippur*, 313–314, and numerous pieces in the *Ne'ilah* service, such as "Enkat m'sal'decha" and "Israel nosha bAdonai" in *Schlußgebet für Jom-Kippur, für Cantor Solo und gemischten Chor*. Out-of-Print Classics Series of Synagogue Music No. 23, Sacred Music Press, New York, (no year).[87]
- Wolf Velvele Schestapol's (1832 Odessa–1872) "Ya'aleh" in Ephros, ed., *Cantorial Anthology of Traditional and Modern Synagogue Music*, Volume II Yom Kippur, 32–36.[88]

Yossele Rosenblatt's (1882 Belaya Tserkov [also spelled Bialacerkow in Holde, 33], Ukraine–1933 Jerusalem) "Chassidic Kaddish"[89] and "Shomer Israel," published by The Joint Distribution Committee of the American Friends for Jewish War Sufferers, NCMXXI.[90]

Abraham Zvi Idelsohn's (1882 Feliksberg [Filzburg near Libau, Kurland], Latvia–1938 Cincinnati, OH) "V'zot haTorah" in *Jewish Song Book for Synagogue, School and Home*, Cincinnati, Ohio, (no year).[91]

Julius Freudenthal's (1805 Braunschweig–1874 Brunswick) "Ein keloheinu" in A. R. Idelsohn, *Jewish Song Book for Synagogue, School and Home*.[92]

Not missing among these selections must be Hugo Chaim Adler's (1894 Mannheim/Antwerp–1955 Worcester, Massachusetts) "El Moleh Rachamim," published by Transcontinental Music Publications, New York, in 1965, which became Cantor Heiser's signature prayer.[93]

Even Cantor Heiser's teacher Aron Friedmann had begun life in the East—in Szaki, Lithuania. Of these luminaries, perhaps only Leo Gollanin and Max Janowski, a very gifted composer and notator,[94] hailed from Western Europe—Gollanin and Janowski (1912–1991) from Germany, though with eastern roots, and Hugo Chaim Adler from Mannheim/Belgium. Most of them practiced Eastern European *hazzanut*, often influenced by the more "modern," hence Western, style of Sulzer and/or Lewandowski, but primarily using the eastern *nusach*. This preference is significant, as Cantor Heiser, like Max Janowski and others, was eager to preserve his Eastern European Jewish heritage while trained to construct a western-style service. His desire for an eastern connection is an interesting reversal of trends, as Eastern European cantors often strove to claim German heritage because it was more "marketable." Janowski was only seven years younger than Cantor Heiser; he also hailed from Berlin, and as in Cantor Heiser's case, one side of his family originated in Eastern Europe. A fascinating article by Neil W. Levin in the Milken Archive of Jewish Music discusses Janowski's initial desire to be seen as German, especially as a newcomer in Chicago's German Jewish community, but his later inclination, during an equally long fifty-year career in Chicago, was to focus almost entirely on Eastern European nusach.[95] In contrast, over his nearly five decades in America, Cantor Heiser was very consistent in the *hazzanut* he chose for his services.

Whether Cantor Heiser was introduced to the music of these giants already in Berlin or only through reissues—or even first issues—of their work in the U.S. is hard to know, but he loyally employed their compositions for festival and High Holy Day services and for special occasions over many years. It is also not known whether Cantor Bloom, his predecessor at B'nai Israel, had any influence on Cantor Heiser's spiritual development or on the way he organized his services during the two years they knew each other, as there are no recordings of Cantor Bloom's *hazzanut*, to my knowledge. Shabbat services were either constructed based on traditional *nusach*, or they followed existing song books by American cantors of eastern origin, such as Israel Goldfarb's [1879–1967][96] and Israel Herbert Levinthal's [1888–1982] *Song and Praise for Sabbath Eve*, which was first published in 1941, or the CCAR's *Shir U'T'filah Union Songster: Songs and Prayers for Jewish Youth* (1960).

Heiser Contemporaries

Because of his early participation in the Conservative Cantors Assembly and his familiarity with the music of the Reform service, one can find a number of contemporaries of Cantor Heiser's in his services, often with eastern roots, among them:

> Israel Alter's (1901 Lemberg–1979 New York) "Yihi ratzon milfanecha" for *Birchat HaChodesh*, arranged by Morris Barash (1903 New York–1977 New York) in *Shirei Israel*, published in 1968.[97]
> Sholom Secunda's (1894 Oleksandriia, Ukraine–1974 New York)[98] choral version of "Pitchu li" for Hallel (1951).
> Sigmund Sabel's (1849 Vienna–1924 New York) "Aleinu" and "V'hayah Adonai" in Nathanson, ed., *Zamru Lo I*, Congregational Melodies and Z'mirot for the Friday Evening Service, 114.
> Abraham Kantor's (Russia) "Na'arizecha" for Shabbat in Nathanson, ed., *Zamru Lo II* Yom Kippur, 107.
> Max Janowski's (1912 Berlin–1991 Chicago) "L'chu N'ran'nah" for Slichot published in 1973.
> Samuel Dubrow's (1916 Philadelphia–1974 Woodmere, New York) "Melech al kol haaretz," and "Adonai, Adonai" for High Holy Days in Nathanson, ed., *Zamru Lo III* Congregational Melodies for the Shalosh R'galim and the High Holidays, 128.
> Zvi Talmon's (1922 Jerusalem–?) "Nedarai lAdonai" in *Pa'amey Hahechal*, Hechal Shlomo, Jerusalem, 1992 (but use here is of earlier version).[99]

Gershon Ephros' (1890 Serotsk, Poland–1978 Perth Amboy, NJ) Hatzi Kaddish for Musaf of Rosh Hashanah, in Ephros, ed., *Cantorial Anthology of Traditional and Modern Synagogue Music*. Volume III Sholosh R'golim, 134.

Moshe Nathanson's (1899 Jerusalem–1981 New York) Hatzi Kaddish arranged for Shalosh R'galim and High Holidays in Nathanson, ed., *Zamru Lo III* Congregational Melodies for the Shalosh R'galim and the High Holidays, 1974, 112. [In *Zamru Lo III*, Nathanson thanks Cantor Heiser for his contribution of music to this series (inside back cover)].

Also, a colleague from the Tri-States region, Cantor Leopold Edelstein (1909 Mitra, Czechoslovakia–1985 Youngstown, OH), was included.[100] He dedicated his composition for "Sim Shalom," published in 1958, to his late wife, Ilonka, who perished at Auschwitz.

Irene Heskes observes what a close-knit community, even family, those interested in Jewish liturgy in the first half of the twentieth century were. She calls Gershon Ephros and Moshe Nathanson "proteges of the father of modern Jewish musical scholarship, Abraham Z. Idelsohn," during their time in Jerusalem preceding World War I.[101] Frigyesi, after great difficulties in her efforts to find a copy of Idelsohn's famous work in communist Hungary, eventually was able to get a copy of Idelsohn's book from an uncle in Israel. Upon studying it, she was somewhat critical as she felt that Idelsohn and others "took a melody for a string of colored beads" to be sorted. She likes her own definition better. "They are fantastic paths of flights drawn on an imaginary map" for the liturgical wanderer on his peregrinations.[102] Whatever the case may be, Ephros and Nathanson put their apprenticeship with Idelsohn to good use after immigrating to the United States. According to Heskes, "both Ephros and Nathanson briefly served as music directors for the Bureau of Jewish Education [in New York] . . . before assuming cantorial duties at congregations." In Jerusalem, Cantor Ephros had assisted Idelsohn in his musical research and collection of liturgical materials, and he followed in that scholarly direction himself after settling in America in 1911. When Ephros published the first of six volumes of Cantorial Anthologies in 1929, Idelsohn wrote a brief preface for it (N. 39).[103] Another music scholar from that period who became deeply involved in the American Jewish liturgy scene was Ismar Elbogen, from Germany, who had also been one of Cantor Heiser's teachers at the *Hochschule für die Wissenschaft des Judentums*, though not for music but for history and literature.

Cantor Heiser's Songprint

One can say that Cantor Heiser constructed his brand of services first in Germany from 1925 until 1939 and then adjusted them to the American liturgical climate between 1942, when he took over as B'nai Israel's *hazzan*, and approximately 1975. During these years he learned new music, now readily available in print, met other musical artists, not least through his membership in the Cantors Assembly, and above all, by participating in numerous concerts and musical programs in partnership with other cantors or musicians, expanding his repertoire and his knowledge. After that he primarily refined what he had created, often at the congregation's request, up until his accident. Edelstein's "Sim Shalom," though published in 1958, was new to the B'nai Israel service in 1988, and may have been the last contemporary composition that Cantor Heiser introduced into his Shabbat service. The melody was not new to him, however, as he had sung it in concert in the 1970s.

From the recording samples available one can see that the choir always followed compositions literally, as did Betty Sue in her solos and in her duets with her grandfather, but Cantor Heiser only stuck to literal renditions when he sang with the choir or in duets or when he rendered music that was composed (Edelstein), seldom with Traditional melodies. Here he was in his glory—improvising, reversing modes, modulating between modes, and above all, interpreting the meaning of every word of a prayer exquisitely.

Cantor Heiser was a master of the soul. He knew how to reach into the depths of his being to bring forth the sounds and feelings that most powerfully conveyed to God his and the congregation's most heartfelt gratitude as well as sincere supplications. Although his Shabbat morning service could be majestic—especially when he led the monthly *Birchat HaChodesh* with his granddaughter Betty Sue and the choir—and his festival services with the help of his granddaughter and the choir spiritually uplifting, it was the High Holy Day services (Slichot and Rosh Hashanah and Yom Kippur) that contained moments of deepest soulfulness. Fortunately, several examples of these special spiritual gems survived on tape so that we can hear for ourselves.

Starting around 1900, many cantors took advantage of a new medium—recordings—bringing Jewish music, including *hazzanut*, into the ordinary Jew's living room. Cantor Heiser, to my knowledge, did not record any of his music professionally. One exception may have been the cantatas he composed with Rabbi Cohen in the 1950s, as we are told that they were broadcast on radio and TV. I have yet to locate any such recordings. Although we do not know why he did not take advantage of recordings, it is possible that professional recording may have been anathema to him. Other cantors had similar reservations about recording their sacred songs and about performing sacred music in secular venues. One of Frigyesi's "informants" noted, "It is impossible to record prayer. Because *kavunes (kavanah)*, which is the only important thing, happens in the present."[104] Cantor Rosenblatt declined to appear on stage for most of his life and took only a minor role in the Al Jolson version of the film *The Jazz Singer*, rather than sing "Kol Nidre," for which he was adored in a synagogue setting. Berlin's Greek Cantor Estrongo Nechama, upon finding out that his entire family had perished in the Holocaust, chose to remain a cantor instead of becoming an opera singer.[105] From his own words we may deduce that Cantor Heiser decided already in his youth to focus on liturgical art rather than on concertizing, which might have focused more on "beauty of sound and formal perfection," which are not the goal but rather "a vehicle of reaching a higher goal."[106] Heschel also points this out in his lecture on "The Vocation of the Cantor," where he states, "He [the cantor] does not stand before the Ark as an artist in isolation, trying to demonstrate his skill or to display vocal feats. . . . His task is to represent as well as to inspire a community." He continues, "It is the task of the Cantor to create the liturgical community, to convert a plurality of praying individuals into a unity of worship."[107]

***

A word about the collection of tapes in my possession. There were fourteen fragments of six different services among Cantor Heiser's tapes that are the primary music source for this study—Slichot, Erev Rosh Hashanah, Kol Nidre, Ne'ilah, Shavuot, and Shabbat. All are services of either major holy days, festivals, or of family *simchas*, such as granddaughter Betty Sue Stein's Bat Mitzvah and granddaughter Shari Stein's confirmation. I recently learned the reason for these eclectic choices: A member of the family acted as a "Shabbes goy" and pushed the button on Cantor Heiser's recording device—after he went to the *bimah*![108]

In some cases, the music breaks off at the crucial moment, which is most regrettable; in other instances, we cannot determine the exact year of the service. For a number of selections, the source of the music is unknown. Is it *nusach*, is it a composition, or is it spontaneous free improvisation? The snippets nevertheless provide us with some excellent examples of Cantor

Heiser's moving and powerful *hazzanut* and give us a good sense of Cantor Heiser's ability to build and deliver successful services. This eavesdropping allows us to assess the spiritual impact of his art on his congregation as well as on a wider audience. The fact that he officiated in the same synagogue for nearly fifty years and that numerous very successful events celebrated the person of *Hazzan* Heiser during his lifetime also provides strong testimony to the effectiveness of his services and the spiritual power of his person. He was loved for his generosity, for his *menshlichkeit*, and—not least—for his artistic talent. This, however, does not mean unconditionally, as we have seen from the minutes from numerous board meetings and executive committee meetings through the years in which congregants criticize aspects of the service and various other matters, including the size and cost of B'nai Israel's beloved choir.

The service discussions are organized in order of the liturgical year, with Shabbat concluding the cycle. Assuming some familiarity with Jewish liturgy by the reader and listener, my main goal is to lead the reader/listener through Cantor Heiser's musical peregrinations—where did he follow Traditional melodies, where compositions, and what are they? And where did he improvise? This exercise will, I hope, not only help to conserve but also to perpetuate Cantor Heiser's *hazzanut*.

To aid the listener in navigating through a particular service, I provide a written guide and commentary to each of the complete service snippets that survived (even though the complete snippets are not available on YouTube), listing all the musical pieces in the order that they appear in the service. This is then followed by a precise step-by-step worksheet, giving both the location in the complete service snippet and in the Silverman prayer book as well as indicating the length of individual clips that have been extricated. Not all clips have been posted, only twenty. In the case of the Erev Rosh Hashanah service, the entire service snippet is provided. In all other cases, only selections marked with an asterisk in the index have been made available, for logistical reasons—to avoid repetitions and overly short pieces and prayers that are primarily davened, as well as often long sermons.

Let us then enter the "chanting" and enchanting world of *Hazzan* Mordecai Gustav Heiser, with all of its power of persuasion, ethereality, human foibles, and accomplishments. We will begin this journey with the Jewish New Year and the service that in my days was almost as important to Congregation B'nai Israel as was Yom Kippur, namely Slichot—the service that begins the penitential season leading up to the *Yamim Noraim* (Days of Awe).

Complete List of Individual Clips Created from Raw Tapes

I. Slichot (1987?)

1. Ashrei (00:01–06:37)
2. Hatzi Kaddish (00:01–03:15)
*3. L'chu n'ran'nah lAdonai (00:01–04:59)
*4. Han'shamah lach (00:01–04:28)
*5. Ta'azin shav'atenu (00:01–04:04)
*6. Lishmoa el harinah (00:01–06:23)
7. Shema Kolenu (00:01–03:37)
*8. Ashamnu (00:01–02:21)
*9. Shomer Israel (00:01–08:42)

II. Erev Rosh Hashanah (No Year)

*10. Entire Erev Rosh Hashanah service (00:01–40:33)
11. Mah Tovu (00:01–02:42)
12. Hashkivenu (00:01–07:00)
13. Hatzi Kaddish (00:01–02:20)
14. Kaddish Shalem (00:01–01:10)
15. Kiddush (00:01–04:46)
16. Shehechianu (00:01–01:30)

III. Yom Kippur Kol Nidre Service (No Year)

*17. Kol Nidre (00:01–14:23)
*18. V'nislach (00:01–02:15)
19. Shehechianu (00:01–02:35)
20. Bar'chu (00:01–01:55)
21. Shema Israel (00:01–03:34)
22. V'rau vanav (00:01–02:40)
*23. Ya'aleh (00:01–02:06)
24. Ki hineh kachomer (00:01–03:58)
25. Adonai, Adonai (00:01–03:52)

IV. Yom Kippur *Ne'ilah* Service (1978)

*26. Amidah and Kedushah (00:01–08:37)
*27. P'sach lonu and Hayom yifneh (00:01–04:12)
*28. Four piyyutim (00:01–08:33)

V. Shavuot Festival Service (Different Years)

29. Pis'chu li, 1979 (00:01–05:22)
30. Kaddish Shalem, 1979 (00:01–01:26)
*31. Torah service, 1979 (00:01–09:32)
*32. Akdamut, 1980 (00:01–05:14)
*33. Return of the Torah service, 1979 (00:01–06:06)
*34. El male rachamim, 1983 (00:01–04:04)
*35. Musaf service, 1980 (00:01–12:02)
36. Adon Olam for festivals, 1983 (00:01–02:04)

VI. Shabbat Morning Service (Different Years)

*37. *Birchat HaChodesh*, 1981 (00:01–08:56)
*38. Sim Shalom, 1988 (00:01–06:38)

* Indicates clip on YouTube for your listening pleasure: YouTube.com, M. G. Heiser

I. Guide to Cantor Heiser's Slichot Service (1987?)

Coming from Berlin, yet committed to Eastern European-type services, Cantor Heiser leaned in one of two directions with his music, either Lewandowski and Sulzer—who, though considered Central Ashkenazi, were seen as reformers of their time, and to a lesser degree Samuel Naumbourg—or Traditional melodies and Eastern European *nusach* or composers with Eastern European roots. He also did not hesitate to intersperse modern compositions by American cantors, often of Eastern European origin, including Hasidic *niggunim*, Israeli or folk melodies, though the overall service was Eastern European. The well-known choral response in his service was new in the nineteenth century synagogue. This particular Slichot service—perhaps more than the other services at our disposal—is very old and at the same time also very new (i.e., modern).

In his study, *Chosen Voices: The Story of the American Cantorate*, Mark Slobin, who mentions Cantor Heiser in his book as a contributor to his project,[109] notes that "Slichot is a particularly weighty service" that begins an entire holiday season—the High Holy Days. B'nai Israel used a booklet entitled "Slichot," published by The Rabbinical Assembly in 1964. The service begins with Rabbi Richard M. E. Marcovitz's introduction; then, as it is not Shabbat anymore and instruments are therefore permitted, the organ prelude introduces the musical offering with the first line of the prayer "Ashrei" (p. 6 in "Slichot" booklet) [Clip 1] (04:44–10:45 side one, full tape; 00:01–06:37 clip, not on YouTube), "Happy are they who dwell in Your house," in a known *nusach* variant described by Slobin as follows: "Because Ashrei sums up the Jewish doctrine of God, the Talmud urges that it be said three times daily (B. Ber. 4b). Hence it is said twice at the morning service and once at the afternoon service (Klein 1979:33)." Slobin likewise notes that "Like other prayers that recur, the Ashrei has variable significance according to the season, which means its musical setting—part of what nusach implies—will also vary."[110] Slobin further explains that several of the ninety-three versions for "Ashrei" available to us are "straight nusach," no embellishment. His thirty-second example, which is the one Cantor Heiser used, varies somewhat from the basic form in that the phrase "Ashrei yoshvei veitecha [od yehallelucha selah]"—the first line of the prayer—lasts longer than the "straight nusach" example and sounds more like a melody than like a chant.[111] Cantor, choir, and organ then continue "silently" until "Zaddik Adonai" (the Lord is righteous), which is just straight melody and organ, with inverted *shtayger*, pleading straightforward, "Shomer Adonai"

(Guardian of Israel, watch over us), with little improvisation, and by the Cantor only, very somber; yet the final "halleluyah" is upbeat and reassuring, ending on a high note. The beginning of the service is very simple and very humble, to set the mood for the penitential season. Rabbi Marcovitz reinforces the mood with words of encouragement, admiration for God's creation, and hope for the New Year if we do *tshuvah, tefillah,* and *zedakah* (repentance, prayer, and charity).

The transition occurs with a solemn and majestic "Hatzi Kaddish" (p. 10) [Clip 2] (16:56–20:09 side one, full tape; 00:01–03:15 clip, not on YouTube), a prayer used as a divider between service sections, and adapted from Musaf of Rosh Hashanah (in Moshe Nathanson, ed., *Zamru Lo III, Congregational Melodies for the Shalosh R'galim and High Holidays,* 134), by Cantor and choir in Traditional, but adapted for High Holy Day mode, without organ, freely improvised by the Cantor, ending in a divine "Amen." This Traditional Hatzi Kaddish is a perfect example of Cantor Heiser's art. Although he follows the established notes for this rendition—one can clearly recognize them—he adds bridging notes so that the melody flows rather than jumps, giving the prayer a soothing effect. Kalib notes that this *nusach* has an Eastern European basis and influenced the West Central European tradition.[112] If the rhythm of the Kaddish lulls the worshipper into comfort, the unexpected grand conclusion with the high "Amen" brings them back to the task at hand and opens their heart to prayer.

After some davening and more remarks by Rabbi Marcovitz, the organ sets the tone, as the choir launches into the first set of prayers, which are compositions of "**L'chu N'ran'nah lAdonai**" (Let us sing to the Lord) [**YouTube, No. 1**] (p. 18) [Clip 3] (22:38–27:37 side one, full tape; 00:01–04:59 clip) by Max Janowski, for Slichot. "L'chu N'ran'nah lAdonai" was published by Friends of Jewish Music in Chicago in 1961, a time when Cantor Heiser was well connected in the world of *hazzanut* and would have been aware of contemporary compositions. The set begins with a soprano solo from the choir, with organ background, then in a cascading wave the entire choir joins in—first the tenors, then the basses, and the altos, followed by a pleading for righteousness and justice, "Zedek u'mishpat" (Janowski), by the Cantor with organ. Cantor Heiser's granddaughter Betty Sue Stein, about 18 years old, chimes in with "Asher b'yado" ([He] who holds us in His Hand) by Janowski, with organ, joined by the choir for a repetition, concluding with Betty Sue's sweet solo voice for a second repetition, "The soul of all life is in God's Hand, the spirit of all human flesh."[113]

Even though part of the same prayer, the mood and the melody change for "**Han'shamah lach**" (The soul is Yours) [**YouTube, No. 2**] (p. 18) [Clip 4] (27:38–32:05 side one, full tape; 00:01–04:28 clip), which is sung in a very moving and elaborate but, alas, unidentified melody by choir and organ, and then by the cantor in a powerful voice, which rises over the choir. Choir, Cantor, and soloists alternate throughout, concluding with a very assertive "l'maan sh'imecha" (for Your Name's sake). Although this service may have been recorded in 1987, nearly fifty years after his arrival from Europe, and twenty years after the congregation formally switched to Sephardic Hebrew, one notices here that Cantor Heiser as well as the American choir sing Ashkenazi pronunciation of Hebrew—"Asanu" instead of the Sephardic "Atanu," for example.

A responsive English reading, "Create me, Your child, anew" (p. 21), led by the Rabbi, follows, concluding with silent meditation and the Cantor's davening.

After the Cantor chants a moving appeal, "**Ta'azin shav'atenu**" (Forgive our transgressions) [**YouTube, No. 3**] (p. 26) [Clip 5] (36:38–40:37 side one, full tape; 00:01–04:04 clip), accompanied by the organ, Yom Kippur, the Day of Atonement, is foreshadowed in the prayer that enumerates God's Thirteen Attributes of Mercy, "Adonai, Adonai" (Deuteronomy 34:6–7) to a Traditional melody notated and arranged by Samuel Dubrow (in Nathanson, ed., *Zamru Lo III*, Congregational Melodies for the Shalosh R'galim and the High Holidays, 128). This prayer, somewhat adjusted musically, is angelically intoned by Betty Sue, accompanied by the organ, then repeated by choir, Betty Sue, and organ; the Cantor concludes the section by davening the rest of the liturgy, ending in the hope that God will answer our prayers.

The service, as a whole, is more modern musically than either Erev Rosh Hashanah or Kol Nidre, yet the prayers are Traditional. This was also the attraction of Salomon Sulzer and Louis Lewandowski in the nineteenth century—to know how to modernize without abandoning the tradition. A very deep "El Melech yoshev" (The King sits [on a throne of Mercy]) is sung by the Cantor, accompanied by the organ, and followed by the choir. The Cantor improvises considerably and concludes this prayer with a delightful "Vayikra" (and proclaimed) in falsetto, and a powerful final "v'Shem Adonai" (to the Lord's name), followed by regular davening. In our working session in Jerusalem, Professor Schleifer concluded that the *falsetto* is beautiful at the right time and for the right words.[114]

As the service continues, Rabbi Marcovitz notes that the next prayer, "**Lishmoa el harinah**" (Hear our plea and our prayer) [**YouTube, No. 4**]

(p. 32) [Clip 6] (47:59–55:24 side one, full tape; 00:01–06:23 clip), is "the epitome of the Slichot service." This particular unidentified composition provides an example of an artful *and* soulful melody with a very complicated musical arrangement for choir, soloists, Cantor, and organ. "The Sabbath has ended, night has come" is begun by the choir in a quiet and pensive tone, then repeated; the melody swells as the soprano takes over from the choir in the second line of the first stanza, "We come before You with earnest plea," accompanied by the organ, only to hand off the lead to the choir again for the refrain. The second stanza, which asks for God's protection, is davened by the Rabbi and congregation. Cantor Heiser takes on the third stanza, beseeching God from the depths of his being, "D'rash na dorshecha" (Receive all who seek Your Presence), with the organ in the background; the choir sings the refrain, musically lifting the weightiness of the foregoing words. In the fourth stanza, the Rabbi and congregation express awe at God's miracles. The fifth stanza, "Yotzer atah" (You created [every living being]), is again sung and improvised by the Cantor in a tender, then strong and soaring voice—with the organ in the background, the choir then follows with the refrain. The sixth stanza is again spoken by Rabbi and congregation. In the seventh stanza, the Cantor continues to plead for God's mercy, with the organ, launching into a beautiful *falsetto* for "Elohim Adonai Zevaot." Unfortunately, Cantor Heiser reused previous tapes when he made practice tapes for students and thus messed up the *falsetto* by breaking in and counting [it is his voice]. We have cut the tape before this spot. The choir and organ conclude the stanza with the refrain, "Hear our plea! Accept our prayer!" The eighth verse is whispered by Rabbi and congregation.

"Shema Kolenu" (p. 36) [Clip 7] (55:39–59:14 side one, full tape; 00:01–03:37 clip, not on YouTube), a prayer pleading with God to hear our supplications, is not sung to any of the well-known melodies but turned into a recitative and improvisation by the Cantor, without organ accompaniment, some of it davened silently. "Al Tashlichenu" (Do not cast us away) is artfully prayed by the Cantor and repeated by the congregation; the Cantor then davens the conclusion. An English reading led by Rabbi Marcovitz follows.

The **"Ashamnu,"** or communal Confession **[YouTube, No. 5]** (p. 40) [Clip 8] (02:21–04:40 side two, full tape; 00:01–02:21 clip), soulfully chanted by Cantor and choir, accompanied by the organ, and joined by the congregation, is a variation on a Hasidic melody heard by Chemjo Vinaver in his childhood and recorded in his *Anthology of Jewish Music*.[115] This spiritual group flagellation is sweetened by the choir's lofty conclusion, followed by the Cantor's davening, and the plea "Hu ya'anenu" (May He answer us), (p. 42), to a popular though unidentified folk melody.

The concluding prayer, "**Shomer Israel**" (Guardian of Israel) [YouTube, No. 6] (p. 47) [Clip 9] (07:20–16:03 side two, full tape; 00:01–08:42 clip), is also part of *Tachanun* [supplications] during the week; here it is sung exquisitely to Yossele Rosenblatt's composition—note for note, as Professor Schleifer says—by Cantor, choir, and organ.[116] The first stanza features choir director Claryne Karsh, a long-time musical associate and friend of Cantor Heiser's, with her rich alto voice, accompanied by the organ and joined by the choir for the repetition. Although the words in the sheet music are Ashkenazi, Cantor Heiser and choir sing Sephardic Hebrew. The Cantor presents a strong and reassuring second stanza "Shomer goy echad" (Guardian of the one people) as well as the third stanza, "Shomer goy kaddosh" (Guardian of the holy people), with a wonderful improvisation, after which he is joined by the choir and supported by the organ. This is all the guidance that Yossele Rosenblatt's composition provides.[117] Cantor Heiser's choir continues with stanzas four and five. In stanza four, choir director Claryne Karsh hauntingly pleads with God for mercy—"mitratzeh b'rachamim"—using the melody from the first stanza and supported by the organ. She is joined by the choir for the repetition, as in the first stanza. Mrs. Karsh then immediately goes into stanza five with "Avinu malkenu" in an unknown and penitent melody and is joined by the choir for an exquisite conclusion of this stanza. Additional stanzas of the hymn are not sung.

Cantor Rosenblatt was a generous human being; he dedicated this composition to and for the benefit of the Jewish War Orphans' Fund following World War I. The information sheet explains that "It costs approximately $100 to maintain a Jewish war orphan in Europe for one year. Every contributor of $100 is entitled to receive the photograph and record of the child cared for through this contribution, and the child is given the name and address of its benefactor, so that direct communication might be established." Individual copies of the sheet music were sold for fifty cents. The *frontis* piece shows an illustration of Cantor Rosenblatt, a poem in Yiddish, and a moving English poem, surrounded by the portraits of 18 children—a not insignificant number, as eighteen is the numerical value for life. The English poem reads:

> I have pondered full deeply again and again:
> What can I do for thee, fatherless child?

What can I give thee, for bread and for spirit?
What can I bring thee—I wondered in vain.
Whatever I do is a drop in the sea,
Whatever I do is too little for thee.

I yearned but to bring thee some service of mine
    But my art weeps and falters before thy young heartbreak:
    But here is a melody made but for thee
    A song with thy prayer in each holy line.
    There is but one help that all Israel has known
    It lies in the 'Guardian of Israel' alone.

Cantor Heiser then launches immediately into the Kaddish Shalem in normal Shabbat *nusach*, which leads to Rabbi Marcovitz's final reading of Psalm 15 and benediction of "Shavua Tov, Shanah Tovah, and Laila Tov!" as well as an organ afterplay.

Slichot Service Order Worksheet, 1987?, Tape No. 16, Rabbi Richard M. E. Marcovitz Officiating, with Organ (as it is not Shabbat anymore)

B'nai Israel Slichot booklet, "Slichot," The Rabbinical Assembly, New York, 1964.
    Note: "M" indicates that melody is identified and sheet music is in hand.
    "?" indicates that melody has not been identified and sheet music is not in hand.

Worksheet Side 1

Rabbi Richard M. E. Marcovitz introduction, then organ prelude (01:27–05:30)

Pg. 6   M "Ashrei," first line only in *nusach*, then silent to "zaddik" (04:44–06:16)
Cantor, choir, and organ (see Mark Slobin, in *Chosen Voices*, ex. 32 262)
? "Zaddik Adonai"—"halleluyah," Cantor and organ (06:17–10:45)
Composition with *shtayger*, up and down
Rabbi Marcovitz comments

Pg. 10   M "Hatzi Kaddish," Cantor, choir, and organ (16:52–20:09)
Traditional *mi Sinai*, but free for Cantor, heavily adapted, beautiful high "Amen."
(In Moshe Nathanson, ed., *Zamru Lo III*, Congregational Melodies for the Shalosh R'galim and the High Holidays, 134)
[See Shalom Kalib, *The Musical Tradition of the East European Synagogue*, Volume One, Part One. Text. Example 89, 58; and Volume One, Part Two. Music. Example 89, 66.]
Rabbi Marcovitz announces silent meditation by congregation (10–16) (20:13–22:36)
Cantor davens quietly

Pg. 18   M "L'chu N'ran'nah lAdonai" (22:38–23:52)
First verse soprano solo by choir member, with organ, then choir joins in cascading fashion ("L'Chu N'ran'nah" for Slichot by Max Janowski, 3–5)

Pg. 18   M "Zedek umishpat," Cantor, with organ (23:53–25:50)
(Max Janowski composition, 5–6)

Pg. 18	M "Asher b'yado"—"kol b'sarish" (25:51–27:37)
	Betty Sue Stein with organ; then choir and organ, then Betty Sue with organ
	(Max Janowski composition, 6–7)
Pg. 18	? "Han'shamah lach" by choir, then solo by Cantor, choir, and organ (27:39–32:05)
	Not Janowski; artful composition, but whose?
Pg. 18	"S'lach lanu"—"avonenu," Cantor davened only (32:06–32:20)
	Rabbi Marcovitz leads responsive reading on 21, then silent meditation on 22, some cantorial davening.
Pg. 26	"Ta'azin shav'atenu," Cantor and organ (36:38–37:15)
Pg. 26	M "Adonai, Adonai," Betty Sue Stein, adapted, with organ (37:16–38:22) then choir, Betty Sue and organ (38:23–39:40)
	Traditional. Notated and arranged by Samuel Dubrow, (in Nathanson, ed., *Zamru Lo III, Congregational Melodies for the Shalosh R'galim and the High Holidays*, 128)
Pg. 26	"V'salach'ta," Cantor davened (39:41–40:37)
Pg. 28	Congregation continues silently with organ
Pg. 30	? "El Melech"—"v'Shem Adonai," Cantor and organ alternating (40:58–46:14)
	with choir, wide tonal range, *shtayger*, "Vaikra" *falsetto*, then davened.
	Rabbi Marcovitz introduces hymn "Lishmoah el harinah" (46:39–47:52)
Pg. 32	? "Lishmoa el harinah" begins with "B'Motzaei m'nuchah" (47:59–55:24)
	Very complicated arrangement, choir, organ, Cantor Heiser
	1st stanza begins with choir, then soprano with organ, then choir
	2nd stanza davened by Rabbi Marcovitz
	3rd stanza Cantor and organ, then choir with organ
	4th stanza davened by Rabbi Marcovitz
Pg. 34	5th stanza Cantor and organ, refrain by choir and organ
	6th stanza davened by Rabbi and Cantor
	7th stanza Cantor and organ, "Adonai Zevaot" *falsetto*, then choir and organ
	(Cantor Heiser messed up tape by counting right in middle of *falsetto*)

	8th stanza silently
	Rabbi Marcovitz announces "Sh'ma Kolenu" (55:25–59:38)
Pg. 36	? "Sh'ma Kolenu," Cantor recitative with improvisation (55:39–59:14)
	No organ, no choir, some prayed silently, Rabbi Marcovitz reading (59:15-end)
	[Tape ends]

Slichot Service Order Worksheet, 1978?, Tape No. 16, Rabbi Richard M. E. Marcovitz Officiating, with Organ

Worksheet Side 2

(Cantor Heiser counting at beginning of tape)

Rabbi Marcovitz reading, maybe continuation from Side 1 (00:58–01:50)

Pg. 41   "Ana Tavo" (Eloheinu, velohei avoteinu), read in English by all (02:02–02:20)

Pg. 40   "Ashamnu," Cantor, choir, organ, then davened by Cantor (02:21–05:00)

Maybe variation on Hasidic melody (see Chemjo Vinaver, *Anthology of Jewish Music*, 1953, 153–154)

Pg. 42   ? "Hu ya'anenu," Cantor, then choir, probably folk tune (05:05–07:18)

Pg. 46   M "Shomer Israel," organ, choir, Cantor (07:20–16:03)

1st stanza Claryne Karsh, alto with organ, then choir and organ, 3

2nd stanza Cantor and organ "Shomer," 4

3rd stanza Cantor "Shomer," then Cantor and choir, all with organ, 5

Great improvisation, great example of *shtaygers*

4th stanza Claryne "Mitratzeh," with organ, then choir and Claryne, with organ, like first stanza

5th stanza Claryne, "Avinu" with organ and choir

This is the end, other stanzas are not sung.

"Shomer Israel" composed by Cantor Josef Rosenblatt, dedicated to and for the Benefit of the Jewish War Orphans Fund.

Note: Text is Ashkenazi, but Cantor Heiser pronounces Separdic Hebrew.

Pg. 50   "Kaddish Shalem," Traditional *nusach* as on Shabbat (16:04–17:08)

Cantor, choir, and organ

Pg. 52   Rabbi Marcovitz concludes service by reading Psalm 15 (17:10–20:46)

Personal meditation, benediction, and organ afterplay (20:47–22:15).

II. Guide to Cantor Heiser's Erev Rosh Hashanah Service (No Date)

Erev Rosh Hashanah was an impressive religious and social event—the B'nai Israel sanctuary, with its 1,500 seats, was packed to capacity, and there was an overflow service for an additional 1,000 people. Since we have a near complete service, mostly consisting of music, I included the **entire Erev Rosh Hashanah service tape [YouTube, No. 7]** [Clip 10] (00:01–40:33 full tape) for our listening pleasure. This particular recording is not dated, but Rabbi Richard Marcovitz was officiating, so it is in the last dozen years of Cantor Heiser's life (1976–1989). And Betty Sue's voice is not as young (her Bat Mitzvah was in 1981), so I would estimate this service to be sometime in the mid-1980s.

On the original cassette tape, which we shortened at the front end, one can hear the chatter of the congregants and the movement of bodies as the congregation sits down for the start of the service, begun by the mixed choir with Louis Lewandowski's "**Mah Tovu**" (How good it is [to dwell in your tents, oh Jacob]) [Clip 11] (00:01–02:42 full tape; 00:01–02:42 clip) (in *Todah W'simrah I: Shabbat*, Out-of-Print Classics Series of Synagogue Music No. 10, 3; also Ephros, ed., *Cantorial Anthology of Traditional and Modern Synagogue Music*. Volume I Rosh Hashonoh, 7). This affirmation that God enjoys being in our midst is reaffirmed by a soprano solo, using the notation for the tenor! Kalib traces the background of the first four bars of this melody to a seventeenth-century Italian aria.[118] Cantor Heiser's granddaughter Betty Sue Stein chimes in with her sweet, clear, and pure soprano voice, "Adonai, ahavti meon" (01:08–01:49). There is no doubt that she means it when she sings, "Lord, I love being in Your House," exactly following the Lewandowski notation (Ephros, ed., *Cantorial Anthology of Traditional and Modern Synagogue Music*. Volume I Rosh Hashonoh, 9), after which the choir picks up with "Va'ani tefilati l'cha" (and I pray to You) in Sephardic pronunciation, even though the Lewandowski sheet music has the Ashkenazi Hebrew (Ephros, ed., *Cantorial Anthology of Traditional and Modern Synagogue Music*. Volume I Rosh Hashonoh, 9).

After some words of welcome by Rabbi Richard Marcovitz, the service continues with the "Bar'chu," or call to worship (04:25–05:05), beginning with a cantorial solo, not in the traditional High Holy Day *nusach*, as one would expect, but on an inverted scale. This leads the worshippers into the depths of their being rather than directly to the heights, no doubt intentionally. Before one can pray, the spiritual door that leads to one's personal holy of holies has to first be unlocked. After the Cantor's "Bar'chu," the choir chimes in with the Traditional High Holy Day *niggun*, "aah-aah-aah," a combination of "Bor'chu" No. 3, arranged by Lewandowski (in Ephros, ed., *Cantorial Anthology of Traditional and Modern Synagogue Music*, Volume I Rosh Hashonoh, 11), and "Bar'chu" (in Nathanson, ed., *Zamru Lo III*, Congregational Melodies for the Shalosh R'galim and the High Holidays, 110); the Cantor then completes the phrase "et Adonai ham'vorach" (the Lord who is blessed) in High Holy Day *nusach* according to Lewandowski (in Ephros, ed., *Cantorial Anthology of Traditional and Modern Synagogue Music*. Volume I Rosh Hashonoh, 11, bottom). Thereafter, all—Cantor, choir, and congregation—join for "Baruch Adonai ham'vorach l'olam vaed" (Praised is the Lord who is blessed for all eternity), again in High Holy Day *nusach*, without organ accompaniment. The congregation is seated. The Cantor picks up the first verse after the "Bar'chu," which begins with "Baruch Atah Adonai" (05:30–08:20) in mid-verse, supported by the choir, in a very beautiful and distinct High Holy Day *nusach*, perhaps improvised, concluding with an improvisational flourish on Lewandowski's "hama'ariv aravim" ([Blessed are you, oh Lord], who brings on evening) ("Bor'chu" No. 3, in Ephros, ed., *Cantorial Anthology of Traditional and Modern Synagogue Music*. Volume I Rosh Hashonoh, 11).

Cantor Heiser picks up the second paragraph, "Ahavat olam" (With everlasting love) preceding the "Shema," with "Ki hem chayenu" (for they are our life), improvising until "V'ahavat'cha" (And your love [may never depart from us]), when he changes to the Lewandowski "Bar'chu" melody (No. 3 in Ephros, ed., *Cantorial Anthology of Traditional and Modern Synagogue Music*. Volume I Rosh Hashonoh, 11), with support from the choir, ending in a lovely improvisational flourish for "ohev amo Israel" (who loves God's people Israel).

The "Shema" (Hear [oh Israel]) (09:20–09:39) itself—the Jewish creed of faith—uses the exact Sulzer melody from the Friday night service (in *Schir Zion, Gesänge für den israelitischen Gottesdienst*, 150th Jubilee Issue, Out-of-Print Classics Series of Synagogue Music No. 6, Joseph Sulzer, ed., 45). According to Kalib, "Its appeal derives from the majesty, dignity, musical beauty and class it lends to the traditional service and liturgical text."[119] The "V'ahavta" verse—"And you shall love the Lord your God with all your heart, with all your soul, and with all your might"—is in the usual congregational Torah *trop*, what I call "Cantor Heiser minhag." The two benedictions following the "Shema" are being recited in an undertone until the middle of the second paragraph, when the Cantor chants the concluding phrases—"L'maan tizkeru" (11:36–12:32) (You will remember [to do all My Commandments and be holy unto your God. I am the Lord your God, who brought you out of the land of Egypt, to be your God; I am the Lord your God])—in a mixture of regular and High Holy Day *nusach*, at the end supported by the choir. The Rabbi interjects an English reading of the liturgical text. The Cantor and choir then conclude this part of the service (simchah rabah v'amru chulam) using the same High Holy Day melodies that they sang for the "Bar'chu." It is a well-organized service!

The prayers that follow (14:27–16:09), "Mi chamochah" (Who is like You, oh Lord?), "Malchutecha" (This is Your Lord), "Adonai imloch l'olam vaed" (The Lord God shall reign forever and ever), and "V'ne'emar" (It is said), are alternated by choir and Cantor in a musical call and response mode, the choir following Sulzer for Rosh Hashanah (in *Schir Zion, Gesänge für den israelitischen Gottesdienst*, Out-of-Print Classics Series of Synagogue Music No. 7, Joseph Sulzer, ed., 231; also Ephros, ed., *Cantorial Anthology of Traditional and Modern Synagogue Music*. Volume I Rosh Hashonoh, 14, and Nathanson, ed., *Zamru Lo III*, Congregational Melodies for the Shalosh R'galim and the High Holidays, 110), while the Cantor majestically improvises on the Sulzer theme, pushing each phrase higher musically as well as spiritually, concluding with "gaal Israel" (redeemer of Israel). The people Israel are climbing the spiritual ladder to God, not only to the tune of Sulzer, but to Lewandowski as well. For this section, their music, based on Tradition, is identical! (See Lewandowski, *Kol Rinnah U'Tefillah*, 83).

With the congregation at this point spiritually receptive to communing with the Divine, the Cantor introduces the "**Hashkivenu**" prayer [Clip 12] (16:34–22:48 full tape; 00:01–07:00 clip), pleading from his depths for a peaceful sleep with a rich improvisation; thereafter, Betty Sue continues the "Hashkivenu" plea for her grandfather [music instructions say this part is for the Cantor] with a disarming, precise rendition of Lewandowski's sophisticated "V'hagen ba'adenu" (No. 85 in *Todah W'simrah Part II: Festgesänge*, Out-of-Print Classics Series of Synagogue Music No. 12, 127; also Ephros, ed., *Cantorial Anthology of Traditional and Modern Synagogue Music*, Volume I Rosh Hashonoh, 22), asking for God's protection. The choir takes over with an exact and strong "Uv'zel k'nafecha tas'tirenu" (May we always sense Your care, text from *Machzor Hadash*, 31) and "U'sh'mor zetenu" (Guard us), (also by Lewandowski, No. 86 in *Todah W'simrah Part II: Festgesänge*, Out-of-Print Classics Series of Synagogue Music No. 12, 128; also Ephros, ed., *Cantorial Anthology of Traditional and Modern Synagogue Music*. Volume I Rosh Hashonoh, 23), followed by the Cantor's impressive improvisation of "U'sh'mor zetenu" (Guard us). His recitation culminates in a sweet *falsetto* for "l'chayim" (to life). After the concluding phrase "Ufros Aleinu" (Spread over us [Your tent of peace]), with "Happoreis," he brings the melody back to the Traditional High Holy Day *nusach* according to Sulzer in *Schir Zion, Gesänge für den israelitischen Gottesdienst*, Out-of-Print Classics Series of Synagogue Music No. 7, Joseph Sulzer, ed., 231; also Nathanson, ed., *Zamru Lo III*, Congregational Melodies for the Shalosh R'galim and the High Holidays, 111), and choir and Cantor conclude with "v'al Yerushalaim" (and on Jerusalem).[120] A good cantor always returns to the *nusach* at the end.

A very catchy and popular but, alas, unidentified "Tik'u bachodesh" (Sound [the shofar] on the new moon) by the choir concludes this part of the service, followed by a majestic **"Hatzi Kaddish"** [Clip 13] (23:32–25:51 full tape; 00:01–02:20 clip) by Cantor and choir, based in part on a traditional version of the Kaddish arranged by Moshe Nathanson for Shalosh Regalim and High Holy Days (in Nathanson, ed., *Zamru Lo III*, Congregational Melodies for the Shalosh R'galim and the High Holidays, 112, and No. 62 "Yehe shmeh raba" (May His great Name [be blessed forever and ever]), in Silverman *Machzor*, 1949/1939, 10, and in *Liturgisches Liederbuch für den Gebrauch der Religionsschulen*, 39), but also improvised and with High Holy Day *nusach*, concluding with one of Cantor Heiser's soul-rending "Amens." This is an excellent example of Cantor Heiser's technique of sketching out notes with gusto—Professor Schleifer noted that "he learned it somewhere and cherishes it."[121] It is also noteworthy that he goes quickly when he improvises because he is sure of himself. He owns the music; it comes from his soul.

The silent "ma'ariv Amidah" follows, concluding with a very upbeat and typical Cantor Heiser **"Kaddish Shalem"** [Clip 14] (31:17–32:25 full tape; 00:01–01:10 clip), using regular Shabbat *nusach*. Rabbi Marcovitz then leads a responsive English reading.

The **Kiddush** [Clip 15] (34:20–39:05 full tape; 00:01–04:46 clip) that evening was B'nai Israel's standard High Holy Day kiddush for Rosh Hashanah by Cantor and choir—with all the bells and whistles. This rendition is by no means ordinary; rather, worshippers at B'nai Israel came to know and expect this Kiddush melody for Rosh Hashanah. I was not able to find it in any of the printed sources, and it may well be Cantor Heiser's own improvisation, perhaps inspired by Sholom Secunda, who wrote an equally elaborate Kiddush and Shehechianu for the Shalosh Regalim. Again, Eli Schleifer commented that "Cantor Heiser knows what he is doing; he relies on himself in his improvisations."[122] The choir introduces "Ki vanu vacharta" (Because You have chosen us) and is joined by the Cantor, who then concludes this section with a solo, affirming God's Word as Truth. Subsequently, Cantor, choir, and congregation alternate "Melech al kol ha'aretz" (Sovereign of all the world), using the Traditional melody notated and arranged by Samuel Dubrow (in Nathanson, ed., *Zamru Lo III, Congregational Melodies for the Shalosh Regalim and the High Holidays*, 223), which, according to Professor Schleifer, is usually used in the service, as indeed it was at B'nai Israel, but not for the Kiddush.[123] However, at B'nai Israel, it was also used in the Kiddush and in the benediction after the Haftarah. The Cantor concludes with a thundering "Melech," acknowledged by the choir with a full and powerful "Amen."

The Kiddush is followed by a beautiful but unidentified "**Shehechianu**" [Clip 16] (39:06–40:32 full tape; 00:01–01:30 incomplete clip) sung four times. "Praised are You, Lord our God, Ruler of the universe, who has kept us in life, sustained us, and enabled us to reach this season" (*Machzor Hadash*, 57). The Cantor begins with "Baruch Atah Adonai," then Betty Sue sings an ethereal "Shehechianu" twice, as does the choir, with everyone joining in. Indeed, the entire congregation is grateful that God has brought us to this day. Although the "Shehechianu" on this tape ends before the prayer is finished, there is a beautiful complete Shehechianu in the Kol Nidre service.

Professor Schleifer concluded that Cantor Heiser is straddling two traditions; musically and linguistically, two directions seek his attention. He comes from the tradition of the Western European *nusach* but tends to use the Eastern. And he now uses Sephardic pronunciation of Hebrew when he learned Ashkenazi Hebrew.[124] However, since Cantor Heiser chose whether to use Ashkenazi or Sephardic pronunciation, no matter in what Hebrew it was written, he seems to have been comfortable with both linguistically, while he clearly leaned toward Eastern European *nusach* in his services, for what I believe were personal reasons connected to his Nazi experience in Germany.

Erev Rosh Hashanah Service Order Worksheet, No Date, Tape No. 13, Rabbi Richard M. E. Marcovitz Officiating, No Organ

Silverman High Holy Day Prayer Book (*Machzor*) Rosh Hashanah—New Year, Yom Kippur—Day of Atonement. Compiled and arranged by Rabbi Morris Silverman, Prayer Book Press, Hartford, CT, 1939, 11th printing, 1949.

(Note: The prayer book I use here is my *machzor* from Tuscaloosa. I do not have the edition used at B'nai Israel. Thus, the page numbers are different.)

I am also in possession of one of Cantor Heiser's Silverman *machzorim*, from 1959/1951, courtesy of the Stein family; the page numbers are the same as in the 1949 version that I am citing.

> Note: "M" indicates that melody is identified and sheet music is in hand.
> "?" indicates that melody has not been identified and sheet music is not in hand.

Worksheet Side 1

Pg. 1   M "Mah Tovu," No. 2 by B'nai Israel choir (00:01–02:42)
with Cantor, choir, and Betty Sue Stein (00:01–01:07)
Louis Lewandowski (In *Todah W'simrah, Part I: Shabbat*, Out-of-Print Classics Series of Synagogue Music No. 10, 3. Also, in Ephros, ed., *Cantorial Anthology of Traditional and Modern Synagogue Music*. Volume I Rosh Hashonoh, 7, several notes changed.)
[See Sholom Kalib, *The Musical Tradition of the Eastern European Synagogue*, Volume One, Part One. Text. Example 128f, 127; and Volume One, Part Two. Music. Example 128f, 130.]

Pg. 1   M (Mah tovu) "Adonai, ahavti meon," Betty Sue (01:06–01:49)
Lewandowski (in Ephros, ed., *Cantorial Anthology of Traditional and Modern Synagogue Music*. Volume I Rosh Hashonoh, 9). Exact!

Pg. 1   M (Mah tovu) "Va'ani s'filosi l'cho," choir (01:50–02:42)
Lewandowski (Ephros, ed., *Cantorial Anthology of Traditional and Modern Synagogue Music*. Volume I Rosh Hashonoh, 9)
Rabbi Marcovitz welcome (02:45–04:00)

Pg. 6   M "Bar'chu" (20 in B'nai Israel *machzor*) (04:27–05:05)
Cantor and choir High Holy Day nusach
Sulzer, (in Nathanson, ed., *Zamru Lo III*, Congregational Melodies for the Shalosh R'galim and the High Holidays, 110; also Lewandowski, in Ephros, ed., *Cantorial Anthology of Traditional and Synagogue Music*. Volume I Rosh Hashonoh, 11).
Cantor Heiser inverts High Holy Day *nusach* at beginning, not all Lewandowski, some parts improvised.

Pg. 6   "Baruch Adonai ham'vorach l'olam vaed," choir (05:06–05:16)

Pg. 6   M ("Bar'chu") "Baruch atah Adonai"—"hama'ariv aravim" (05:30–08:20)
Cantor and choir
Lewandowski (No. 111 in *Kol Rinnah UT'fillah*, 81; also in Ephros, ed., *Cantorial Anthology of Traditional and Modern Synagogue Music*. Volume I Rosh Hashonoh, 11), and High Holy Day *nusach*.
Improvisation and flourishes.

Pg. 6   M ("Bar'chu") "Ahavat olam" . . . "Ki hem chayenu"—"ohev amo Israel" (08:30–09:19)
Cantor and choir, pivots to different scale
Lewandowski (in Ephros, ed., *Cantorial Anthology of Traditional and Modern Synagogue Music*. Volume I Rosh Hashonoh, 11), and High Holy Day *nusach*

Pg. 7   M "Shema Israel," choir (09:20–09:39)
Salomon Sulzer Friday night service (in *Schir Zion, Gesänge für den israelitischen Gottesdienst*, Joseph Sulzer, ed., 150th Jubilee Issue, Out-of-Print Classics Series of Synagogue Music No. 6, 45), exactly!
[See Sholom Kalib, *The Musical Tradition of the Eastern European Synagogue*, Volume One, Part One. Text. Example 99c, 71; and Volume One, Part Two. Music. Example 99, 80.]

Pg. 7   "V'ahavta et Adonai," Cantor and congregation (09:40–10:59)
In Torah *trop*

Pg. 8   "V'hayah im shamoa," silently (11:00–11:35)

Pg. 8   "Vayomer Adonai el Moshe lemor," silently
"L'maan tizkeru"—"Adonai Eloheichem" (11:36–12:19)

               Cantor Heiser *trop*
               "Adonai Eloheichem Emet," High Holy Day nusach,
               Cantor, then choir (12:20–12:32)
               Rabbi Marcovitz and congregation reading on 25 in B'nai Israel
                   Machzor (12:33–13:37)

Pg. 9   M ("Emet v'emunah" . . .) "Umalchuto"—"chulam," Cantor
               and choir (13:38–14:27)
               Traditional High Holy Day *nusach* (Sulzer in Ephros, ed.,
                   *Cantorial Anthology of Traditional and Modern Synagogue
                   Music.* Volume I Rosh Hashonoh, 14–15; also Lewandowski
                   No. 81 in *Todah W'simrah* No. 12, 125, and No. 116 in *Kol
                   Rinnah UT'fillah*, 82–83).

Pg. 9   M "Mi chamochah," choir (14:27–14:48)
               Salomon Sulzer (in *Schir Zion*, No. 7, 231; also Ephros, ed.,
                   *Cantorial Anthology of Traditional and Modern Synagogue
                   Music.* Volume I Rosh Hashonoh, 14; also Nathanson, ed.,
                   Zamru Lo III, Congregational Melodies for the Shalosh
                   R'galim and High Holidays, 110), and Lewandowski (No.
                   116 in *Kol Rinnah UT'fillah*, 83).

Pg. 9   M (Mi chamochah) "Malchutecha," Cantor (14:47–15:13)
               Sulzer (in Ephros, ed., *Cantorial Anthology of Traditional and
                   Modern Synagogue Music.* Volume I Rosh Hashonoh, 14–15),
                   and Lewandowski (No. 116 in *Kol Rinnah UT'fillah*, 83),
                   with flourish at end.

Pg. 9   M (Mi chamochah) "Adonai imloch l'olam vaed," choir
               (15:14–15:24)
               Sulzer (in Ephros, ed., *Cantorial Anthology of Traditional and
                   Modern Synagogue Music.* Volume I Rosh Hashonoh, 15,
                   first note different; also in *Schir Zion*, No. 7, 231), and
                   Lewandowski (No. 116 in *Kol Rinnah UT'fillah*, 83).

Pg. 9   M "V'ne'emar"—"gaal Israel," Cantor and choir (15:24–16:09)
               Improvisation on *nusach*, but ends with Sulzer, arranged by
                   Gershon Ephros (in Ephros, ed., *Cantorial Anthology of
                   Traditional and Modern Synagogue Music.* Volume I Rosh
                   Hashonoh, 15), and Lewandowski (No. 116 *in Kol Rinnah
                   UT'fillah*, 83–84).

Silent prayer

Pg. 10   "Hashkivenu"—"Sh'mecha," Cantor Heiser solo (16:34–18:15)

Like earlier beginnings, High Holy Day *nusach*, then own improvisation, with *shtayger*.

Pg. 10   M "V'hagen ba'adenu"—"u'mea'chareinu," Betty Sue solo (18:16–19:28)
Exquisite!
Lewandowski (No. 85 in *Todah W'simrah Part II: Festgesänge*, Series No. 12, 127; also Ephros, ed., *Cantorial Anthology of Traditional and Modern Synagogue Music*. Volume I Rosh Hashonoh, 22–23), perfect!

Pg. 10   M "Uv'zel k'nafecha tas'tirenu"—"v'ad olam," choir (19:28–20:34)
Lewandowski (No. 86 in *Todah W'simrah Part II: Festgesänge*, Out-of-Print Classics Series of Synagogue Music No. 12, 128; also Ephros, ed., *Cantorial Anthology of Traditional and Modern Synagogue Music*. Volume I, Rosh Hashonoh, 23), exact!

Pg. 10   M "U'sh'mor zetenu"—"v'ad olam," Cantor extensive recitative (20:35–21:47)
"l'chayim" *falsetto* and word repetition

Pg. 10   M "Ufros Alenu"—"sukkat shlomecha," Cantor only (21:47–22:00)

Pg. 10   M "Baruch Atah Adonai"—"Yerushalaim" (22:01–22:48)
Cantor and choir in High Holy Day *nusach*
Sulzer (in *Schir Zion*, No. 7, 231; Nathanson adaptation in *Zamru Lo III*, Congregational Melodies for the Shalosh R'galim and the High Holidays, 111, somewhat more adapted by Cantor Heiser).

Pg. 10   ? "Tik'u bachodesh," choir (22:49–23:31)
First two notes from "Tik'u" (No. 61 in *Liturgisches Liederbuch*, 39)

Pg. 10   M "Hatzi Kaddish," Cantor and choir (23:32–25:51)
Beginning Traditional (in Nathanson, ed., *Zamru Lo III*, Congregational Melodies for the Shalosh R'galim and for the High Holidays, 112), then own and High Holy Day *nusach*, also "Yehe shmeh raba" (No. 62 in *Liturgisches Liederbuch*, 39), beautiful high "Amen."

Pg. 11   Silent Amidah (30–39 in B'nai Israel *machzor*) (25:52–31:15)

Pg. 16   Kaddish Shalem, Cantor and choir (31:17–32:25)
Shabbat *nusach*, very upbeat.

	Rabbi Marcovitz leads responsive reading on 45 in B'nai Israel *machzor* (32:26–34:14)
Pg. 19	? Kiddush (46 in B'nai Israel *machzor*) "Baruch Atah Adonai"—"mitzraim" (34:20–36:45) Cantor and choir, improvised.
Pg. 19	? (Kiddush) "Ki vanu vacharta," choir, then Cantor and choir (36:46–37:25)
Pg. 19	? (Kiddush) "U'd'varcha emet," Cantor and choir (37:26–37:47)
Pg. 19	M (Kiddush) "Melech al kol haaretz" with improvisation (37:48–39:05)

Cantor and choir: Five times, last time Cantor only (strong voice).

Traditional. Notated and arranged by Samuel Dubrow (in Nathanson, ed., *Zamru Lo III, Congregational Melodies for the Shalosh R'galim and the High Holidays*, 223).

Pg. 19   ? "Shehechianu" Cantor, then "Shehechianu" repeated (39:06–40:32)

Four times: Betty Sue twice and then choir twice.
Melody is similar to High Holy Day Kiddush.
Beautiful, perhaps Cantor Heiser's own.

[Tape ends before end of prayer.]

Not recorded are "Aleinu," 22; Mourner's Kaddish, 23, and "Yigdal," 25 in the Silverman *machzor*.

III. Guide to Cantor Heiser's Yom Kippur Kol Nidre Service (No Date)

There is no date for this service, although Meyer Gisser (1920–1986), president of B'nai Israel (1977–1980), was still alive. In the service, Rabbi Marcovitz honors him as one of the past presidents who stand before the Open Ark, so the service was held between 1980 and 1986. No organ is used; Cantor Heiser uses pitch pipe throughout.

The 1949 Silvermann *machzor* in my possession does not begin the Kol Nidre service for Erev Yom Kippur with "Mah tovu." But at B'nai Israel the service started with Lewandowski's "Mah tovu" for High Holy Days and Shalosh Regalim with Cantor and choir (*Todah W'Simrah, Part I: Shabbat*, Out-of-Print Classics Series No. 10, 3; also No. 2 Ephros, ed., *Cantorial Anthology of Traditional and Modern Synagogue Music*. Volume I Rosh Hashonoh, 7)—a B'nai Israel favorite (discussed under Erev Rosh Hashanah). It set the mood for the evening, which, though more somber than Rosh Hashanah, was just as festive and pregnant with anticipation. This hymn is followed by a prayer by Rabbi Marcovitz and a reading of the names of past presidents who are no longer living and then, before the open Ark, the names of living past presidents.

The Cantor then introduces the Kol Nidre section with "Or zaruah l'zaddik"—"Light is sown for the righteous, joy for the upright in heart,"[125] also not in this place in the 1949 Silverman *machzor*, but a standard prayer for the procession of the Torah scrolls even in today's Kol Nidre service. Not only Jews, but Christians as well, know that the introspective and contrite "**Kol Nidre**" (All Vows) prayer **[YouTube No. 8]** [Clip 17] (09:05–23:27 side A, full tape; 00:01–14:23 clip), beseeching the Almighty to forgive our trespasses against God in the past year (or is it in the next?) is the heart of the evening service that begins a twenty-five-hour fast marathon for repentant Jews. Business before holiness, and so the court is convened as the choir begins the renowned Lewandowski melody with "ah-ah-aaah, ah-ah-aaah," followed by a solemn and heartfelt "Kol Nidre" by the Cantor. Emphasizing every single word, he establishes the ground rules for the legal proceedings in a strong but neutral voice. "By the authority of the Heavenly Tribunal, and of the Court below, with Divine sanction and with the sanction of this holy congregation, we declare it lawful to pray together with those who have transgressed."[126] The choir underscores the seriousness of our transgressions with "Nid'rana" (Our vows [to God]), after which the Cantor continues with the legal formula that annuls any vows (in this version) that will be made "from this Day of Atonement unto the next Day of Atonement." Some versions of the prayer state a different time frame, "from the last Day of Atonement until this Day of Atonement"—whichever, may it be for our good, sung by the Cantor in a strong voice. The choir alternates phrases with the Cantor—"the vows shall be absolved, released, annulled, made void," in all possible ways of stating the obvious, to convince God of our sincerity, and then a final firm statement by choir and Cantor. First a gentle "Nid'rana" by the choir, carried by the Cantor, who states firmly "[Our vows] shall not be vows, and our bonds shall not be bonds," interwoven with a sweet "aaah" by the choir, after which the Cantor completes his plea to God that "Our oaths shall not be oaths" in a grave and repentant voice.

Kol Nidre is sung three times. The first repetition differs from the first rendition by the Cantor's strong voice—like Azazel, the scapegoat, who carried the sins of the people into the wilderness, so the Cantor carries not only his own sins, but those of his congregation as well. Nevertheless, he is not crushed, he is not daunted, he bears his load—with joy, it seems, with many flourishes throughout, and the choir sweetens the burden with their lovely and elaborate musical support. The third rendition is throughout elaborate, beautiful, and majestic. The Cantor is quite certain that God will allow us another year of spiritual life, and his prayer is more a thanksgiving than a plea at this point. The choir underscores his soulful declamations with a full complement of voices. Cantor Heiser concludes Kol Nidre with an almost triumphant, high "our oaths shall not be oaths," giving us more than hope that we may begin the New Year with a clean slate.

Kalib notes that the prayer text is very old and that the prayer was sung three times so that latecomers had a chance to hear it.[127] As it should, the prayer began with contrition and continued to a tranquility that derives from the Cantor's inner certainty that God is on our side; hence, the concluding statement is assertive, shouting to all the world that God will indeed forgive our iniquities. The melody for Kol Nidre is Traditional—it is a *mi Sinai* tune, but over the years it has been arranged by many different choir masters and composers. This particular rendition was not easy to place, even though it sounds like Lewandowski. It is at least in part Lewandowski, just Cantor Heiser's version of Lewandowski. The Cantor's first four measures follow exactly Lewandowski (No. 107 in *Kol Rinnah UT'fillah*, Series No. 9, 79, and No. 68 in *Todah W'simrah II: Festgesänge* No. 12, 109). Thereafter he periodically returns to key notes in Lewandowski, at the beginning and end of a particular phrase, also echoed by the choir, but in between he is in his own creative sphere with suitable and enhancing improvisations, very much in the tradition of twentieth-century cantors such as Yossele Rosenblatt, Richard Tucker, and others. As this music was second nature to him, he could take liberties in his delivery as he saw fit. This version of Kol Nidre is probably a Cantor Heiser original based on the *mi Sinai* melody and on Lewandowski.

In a letter from his friend Hans to Mrs. Heiser after Cantor Heiser's death, Hans commented how deeply Cantor Heiser's music had affected him in Germany and that he had dictated Cantor Heiser's Lewandowski renderings to their choir master and had them performed in his synagogue in England.[128] Also, Cantor Heiser almost surely learned this particular version from one of his teachers. We know that Leo Gollanin, a student of Lewandowski's, sang Kol Nidre in the New Synagogue in Berlin in 1932—there is a recording of the rehearsal in the Spielberg Collection at the U.S. Holocaust Memorial Museum in Washington, D.C.[129]—at a time when Cantor Heiser had concluded his studies with Gollanin and was himself officiating at services in the Old People's Home where Hans became his student. Likewise, Cantor Felix Asch was one of his teachers, and Asch had recorded "Kol Nidre" already in 1902. There are many fascinating influences on Cantor Heiser's art!

The service continues with **"V'nislach" [YouTube, No. 9]** [Clip 18] (23:35–24:35 full tape; 00:01–02:15 clip), a paragraph only for Yom Kippur. "And the congregation of Israel shall be forgiven, as well as the stranger that dwelleth among them, since the people have transgressed unwittingly."[130] This is a big assumption and signals that God has trust in the Jewish people as well. The prayer is sung by the Cantor exactly in Lewandowski's composition, No. 108 (in *Kol Rinnah UT'fillah*, Out-of-Print Classics Series of Synagogue Music No. 9, 80, and No. 71 in *Todah W'simrah Volume II, Part II: Festgesänge*, Out-of-Print Classics Series of Synagogue Music No. 12, 121–22), and repeated by the choir. The Cantor continues with "S'lach na" (Forgive us) (24:36–25:15), also Lewandowski, No. 109 and No. 73. The choir concludes with three beautiful and soulful renditions of Lewandowski's "Vayomer Adonai, salachti kidvarecha" (God said, "I have forgiven as you have asked") (25:16–25:48), all in the Kol Nidre section of *Kol Rinnah UT'fillah*, (Out-of-Print Classics Series of Synagogue Music No. 9, No. 109, 81, and No. 73 in *Todah W'simrah II: Festgesänge*, 122–123).

The "business" part of the pre-Yom Kippur service concludes with the same lovely "Shehechianu" [Clip 19] (25:49–28:23 side A, full tape; 00:01–02:35 clip, not on YouTube) that concluded the Erev Rosh Hashanah service. The Cantor shares this prayer with his granddaughter Betty Sue Stein and with the choir. A beautiful improvisation expresses our gratitude for God's sustaining us—"v'higianu"—in falsetto, allowing the congregation to concentrate on God's mercy and grace at the beginning of this new year. There is a brief break in the service, after which the Rabbi transitions to the evening service with a responsive reading of Psalm 130 in English.

A festive "Bar'chu" [Clip 20] (31:27–32:26 side A, full tape; 00:01–01:55 clip, not on YouTube) begins the actual "day" of Yom Kippur (see Erev Rosh Hashanah for discussion of liturgy). This is followed by a recitation of the Traditional mode "Shema" [Clip 21] (34:35–35:14 side A, full tape; 00:01–03:34 clip, not on YouTube), "Hear oh Israel," arranged by Sulzer (in *Schir Zion, Gesänge für den israelitischen Gottesdienst,* Out-of-Print Classics Series of Synagogue Music No. 6, 150th Jubilee Issue, 45). From the "Bar'chu" until the Hatzi Kaddish before the silent Amidah, the service is the same as the Erev Rosh Hashanah service we already explored—with two exceptions. During Temple times, on this day the High Priest entered the Holy of Holies and uttered the words traditional Jews do not utter all year long: "Baruch Shem K'vod Malchuto l'olam vaed"—"Praised be God's glorious Name forever and ever," and the Cantor leads the choir in proclaiming this praise. The "Shema" and the normal "V'ahavta" (And you shall love [the Lord your God]) are framed by the benediction "Ahavat Olam" (You love [Israel] forever), using the High Holy Day *nusach*, at the front end, and by a silent "V'hayah im shamoa" (If you hear [my Commandments] it shall come to pass) following, culminating in "Adonai Eloheichem Emet" (In truth Adonai is your God) in High Holy Day *nusach* by the Cantor and repetition by the choir. This is followed by an English reading led by the Rabbi.

Cantor Heiser begins the section "Emet v'emunah" with an improvisation of "V'rau vanav" [Clip 22] (38:43–41:22 side A, full tape; 00:01–02:40 clip, not on YouTube) "when they [the children of Israel] saw [God's might]" at the Yam Suf, then the choir joins him in High Holy Day mode, following Lewandowski (in *Kol Rinnah UT'fillah,* 82–3). "Mi chamochah" (Who is like you, oh Lord?) (39:41–40:04) exactly follows Lewandowski's composition (in *Kol Rinnah UT'fillah,* 83, and No. 83 in *Todah W'simrah II: Festgesänge,* 126)—it can also be found in Ephros, ed., *Cantorial Anthology of Traditional and Modern Synagogue Music.* Volume I Rosh Hashonoh, 14—by Sulzer! (Nathanson, ed., *Zamru Lo III,* Congregational Melodies for the Shalosh R'galim and the High Holidays, 110, and Sulzer in *Schir Zion* No. 7, 231). This is another one of the instances where Sulzer's melody has become nearly a *mi Sinai* tune and was untouchable. Likewise, "Malchutecha" (This is your God) (40:05–40:26), a cantorial solo, follows Lewandowski (No. 116, in *Kol Rinnah UT'fillah*, 83, and Sulzer, in Ephros, ed., *Cantorial Anthology of Traditional and Modern Synagogue Melodies*. Volume I Rosh Hashonoh, 15), with some personal flourishes. "Adonai imloch" (the Lord God [shall reign forever and ever]) (40:27–40:38) by the choir exactly follows Lewandowski (in *Kol Rinnah UT'fillah*, 83, or Sulzer in Ephros, ed., *Cantorial Anthology of Traditional and Modern Synagogue Melodies*. Volume I Rosh Hashonoh, 15). This section concludes with the Cantor improvising on "V'ne'emar" (40:39–41:22), based on Lewandowski (in *Kol Rinnah UT'fillah*, 83, and Sulzer in Ephros, ed., *Cantorial Anthology of Traditional and Modern Synagogue Melodies*. Volume I Rosh Hashonoh, 15), praising the Redeemer of Israel, concluding with an embellished "gaal Israel." In this section one can again see Cantor Heiser's method of improvisation at work. He is very confident with the old *nusach*, in this case the High Holy Day *nusach*; there is no need for caution, he knows what he is doing, and he does not hesitate to improvise.

The "Hashkivenu" prayer is enhanced with an angelic "Vhagen ba'adenu" (to "umea'chareinu") (41:32–42:44) by Betty Sue, followed by the choir from "Uv'zel" to "v'ad olam" (42:45–43:59), both Lewandowski (No. 85 and No. 86 in *Todah W'simrah II: Festgesänge*, 127–129). Cantor Heiser then returns to "Ush'mor zetenu" with a lovely improvisation, concluding with the High Holy Day *nusach* and joined by the choir from "Baruch Ata Adonai" until the end, concluding with a powerful cantorial "v'al Yerushalaim." The solemnity of the day is not forgotten—this is the second exception, as the Cantor proclaims, "On this day shall atonement be made for you, to cleanse you: from all your sins before the Lord shall ye be clean" (Silverman *Machzor*, 217) (45:37–46:31). This is affirmed by a choral repetition. The concluding prayer is a beautiful, albeit interrupted Hatzi Kaddish by the Cantor, which is followed by a long sermon by Rabbi Marcovitz.

After the Hatzi Kaddish, the tone of the service changes. If we heard High Holy Day *nusach*, Lewandowski and Sulzer exclusively so far, the selections in the second part of the evening service are more modern—primarily Wolf Schestapol and Max Janowski. We are already familiar with Janowski's "L'chu N'ran'nah" (28:07–35:12) from Slichot, including "Zedek u'mishpat" and "Asher b'yado." The two following prayers, "Han'shamah lach," also in the Erev Rosh Hashanah service, and "L'maan shim'cha," are not by Janowski, and no composer has been identified. Wolf Schestapol contributed "**Ya'aleh**" ("Rise") **[YouTube No. 10]** [Clip 23] (25:50–27:55 side B, full tape; 00:01–02:06 clip), a *piyyut* pleading that our prayers may rise to God's ear, arranged by M. Graumann (1871–1933) in Ephros, ed., *Cantorial Anthology of Traditional and Modern Synagogue Music*. Volume II Yom Kippur, 32–36, by choir, cantor, and congregation.

Likewise, "Ki hineh kachomer" (Behold, we are as clay [in the hands of the Potter]) [Clip 24] (42:41–46:40 side B, full tape; 00:01–03:58 clip; not on YouTube),[131] perhaps by Zvi Talmon in *T'ruot Hahekhl* [p. 33], sounds somewhat dissonant after the harmonious service that preceded it. The prayer, before the open Ark, with the congregation standing, implores God to remember the covenant "Labrit habet" and not our sins.

Both selections are markedly different in many ways: The melodies are not Traditional, but modern; the tonality is not as comfortable—to the audience, but also to the choir, if not to the Cantor. This leads to a more hesitant and tentative delivery and, as a result, less improvisation by the Cantor, as both he and the choir stick close to the notes on the page. The gusto and enthusiasm in the Traditional *nusach*, which often translates into a spiritual experience, as with the Hatzi Kaddish, for example, is much more measured, as Cantor and choir are more literal in their presentation.

So why include these hymns in the service? And why use compositions that diverge so markedly in style from the Traditional *nusach*? Both are important hymns for Yom Kippur, and there are a variety of compositions to choose from. In the case of "Ya'ale," it may have been sentimentality—Cantor Heiser may have brought this composition with him from Germany—and in the case of "Ki hineh kachomer," an admiration for the composer, if it is indeed Dr. Zvi Talmon (Monsohn) from Jerusalem, who started the choir at Hechal Shlomo, the Great Synagogue in Jerusalem, and directed it still in the 1990s. But there may also be another more practical reason—the congregation's demand for modernization of the service.

A lovely contribution to the service before "Ki hineh kachomer" is the slightly adapted Traditional "Adonai, Adonai," [Clip 25] (37:55–41:10 side B, full tape; 00:01–03:52 clip, not on YouTube) notated and arranged by Samuel Dubrow (in Nathanson's *Zamru Lo III*, Congregational Melodies for the Shalosh R'galim and the High Holidays, 128). The Cantor sets up the prayer by leading us to the place where God walks before us. We, God's children, pronounce God's Thirteen Divine Attributes of Mercy. These attributes are repeated three times, starting with Betty Sue, who, in her childhood innocence, delivers an absolutely gorgeous rendition, clear as a pearl. The first repetition follows by choir and congregation. The second repetition—so the third rendition—is unique. As the Cantor chants the prayer in Hebrew, Rabbi Marcovitz does a parallel reading, also in Hebrew.

The tape ends with "El melech yoshev"—"God our King, sits [on a throne of Mercy]" (46:52–47:15), davened by the Cantor.

Unfortunately, none of the recordings contain one of Cantor Heiser's and the B'nai Israel choir's favorite and most heart-rending preparatory prayers for the *Viddui*, the paragraph "Ana tavo" according to Lewandowski (No. 112, *Todah W'simrah II: Festivals*, 155), which Betty Sue Stein sang in a heavenly voice.[132] But I was able to find a rendition of the prayer on YouTube for our listening pleasure.

Yom Kippur Kol Nidre Service Order Worksheet, No Date, Rabbi Richard M. E. Marcovitz Officiating, Silverman Machzor, No Organ, Cantor Uses Pitch Pipe

>Note: "M" indicates that melody is identified and sheet music is in hand.
>
>"?" indicates that melody has not been identified and sheet music is not in hand.

Worksheet Side 1

>M "Mah tovu" (00:08–01:07)
>Not in Silverman *machzor* for this service, but on page 1 of *machzor*.
>B'nai Israel Choir
>Lewandowski (in *Todah W'simrah*, Part I: Shabbat, Out-of-Print Classics Series of Synagogue Music No. 10, 3)
>(Mah tovu) "Adonai" Betty Sue Stein, beautiful (01:08–01:45)
>Then choir and congregation (01:46–02:37)
>Rabbi Marcovitz petition for personal forgiveness (02:38–04:15)
>Recalls personal history of congregation (04:16–07:25)
>Rabbi Marcovitz introduces "Or Zarua" (350 in B'nai Israel *machzor*)
>? "Or zarua" by Cantor (Psalm 97) (07:30–09:00)
>Repeated three times, perhaps own improvisation.

Pg. 207 M "Kol Nidre" (352 in B'nai Israel *machzor*), *mi Sinai* melody (09:05–13:59)

>1. Choir begins "ah, ah,. . . . ," then Cantor "Kol Nidre" to "u'sh'vuot," then choir; then Cantor to "nafshatana" and beyond to "l'tovah," majestic; choir shares to "sharan." "Sh'vitin" choir; then Cantor "b'telin um'vutalin, lo shririn v'lo kayamin." "Nidrana" choir, then Cantor to "sh'vuot"
>2. Choir, then Cantor (strong voice), alternating with choir (14:05–18:43)
>   More elaborate, but tranquil.
>3. Cantor and choir, very elaborate, confident, beautiful, majestic. (18:44–23:27)
>   High "sh'vuot'" by Cantor Heiser at end.
>   Lewandowski (No. 68 in *Todah W'simrah*, Part II: *Festgesänge*,

Out-of-Print Classics Series of Synagogue Music No. 12, 109), first four measures, then only some of it; also Lewandowski (No. 107 in *Kol Rinnah UT'fillah*, Out-of-Print Classics Series of Synagogue Music No. 9, 79).
[See Sholom Kalib, *The Musical Tradition of the Eastern European Synagogue*. Volume One, Part One. Text. Example 39, 25, and Example 91, 59; and Volume One, Part Two. Music. Example 39, 28, and Example 91, 67.]
Rabbi Marcovitz davens (23:28–23:34)

Pg. 207 M "V'nislach" Cantor, then choir: exact! (23:35–24:35)
Lewandowski, No. 71 in *Todah W'simrah Part II: Festgesänge*, Out-of-Print Classics Series of Synagogue Music No. 12, 121–22. See also Lewandowski, No. 108 in *Kol Rinnah UT'fillah*, iSeries No. 9, 80.

Pg. 207 M "S'lach na," Cantor Heiser (24:36–25:15)
Lewandowski (No. 73 in *Todah W'simrah Part II: Festgesänge*, Out-of-Print Classics Series of Synagogue Music No. 12, 122. See also Lewandowski, No. 109 in *Kol Rinnah UT'fillah*, Out-of-Print Classics Series of Synagogue Music No. 9, 81). Exact!

Pg. 207 M "Vayomer Adonai," three times by choir (25:16–25:48)
See Lewandowski (in *Kol Rinnah UT'fillah*, No. 109, 81, and *Todah W'simrah II: Festgesänge*, No. 73, 122 and 123)

Pg. 207 ? "Shehechianu," Cantor to "olam"; (25:49–28:23)
Betty Sue 2x "Shehechianu," then 3 and 4 by choir, then 5 by Cantor Heiser with improvisation and "v'higianu" in falsetto.

There is a break before the Ma'ariv Service.
Rabbi Marcovitz remarks (29:55–30:34)
Responsive reading of Psalm 130 (359) (30:35–31:14)

Pg. 213 M "Bar'chu" (360) (31:27–32:26)
Cantor inverted *nusach*, choir to "vaed," then Cantor Traditional (Sulzer in Nathanson, ed. *Zamru Lo* III, Congregational Melodies for the Shalosh R'galim and the High Holidays, 110; Lewandowski, in Ephros, ed., *Cantorial Anthology of Traditional and Modern Synagogue Music*, Volume I Rosh Hashonoh, 11, adapted).
Cantor repeats, then davening.

Pg. 213   M "U'ma'avir"—"aravim," Cantor and choir (32:35–33:22)
High Holy Day *nusach* davened, part Lewandowski (No. 111 in *Kol Rinnah UT'fillah*, 81; also No. 76 in *Todah W'simrah II: Festgesänge*, all but "Baruch Ata Adonai" toward end; also, Ephros, ed., *Cantorial Anthology of Traditional and Modern Synagogue Music*, Volume I Rosh Hashonoh, 11).

Pg. 213–14   "Ahavat" (361) (34:03–34:34)
Second benediction before the Shema is led by Rabbi Marcovitz in English together, then Cantor "V'ahavatecha"—"ohev amo Israel," regular melody with High Holy Day *nusach* at end

Pg. 214   M "Shema" (34:35–35:14)
Cantor, choir, and congregation together; then "Baruch Shem K'vod" Cantor and everybody.
Traditional, by Salomon Sulzer (in *Schir Zion, Gesänge für den israelitischen Gottesdienst*, Out-of-Print Classics Series of Synagogue Music No. 6, 150th Jubilee Issue, 45), slightly adjusted.

Pg. 214   "V'ahavta," everybody, regular Torah *trop* (35:15–36:26)

Pg. 215–16   "V'hayah im shamoa," silent to "Adonai Eloheichem Emet" (36:27–37:20)
Sung by Cantor in High Holy Day *nusach*, then choir repeats "Emet" (37:21–37:33)
Rabbi Marcovitz and congregation reading together (37:35–38:42)

Pg. 216   M (Emet v'emunah) "v'rau vanav"—"v'amru chulam" (38:43–39:40)
Cantor and choir in High Holy Day *nusach*
(Lewandowski No. 116 in *Kol Rinnah UT'fillah*, 82–3)

Pg. 216   M "Mi chamochah"—"oseh fele," choir (39:41–40:04)
Lewandowski exactly! (No. 116 in *Kol Rinnah UT'fillah*, 83; also No. 83 in *Todah W'simrah II: Festgesänge*, 126–127; and Ephros, ed., *Cantorial Anthology of Traditional and Modern Synagogue Music*. Volume I Rosh Hashonoh, 14 [but Sulzer!]; Nathanson, ed. *Zamru Lo III, Congregational Melodies for the Shalosh R'galim and the High Holidays*, 110, and Sulzer, in *Schir Zion*, No. 7, 231.)

Pg. 216　M "Malchutecha," Cantor solo (40:05–40:26)
Lewandowski (No. 116 in *Kol Rinnah UT'fillah*, 83, but improvised. Also, Sulzer in Ephros, ed., *Cantorial Anthology of Traditional and Modern Synagogue Music*. Volume I Rosh Hashonoh, 15)

Pg. 216　M "Adonai," choir (40:27–40:38)
Lewandowski exactly! (No. 116 in *Kol Rinnah UT'fillah*, 83. Also, Sulzer in Ephros, ed., *Cantorial Anthology of Traditional and Modern Synagogue Music*. Volume I Rosh Hashonoh, 15.)

Pg. 216　M "V'ne'emar"—"gaal Israel" (40:39–41:22)
Cantor Heiser, supported by choir, embellished.
(Lewandowski, No. 116 in *Kol Rinnah UT'fillah*, 83–84, and Sulzer, in Ephros, ed. *Cantorial Anthology of Traditional and Modern Synagogue Music*. Volume I Rosh Hashonoh, 15.)
Rabbi Marcovitz announces "Hashkivenu" prayer (41:23–41:31)

Pg. 216　M "Hashkivenu" (366) (41:32–42:44)
Betty Sue, "V'hagen"—"umea'chareinu," exact!
(Lewandowski, No. 85 in *Todah W'simrah Part II: Festgesänge*, Out-of-Print Classics Series of Synagogue Music No. 12, 127; also, Ephros, ed. *Cantorial Anthology of Traditional and Modern Synagogue Music*. Volume I Rosh Hashonoh, 22–23.)

Pg. 216　M "U'vzel"—"atah," choir (42:45–43:15)
Lewandowski, exact! (In Ephros, ed., *Cantorial Anthology of Traditional and Modern Synagogue Music*. Volume I Rosh Hashonoh, 23–24; also, *Todah W'simrah Part II: Festgesänge*, 128–129.)

Pg. 216　M "U'sh'mor zetenu" (43:16–44:32)
Choir, then Cantor improvised, then choir to "v'ad olam" (Ephros, ed., *Cantorial Anthology of Traditional and Modern Synagogue Music*. Volume I Rosh Hashonoh, 23–24, also *Todah W'simrah Part II: Festgesänge*, 128–129.)

Pg. 216　"Ufros aleinu," Cantor Heiser improvisation, then High Holy Day *nusach* (44:33–44:59)

Pg. 216　M "Hapores sukkat shalom"—"v'al Yerushalaim" (45:00–45:36)
Choir, then Cantor
Traditional (in Nathanson, ed., *Zamru Lo III, Congregational Melodies for the Shalosh R'galim and the High Holidays,*

111; also, Sulzer, *Schir Zion*, No. 7, 231, and No. 59, "Mi-chomauchoh," in *Liturgisches Liederbuch*, 39).

Pg. 217   ? "Ki vayom" unknown composition; Cantor, then choir (45:37–46:31)

Pg. 217   "Hatzi Kaddish" (46:32–47:08)
High Holy Day *nusach*, incomplete to "u'viz'man kariv"
(Melody No. 59, "Mi-chomauchoh," in *Liturgisches Liederbuch*, 39; also, Nathanson, ed. *Zamru Lo III*, for Shalosh R'galim and High Holidays, 112)
[Tape ends here.]

Yom Kippur Kol Nidre Service Order Worksheet, No Date, Rabbi Richard M. E. Marcovitz Officiating, Silverman Machzor, No Organ, Cantor Uses Pitch Pipe

Worksheet Side 2

(Lost partial repetition of Hatzi Kaddish)

P. 217   Hatzi Kaddish continued from "Yitbarach"—"v'imru Amen" by Cantor Heiser (00:07–01:34)
High Holy Day *nusach*, beautiful!
Silent Amidah (370–383), then long sermon by Rabbi Marcovitz (01:36–25:48)

Pg. 227   M "Ya'aleh" (25:50–27:55)
First choir, then Cantor alternates with Rabbi and congregation, then silent
Composition by Wolfele Schestapol (in Ephros, ed. *Cantorial Anthology of Traditional and Modern Synagogue Music*. Volume II Yom Kippur, 32–36), accurate.
Rabbi Marcovitz announces "L'chu n'ran'nah lAdonai" (28:00–28:06)

Pg. 229   M "L'chu n'ran'nah lAdonai" (last line on page 386 in B'nai Israel *machzor*) (28:07–29:03)
Cantor, then choir exactly
(Max Janowski, "L'Chu n'ran'nah" for Slichot, 3–5)

Pg. 230   M "Zedek umishpat," Cantor Heiser (29:04–30:11)
(Max Janowski, see Slichot, 5–6)

Pg. 230   M "Asher b'yado" (30:12–31:36)
Betty Sue to 30:53, then choir repeats.
(Max Janowski, see Slichot, 6–7)

Pg. 230   ? "Han'shamah lach," first choir, then Cantor Heiser (31:37–34:02)
Very expressive and eloquent.
NOT Janowski. Unidentified.

Pg. 230   ? "L'ma'an shim'cha" (34:03–35:12)
Male soloist, then choir (male vocalist and Klaryne Karsh) to "ki rav hu."
Cantor davens to "zedakah."

          Not Janowski. Unidentified.
          Rabbi Marcovitz and congregation responsive reading
              (35:13–37:01)
          (389–391, Psalm 103)
          Rabbi Marcovitz announces "El erech apaim" (37:02–37:16)

Pg. 235   "El erech apaim," responsively by *Hazzan* and congregation
             (37:18–37:53)
          Cantor davens to "vayikra." (392)

Pg. 235   M "Adonai, Adonai" three times
          1. Betty Sue, slightly adjusted (37:54–38:47)
          2. Choir and congregation (38:48–39:46)
          3. Cantor and Rabbi parallel chanting/reading in Hebrew
              (39:47–41:10)
          Rabbi's reading of Hebrew text is not obvious in this *Machzor*.
          Notated and arranged by Samuel Dubrow (in Nathanson, ed.,
              Zamru Lo III, Congregational Melodies for the Shalosh
              R'galim and High Holidays, 128)
          Cantor davens conclusion of prayer.
          Rabbi Marcovitz introduces *piyyut* (41:11–42:40)

Pg. 235   "Ki hineh kachomer" (394 in B'nai Israel *machzor*), responsively
             (42:41–46:40)
          1. Choir,
          2. Cantor "gallachish" [priest-like],
          3. Choir,
          4. Cantor,
          5. Choir very flowery, not all verses.
          See compositions by Zvi Talmon in T'ruot Hahekhl, 33.
          (Professor Eli Schleifer, HUC Jerusalem, has book.)
          Rabbi Marcovitz announces "El melech yoshev" (46:41–46:50)

Pg. 235   "El melech yoshev" (396 in B'nai Israel *machzor*), Cantor davens
             (46:52–47:15)

[Tape ends here. Remainder of Kol Nidre service is not recorded.]

IV. Guide to Cantor Heiser's Yom Kippur Ne'ilah Service (1978)

Just as there is no recording of the daytime Rosh Hashanah service, there also is no tape of the daytime Yom Kippur service. We do, however, have a fairly extensive section of the *Ne'ilah* service, which ends a day of introspection, prayer, and penitence.

Cantor Heiser chose an all-male choir for the Yom Kippur *Ne'ilah* service, not his beloved mixed choir, thereby reverting to the more observant tradition of separating the sexes, which he encountered in Berlin and England. One of the letters of recommendation from Berlin mentioned that these services were in the Orthodox tradition. His recommendation from the Kitchener Refugee Camp mentioned that he trained a choir from the 3,000 men there. *Ne'ilah* was the only service for which he used an all-male choir in Pittsburgh. This may be one of the oldest services we have, as it dates from 1978, when B'nai Israel began its seventy-fifth year of existence. Another possibility is that he used only a partial choir to save money. The board minutes often contain discussions of the cost of the choir, especially in the later years when the congregation was struggling financially.

Approximately one hour before the sun sets, the race to the finish begins with a few announcements by the Rabbi and a special "Ashrei," followed by the silent Amidah or Standing Prayer. The tape of Cantor Heiser's service begins with the repetition of the Amidah prayer, "**Baruch Atah Adonai**" [YouTube No. 11] (722) [Clip 26] (02:24–11:02 full tape; 00:01–08:37 clip) in the Traditional Eastern European *nusach* (arranged by Baruch Schorr, for the concluding "N'ilo" service, in Ephros, ed., *Cantorial Anthology of Traditional and Modern Synagogue Music*. Volume II Yom Kippur, 299). As it is imperative for most congregations that the service conclude with the setting of the sun, the service is conducted hurriedly. It is obvious that Cantor Heiser has performed this service often, as he is completely at ease rushing through the various prayers with a strong and certain voice. What follows the Schorr arrangement, however, is not precise in any way—"Misod" (with the words of the wise) seems to be based on a Traditional melody in the Baer Collection, arranged by Gershon Ephros (Ephros, ed., *Cantorial Anthology of Traditional and Modern Synagogue Music*. Volume II Yom Kippur, 203); No. 22 "Zach'renu" (Remember us [for life]) by Gershon Ephros can be found in Ephros, ed., *Cantorial Anthology of Traditional and Modern synagogue Music*. Volume I Rosh Hashonoh, 44 (only the word "zach'renu" is used in Ephros melody), and "Melech ozer" (Our King, our Protector), Traditional from the Grauman Collection (also in Ephros, ed., *Cantorial Anthology of Traditional and Modern Synagogue Music*. Volume I Rosh Hashonoh, 45), is heavily adapted. "Atah gibor" (You are mighty) may also be Traditional from the Graumann Collection, and while "M'chalkel chayim b'chesed" (You sustain life with loving kindness) sounds Traditional, I was not able to track it down. Much of this section is davened and improvised by the Cantor and supported by a male choir. In contacting organizations to request permission to use their material, I actually "met" a cantor who had sung with Cantor Heiser on the holidays, also in the all-male *Ne'ilah* choir.

The Kedushah changes the tone of the service, as the Traditional music for the High Holy Days and music composed specifically for *Ne'ilah* and for the High Holy Days is interspersed with Friday night and Shabbat melodies. Cantor Heiser relies on Lewandowski for "Kakatuv" (as it is written) but not entirely (*Todah W'simrah Part II: Festgesänge*, Out-of-Print Classics Series of Synagogue Music No. 12, Volume 2, 179); "Kadosh, kadosh, kadosh" (Holy, holy, holy) (07:53–08:08) is Sulzer's (in *Schir Zion, Gesänge für den israelitischen Gottesdienst*, 150th Jubilee Issue, Out-of-Print Classics Series of Synagogue Music No. 6, Joseph Sulzer, ed., 85, and Nathanson, ed., *Zamru Lo II*, Congregational Melodies and Z'mirot for the entire Sabbath Day, 114); and the "Shema" (08:46–09:05) is Goldfarb's (in Israel Goldfarb and I. H. Levinthal, *Song and Praise for Sabbath Eve*, 9). "V'hayah Adonai" is Goldfarb (in Goldfarb and Levinthal, *Song and Praise for Sabbath Eve*, 56), and "Imloch Adonai l'olam" (10:24–10:40) is Sulzer (in *Shir U'Tefilah Union Songster*, 314, also Nathanson, ed., *Zamru Lo II*, Congregational Melodies and Z'mirot for the entire Sabbath Day, 115, and the *Union Hymnal*, CCAC, 1949, 451). The Cantor concludes the Kedushah by davening "L'dor vador," still in the *Ne'ilah nusach* yet indicating that this service is already moving toward the ordinary.

But not quite. Once more we return to the special mood of the closing of the gates, as the Cantor intones **"P'sach lonu,"** and **"Hayom yifneh," [YouTube No. 12]** [Clip 27] (16:23–20:35 full tape; 00:01–04:12 clip), in *mi Sinai nusach*, arranged by Israel Schorr [son of Baruch Schorr] (in Ephros, ed., *Cantorial Anthology of Traditional and Modern Synagogue Music*. Volume II Yom Kippur, 304), each verse repeated by the male choir.

> O keep open for us Your gate of mercy,
> At the time of the closing of the gate
> Now that the day is waning.
> The day is passing;

The sun is setting;
O let us enter Your gate at last.
O God, we beseech You.

Here Cantor Heiser uses the Ashkenazi pronunciation of Hebrew, which Schorr also uses for the sheet music. Although "Ono El no" (We beseech You, oh God) is part of the same hymn, and the melody is identical to Israel Schorr's until the last part of the verse, this stanza is called Traditional, arranged by David Nowakowsky (1848–1921) in Ephros, ed., *Cantorial Anthology of Traditional and Modern Synagogue Music.* Volume II Yom Kippur, 307.

Forgive, pardon, take pity;
Grant us atonement;
Subdue our sin and iniquity.[133]

Following "Adonai, Adonai," notated and arranged by Samuel Dubrow (in Nathanson, ed., *Zamru Lo III,* Congregational Melodies for the Shalosh R'galim and the High Holidays, 128), we are treated to the **Four Piyyutim [YouTube No. 13]** (734) [Clip 28] (23:25–30:22 full tape; 00:01–08:33 clip) from which only the first few lines have survived. Each has a distinct melody, which is Traditional and arranged by David Nowakowsky (in Ephros, ed., *Cantorial Anthology of Traditional and Modern Synagogue Music.* Volume II Yom Kippur, 311–314). The melodies are complicated and intriguing, different from any other kind of melody. The Cantor sings each one by himself—"Enkas m'sal'decha" (May the prayers of all Your faithful); "Yisroel nosha bAdonoi" (Israel shall be saved by the Lord); "Yach'bienu" (May God shelter us); and "Yash'mienu" (Let us hear ['I have pardoned']) in Ashkenazi pronunciation—and the choir repeats each verse. This series of poems concludes with "Adonai, Adonai" (30:34–33:18), this time not arranged by Samuel Dubrow, but by David Nowakowsky, in a unique melody for *Ne'ilah* (Nos. 10 and 10b in *Schlußgebet für Yom Kippur,* Out-of-Print Classics Series of Synagogue Music No. 23, 12 and 14; see also Ephros, ed., *Cantorial Anthology of Traditional and Modern Synagogue Music.* Volume II Yom Kippur, 314–315), repeated by the choir.

After a congregational reading on 735–737 led by Rabbi Marcovitz, the *Ne'ilah* service concludes with the assurance that God has forgiven us, in Jakob Beimel's humble, yet triumphant melody for "Ki anu amecha" (For we are Your people), No. 2 in Nathanson, ed., *Zamru Lo III,*

Congregational Melodies for the Shalosh R'galim and the High Holidays, 197, a final "Ashamnu" or "Viddui" (Confession) in the Eastern European mode and a communal reading. Cantor Heiser's version of David Nowakowsky's "Atah noten Yad l'foshim" (You help the transgressors) in *Schlußgebet für Yom Kippur*, 25, supported by the choir, is absolutely beautiful, with a moving recitative, "Mah anu meh chayenu" (What are we? What is our life?), concluding with an exquisite final plea "rachem alenu" (have mercy upon us) in *falsetto*, at which point the tape ends.[134]

Missing is the remainder of the Amidah, Avinu Malkenu, Kaddish Shalem, and the sounding of the Shofar, followed by "Next Year in Jerusalem," as well as Havdalah and Ma'ariv.

This service is an interesting mixture. It is Traditional *nusach*, part improvised, part late nineteenth-century Eastern European style. Also traditional on the Jewish religious spectrum is the male choir, and the service is dramatic in its choice of composers—Nowakowsky on the one hand and Goldfarb on the other. One may agree with Professor Eliyahu Schleifer when he notes that in the organization of this service one can see that Cantor Heiser is a master of his craft; his style is both declamatory as well as melodic, and he is very imaginative in his recitatives.[135] The service is also an appropriate conclusion to solemn and uplifting High Holy Days at Congregation B'nai Israel.

Yom Kippur Ne'ilah *Service Order Worksheet, 1978, Tape No. 11, Rabbi Richard M. E. Marcovitz Officiating, Silverman* Machzor, *No Organ*

Note: "M" indicates that melody is identified and sheet music is in hand.

"?" indicates that melody has not been identified and sheet music is not in hand.

Worksheet Side 1

Pg. 448   "Ashrei"

Pg. 451   Silent Amidah
[Tape begins here]
(Ark open for entire service) Remarks by Rabbi Marcovitz (01:05–02:23)

Pg. 459   M "Baruch Atah Adonai"—"b'ahavah" (02:24–03:41)
(722 in B'nai Israel *machzor*)
Cantor and male choir
Traditional, arranged by Baruch Schorr ("N'ilo," concluding service, in Ephros, ed., *Cantorial Anthology of Traditional and Modern Synagogue Music.* Volume II Yom Kippur, 299).

Pg. 459   M "Misod," Cantor and male choir (03:42–04:27)
Traditional, from the Baer Collection, arranged by Gershon Ephros (in Ephros, ed., *Cantorial Anthology of Traditional and Modern Synagogue Music.* Volume II Yom Kippur, 203), not exact.

Pg. 459   M "Zach'renu," Cantor and male choir (04:28–04:49)
G. Ephros (in Ephros, ed., *Cantorial Anthology of Traditional and Modern Synagogue Music.* Volume I Rosh Hashonoh, 44), only the word "zach'renu."

Pg. 459   M "Melech ozer"—"Magen Avraham" (04:50–05:09)
Cantor, then male choir
G. Ephros (in Ephros, ed., *Cantorial Anthology of Traditional and Modern Synagogue Music.* Volume I Rosh Hashonoh, 45), only some of it.

Pg. 460   M "Atah gibor," Cantor and male choir (05:10–05:24)
G. Ephros (in Ephros, ed., *Cantorial Anthology of Traditional and*

Modern Synagogue Music. Volume I Rosh Hashonoh, 45).
Not very close.

Pg. 460   "M'chalkel chayim b'chesed"—"umatzmiach y'shuah" (05:25–06:05)
Cantor and male choir

Pg. 460   "Mi chamochah"—"hametim," Cantor and male choir (06:06–06:50)

Pg. 460   "Imloch Adonai l'olam"—"El na," Cantor davened (06:51–06:59)

Pg. 460   "Shema na s'lach na," Cantor solo (07:00–07:19)

Pg. 460   "U'v'chen ul'cha," Congregation and Cantor davened (07:20–07:32)

Pg. 461   M "Kakatuv"—"v'amar" (07:41–07:52)
Cantor Heiser only, then with choir
Lewandowski (No. 165 in *Todah W'simrah Part II: Festgesänge*, Out-of-Print Classics Series of Synagogue Music No. 12, 179), not totally, end improvised.

Pg. 461   M "Kadosh, kadosh, kadosh," Cantor and male choir (07:53–08:08)
Sulzer (in *Schir Zion*, 150th Jubilee Issue, Out-of-Print Classics Series of Synagogue Music No. 6, 85; also Nathanson, ed., *Zamru Lo II. Congregational Melodies and Z'mirot for the entire Sabbath Day*, 114.)

Pg. 461   "Kvodo," Cantor only, embellished (08:09–08:23)

Pg. 461   M "Baruch kvod Adonai," Cantor and male choir (08:24–08:31)
(In Nathanson, ed., *Zamru Lo II. Congregational Melodies and Z'mirot for the entire Sabbath Day*, 114.) Some adjustment.

Pg. 461   "Mimkomo," Cantor only (08:32–08:45)

Pg. 461   M "Shema Israel" (08:46–09:05)
Cantor, male choir and congregation
Goldfarb (in I. Goldfarb and I. H. Levinthal, *Songs and Praise for Sabbath Eve*, 9).

Pg. 461   "Echad hu Eloheinu," Cantor only (09:06–09:22)

Pg. 461   M "Ani Adonai Eloheichem," Cantor, choir, and congregation (09:23–09:30)

Pg. 462   "Adir adirenu," Cantor only (09:31–09:39)

Pg. 462 M "V'hayah Adonai," Cantor and male choir (09:40–10:18)
(In I. Goldfarb and I. H. Levinthal, *Song and Praise for Sabbath Eve*, 56.)

Pg. 462 "U v'divrei kadshecha," Cantor only (10:19–10:23)

Pg. 462 M "Imloch Adonai l'olam," Cantor and male choir (10:24–10:40)
Sulzer (in *Shir U'Tefilah Union Songster: Songs and Prayers for Jewish Youth*, CCAR, 1960, 314; also, *Union Hymnal*, CCAR, 1949, 451; also, Nathanson, ed., *Zamru Lo II*, Congregational Melodies and Z'mirot for the entire Sabbath Day, 115.)

Pg. 462 "L'dor vador," Cantor only *nusach* (10:44–11:02)

Pg. 462 "Chamol al ma'aseicha," Cantor only (11:03–12:16)

Pg. 462 "Uv'chen ten pach'decha," Cantor, then choir (11:17–11:55)

Pg. 463 "Uv'chen ten kavod," Cantor, then choir (11:56–12:12)

Pg. 463 "Simchah L'arzecha," Cantor Heiser, popular melody (12:13–12:29)

Pg. 463 "Uv'chen: Zaddikim yir'u v'yismachu," Cantor Heiser, popular (12:30–13:00)

Pg. 463 "V'timloch Atah Adonai," Cantor Heiser only *nusach* (13:01–13:16)

Pg. 463 M "Imloch Adonai l'olam," Cantor and male choir (13:17–13:36)
Sulzer (in *Shir U'Tefilah Union Songster: Songs and Prayers for Jewish Youth*, CCAR, 1960, 314; also, Nathanson, ed., *Zamru Lo II*, Congregational Melodies and Z'mirot for the entire Sabbath Day, 115).

Pg. 463 "Kadosh Atah"—"Hamelech Hakadosh" (13:37–14:15)
Cantor High Holy Day *nusach*, then choir and Cantor

Pg. 463 "Atah b'chartanu," Cantor davens only (14:16–14:34)

Pg. 463 "Vatiten lanu"—"zecher b'yitziat mizrayim," Cantor only (14:35–14:53)

Pg. 464 "Eloheinu v'Elohei" (Ya'aleh v'yavo), Cantor only (14:54–15:26)

Pg. 464 "Zach'renu Adonai Eloheinu" (15:27–16:22)
Cantor special melody and choir "Amen"

Pg. 464 M "Petach lanu" (16:23–20:35)
mi Sinai by Cantor, then choir repeats verse

Traditional, arranged by Israel Schorr (see Ephros, ed., *Cantorial Anthology of Traditional and Modern Synagogue Music*. Volume II Yom Kippur, 304). Ashkenazi pronunciation.

Pg. 464 M "Hayom yifneh" Cantor, then choir repeats verse
Traditional, arranged by Israel Schorr (see Ephros, ed., *Cantorial Anthology of Traditional and Modern Synagogue Music*. Volume II Yom Kippur, 304).

Pg. 464 M "Ono El no" Cantor, then choir repeats verse
Traditional, arranged by D. Nowakowsky (in Ephros, ed., *Cantorial Anthology of Traditional and Modern Synagogue Music*. Volume II Yom Kippur, 307).

Pg. 465 "El melech yoshev"—"vayikra," Cantor davens (20:36–21:15)

Pg. 465 M "Adonai, Adonai," Cantor, choir, and congregation (21:16–22:19)
Traditional. Notated and arranged by Samuel Dubrow (in Nathanson, ed. *Zamru Lo III*, Congregational Melodies for the Shalosh R'galim and High Holidays, 128).
Cantor davens to end.
Rabbi Marcovitz explains fragments of four *piyyutim* that will follow (22:21–23:23)

Pg. 469 M "Enkat m'sal'decha" (23:25–24:51)
(734 in B'nai Israel *machzor*) Cantor solo melody, then choir repeats verse
Traditional, arranged by David Nowakowsky (in Ephros, ed., *Cantorial Anthology of Traditional and Modern Synagogue Music*. Volume II Yom Kippur, 311).
Cantor Heiser sings Ashkenazi pronunciation—<u>Enkas, not Enkat.</u>

Pg. 469 M "Israel nosha bAdonai," Cantor solo, then choir repeats verse (24:52–26:44)
Traditional, arranged by D. Nowakowsky (in Ephros, ed., *Cantorial Anthology of Traditional and Modern Synagogue Music*. Volume II Yom Kippur, 311 and 312).

Pg. 469 M "Yach'bienu zel Yado," Cantor solo, then choir repeats verse (26:50–28:27)
Traditional, arranged by D. Nowakowsky (in Ephros, ed., *Cantorial Anthology of Traditional and Modern Synagogue Music*. Volume II Yom Kippur, 312 and 313).

Pg. 469 M "Yash'mienu," Cantor solo, then choir repeats verse
(28:28–30:25)
Traditional, arranged by D. Nowakowsky (in Ephros, ed., *Cantorial Anthology of Traditional and Modern Synagogue Music.* Volume II Yom Kippur, 313 and 314).
Cantor davens to end.

Pg. 470 M "Adonai, Adonai," Cantor solo, then choir repeats
(30:34–33:21)
Traditional, arranged by D. Nowakowsky (in Ephros, ed., *Cantorial Anthology of Traditional and Modern Synagogue Music.* Volume II Yom Kippur, 314 and 315. Also, in D. Nowakowsky, *Schlußgebet für Yom Kippur,* Out-of-Print Classics Series of Synagogue Music No. 23, 12 and 14 [Nos. 10 and 10b respectively] *Ne'ilah* service).
Cantor davens to end.
Rabbi Marcovitz (735–737) responsive reading (33:22–35:35)

Pg. 471 M "Ki anu amecha," No. 2, Cantor and congregation
(35:36–37:33)
Composition by J. Beimel (in Nathanson, ed. *Zamru Lo III,* Congregational Melodies for the Shalosh R'galim and High Holidays, 197).
Cantor davens to end

Pg. 471 "Ashamnu," Cantor and congregation (37:34–39:07)
Eastern European
Cantor davens to end.
Rabbi Marcovitz leads congregational reading (39:08–42:20)
(741 in B'nai Israel machzor)

Pg. 472 M "Atah noten Yad l'foshim," Cantor solo, later choir (42:25–45:43)
(In D. Nowakowsky, *Schlußgebet für Yom Kippur,* Out-of-Print Classics Series of Music No. 23, 25), but Cantor Heiser's version, with exquisite recitative "Mah anu, meh chayenu" (What are we? What is our life?), supported by choir.

Pg. 472 "Atah hiv'dalta enosh" (45:44–47:06)
Cantor solo, very expressive; then with choir; then Cantor to "rachem aleinu" in beautiful falsetto
[See Kalib, *The Musical Tradition of the Eastern European Synagogue.* Volume One. Part One. Text. Ex. 119 g, 117; and Volume One. Part Two. Music. Ex. 119 g, 117.]

[Tape ends here.]

Not recorded are "Modim anachnu lach," 473–474; "Sim Shalom" and "B'sefer chayim," 475; "Avinu Malkenu," 476; "Kaddish Shalem," and concluding prayers, as well as Ma'ariv service, Havdalah, and blowing of Shofar, 478ff in Silverman *Machzor*.

V. Guide to Cantor Heiser's Shavuot Festival Services (1979)

There are no recordings of Passover or Sukkot, although there is a cassette tape, poor in technical quality, of the songs at the end of the Passover *seder*, a very popular event at B'nai Israel. There are, however, several fragments from a Shavuot service—Hallel, Torah service, chanting of the Torah and Haftarah, return of the Torah service, and Musaf service—all from 1979. It is easy to understand why—1978–1979/5738–5739 was the seventy-fifth anniversary of Congregation B'nai Israel, and for a number of years Confirmation at B'nai Israel took place on Shavuot. There is also a 1980 Shavuot Musaf service because it was the year of Shari Stein's Confirmation, and a 1983 Yizkor (Memorial) service with Hugo Chaim Adler's "El Mahle Rachamim," Cantor Heiser's signature prayer.

During the *haggim* (festivals), the congregation swayed like poppies in a field of grain while the gentle breeze of the choir, accentuated by periodic heart-rending solos by Canter Heiser's granddaughter Betty Sue Stein or the choir director, Claryne Karsh, rang out from the balcony, or duets by Cantor and either soloist engulfing the entire congregation in a powerful communal prayer experience. There was no question in anyone's mind that God was listening.

The Hallel [V (a) 1979] begins with a cheerful but unidentified "Halleluyah" composition by choir and organ and a welcome to the Confirmation class of 5739/1979, in the seventy-fifth year of B'nai Israel, by Rabbi Richard M. E. Marcovitz. Cantor Heiser leads the Hallel prayer, supported by the choir. Until "Pitchu li" most of the liturgy is davened by the Cantor, causing Professor Schleifer to comment that Cantor Heiser's style here is "gallachish," like a priest in a church.[136] This monotony is interrupted by an English reading, followed by "Nedarai LAdonai" (09:51–10:21) to a tune that resembles some of Zvi Talmon's "Nedarai LAdonai" in *Pa'amey Hahechal*, Compositions for Cantor and Choir, as sung at Hechal Shlomo, Jerusalem.[137] After some more davening by the Cantor and an English reading of Psalm 118, choir and organ pick up with "Pis'chu li" (Open to me [the gates of the righteous]) [Clip 29] (12:36–16:45 part I, side 1, full tape; 00:01–05:22 clip, not on YouTube) by Sholom Secunda for Mixed Voices with piano accompaniment. Copyrighted in 1951, this music is composed in the popular styles of Israel at the time; it was printed by Mills Music, Inc. in New York. Sholom Secunda was one of Cantor Heiser's favorite contemporary composers, whose compositions he enjoyed performing, especially at concerts. Betty Sue, who was all of ten, gets the congregation's attention as she chimes in with a very sweet but sophisticated "Od'cha" (I will give thanks to You), "Even Ma'asu habonim" (The stone which the builders rejected), and "Me'et Adonai" (By the Grace of God) (13:11–15:32), all by Secunda, each time repeated by the choir. The choir concludes this section with "Zeh hayom asah Adonai" (This is the day the Lord has made) (15:30–16:45), also by Secunda, followed, after some more davening, by a very upbeat "Kaddish Shalem" [Clip 30] (18:01–19:24 part I, side 1, full tape; 00:01–01:26 clip, not on YouTube) in Shabbat *nusach* by Cantor and choir.

The **Torah service [YouTube No. 14]** [Clip 31] (19:39–34:05 part II, side 1, full tape; 00:01–09:32 clip) [V (b) 1979] on the Shalosh Regalim consisted of compositions by Avraham Dunajewski, Salomon Sulzer, Louis Lewandowski, and Samuel Naumbourg. It was a very "sunny" service—festive, lighthearted, and cheerful. Although the technical quality of the recording we have is somewhat uneven in sound, I am nevertheless including clips from it as an example of the wonderful collaboration between Cantor and choir. The service begins with the choir singing Dunajewski's "Ein kamocha" (There is none like You) (19:39–23:34) in Ephros, ed., *Cantorial Anthology of Traditional and Modern Synagogue Music*. Volume III Sholosh R'golim, 243–46, followed by three fine soprano solos, "Av harachamim" (Father of Mercy) (21:03–21:42),[138] "Tivneh chomot" (Who will rebuild the walls [of Jerusalem]) (21:43–22:21), and "Ki v'cha" (In You alone) (22:22–23:34), each repeated by the choir (Ephros, ed., *Cantorial Anthology of Traditional and Modern Synagogue Music*. Volume III Sholosh R'golim, 247–49).[139] These are followed by Louis Lewandowski's "Vayihi binsoa haaron" (When the Ark moved forward) (23:35–24:03) in *Todah W'simrah Part II: Festgesänge*, Vol. 1, Series No. 11, 24, sung soulfully by the Cantor, then organ and choir. Dignified and joyful, this section is the heart of the Torah service. "For out of Zion goes the Torah" (Ki mi Zion teze Torah) (24:25–24:59) never sounded more promising. In the sheet music, Lewandowski instructs the choir director that the choir should sing this repeatedly, first pianissimo, then piano, and finally forte while the Torah scrolls are taken from the Ark.[140] In this version of the Torah service, it is only sung once. God's Thirteen Attributes, "Adonai, Adonai" (25:39–29:15) are sung by the Cantor to Samuel Naumbourg's artful melody (in Ephros, ed., *Cantorial Anthology of Traditional and Modern Synagogue Music*. Volume I Rosh Hashonoh, 12–13), repeated by the choir and accompanied by the organ. The first repetition is spoken in English by the Rabbi, with the second again chanted by the Cantor, then choir and organ. A nearly inaudible English reading follows before the scroll is taken from the Ark.

Lewandowski reigns for the "Shema," "Echad Eloheinu," "Gadlu lAdonai," and "L'cha Adonai" (30:44–34:05) with beloved melodies by Cantor and choir (in *Todah W'simrah Part II: Festgesänge*, Out-of-Print Classics Series of Synagogue Music No. 11, Volume 1, 57–58, also in Ephros, ed., *Cantorial Anthology of Traditional and Modern Synagogue Music*. Volume III Sholosh R'golim, 266–271).

Shavuot is the only time of the year when we chant the piyyut "**Akdamut**" [YouTube No. 15] [Clip 32] (38:29–42:15 side one, full tape; 00:01–05:14 clip; actually recorded on Tape No. 6 Shavuot 1980, Side One, 11:19–16:35) [V (b) 1979, also V (e) 1980] as an introduction to the chanting of the Ten Commandments.[141] To Kalib's thinking, "Akdamut and its melody serve as the conceptual as well as musical *leitmotif* of the Festival of Shavuot."[142] I will here give a flavor of the poem by including ten lines from the Artscroll translation.

> In introduction to the Words [Ten Commandments],
> and commencement of my speech,
> I begin by taking authorization and permission.
> In two and three sections, I shall commence with trembling,
> With permission from Him Who created everything and shields it
>   till its hoary age.
> His is eternal strength that could not be described –
> Even if the heavens were parchment, and the forests quills,
> If the earth's inhabitants were scribes and recorders of initials –
> The glory of the Master of heaven and the Ruler of earth.
> In isolation He established the earth and controlled [its expansion]
>   with constraints,
> He perfected it without fatigue and without weariness,
> And with a letter, slight and lacking substance.
> [. . . .][143]

Cantor Heiser thoroughly enjoyed chanting a large section of "Akdamut." The *piyyut* is in Aramaic and the melody is *mi Sinai nusach*. At B'nai Israel the *piyyut* is chanted responsively by Cantor and Rabbi and congregation.

After the completion of the Torah reading and the chanting of the Haftarah, the **Return of the Torah service** [YouTube No. 16] [Clip 33] (30:10–36:13 side two, full tape; 00:01–06:06 clip) [V (c) 1979 and V (f) 1980] begins with an improvisation on Salomon Sulzer's "Yehallelu" (Let them praise) (30:10–30:27) by the Cantor, followed by the choir's rendition of Sulzer's "Hodo al Eretz" (His Glory is above the earth) (30:28–31:12) in *Schir Zion*, 150th Jubilee Issue, Out-of-Print Classics Series No. 6, 104, also Ephros, ed., *Cantorial Anthology of Traditional and Modern Synagogue Music.* Volume III Sholosh R'golim, 275.[144] This hymn is immediately followed by the choir's popular version of Naumbourg's "S'u shearim" (Lift up your heads, you gates) in *Z'mirot Israel: Chants Religieux des Israelites*, Out-of-Print Classics Series of Synagogue Music No. 14, 195, also Ephros, ed., *Cantorial Anthology of Traditional and Modern Synagogue Music.* Volume III Sholosh R'golim, 276–281, carried by the choir's soprano. It is melodies like these that gave Naumbourg the reputation of transforming entertainment and operatic tunes into sacred melodies. Kalib notes that to Naumbourg, "this music effectively expressed and projected the spirit of the text."[145] The Torah service concludes with a lovely "Ki lekach tov" (Because I gave you good [things]) (34:15–35:03) by a young Betty Sue wishing the congregation "Shalom," followed by a solemn "Hashivenu" (Turn us) (35:04–36:13) by the choir, both by Lewandowski (in *Todah W'simrah, Part I: Shabbat*, Out-of-Print Classics Series No. 10, 128–29). Presentations by the confirmands about the meaning of the synagogue through the ages follow.

The memorial service occurs in the Jewish community during four services annually—Passover, Shavuot, Sukkot, and Yom Kippur. It is a short but solemn service, usually before the return of the Torah scrolls to the Ark. The rabbi often takes the opportunity for a longish sermon before beginning the memorial service, rather than after the return of the Torah, which is a more usual spot for the sermon—no doubt because the turnout is the largest at that point. Even members who do not come to services often, or stay for an entire service, will come to honor their departed loved ones. Most congregations have Memorial Booklets with the text for the various prayers and the names of congregants' family members. B'nai Israel used such a booklet, which I do not have, but we do have a brief snippet of one of Cantor Heiser's memorial services from 1983 [V (g)].

This particular *hazkarah* seems to have taken place after the Musaf service; it was the final section of this particular festival service and began with an introduction by Rabbi Marcovitz and the hymn "Shviti Adonai" (I have set the Lord [always before me]) in the booklet by the B'nai Israel choir. The Rabbi then introduces the various prayers in memory of a father, mother, husband, wife, son, daughter, or other relatives and friends, and Jewish martyrs, which are recited silently by each congregant individually. Rabbi and congregation (4) read Psalm 1 out loud, followed by another reading by the Rabbi (7), and a responsive reading on 9. Then individual memorial plaques in memory of a loved one are dedicated by congregants; the Rabbi announces the names and who is donating the memorial plaques. At the conclusion of this ceremony, the congregation rises for the individual recitation of *Yizkor* prayers for father, mother, other family and friends, which concludes with the remembering of Israel's martyrs, read by the Rabbi.

Following the individual *Yizkor* prayers, the congregation rises for the chanting of the **El Male Rachamim** prayer [YouTube No. 17] [Clip 34] (14:05–18:06 full tape; 00:01–04:04 clip), or Eyl Moleh Rachamim, as Hugo Chaim Adler spells it (Transcontinental Music Publications, New York, 1965), chanted by *Hazzan* Heiser, accompanied by the organ, and supported very gently by the choir. "May their resting place be in the Garden of Eden—therefore may the Master of mercy shelter them in the shelter of His wings for eternity."[146] Cantor Heiser sweetly guides the mourner's soul to the comforting thought that their loved ones' souls will be bound up in the bonds of eternal life—a consolation to those who are left behind. The prayer concludes with a second consolation when choir and Cantor ask the congregation to join in with a soothing and uplifting "Amen." In addition to praising God and pleading with God, Cantor Heiser was at his best in comforting his congregants, and he became not only Congregation B'nai Israel's favorite clergy to precent at this service, but much of Pittsburgh's. For a number of years, hardly any community or city-wide event requiring "El Male Rachamim" took place without Cantor Heiser's soulful rendition of this prayer.

The service, on the second day of Shavuot, which is the seventh day of Sivan, continues with the Rabbi's mentioning the names of those who died during the past year, leading into a communal recitation of Psalm 23, "The Lord is my Shepherd," led by the Rabbi, followed by a communal Kaddish.

The entire worship service concludes with the hymn, "Adon Olam" (Master of the Universe) [Clip 36] (20:50–22:55 full tape; 00:01–02:04 clip, not on YouTube) sung by the choir to Sulzer's melody for festivals (in *Schir Zion*, 150th Jubilee Issue, Out-of-Print Classics Series No. 6, 57). After a final blessing, the Rabbi dismisses the congregation with a "Hag Sameach and Good Yom Tov!" followed by an organ afterplay as the congregants leave the sanctuary.

To return to what was the traditional order of the service at B'nai Israel, we will now continue with a discussion of the Musaf service [V (d) 1980]. As previously mentioned, at B'nai Israel, Confirmation often took place on

Shavuot. Shavuot 1980/5741 was the year of Cantor Heiser's oldest granddaughter Shari Stein's Confirmation, which is why a family member taped the service. Shari chanted the brachot before and after the Maftir portion and the Haftarah on that day.

Following the return of the Torahs to the Ark, the **Musaf service 1980 [YouTube No. 18]** [Clip 35] (30:14–41:44 full tape; 00:01–12:02 clip) begins with a new tape [V (d) 1980]. Cantor Heiser chants the Hatzi Kaddish in Shabbat *nusach*, accompanied by the choir. He makes a mistake, but quickly catches his error and precedes without any hesitation. The Amidah prayer (31:13–32:30) is also chanted in regular Shabbat *nusach*, by Cantor and choir. He breezes through the prayer fairly quickly, as he has chanted this for only about sixty years, lingering only on "Somech noflim" (32:31–33:20) by Lewandowski (in *Todah W'simrah Part I: Shabbat*, Out-of-Print Classics Series of Synagogue Music No. 10, 142).

The Musaf Kedushah is Cantor Heiser's creation. For it, he chose or adapted melodies that he probably knew already in Germany. When listening to the interplay between choir and Cantor, or Cantor and soloist, one notices a familiarity and level of comfort with each other and with the music that results in a harmonious and easy give and take throughout. All elements available are featured—choir and soloists. One gets the sense of being witness to the creation of a great work of art. The choir begins the Musaf Kedushah with "Na'arizecha" (33:30–34:38). The first three notes are from Nathanson (in Nathanson, ed., *Zamru Lo II*, Congregational Melodies and Z'mirot for the entire Shabbat Day, 107). "Kakatuv" ever so briefly uses Lewandowski's festival melody (in *Todah W'simrah Part II: Festgesänge*, Out-of-Print Classics Series of Synagogue Music No. 12, Volume 2, 179), and then climaxes in "Kadosh, kadosh, kadosh" (34:39–35:00) to Sulzer (in *Schir Zion*, 150th Jubilee Issue, Out-of-Print Classics Series of Synagogue Music No. 6, 85). This sets the stage for a most soulful, though unidentified duet between Cantor Heiser and Claryne Karsh, tenor and alto, fully convincing those who listen that indeed "God's Glory pervades the universe." The full choir confirms that we are to praise God's Glory in God's heavenly abode, leaning ever so slightly on Sulzer (No. 81 in *Schir Zion*, No. 6, 85).

If Cantor Heiser and Claryne Karsh opened the hearts of the congregants, Betty Sue, in what follows, creates a fine ethereality with her sweet, though unidentified rendition of "Mimkomo" (From God's heavenly abode may God turn in Mercy and bestow Grace unto the people who, reciting the Shema evening and morning, twice daily, proclaim in love the unity of God's name) (36:35–37:40).[147] And the entire choir, as well as the congregation, chime in to attest, "Hear, oh Israel, the Lord our God, the Lord is One" (37:41–38:08), by Israel Goldfarb (in I. Goldfarb and I. H. Levinthal, *Song and Praise for Sabbath Eve*, 9. The Cantor then davens, "He is our God," which God confirms through Betty Sue's innocent voice, "Ani Adonai Eloheichem," also in the Sulzer mode. This is again emphasized by Betty Sue with a composition whose beginning seems to be based on Baruch Schorr's 1906 work, published in *N'Ginoth Baruch Schorr*—"Adir Adirenu" (You are our Almighty God) (38:43–39:07). The rest is not identified. This conviction, that the Lord is Israel's Almighty God, is affirmed by the choir's joyful confirmation, "V'hayah Adonai" (The Lord shall be [Sovereign over all the earth]), to Israel Goldfarb's Traditional melody (in Goldfarb and Levinthal, *Song and Praise for Sabbath Eve*, 56). Cantor and choir confirm that "The Lord shall reign forever"—"Imloch Adonai l'olam" to Sulzer (in *Shir UT'fillah Union Songster*, 314). The Festival Musaf Kedushah concludes with an exquisite duet between Cantor Heiser and his granddaughter, "L'dor vador" (Unto all generations [we shall declare Your greatness]), to an unknown composition. The Cantor (40:25–42:14) concludes this truly holy exchange with a final expression of gratitude, "Blessed are You, oh Lord, the holy God"—"Baruch Atah Adonai, haEl haKadosh," in festival *nusach*.

After the silent Amidah, the tape ends with a spirited Kaddish Shalem by the Cantor in Shabbat *nusach*, supported by the choir and organ.

The festival services, more than any other, were spiritual comfort food for the congregants of B'nai Israel; they affected the congregation like rich chicken soup—comforting and enjoyable. One may also notice that on festivals there is less improvisation by the Cantor and a heavier participation by the choir or soloists than on the High Holy Days. The service flows, almost by itself, even though these services only happen three times a year. And the large attendance on the festivals in the later years, even when it was not Confirmation, would be any twenty-first-century Conservative synagogue's envy.

V (a) Shavuot Hallel Service Order Worksheet, 1979, Tape No. 17, Side 1, Part One, Rabbi M. E. Marcovitz Officiating, Silverman Siddur, Confirmation Class of 5739, 75th Year of B'nai Israel, with Organ

Note: "M" indicates that melody is identified and sheet music is in hand.

"?" indicates that melody has not been identified and sheet music is not in hand.

Worksheet Side 1, Part One

(No page number) "Halleluyah," unidentified composition by choir and organ (00:23–02:07)

Rabbi Marcovitz welcomes the confirmation class of 5739/1979 (02:18–03:14)

Pg. 110 Hallel (Psalms 113–118)

M "Baruch Atah Adonai," Cantor solo, then choir "Amen" (03:16–04:35)

Pg. 110 "Halleluyah," silent, then Cantor only "Hamashpili lirot" (04:42–05:25)

Pg. 111 "Mah lecha hayam," Cantor davens (05:35–06:18)

Pg. 111 Psalm 115:1–11 in English by Rabbi and congregation (06:38–07:38)

Last line davened by Cantor Heiser

Pg. 112 "B'ruchim atem lAdonai," Cantor solo (07:48–08:39)

Bottom silent, Cantor last two lines, starting with "he'emanti" (08:54–09:17)

Pg. 113 "Ana Adonai ki ani av'decha," Cantor only, improvised (09:18–09:38)

Pg. 113 "L'cha ez'bach," Cantor only, davened (09:39–09:50)

Pg. 113 "Nedarai LAdonai"—"halleluyah" (09:51–10:21)

Composition by Cantor Zvi Talmon, Hechal Shlomo (in *Pa'amey Hahechal*, Jerusalem, 1992, in part only and an earlier version).

Pg. 113 "Ki gavar aleinu," Cantor only composition (10:22–10:37)

Pg. 113 "Hodu LAdonai ki tov," Cantor only composition (10:38–11:00)

Pg. 114 "Min hametzar," Cantor only improvisation (11:01–11:10)

Pg. 114 English Psalm 118 (11:12–12:35)
Rabbi Marcovitz responsive with congregation

Pg. 114 M "Pitchu li sha'arei Zedek," composition organ and choir (12:36–13:10)
Sholom Secunda, "Pis'chu Li", for Mixed Voices (Mills Music Inc., New York, 1951), popular style of Israel.

Pg. 115 M "Od'cha ki anitani" (13:11–14:06)
Betty Sue, age 10; then choir repeats (Secunda, 1951, 3)

Pg. 115 M "Even ma'asu habonim" (14:07–14:36)
Betty Sue; then choir repeats (Secunda, 1951, 5)

Pg. 115 M "Me'et Adonai haitah zot" (14:39–15:32)
Betty Sue; then choir repeats (Secunda, 1951, 5)

Pg. 115 M "Zeh hayom asah Adonai," Choir (15:33–16:45)
(Secunda, 1951, 7–8)

Pg. 115 "Ana Adonai," Cantor, then davened (16:48–17:19)

Pg. 115 M "Ki lekach tov," Cantor davens, then choir (17:22–18:00)
Lewandowski (in *Todah W'simrah, Part I: Shabbat*, Out-of-Print Classics Series of Synagogue Music No. 10, 128)

Pg. 116 "Kaddish," Cantor and choir (18:01–19:24)
Shabbat *nusach, very upbeat*

Pg. 117 Rabbi Marcovitz announces Torah service on 117 (19:25–19:37)
(End of Tape 17, Side 1, Part One)

V (b) Shavuot Torah Service, Torah and Haftarah Readings, Return of Torah Service Order Worksheet, 1979, Tape No. 17, Side 1, Part Two, Rabbi Richard M. E. Marcovitz Officiating, Silverman Siddur, 75th Year of B'nai Israel, with Organ

>Note: "M" indicates that melody is identified and sheet music is in hand.
>
>"?" indicates that melody has not been identified and sheet music is not in hand.

Worksheet Side 1, Part Two

Torah service

Pg. 117   M "Ein kamocha," choir to "bashalom" (19:39–21:02)
Avraham Dunajewski (in G. Ephros, ed., *Cantorial Anthology of Traditional and Modern Synagogue Music*. Volume III Sholosh R'golim, 243–46).

Pg. 117   M (Ein kamocha) "Av harachamim"—"et Zion" (21:03–21:42)
Female soloist (soprano), then choir
Avraham Dunajewski (in Ephros, ed., *Cantorial Anthology of Traditional and Modern Synagogue Music*, Volume III Sholosh R'golim, 247).
[Sholom Kalib, *The Musical Tradition of the Eastern European Synagogue*, Volume One, Part One. Text. Example 164c, 198; and Volume One, Part Two. Music. Example 164c, 194].

Pg. 117   M (Ein kamocha) "Tivneh chomot Yerushalaim" (21:43–22:21)
Female soloist (soprano), then choir
Avaraham Dunajewski (in Ephros, ed., *Cantorial Anthology of Traditional and Modern Synagogue Music*. Volume III Sholosh R'golim, 247).

Pg. 117   M (Ein kamocha) "Ki v'cha l'vad" (22:22–23:34)
Female soloist (soprano), then choir
Avraham Dunajewski (in Ephros, ed., *Cantorial Anthology of Traditional and Modern Synagogue Music*. Volume III Sholosh R'golim, 248–49).

Pg. 117   M "Vayihi binsoa," Cantor and organ, then choir (23:35–24:03)
Louis Lewandowski (in *Todah W'simrah Part II: Festgesänge,*

Volume 1, Out-of-Print Classics Series of Synagogue Music No. 11, 24).

Pg. 117 M (Vayihi binsoa) "Kumah Adonai, v'yafuzu oyvecha" (24:04–24:24)
Female vocalist, choir, and organ
Lewandowski (in *Todah W'simrah*, Part II for Festivals, Volume 1, Out-of-Print Classics Series of Synagogue Music No. 11, 24).

Pg. 117 M (Vayihi binsoa) "Ki mi Zion" (24:25–24:59)
Female vocalist, choir, and organ
Lewandowski (in *Todah W'simrah*, Part II: *Festgesänge*, Volume 1, Out-of-Print Classics Series of Synagogue Music No. 11, 25).
[See Kalib, *The Musical Tradition of the Eastern European Synagogue*. Volume One. Part One. Text. Ex. 99e, 71 and 198; and Volume One. Part Two. Music. Ex. 99e, 81.]

Pg. 117 M "Baruch shenatan"—Same melody as "Ki mi Zion" (25:00–25:38)
Female vocalist, choir, and organ
Lewandowski (in *Todah W'simrah*, Part II for Festivals, Volume 1, Out-of-Print Classics Series of Synagogue Music No. 11, 25).

Pg. 118 M "Adonai, Adonai," No. 1, three times (25:39–29:10)
1. Cantor, choir, and organ (25:29–27:15)
(Not very loud because Cantor is facing toward the Holy Ark)
Naumbourg (in Ephros, ed., *Cantorial Anthology of Traditional and Modern Synagogue Music*. Volume I Rosh Hashonoh, 12–13).
2. Rabbi Marcovitz in English (27:16–27:34)
3. Cantor (not very loud) and choir, also organ (27:35–29:10)
Reading before the Ark by student (not very loud) (29:12–30:20)

Pg. 123 M "Shema Israel," Cantor with organ, then choir repeats (30:44–31:28)
Lewandowski (in *Todah W'simrah* Part II: *Festgesänge*, Volume 1, Out-of-Print Classics Series of Synagogue Music No. 11, 57 and 58; also No. 58 in *Todah W'simrah* Part I: *Shabbat*, Out-of-Print Classics Series of Synagogue Music No. 10, 115, and

Ephros, ed. *Cantorial Anthology of Traditional and Modern Synagogue Music.* Volume III Sholosh R'golim, 266).

Pg. 123 M "Echad Eloheinu," Cantor, then choir repeats (31:31–32:13)
Lewandowski (in *Todah W'simrah Part II: Festgesänge*, Volume 1, Out-of-Print Classics Series of Synagogue Music No. 11, 57 and 58; also No. 59 in *Todah W'simrah Part I: Shabbat*, Out-of-Print Classics Series No. 10, 115, and in Ephros, ed., *Cantorial Anthology of Traditional and Modern Synagogue Music.* Volume III Sholosh R'golim, 266).

Pg. 123 M "Gadlu lAdonai," Cantor and organ, end adjusted (32:14–32:36)
Lewandowski (in *Todah W'simrah Part II: Festgesänge*, Volume 1, Out-of-Print Classics Series of Synagogue Music No. 11, 57; also in Ephros, ed. *Cantorial Anthology of Traditional and Modern Synagogue Music.* Volume III Sholosh R'golim, 267).

Pg. 123 M "L'cha Adonai hag'dulah," choir and organ (32:37–34:05)
Lewandowski (in *Todah W'simrah Part II: Festgesänge*, Volume 1, Out-of-Print Classics Series of Synagogue Music No. 11, 58 and 59; also in Ephros, ed., *Cantorial Anthology of Traditional and Modern Synagogue Music.* Volume III Sholosh R'golim, 267–271), exact!
"Misheberach," Prayer for the sick by Rabbi Marcovitz (34:13–35:29)
Student gives drash (remarks) on Torah reading (35:30–37:08)
Rabbi Marcovitz explains "Akdamut" piyyut (37:09–38:20)
About the Greatness of God

Pg. 185–186 Student chants two pages of "Akdamut" responsively to *mi Sinai* tune with Rabbi and congregation (38:29–42:15)
Cantor Heiser calls up five students to read five aliyot (42:37–46:40)
Torah portion is Exodus 19:1–20:22.
First *aliyah* (19:1–6), then 2nd *aliyah* (19:7–13) for a bride and groom; beautiful blessing by *Hazzan*
There are three more *aliyot* on Side Two of Tape No. 17.
Torah reading is on p. 50 of Festival reading book.

[End of Tape No. 17, Side 1, Part Two].

V (c) Shavuot Return of Torah Service Order Worksheet, 1979, Tape 17, Side 2, Part One, Rabbi Richard M. E. Marcovitz Officiating, Silverman Siddur

Starts with Rabbi blessing couple before second *aliyah*, and Torah readings 3. (Ex. 19:14–19), 4. (Ten Commandments: Ex. 19:20–20:13), and 5. (Ex. 20:14–22).

Tape interrupts during fifth *aliyah*; someone speaks. Maftir is lost.

> Note: "M" indicates that melody is identified and sheet music is in hand.
> "?" indicates that melody has not been identified and sheet music is not in hand.

Worksheet Side 2, Part 1

Haftarah for Shavuot Day 1, Ezekiel 1:1–28, 3:12 (12:16–23:40)
    Shared by several students

Responsive reading by student and congregation (23:59–25:27)

Youngsters sing a Hebrew song, "Avinu she bashamayim" (25:35–26:48)

P. 130   Prayer for our country by student (26:56–27:44)

P. 132   "Ashrei" in English responsively (27:45–29:46)

    Return of Torah Service

Pg. 133   M "Yehallelu," Cantor Heiser, choir, and organ (30:10–30:27)
        Beginning improvised, then Sulzer (Ephros, ed., *Cantorial Anthology of Traditional and Modern Synagogue Melodies*. Volume III Sholosh R'golim, 275).

Pg. 133   M "Hodo al Eretz," Choir with organ (30:28–31:12)
        Sulzer (in *Schir Zion*, 150th Jubilee Issue, Out-of-Print Classics Series No. 6, 104; Ephros, ed., *Cantorial Anthology of Traditional and Modern Synagogue Music*. Volume III Sholosh R'golim, 275), is close interpretation.
        [See Sholom Kalib, *The Musical Tradition of the Eastern European Synagogue*. Volume One. Part One. Text. Example 99f, 72 and 198; and Volume One. Part Two. Music. Example 99f, 81–82.]

Pg. 135 M "S'u shearim," Choir, soprano solo, and organ (31:13–34:02)
 Naumbourg (in *Z'mirot Israel: Chants Religieux des Israelites*, Out-of-Print Classics Series No. 14, 195; also Ephros, ed., *Cantorial Anthology of Traditional and Modern Synagogue Music*. Volume III Sholosh R'golim, 276–81).
 [See Sholom Kalib, *The Musical Tradition of the Eastern European Synagogue*, Volume One. Part One. Text. Example 100, 76–77; and Volume One, Part Two. Music. Example 100, 82.]

Pg. 136 "Uv'nuchah yomar," Cantor davens (34:03–34:14)

Pg. 136 M "Ki lekach tov," Betty Sue, age 10, with organ (34:16–35:03)
 Lewandowski (No. 76 in *Todah W'simrah I: Shabbat*, Out-of-Print Classics Series of Synagogue Music No. 10, 128).

Pg. 136 M "Hashivenu," Choir, soprano solo, and organ (35:04–36:13)
 Lewandowski (No. 76 in *Todah W'simrah I: Shabbat*, Out-of-Print Classics Series of Synagogue Music No. 10, 129).

Speeches by students (36:19–46:39)

[End of Tape 17, Side 2, Part One].

V (d) Shavuot Festival Musaf Service Order Worksheet, 1980, Tape No. 18, Rabbi Richard M. E. Marcovitz Officiating, Silverman Siddur, with Organ, Shari Stein Confirmation

>Note: "M" indicates that melody is identified and sheet music is in hand.
>
>"?" indicates that melody has not been identified and sheet music is not in hand.

Worksheet Side 1

Rabbi Richard M. E. Marcovitz remarks before Musaf service (29:18–30:12)

Pg. 146 "Hatzi Kaddish," Organ and Cantor (30:14–31:12)
(Cantor makes a mistake, but corrects himself.)
Traditional, very upbeat, with choir.

Pg. 147 "Musaf Amidah"—"Baruch Atah Adonai" (31:13–32:30)
Cantor, supported by choir and organ

Pg. 147 "M'chalkel," Cantor davens (32:22–33:30)

Pg. 147 M "Somech noflim," Cantor Heiser and choir (32:31–33:20)
Lewandowski (No. 80 in *Todah W'simrah, Part I: Shabbat*, Out-of-Print Classics Series of Synagogue Music No. 10, 142), only small piece and not precise, mostly Cantor davened.

Pg. 147 "V'ne'eman," Cantor and choir (32:55–33:21)

Pg. 148 M Musaf Kedushah, "Na'arizecha," Organ and choir (33:30–34:38)
(Nathanson, ed., *Zamru Lo II*, Congregational Melodies for the Shalosh R'galim and for the High Holidays, 107, first line only.)

Pg. 148 M "Kakatuv," Cantor Heiser and choir with organ
Lewandowski (in *Todah W'simrah Part II: Festgesänge*, Out-of-Print Classics Series No. 12, Volume 2, 179, first line).

Pg. 148 M "Kadosh, kadosh, kadosh," Cantor and choir (34:39–35:03)
Sulzer (in *Schir Zion*, 150th Jubilee Issue, Out-of-Print Classics Series No. 6, 85).

Pg. 148 ? "K'vodo" (35:04–36:23)
Cantor and Claryne Karsh (duet), with organ, then choir, not

identified, beautiful and moving, high and powerful "kvodo" by Cantor Heiser.

Pg. 148 M "Baruch k'vod Adonai," Choir (36:24–36:34)
Sulzer (in *Schir Zion*, 85), adapted.

Pg. 148 ? "Mimkomo" (36:35–37:40)
Betty Sue and organ, not identified, beautiful.

Pg. 148 M "Shema Israel," Everyone (37:41–38:08)
Israel Goldfarb (in I. Goldfarb and I. H. Levinthal, *Song and Praise for Sabbath Eve*, 9).

Pg. 148 "Hu Eloheinu," Cantor only (38:09–38:32)

Pg. 148 "Ani Adonai Eloheichem," Choir and organ (38:33–38:42)
In Sulzer style

Pg. 148 M "Adir Adirenu" (38:43–39:07)
Betty Sue, beautiful.
Baruch Schorr (No. 130 in *N'Ginoth Baruch Schorr*, herausgegeben von Israel Schorr, 1906, 130), adapted.

Pg. 148 M "V'hayah Adonai" (39:08–39:52)
Betty Sue and choir with organ
Israel Goldfarb (in I. Goldfarb and I. H. Levinthal, *Song and Praise for Sabbath Eve*, 56).

Pg. 148 "Uv'divrei kod'shecha," Cantor only (39:53–40:01)

Pg. 148 M "Imloch," Choir and organ (40:02–40:20)
S. Sulzer (in *Shir U'Tefilah Union Songster*, 314).

Pg. 148 ? "L'dor vador" (40:25–42:14)
Betty Sue and Cantor (duet), very sweet, not identified.
Cantor and choir conclude.

Pg. 149–155 Long silence; congregation is finishing Musaf Amidah.

Pg. 156 "Kaddish Shalem" (44:47–45:53)
Cantor and choir Shabbat *nusach*, with organ

[Tape No. 18, Side 1 ends here.]

Not recorded are "Ein Keloheinu," by Julius Freudenthal (in A. Z. Idelsohn, *Jewish Song Book for Synagogue, School, and Home*. Cincinnati, OH, 113), 157; "Aleinu," by Sigmund Sabel (in Nathanson, ed., *Zamru Lo I: Congregational Melodies for the Shalosh R'galim and the High Holidays*, 112); "Va'anachnu," by Sigmund Sabel (in Nathanson, ed., *Zamru Lo I: Cong-*

regational Melodies for the Shalosh R'galim and the High Holidays, 113), and "V'hayah Adonai," by Israel Goldfarb (in I. Goldfarb and I. H. Levinthal, *Song and Praise for Sabbath Eve*, p. 56); also S. Sabel (in Nathanson, ed., *Zamru Lo I: Congregational Melodies for the Shalosh R'galim and the High Holidays*, 114).

(Memorial service follows here.)

V (e) Shavuot Service Order Worksheet, 1980, Tape No. 6, Side 1, Rabbi Richard M. E. Marcovitz Officiating, Silverman Siddur, Shari's Confirmation, piyyut Akdamut, Day One of Shavuot

Note: "M" indicates that melody is identified and sheet music is in hand.

"?" indicates that melody has not been identified and sheet music is not in hand.

Worksheet Side 1

[Tape begins with some Yiddish songs, like "Rosinen und Mandeln," very poor quality.]

Rabbi Marcovitz sermon (loud background noise) (05:13–11:10)

Rabbi Marcovitz introduces *piyyut* "Akdamut" (11:11–11:18)

Pg. 185–186 "Akdamut" (11:19–16:32)
 Cantor Heiser and Rabbi and congregation alternately
 [See Sholom Kalib, *The Musical Tradition of the Eastern European Synagogue*, Volume One. Part One. Text. Examples 144c and d, 142; and Volume One, Part Two. Music. Example 144 c, 151.]

Rabbi Marcovitz introduces Torah reading (16:36–17:05)

Torah reading by Cantor Max Haalman, 5 *aliyot* (17:07–31:47)

Hatzi Kaddish by Max Haalman (31:48–33:08)

Cantor Haalman calls *magbiah* and *golel* for *Sefer Rishon* (33:11–33:41)

Cantor Haalman calls *maftir* for reading from second scroll (33:45–34:09)

[Tape No. 6, Side 1 ends.]

V (f) *Shavuot Service Order Worksheet, 1980, Tape No. 6, Side 2, Rabbi Richard M. E. Marcovitz Officiating, Silverman* Siddur, *Shari's Confirmation, with Organ*

Note: "M" indicates that melody is identified and sheet music is in hand.

"?" indicates that melody has not been identified and sheet music is not in hand.

Worksheet Side 2

Shari Stein chants *brachot* before *maftir aliyah* (00:20–00:39)

Cantor Max Haalman chants *maftir* (00:40–01:28)

Shari Stein chants *brachot* after *maftir aliyah* (01:29–01:42)

Cantor Haalman calls *magbiah* and *golel* for *Sefer Sheni* (01:43–02:12)

Rabbi Marcovitz recites 'V'zot HaTorah' in English (02:13–02:25)

Rabbi Marcovitz comments before Shari chants the Haftarah (02:27–05:00)

Shari Stein chants Haftarah [Ezekiel 1:1–28, 3:12] (05:02–16:13)

Prayers for country, for Israel, and for World Peace by confirmands (16:20–20:05)

Pg. 132   Ashrei to standard Shabbat melody, by confirmands (20:25–22:33)

Return of Torah service

Pg. 133   M "Yehallelu," Cantor Heiser and organ (22:48–23:08)

Pg. 133   M "Hodo al Eretz," Choir with organ (23:09–23:58)

Pg. 135   M "S'u shearim," Organ and choir, soprano solo (24:00–26:56)

Pg. 136   "Uv'nuchah yomar," Cantor only (26:57–26:59)

Pg. 136   M "Ki lekach tov," Betty Sue, age 12 (27:00–27:56)

Pg. 136   M "Hashivenu," Choir and organ (27:57–29:16)

(Same sources as for Return of Torah service for Shavuot 1979 (c).

[Tape No. 6, Side 2 ends].

V (g) Yizkor *Shavuot Service Order Worksheet, 1983, Tape No. 9, Rabbi Richard M. E. Marcovitz Officiating,* Silverman *Siddur, Day Two, 7 Sivan, with Organ*

There is a *Yizkor* booklet which I do not have. Dedication of memorial plaques.

> Note: "M" indicates that melody is identified and sheet music is in hand.
> "?" indicates that melody has not been identified and sheet music is not in hand.

Worksheet Side 1

Rabbi Marcovitz comments (00:23–00:40)

Pg. ?   ? "Shviti Adonai" by choir (00:41–02:04)

Pg. ?   Rabbi Marcovitz introduction to memorial prayers (02:05–05:25)
Several readings (05:26–09:00)
Dedication of memorial plaques (09:01–11:42)
Cantor leads individual memorial prayers (11:43–14:00)

Pg. ?   M "El male rachamim," Organ, Cantor Heiser, and choir (14:05–18:06)
Beautiful, tender and moving.
Hugo Chaim Adler, "Eyl Moleh Rachamim" (in *Yamim Noraim*, Transcontinental Music Publications, 1965, Music Box 3, HUC-JIR Library, Jerusalem).
Rabbi Marcovitz reading (18:08–19:05)

Pg. 15   Rabbi Marcovitz reading of Psalm 23 (19:06–19:56)

Pg. 16   Mourner's Kaddish by all (19:57–20:46)
Rabbi Marcovitz announces concluding hymn (20:47–20:53)

Pg. 162   M "Adon Olam," Organ and choir (20:54–22:55)
Sulzer (in *Schir Zion*, 150th Jubilee Issue, Out-of-Print Classics Series of Synagogue Music No. 6, 57).
Rabbi Marcovitz gives final blessing (22:56–23:53)
Organ afterplay (23:54–25:23).

VI. (a) Guide to Cantor Heiser's Shabbat Service (May 2, 1981/28 Nisan 5741)

We only have sections of two Shabbat services—one from Betty Sue Stein's Bat Mitzvah on May 2, 1981, and the other from November 5, 1988. This latter service is probably the last one that was recorded, as Cantor Heiser's accident happened in the spring of 1989. In any case, it is the last one at my disposal.

Betty Sue's Bat Mitzvah was on Shabbat Kedoshim, which was also Cantor Heiser's Bar Mitzvah portion, as his birthday was on May 8. Cantor Heiser has the second *aliyah*, and Leviticus 19:26 in the Torah is read beautifully by Sexton, or Shamash Rev. Max Haalman, who also recites the Hatzi Kaddish after the *acharon aliyah*. Cantor Heiser then calls up Betty Sue, *Ha Bachurah* Bat Mitzvah *Bayla Rivka bat Reb Avraham Josef*, for the *maftir aliyah*. Betty Sue chants the *maftir*, followed by the congregational singing of "V'zot haTorah" (This is the Torah) by Abraham Zvi Idelson (in Nathanson, ed., *Zamru Lo II*, Congregational Melodies and Z'mirot for the entire Sabbath Day, 89), as the Torah scroll is lifted. Grandmother Elly Heiser, a *bat cohen*, speaks on the prophetic portion from Ezekiel, also from a priestly family, before Betty Sue chants the *Haftarah*, Ezekiel XX:2–20.[148] This recitation is followed by the Prayer for our Country by mother Judith Stein and the Prayer for Israel, in Hebrew and English, by sister Shari Stein.

Since it is the Shabbat before the new month begins, the Blessing for the New Month or **Birchat HaChodesh [YouTube No. 19] [Clip 37]** (42:22–46:54 full tape; 00:01–08:56 clip) (01:40–10:05 on Tape No.) is chanted at this point. At B'nai Israel, the Shabbat service that included the Prayer for the New Month was always very festive, and this one even more so as it is a double celebration. This rendition is unusually powerful and meaningful, based on a composition by Israel Alter in *Shirei Israel* and arranged for choir and organ by Morris Barash. The Barash arrangement was published by the Cantors Assembly of America in 1968. Included are recitatives for the *Hazzan* with piano or organ accompaniment. As already indicated, Cantor Heiser's renditions of Jewish liturgical music went straight to the heart. His sensitivity to the occasion, to the religious meaning of a hymn, even each word in a prayer, and to the richness of the voices at his disposal all contributed to a powerful spiritual experience.

The text for "Birchat HaChodesh" is the same for most congregations, across denominations, but there are numerous melodic settings. Cantor Heiser was a master of manipulation of the human heart, and perhaps also of the heart of God, and his ability to make the most of the voices at his disposal benefited the congregation greatly. In this prayer for the New Month of Iyar, he features the purity of his granddaughter's young voice; the continuity, even longevity of his own, single and in combination, is accentuated by the vivaciousness of the mixed choir. Every note is purposefully expressed to maximize the emotional impact of the prayer on God and on the congregation.

The prayer begins: "Yihi ratzon milfanecha—May it be Your will, Oh Lord our God and God of our ancestors, to renew us this coming month for our good and for blessing. Oh grant us long life, a life of peace, of goodness, of blessing, of sustenance, of bodily vigor."[149] After individual congregational recitation of the first paragraph, these words are sung by Cantor Heiser's granddaughter Betty Sue Stein in her clear voice of twelve. The fresh, pure, and innocent quality of the young voice is meant to open the minds and hearts of the supplicants who are beseeching God for a good month. The pure voice is also meant to open the heart of God Almighty, the Source of Goodness, which we cannot take for granted. And finally, it is a granddaughter pleading for a long life and bodily vigor for all, but especially for her by then 76-year-old Papa.

After this somewhat adapted opening passage, the youthful voice is joined by the mature voice of the grandfather, Cantor Heiser, and together young and old plead with God for "a life marked by reverence for You and the dread of sin" (Chayim sheyesh bahem yirat shamayim v'yirat chet) and the request is repeated by both a second time, exactly following Alter's composition; then the voice of authority, the precentor or intermediary for the congregation, continues pleading on behalf of all, "chayim sheeyn bahem bushah uch'limah"—"a life free from shame and reproach, a life of abundance and honor, a life in which the love of the Torah and the fear of heaven shall ever be with us, a life in which all the desires of our hearts shall be fulfilled for our good. Amen."[150] Here it is the voice of experience in intercession with God that takes over, the personal integrity of the *hazzan* vouchsafes for the goodness of the entire congregation.

Each individual then silently prays for the good of all Israel, "May the One who wrought wondrous deeds for our fathers (Mi she asah nisim la'avoteinu) and redeemed them from slavery unto freedom, soon redeem us and gather our exiled fellow Jews from the four corners of the earth, for all Israel is one fellowship; and let us say, Amen."[151] This is repeated out loud and for all by the Cantor, who emphasizes the words "freedom" (cherut) and "will redeem" (ig'al) in his rendition. Toward the end of the paragraph, he draws in the support of the congregation, who join him in affirming that "all Israel is one fellowship" (chaverim kol Israel). This statement is affirmed even by those who know no Hebrew, and the choir and the entire congregation answer "Amen."

Rabbi Marcovitz then announces that the new month of Iyar begins the following week on Monday and Tuesday, and he prays that God grant the entire house of Israel a good month. The formulaic statement, "Rosh Hodesh Iyar" (The New Month of Iyar will begin on Monday and Tuesday. May this New Month bring blessing to us and to all Israel) is repeated by the Cantor as the spokesperson for the congregation.[152]

The concluding paragraph, "Y'chadeshehu," which asks for God's blessing is sung by the choir to a majestic, dare we say triumphant, Lewandowski composition No. 25, "Neumondsweihe" (in *Liturgisches Liederbuch für den Gebrauch der Religionsschulen*, Berlin, 1912, 14, and No. 66 in *Todah W'simrah Part I: Shabbat*, Out-of-Print Classics Series of Synagogue Music No. 10, 121). The *Hazzan* uses all of his vocal powers of persuasion when he pleads for "life and peace" (l'chayim u'l'shalom) in his most heart-rending voice, with which the congregation concurs by singing "Amen." This is repeated for "gladness and joy" (l'sasson u'l'simchah), again affirmed by the congregation with "Amen," and a final plea for "salvation and comfort" (lishua ul'nechamah), to which choir and congregation respond with a final "Amen." The words in the Silverman *siddur* read, "May the Holy One, blessed be God, renew this month for us and for all God's people, the house of Israel, for life and peace, for gladness and joy, for salvation and comfort, and let us say, Amen."[153]

Following the Prayer for the New Month in the service order, Betty Sue's sister Adele Stein chants "Ashrei" to the popular melody of "Shir HaKavod," but it is incomplete as someone taped over the service. The service for returning the Torah to the Ark is every bit as festive as is such a service for the *haggim*, with the choir, Cantor Heiser, Betty Sue, and soprano solos to melodies by Sulzer and Lewandowski—Naumbourg's "S'u shearim" is, of course, not sung, as it is not a festival, but rather "Hodo al eretz" to Sulzer (in *Schir Zion*, 150th Jubilee Issue, Out-of-Print Classics Series of Synagogue Music No. 6, 104).

In her speech, Betty Sue acknowledges that she began to sing with her grandfather at age seven, in 1975, when she had to stand on a box to sing her first solo.[154] "Judaism has always been a way of life for me. . . . At my Bat Mitzvah, as I pledge my loyalty to God and His Commandments, I feel that God is near me. I pray that He may guide me in the years to come. May He watch over me and my family and those who came to celebrate with me on this important day in my life. This coming Rosh HaShanah it will be six years since I was put on a box to sing my first solo here at B'nai Israel with my grandfather. Not many grandchildren have that honor, and I hope that I can continue to bring as much pleasure with my voice as my Papa has done with his. I thank God for my wonderful parents, my sisters, and my four wonderful grandparents.... I set the Lord before me always. Amen."[155]

Before the Priestly Blessing, Rabbi Marcovitz highly praises Betty Sue's "gift of a voice . . . like a pearl" (that we all enjoyed until 1989 in a congregational setting). He continues, "I detected a little more nervousness in your Papa.... You have been given a gift, a gift of a voice, what a magnificent gift it is.... That gift that you have been given is like a pearl, a pearl is a very special stone.... Today you are standing on your own two feet [not on a box]."[156]

The recording ends here with the family reciting "Shehechianu," the prayer that celebrates persisting until this day, and with Rabbi Marcovitz's sermon.

Shabbat Service Order Worksheet, (May 2, 1981/ 28 Nisan 5741), Tape No. 14, Betty Sue Stein's Bat Mitzvah, Rabbi Richard M. E. Marcovitz Officiating, Silverman Siddur

Side 1, Silverman *siddur. Parshah Kedoshim, Lev. 19:18* (503 Hertz
  Chumash). Betty Sue's Bat Mitzvah and Cantor Heiser's
  Bar Mitzvah anniversary. (His birthday was May 8.)

  Note: "M" indicates that melody is identified and sheet music is
  in hand.
  "?" indicates that melody has not been identified and sheet
  music is not in hand.

Worksheet Side 1

Prayer for the sick (*misheberach*) by Rabbi Marcovitz (00:14–01:45)
Introduction to Torah reading by Rabbi Marcovitz (01:46–04:50)
More than 7 *aliyot* (10), begins with Lev. 19:23, *Hertz Chumash*
Cantor Heiser has *aliyah* 2, *Sheni*, Lev. 19:26 (06:44–08:01)
Some other members of Heiser family have *aliyot*.
Beautiful Torah reading (*leyning*) by Cantor Max Haalman, *shamash*
Hatzi Kaddish by Cantor Haalman
Hazzan Heiser calls up granddaughter Betty Sue—HaBachurah Bat
  Mitzvah *Bayla Rivka bat Reb Abraham Josef*, for the *maftir
  aliyah* (21:13–21:58)
Betty Sue chants the *maftir*, Hertz Chumash, 508 (22:00–23:30)
Cantor Haalman calls up *hamagbiah v'hagolel* [persons who lift and dress
  the Torah scroll]
Congregation rises, everyone sings "V'zot haTorah" (24:05–24:28)
A. Z. Idelson (in Nathanson, ed., *Zamru Lo II*, Congregational Melodies
  and Z'mirot for the entire Sabbath Day, 89)
Elly Heiser, Betty Sue's grandmother, is a *bat cohen*; she speaks on Ezekiel
  before Betty Sue chants the *Haftarah* (24:49–27:45)
Betty Sue chants Ezekiel XX:2–20, Hertz Chumash, 511 (28:08–38:04)
  Beautiful and accomplished

Pg. 130 Prayer for our country by Judy Stein (38:46–39:40)

Pg. 131 Prayer for Israel in Hebrew and English by Shari Stein
  (40:21–41:24)

(Note: Entire Prayer for the New Month is on Tape No. 19, Side 2.)

Rabbi Marcovitz explains the Prayer for the New Month (41:33–42:22)

Pg. 129 M Prayer for the New Month "Birchat HaChodesh" (42:23–42:50)
Monday and Tuesday will be the new month of Iyar

[From here to end of Tape No. 14, Side 1 is repeated on Tape No. 19, Side 2, starting below.]

Pg. 129 M "Yihi ratzon milfanecha" (01:10 on Tape 2) (42:52–44:38)
All pray silently, then Betty Sue solo.
"Birchat HaChodesh" by Israel Alter, arrangement by Morris Barash (in *Shirei Israel*, published by Cantors Assembly, New York, 1968), adapted, beautiful rendition.

Pg. 129 M "Chayim she yesh bahem" (44:39–46:54)
Betty Sue and Cantor duet, then Cantor solo to "shet'hi vanu" (Israel Alter exactly), 21–23, then Tape 14, Side 1 runs out.

Shabbat Service Order Worksheet (May 2, 1981/28 Nisan 5741), Tape No. 19, Betty Sue Stein's Bat Mitzvah, Rabbi Richard M. E. Marcovitz officiating, Silverman Siddur

> Note: "M" indicates that melody is identified and sheet music is in hand.
> "?" indicates that melody has not been identified and sheet music is not in hand.

Worksheet Side 2

> This tape begins with Rabbi Marcovitz explaining the Prayer for the New Month (which follows in its entirety), then congregation reads silently (00:20–01:38)

Pg. 129   M "Yihi ratzon milfanecha," Betty Sue Stein solo (01:40–03:22)
"Birchat HaChodesh" by Israel Alter, arrangement by Morris Barash (in *Shirei Israel*, published by Cantors Assembly, New York, 1968), adapted, beautiful rendition.
M "Chayim she yesh bahem," Cantor Heiser and Betty Sue duet (03:23–04:29)
Then Cantor recitative, "Chayim . . . " to "shet'hi vanu . . . amen." (04:30–05:58)
Alter exactly, 21–23.

Pg. 129   "Mi she asah nisim," Cantor solo improvised (06:09–06:47)

Pg. 129   "Chaverim," popular melody (06:48–07:35)
Cantor and congregation, then Cantor solo, and choir
Rabbi Marcovitz announcing the month of Iyar (07:36–07:59)

Pg. 129   "Rosh Hodesh Iyar," Cantor Heiser solo, beautiful (08:00–08:30)

Pg. 129   M "Y'chadeshehu," choir with Cantor, glorious (08:35–10:05)
Lewandowski, No. 66 (in *Todah W'simrah Part I: Shabbat*, Out-of-Print Classics Series of Synagogue Music No. 10, 121; Also Lewandowski No. 25 "Neumondsweihe (in *Liturgisches Liederbuch für den Gebrauch der Religionsschulen, Berlin 1912*, 14)
Rabbi Marcovitz announces prayer "Ashrei" (10:09–10:22)

Pg. 132   "Ashrei," led by Adele Stein (incomplete) (10:24–12:00)
To melody of "Shir HaKavod"

(Break in tape; someone taped over service.)

Adele continues to end. (21:30–22:15)

Return of the Torah Service

Pg. 133   M "Yehallelu," Cantor solo, then choir (22:22–22:37)
          Sulzer (in *Schir Zion*, 150th Jubilee Issue, Out-of-Print Classics
             Series of Synagogue Music No. 6, p. 104; also Ephros, ed.,
             *Cantorial Anthology of Traditional and Modern Synagogue
             Music*. Volume III Sholosh R'golim, 275).

Pg. 133   M "Hodo al eretz," choir (22:38–23:17)
          Sulzer (in *Schir Zion*, 150th Jubilee Issue, Out-of-Print Classics
             Series of Synagogue Music No. 6, 104, not first line); also in
             Ephros, ed., *Cantorial Anthology of Traditional and Modern
             Synagogue Music*. Volume III Sholosh R'golim, 275).

Torah procession

Pg. 134   ? "Havu LAdonai" (23:18–25:50)
          Cantor alternating with choir and congregation

Pg. 136   "Uv'nuchah yomar," Cantor davens (25:51–26:02)

Pg. 136   M "Ki lekach tov," Betty Sue (26:03–26:45)
          "Hashivenu" choir, with female soloist (26:46–27:58)
          Lewandowski (in *Todah W'simrah Part I: Shabbat*, Out-of-Print
             Classics Series of Synagogue Music No. 10, 128).

Betty Sue's Bat Mitzvah speech, very touching (29:07–31:24)
          Mentions that nearly six years ago she stood on a box to sing
             with her grandfather

Rabbi Marcovitz's Bat Mitzvah remarks to Betty Sue (31:48–37:54)
          "Gift of a voice" . . . "like a pearl"
          Priestly Blessing for Betty Sue by Rabbi Marcovitz, spoken
             (37:55–38:25)
          Shehechianu, spoken by everyone (38:57–39:24)
          Rabbi Marcovitz sermon (39:34–46:58)

[End of Tape 19, Side 2].

VI. (b) Guide to Cantor Heiser's Shabbat Musaf Service, (November 5, 1988)

The second snippet that survived is the Shabbat Musaf service from November 5, 1988. Why the choir was employed I cannot say for certain, as it was not used every Shabbat. With one exception that I will discuss below, the lovely music is that of an "ordinary" Shabbat. Cantor Heiser sings an adaptation of his teacher Aron Friedmann's Hatzi Kaddish (in Schir Lisch'laumau, 149), then he launches into the Shabbat *nusach* for the Musaf Amidah prayer at lightning speed and into a *hecha kedushah* with a brief "Somech noflim, rofe cholim" by Lewandowski (in Todah W'simrah, Part I: Shabbat, Out-of-Print Classics Series of Synagogue Music No. 10, 112). "Na'arizecha" is davened by the Cantor, followed by Sulzer's "Kadosh, kadosh, kadosh" by choir and Cantor. The "Shema" is sung to Israel Goldfarb's melody (in I. Goldfarb and I. H. Levinthal, Song and Praise for Sabbath Eve, 9), and then followed by his own composition for "Hu Eloheinu" (He is our God) (10:05–10:42). A slightly adapted "Imloch Adonai l'olam" by Sulzer (in *Shir U'Tefilah Union Songster*, 314) concludes the section of the service that is sung; the rest of the Amidah is silent. The service picks up again with "Birkat Kohanim," or the Priestly Blessing, which is unidentified but sounds Hasidic in nature, and concludes with an exquisite falsetto by the Cantor at the beginning of the third blessing, "Isa Adonai."

After the Priestly Blessing in this particular service, Cantor Heiser interjects a contemporary composition by his friend and colleague Cantor Leopold Edelstein from Austria/Czechoslovakia, who lived in Youngstown, Ohio, after World War II. The composition, **"Sim Shalom**—A Prayer for Peace, from the Saturday Morning Liturgy," **[YouTube No. 20]** [Clip 38] (15:44–20:22 full tape; 00:01–06:38 clip) for Mixed Chorus and Organ or Piano, was printed by Metro Music in New York in 1958. The date of November 5 may have been the reason for this special musical selection for the service, as it was close to the anniversary of Kristallnacht, November 9–10. As discussed earlier, both Cantor Heiser and Cantor Edelstein had personal experience with the Holocaust. Since this was the premiere of Edelstein's "Sim Shalom" in a B'nai Israel service—though not the first time that Cantor Heiser had sung it—this may well have been why Cantor Heiser employed the choir for that Shabbat service.

The choir starts off with a very gentle "Sim Shalom tovah u'vrachah" (Grant peace, goodness, and blessing), followed by Cantor Heiser. The first two words, "Sim Shalom" are set in a high f sharp, no doubt on purpose, as shalom is something the world has not achieved in all the years since the Holocaust, and we continue to pray for it with all of our strength. Peace is an almost impossible task to achieve, just as it is to sing these two words without great effort. This is clearly obvious from Cantor Heiser's offering. He had just sung an equally high "Isa Adonai" in the previous Priestly Benediction flawlessly, yet starting a new and very different musical composition with such a high note at the end of a long Shabbat morning service and with such a lofty purpose proved to be a challenge and required considerable vocal effort. As the prayer continued, the level dropped somewhat and Cantor Heiser was quite comfortable again, as was the choir with what sounds like Hasidic melodies. Cantor and choir conclude with a powerful "May the Lord bless God's people Israel with peace" (Ham'varech et amo Israel ba'shalom), almost as if to reassure the worshippers that God can indeed bestow peace on us in spite of what is going on in the world. Cantor Heiser's courage and effort in presenting such a different and difficult composition at age eighty-three is admirable.

After "Sim Shalom" the service concludes with an excellent Shabbat Kaddish Shalem, the regular slightly adjusted Shabbat "Ein keloheinu" melody by Julius Freudenthal (in A. Z. Idelsohn, *Jewish Song Book*, Cincinnati, 1928, 113), of which Kalib says that it is not *nusach*, but a popular tune, considered to be a post-service *niggun* [See Kalib: *The Musical Tradition of the Eastern European Synagogue*, Volume One. Part One, Text, 108]. Sigmund Sabel's "Aleinu" (in Nathanson, ed., *Zamru Lo I. Congregational Melodies and Z'mirot for the Friday Evening Service*, 112); Sulzer's Traditional "Va'anachnu korim;" and Goldfarb's "V'hayah Adonai" (both in I. Goldfarb and I. H. Levinthal, *Song & Praise for Sabbath Eve*, 56) conclude the service.

All but the Edelstein melody—whether Traditional, Sulzer, Feudenthal, Sabel, or Goldfarb—are very familiar melodies to the congregation. And in the service of keeping worship fresh, Edelstein's "Sim Shalom" fills that requirement. On the whole, congregants are totally in their comfort zone singing along with the Cantor and choir; the melodies are uplifting, creating a feeling of serenity, a feeling of rest and of peace for Shabbat. Yet Edelstein's composition provides the reminder that no matter how safe and secure we feel, there is always a risk, a danger, to Jewish existence. We will only experience total peace when the Messiah comes.

Shabbat Musaf Service Order Worksheet, (November 5, 1988), Tape No. 15, Silverman Siddur, Rabbi Richard M. E. Marcovitz Officiating

> Note: "M" indicates that melody is identified and sheet music is in hand.
> "?" indicates that melody has not been identified and sheet music is not in hand.

Worksheet Side 1

Rabbi Marcovitz sermon continues (00:19–15:41)

Rabbi Marcovitz introduces Musaf Service (05:42–06:12)

Pg. 137 "Musaf Hatzi Kaddish," Cantor and choir (06:12–07:09)
Very fast and comfortable

Pg. 137 Musaf Amidah, "Baruch Atah Adonai," Cantor, choir (07:10–07:58)
Shabbat *nusach*

Pg. 138 M "Somech noflim," Cantor and everyone (07:59–08:54)
Lewandowski (in *Todah W'simrah, Part I: Shabbat*, Out-of-Print Classics Series No. 10, 112), brief phrase only, then *nusach*.

Musaf Kedushah

Pg. 138 "Na'arizecha," davened by the Cantor (08:43–08:54)

Pg. 139 M "Kadosh, kadosh, kadosh," choir, Cantor (08:55–09:10)
Sulzer (in Nathanson, ed. *Zamru Lo II. Congregational Melodies and Z'mirot for the entire Sabbath Day*, 114; also *Schir Zion*, 150th Jubilee Issue, Out-of-Print Classics Series of Synagogue Music No. 6, 85).

Pg. 139 M "K'vodo," Cantor only (09:14–09:23)

Pg. 139 M "Baruch k'vod Adonai," choir (09:24–09:31)
Lewandowski (in Nathanson, ed., *Zamru Lo II. Congregational Melodies and Z'mirot for the entire Sabbath Day*, 114), changed.

Pg. 139 ? "Mimkomo," Cantor Heiser *nusach* (09:32–09:46)

Pg. 139 M "Shema Israel," everyone (09:47–10:05)

Israel Goldfarb (in I. Goldfarb and I. H. Levinthal, *Song and Praise for Sabbath Eve*, 9).

Pg. 139 "Hu Eloheinu," Cantor and congregation (10:06–10:46)
Cantor Heiser's own composition

Pg. 139 "Ani Adonai Eloheichem," choir (10:47–10:55)

Pg. 139 "Uv'divrei kodsh'cha," Cantor Heiser (10:56–10:59)

Pg. 139 M "Imloch Adonai l'olam," choir (11:00–11:40)
Sulzer (in *Shir U'Tefilah Union Songster*, 314, and Nathanson, ed., *Zamru Lo II*, Congregational Melodies and Z'mirot for the entire Shabbat Day, 115).
Cantor davens to end, choir sings "Amen,"
Silent Amidah (11:41–13:37)
Rabbi Marcovitz introduction to Priestly Blessing (13:38–13:47)

Pg. 144 Birkat Kohanim, "Eloheinu velohei avoteinu"
Cantor, choir "Ken yihi ratzon," and Rabbi Marcovitz in English (13:48–15:02)
Hasidic, beautiful Cantor *falsetto* for "Isah Adonai"
Rabbi Marcovitz announces "Sim Shalom" prayer (15:03–15:41)

Pg. 145 M "Sim Shalom" (15:44–22:22)
Composed by Cantor Leopold Edelstein of Youngstown, Ohio (Austrian by birth), in "traditional style," complicated; first choir, then Cantor Heiser alternating with choir.

Pg. 156 "Kaddish Shalem," Cantor at lightning speed and choir (22:23–23:12)

Pg. 157 M "Ein keloheinu," Cantor and choir (23:17–24:44)
Julius Freudenthal (in Idelsohn, *Jewish Song Book*, Cincinnati, Ohio, 1928, 113). According to Sholom Kalib, this is not *nusach* but a post-service *niggun*. [See Kalib, *The Musical Tradition of the Eastern European Synagogue*, Volume One, Part One. Text. Example 111, 108; and Volume One, Part Two. Music. Example 112, 113.]

Pg. 158 M "Aleinu"—"k'chol hamonam," Cantor and choir (24:45–25:18)
Sigmund Sabel (in Nathanson, ed., *Zamru Lo I*. Congregational Melodies and Z'mirot for the Friday Evening Service, 112).

Pg. 158 M "Va'anachnu korim," Cantor and choir (25:19–25:44)
Sulzer (in *Shir U'Tefilah Union Songster*, 303 A); also Sulzer,

"Va'anachnu" No. 2 (in Ephros, ed., *Cantorial Anthology of Traditional and Modern Synagogue Music*. Volume III Sholosh R'galim, 66); I. Goldfarb (in I. Goldfarb and I. H. Levinthal, *Song and Praise for Sabbath Eve*, 56).

Rabbi Marcovitz reading (25:52–26:16)

Pg. 158   M "V'ne'emar v'hayah Adonai," Cantor and choir (26:17–27:20)

Israel Goldfarb (in I. Goldfarb and I. H. Levinthal, *Song & Praise for Sabbath Eve*, 56); also Sabel (in Nathanson, ed., *Zamru Lo I*, Congregational Melodies and Z'mirot for the Friday Evening Service, 114), but altered.

Pg. 161   Rabbi Marcovitz announces Mourners Kaddish and reads names of yahrzeits (27:21–28:13)

Mourners Kaddish by all (28:14–29:00)

[Tape 15, Side 1 ends here.]

Not recorded is "Adon Olam," 162 in Silverman *siddur*.

CONCLUSION

Hazzan Mordecai Gustav Heiser, the Sweet Singer of Congregation B'nai Israel in the East End of Pittsburgh, Pennsylvania, rests in the B'nai Israel cemetery on Blackadore Road in Penn Township with his spouse of fifty-four years, Elly Hochmann Heiser. On July 22 (13 of Av), 2021, we lost their only child, Judith Heiser Stein, wife of Alvin Stein.

But death is no impediment to the survival of Cantor Heiser's spirit in his art of liturgical Jewish music, *hazzanut*, because in many instances versions of it existed already before his lifetime and have continued in practice after his passing. Mark Slobin notes that "We must turn to portraits of individuals to understand how the cantorate worked."[1] And so we have. Cantor Heiser's peregrinations through the vast soundscape of Jewish music—Jewish folksongs, Hasidic *niggunim*, songs of the *chalutzim*, Yiddish songs, and his beloved *hazzanut*—provide a brief glimpse into one artist's rich and joyous renditions of these ancestral cultural treasures as well as the powerful creative spirit of contemporary Jewish musical art, and thereby enrich the entire tapestry of Jewish culture and history.

Cantor Heiser was the messenger not only of his own prayers but also those of his entire congregation for nearly half a century. Political events—worldwide and in the U.S., and the Jewish community's interaction with these events—came and went. Newspaper coverage by the Pittsburgh Jewish press over these years helps us revisit the early years of the Zionist movement and its development, especially through the 1940s until the creation of the State of Israel in 1948, again with a front row seat through Cantor Heiser's involvement in the Pittsburgh Jewish community. As a longtime enthusiastic supporter of Zionism, Cantor Heiser celebrated the creation of the State of Israel in song, and he and his wife visited Israel at least five times.

Cantor Heiser's support of the founding of the Cantors Assembly in 1947 and beyond attests to American cantors' desire to form professional organizations that provided a support network for those individuals who chose to dedicate their lives to the beautification of worship services in all of the denominations within American Judaism. Not only did they enrich their own professional and personal lives through these collaborative venues, but the experiences of their congregants and community as well. Furthermore, Cantor Heiser and his colleagues contributed tremendously to the cultural life of the entire Jewish community, and, beyond that, the city of Pittsburgh and the Tri-State region of Western Pennsylvania, Ohio, and West Virginia as well. His certificate as *Hazzan* in 1954, in addition to his certification from cantorial school in Berlin in 1929, legitimized him as a properly trained precentor for Jewish sacred music.

A recital at Carnegie Recital Hall in New York must have been every aspiring singer's dream—even the biggest star of them all, Cantor Yossele Rosenblatt, appeared in that venue—and Cantor Heiser joined this distinguished group of vocal artists with a concert in 1949. While always a sacred singer, he thoroughly enjoyed concerts that included his repertoire from Germany, both secular and religious, and he thrived on concerts in which he collaborated with other artists, often for the benefit of B'nai Israel, the Cantors Assembly, the Zionist Organization of America, and many other philanthropic funds.

For his entire long career, Cantor Heiser delighted congregants and audiences with his beautiful and soulful music, but underneath it all there always lurked the memory of those terrible years from 1933 to 1939 when the Nazis first came to power. They robbed him initially of a full education and certification as rabbi, then of his job as cantor of the Berlin-Lichtenfelde-Lankwitz congregation, his home, his community, and eventually his family. Nine members of his family were murdered by the Nazis, and perhaps more. As he wrote the names into one of his prayer books, he was reminded of their loss every time he prayed. The sad and frustrating correspondence across the ocean after the Heisers' arrival in Pittsburgh in 1940 is another reminder of how much those left behind suffered and, ultimately, how painfully slow they were led to their deaths. He never forgot—although he seldom spoke about the family's Holocaust experience and his incarceration in Sachsenhausen—nor did the family. Still in 1999, his daughter, Judith, would write after her first visit to Berlin in that year (and ten years after her father's death) that now she wasn't afraid of Germans anymore. What a terrible way to go through life.

The United States Holocaust Memorial Museum in Washington, D.C. admonishes us to collect and share the story of each Jewish person who fell victim to this life struggle under the Nazis, for these stories are part of Jewish history and culture and contribute to a greater and deeper understanding of the entire Jewish people. And not only the experiences of Jews whose lives were impacted by the Holocaust matter, but also the stories of all those who became victims of the Nazis' cruelty, such as Sinti and Roma, Gays, Jehovah's Witnesses, Polish intellectuals, Russian POWs, and the mentally and physically challenged. They all belong to the larger picture of genocide as well.

Cantor Heiser was a committed Jew who served his community in Germany, England, and the United States as a sincere representative before the Almighty. He had a rich and rewarding spiritual life, and thousands who heard him sing at one point during their journey through life remember the encounter as an enriching experience. Most of them—the Binstocks, Horns, Caplans, Finkelsteins, Ainsmans, Louiks, Marcusons, Adlers, Katzes, and many other families—are no longer able to bear witness to Cantor Heiser's spiritual power. So it seems right to preserve and share the life and work of a man who brought so much joy, comfort, and spiritual fulfillment to so many over the course of his life while at the same time carrying the tremendous burden of his family's and community's tragic losses. This service of joy and beauty may have made it easier for him to cope with these disturbing memories.

There are not many micro studies of any cantor and his work, perhaps with the exception of those who ascended to secular stardom in the world of opera, theater, or cinema. As outsiders, this glimpse into the life and art of one particular sacred singer allows us to learn about the ins and outs of the little-known world of the cantorate. There is currently a readership and listenership of young professionals who search for examples of "how it used to be done." Recently, a young rabbi from a nearby state emailed me to ask whether there was more of Cantor Heiser's music, as he enjoys listening to professional cantors. Unfortunately there is not much more. From the incomplete tapes, we culled thirty-eight usable musical snippets, twenty of which became the foundation for this book. With so many different types of synagogues and different services even within one synagogue today, those who never experienced a more formal, choreographed service based mostly on the Tradition have an interest in learning about this liturgy, as do Jews in general and non-Jews who have an interest in liturgy, Jewish and otherwise, in Jewish music and in music in general, and in Jewish history, culture, and life as such as well.

The exploration of Cantor Heiser's art also allows for a peek into the lives and times of several cantors whose music he presented, including classmate Professor and Rabbi Emil Fackenheim's Berlin phase, which paralleled Cantor Heiser's, and a look at such historical phenomena as European Jewry, East and West; American Jewry, the Holocaust, Zionism, and even the birth of the modern state of Israel—on the specific examples of the

Hochschule für die Wissenschaft des Judentums in Berlin and the Cantors Assembly of the Jewish Theological Seminary in New York, as well as such cultural institutions as the Friendship Club in Pittsburgh, NBC's "The Living Word" radio and television broadcasts, the work of the Zionist Organization of America (Pittsburgh chapter), visits to the state of Israel, which came into being eight years after Cantor Heiser came to a very Israel-committed Jewish community in the city of Pittsburgh, and the celebration of milestones and honors in one Jewish person's life. Always, always, the Holocaust hovered over these successes in the form of the "El Male Rachamim" prayer, at annual Holocaust Memorial Day ceremonies, congregational Memorial services, and communal as well as city-wide commemorations.

Technically, the invention of YouTube has made it much easier to post music clips on electronic media so that publishers don't have to worry about making CDs and pockets for them in a book (a costly undertaking), and diverse listeners can freely enjoy the offerings of *hazzanut*—for free. This in itself is a breakthrough in communications and a step forward in the way we share resources. When it came to sacred music, though, Cantor Heiser was very traditional; he did not professionally record any of his repertoire. This does not mean that he objected to the large number of newspaper announcements of his services and concerts during his lifetime—that was a necessity in the profession. Nor was he put off by the many honors that were bestowed on him during his lifetime. These tributes were not his alone but also the congregation's and the community's. What was good for him personally benefitted the congregation, and the congregation was his ultimate concern. With the loss of a number of Eastern European cantors in the Holocaust, and many others then not necessarily recording their music, Cantor Heiser's surviving amateur recordings are precious. This book not only honors him but also a tradition that was greatly violated and decimated by historical events.

To research this subject, to revisit the life and art of my teacher and my friend, to sing some of his melodies for the past three decades, and now to write about this music has been a great honor, privilege, and joy; it has been hard yet rewarding work. It is my hope that the reader/listener will enjoy the fruits of my labor.

At the conclusion of the recitation or study of a Book of the Torah, it is customary to say or chant the blessing, *Hazak, hazak, v'nithazek!* (Be strong, be strong, and we shall be strengthened).

GLOSSARY

Abitur (Hochschulreife)—Final examination at academic-track high school

Aliyah—Going up (lit.), immigrating to Israel, honor during synagogue service

Ashkenaz—Germany

Ashkenazi(c), Ashkenazim—German, also all of European Jewry

Aufgebotsverzeichnis—Register of marriage applicants

Aufruf—Religious act of calling up bride and groom for a blessing before the wedding

Baal Kore—Torah reader

Bachur(ah), bocher—Boy, girl

Bar—Aramaic for *ben* (son)

Bar mitzvah—Son of the Commandments, coming-of-age ceremony for Jewish boy, traditionally at age 13

Bat—Daughter

Bat mitzvah—Daughter of the Commandments, coming-of-age ceremony for Jewish girl, traditionally at age 12

Beit haT'filah—House of prayer

Beit haMidrash—House of study

Beit haKnesset—House of assembly

Beshert—Meant to be, destined (Yiddish)

Bimah—Pulpit, platform

Birkat Hachodesh, Birkat Hahodesh—Prayer for the new month

Birkat hamazon—Prayer of thanksgiving after meal

B'nai Israel—Sons (Children) of Israel

Brachot—Blessings

Brautstrauss—Wedding bouquet

Chalutz(im)—Pioneer(s) in pre-state Land of Israel

Chacham—Wise (learned) person

Chevra Shas—Society for the Study of *Talmud*

Centralverein für die Juden in Deutschland—Central Organization for Jews in Germany

Cohen—One from the Priestly caste

Daven (verb)—Pray (Yiddish)

Führungszeugnis—Character reference

Geburtsschein—Birth certificate

Gesamtarchiv der deutschen Juden—Main archive of German Jews

G'mar Chatimah Tovah—Greeting "May You Be Sealed for Good" between Rosh Hashanah and Yom Kippur

Haftarah—Prophetic portion on Shabbat and holidays

Hag(gim)—Festival(s)

Hanukkah, *Chanukkah*, Chanuka, Hanuka—Dedication, Festival of Lights

Havdalah—Separation ceremony between holy time and ordinary time such as Shabbat and weekday

Hazkarah—Memorial service

Hazzan, Chazen, Chazzn—Officiant in religious ceremony, cantor, precentor, prayer leader

Hazzanut, Chasonus—Jewish liturgy

Hilfsverein der Juden in Deutschland—Aid Society for Jews in Germany

HIAS (Hebrew Immigrant Aid Society)—Refugee Protection Organization

Hiddur mitzvah—Beautification of the Torah

Hochschule für die Wissenschaft des Judentums—non denominational Jewish college

Israelitische Religionsverein—Jewish religious organization

Kabbalat Shabbat—Ceremony for welcoming Shabbat on Friday afternoon

Kashrut—Dietary laws

Kavanah—spiritual intent, concentration

Königstädtische Oberrealschule—Name of higher trade school in Berlin

Kristallnacht—Crystal Night, Night of Broken Glass; November 9, 1938, when Nazis burned down many synagogues, destroyed Jewish property, and harassed, arrested and killed Jews

Kultusverwaltung der jüdischen Gemeinde zu Berlin—Main administration of Jewish community in Berlin

Leyn (Yiddish)—Chanting of the Torah in prescribed tune (*trop*)

L'Shanah Tovah Tikatevu—Greeting "May you be inscribed for a good year" up to Rosh Hashanah

Machzor(im)—High Holy Day (Rosh Hashanah and Yom Kippur) prayer book(s)

Mashgiach—Ritual kitchen supervisor

Megillah—One of Five Books, not including the Torah, that are kept and read on a scroll (Book of Ruth, Ecclesiastes, Song of Songs, *Eicha* [Lamentations], and Book of Esther)

Melave Malke— Fourth meal at the conclusion of Shabbat, escorting the Queen

Menshlich(keit)—Humane, humaneness

Midrash—Free interpretation of biblical stories

Mincha—Afternoon prayer service

Minyan(im)—Quorum (pl.) of ten

Mizrachi—Middle Eastern, Mediterranean

Mohel—Jewish ritual circumciser

Musaf(im)—Additional service, final service in traditional Shabbat, Festival and High Holy Day worship service

Musikdirektor—Director of a musical body

Ne'ilah—Concluding service on Yom Kippur

Nusach (Nus'chaot pl.)—Traditional mode(s) in Jewish liturgy

Oberkantor—Senior Cantor

Parshah—Portion

Pogrom—Persecution

Prediger—Preacher

Probevortrag—Trial lecture [sermon]

Reichsvertretung—Jewish representatives to German Reich

Rosh Hashanah—Jewish New Year

Sammeltransport—Group transport

Seelsorger—Minister

Seudah shlishit—Third meal on Saturday afternoon

Sephard—Spain

Sephardic—Spanish, but also Mediterranean

Shabbat—Jewish day of rest from Friday evening to Saturday evening

Shacharit (Shacharis)—Morning Prayers

Shaliach Tzibur (Sheliach Tsibbur)—Messenger [of the congregation]

Shamash(im)—Helper(s)

Shavuot—Pentecost, or the Receiving of the Ten Commandments

Shtayger—A Jewish "ladder" (mode) of musical notes

Shul—Place of learning and prayer, synagogue

Siddur—Prayer book (not including Rosh Hashanah and Yom Kippur)

Simcha—Celebration

Simchat Torah—holiday, Celebration of the Torah

Slichot—Penitential service

Standesamt—German office for personal status matters

Synagogue—Jewish house of worship, *shul*

Ta'amim—*Trop* signs for Torah chanting

Talmud—Jewish religious and legal text from approximately sixth century C.E. made up of Mishnah [200 C.E.] and Gemarah [400–600 C.E.]

Tanach (Tenach)—The Hebrew Bible made up of *Torah* [Five Books of Moses], *Nevi'im* [Prophets], and *Chetuvim* [Writings]

Torah (Thora)—Five Books of Moses [Genesis, Exodus, Leviticus, Numbers, and Deuteronomy]

Trop—Chant

Tsaddik—Leader of Hasidic group

World Zionist Organization—umbrella organization for Zionist activities

Yahrzeit—Hebrew anniversary of a person's death

Yizkor—Memorial (service)

Yom HaShoah—Holocaust Memorial Day

Yom Kippur—Day of Atonement

Zionist Organization of America (ZOA)—Organization for the support of the State of Israel

Z'mirot (Z'miros)—Table songs

NOTES

Preface

1. About Professor Eliyahu Schleifer, see Judah M. Cohen's *The Making of a Reform Jewish Cantor* (Indiana University Press, Bloomington, 2009). See also Professor Schleifer's extensive publications—among them, Amit Klein in collaboration with Professor Eliyahu Schleifer and Professor Edwin Seroussi, Jewish Music Research Centre, Hebrew University, Jerusalem, "Harmonizing Theory with Creativity: Cantor Leib Glantz's Musical Agenda," in Jerry Glantz, ed., *Leib Glantz—The Man Who Spoke to God* (Tel Aviv Institute for Jewish Liturgical Music, Tel Aviv, 2008, 145–174). Also Eliyahu Schleifer, "Jewish Liturgical Music from the Bible to Hasidism," in Lawrence A. Hoffman and Janet R. Walton, eds., *Sacred Sound and Social Change: Liturgical Music in Jewish and Christian Experience* (University of Notre Dame Press, Notre Dame/London, 1992, 13–58). Further, Eliyahu Schleifer's "Jewish Musical Culture—Past and Present" in *The World of Music*, Volume 37, No. 1, 1995 (59–72). See also Eliyahu Schleifer, ed., *Jewish Miniatures*, Vol. 136A, Louis Lewandowski Festival, *Samuel Naumbourg: The Cantor of French Jewish Emancipation* (Centrum Judaicum, Hentrich & Hentrich, Berlin, 2015). Volumes on Sulzer and Lewandowski by other authors were also published. The Lewandowski Festival has taken place since 2011. The 2015 program focused exactly on the composers and music of the Eastern European Choral Shul of interest here. The concluding concert in 2015 took place at the Rykestrasse Synagogue in Berlin. On December 17, 2020, Professor Schleifer, who is a member of the Advisory Board of the Lewandowski Festival, delivered words of welcome electronically from Jerusalem for the opening concert of that year's festival. On August 10, 2022, the World Congress for Jewish Studies organized a session in Jerusalem, "Traditional Music for the Reform Synagogue," honoring Cantor Schleifer for his "lifetime contributions to Reform Liturgy" in the form of his many compositions. Press release from HUC/JIR, Jerusalem, August 12, 2022.

Introduction

1. I would like to point the reader to another study, so similar yet so different from this one, by Judit Niran Frigyesi, an ethnomusicologist. Her research took place in Budapest, and to a lesser degree in Prague, in the 1970s, yet the volume was published in 2018 in English (2014 in Hungarian). Reading through the poetic rendition of her experiences, I could only shake my head in amazement. Here I am in a free country following the magical liturgical journey of one cantor, while Judit put her life in danger by sneaking into the forbidden shtiebls and synagogues of Budapest under a Communist regime to capture the sounds of a group of men who tried to keep the tradition alive. What a treasure! My thanks to my anonymous reviewer who pointed this study out to me. Judit Niran Frigyesi, *Writing on Water: The Sounds of Jewish Prayer*. Central European University Press, Budapest-New York, 2018.

2. In 2021 and 2022, Rachel Brown, my student at the University of Tennessee for a very brief time before graduation, took over the task of cantor for our congregation on the High Holy Days. She began to learn the *Ne'ilah* service that I had davened for nearly three decades, so that elements of Cantor Heiser's music continue into the next generation.

3. See Berlin map with some of the addresses of the Heiser and Hochmann families. My thanks to Eric Arnold, Greg March, and Michelle Brannen at UT's Hodges Library for their help in creating a map of Berlin that the publisher could implement.

4. Rena Sufrin Kennedy and I have corresponded at length about the Heiser genealogy. A few years ago, she sent me her version of the family tree. Among the information is the fact that Selma Brauer was from Kovno, something I had not been aware of before. My sincere thanks to Rena for sharing her work with me.

5. Some excellent studies of *hazzanut* include works by a number of authors: the father of Jewish liturgical history, Abraham Z. Idelsohn, *Jewish Liturgy and Its Development*. Dover Publications, Inc., New York, 1995/1932; Ismar Elbogen, *Jewish Liturgy: A Comprehensive History*. Translated by Raymond P. Scheindlin. Jewish Publication Society, New York and Philadelphia, 1993; Mark Slobin, *Chosen Voices: The Story of the American Cantorate*. University of Illinois Press, Urbana and Chicago, 2002/1998; Marsha Bryan Edelman, *Discovering Jewish Music*. The Jewish Publication Society, Philadelphia, 2003/5763; Leib Glantz's excellent collection of essays as well as laudations to his life and work in Jerry Glantz, ed., *Leib Glantz—The*

Man Who Spoke to God; and Sholom Kalib, *The Musical Tradition of the Eastern European Synagogue*. Volume One. Introduction: History and Definition, Volume One, Part One (Text) and Volume One, Part Two (Music). Syracuse University Press, Syracuse, New York, 2002. Each of them comes at the topic from a different point of view, and while Slobin and Edelman cover the topic in a very similar way, Frigyesi and Glantz are worlds apart. Elbogen precedes Idelsohn, and Kalib is in a class all of his own. And yet, there is something that binds all of these scholars despite their differences—their interest in and love for *hazzanut*.
6. Judith Vander. *Songprints: The Musical Experience of Five Shoshone Women*. University of Illinois Press, Urbana and Chicago, 1988.

Chapter 1

1. Sholom Kalib, *The Musical Tradition of the Eastern European Synagogue*. Volume One. Introduction: History and Definition, Part One. Text. 29.
2. Gilya Gerda Schmidt, *Süssen Is Now Free of Jews: World War II, the Holocaust, and Rural Judaism*. Fordham University Press, New York, 2012.
3. *Jüdische Frontsoldaten aus Württemberg und Hohenzollern*. Württembergischer Landesverband des Centralvereins deutscher Staatsbürger jüdischen Glaubens. J. Fink, Stuttgart, 1926.
4. The origin of the term cantor and his role may well be Christian, derived from *cantare*, to chant or sing. During the Middle Ages, there was a Schola Cantorum in the Church that taught musicianship. Several scholars point out that Johann Sebastian Bach was a cantor in the Church. The term *hazzan*, in Judaism today comparable to cantor, is of Jewish origin and originally meant a functionary. See *Encyclopedia Judaica*, Vol. 12, Min-O, Macmillan, New York and Jerusalem, 1972, 588. It seems that there is a general consensus that the role of the cantor/*hazzan* originated in the Levitical singers in the Temple in Jerusalem, but not the music.
5. See Eliyahu Schleifer, "Jewish Liturgical Music from the Bible to Hasidism," in Lawrence A. Hoffman and Janet R Walton, eds., *Sacred Sound and Social Change*. Liturgical Music in Jewish and Christian Experience, 14–22.
6. Bezalel Narkiss. In *Hebrew Illuminated Manuscripts*. Macmillan, New York, 1969, Narkiss describes *hiddur mitzvah* as "adornment of the implements involved in performing rituals." 13. Also Slobin, *Chosen Voices*, 263. Vivian B. Mann, ed., *Jewish Texts on the Visual Arts*. Cambridge University Press, Cambridge, 2000, explains the principle of *hiddur mitzvah* as

"the requirement of fulfilling a commandment in the finest way possible." 124; Gilya Schmidt, *The Art and Artists of the Fifth Zionist Congress, 1901. Heralds of a New Age.* Syracuse University Press, Syracuse, NY, 2003, 16. In *Etz Chaim Chumash*, *hiddur mitzvah* is defined as "an esthetically pleasing context," 554. Charles Davidson speaks of "the beautification of the commandment," in Charles Davidson, *From Szatmar to the New World: Max Wohlberg. American Cantor.* The Jewish Theological Seminary, New York, 2001, 109–110.

7. Glantz on *nusach* deriving from biblical cantillation modes, in Jerry Glantz, ed., *Leib Glantz—The Man Who Spoke to God*, 330. Also, Kalib, *The Musical Tradition of the Eastern European Synagogue.* Volume One. Introduction: History and Definition. Part One. Text. and Volume One, Part Two. Music. Kalib even identifies individual *ta'amim* as the foundation for certain phrases of *nusach*.

8. For an incredibly informative and detailed study of Eastern European Ashkenazi liturgy, see Sholom Kalib, *The Musical Tradition of the Eastern European Synagogue*, Volume One, Part One. Text. and Part Two. Music.

9. Throughout this manuscript, I will use the terms "cantor" and "*hazzan*" interchangeably, although one could make a distinction, as Cantor Heiser's CA certificate in 1954 shows. Before receiving his certificate, he was called either Cantor or Minister or Reverend, the last two borrowed from Christian clergy, but hardly ever *hazzan*. The training for it was of a formal nature at JTS, and afterward, he was then recognized as a member of an elite club of *hazzanim*.

10. Frigyesi, *Writing on Water*, 68–69.

11. Jewish Virtual Library, A Project of AICE, "Virtual Jewish World: Berlin Germany." Online, accessed 12/1/2022.

12. Steven Aschheim, *Brothers and Strangers*. University of Wisconsin Press, Madison, Wisc., 1982. This study presents a rather troubling picture of the relationship between West European, especially German, Jews and East European Jews, and specifically in Berlin.

13. Short biography in third person on official stationary. "Hazzan Mordecai G. Heiser was born in Kovno, Lithuania; came to Berlin as a very young child, etc." Stein Collection.

14. This information is found in documents that are in the possession of the Stein family in Pittsburgh, PA. Further references will be to "Stein Collection." Also letter from Helene Thill, *Jüdische Kultusgemeinde Koblenz*, dated May 2, 1999; Reinhard Pfaff, Standesamt Nassau, in letter dated July 7, 2000, and information from Weissensee Cemetery in Berlin. Stein

Collection. Selma Brauer's origin can be found in the Heiser/Stein family tree constructed by Rena Sufrin Kennedy.
15. Helene Thill letter, dated May 2, 1999. Stein Collection. The Koblenz Memor Book says that he was deported from Theresienstadt to Treblinka [not Minsk] on September 19, 1942. In *Gedenkbuch: Opfer der Verfolgung der Juden unter der nationalsozialistischen Gewaltherrschaft in Deutschland 1933–1945*. Herausgegeben vom Bundesarchiv. Zweite, wesentlich erweiterte Auflage, Volume II. Bundesarchiv, Koblenz, 2006, 1250. Further mention will be to Koblenz Memor Book.
16. Weissensee Cemetery information. Stein Collection.
17. Gustav Heiser, *Geburtsschein*. Stein Collection.
18. See also Gustav Heiser, *Geburtsurkunde*. Stein Collection.
19. Helene Thill letter, dated May 2, 1999; see also Eleonore and Hugo birth certificates. Stein Collection.
20. Helene Thill letter, dated May 2, 1999. Stein Collection. Information on family can also be found in Koblenz Memor Book, which states that Hugo died in Riga; death date is November 30, 1941. Volume II, 1250.
21. Helene Thill letter, dated May 2, 1999. Stein Collection. Koblenz Memor Book gives the death date as November 30, 1941. Volume II, 1250.
22. Birth and death certificates. Stein Collection.
23. Excerpt from birth register. Stein Collection. My thanks to the late Werner Runschke, Süssen City Archive Director, for helping to decipher the handwritten document.
24. "Scheunenviertel: History, Architecture, and Sights," by Alex McKerrel, online, accessed 12/6/22.
25. Helene Thill letter, dated May 2, 1999. Stein Collection.
26. Gustav Heiser *Führungszeugnis*, 1939. Stein Collection.
27. Heiser *Abgangs-Zeugnis*, Stein Collection. It appears that the graduation date has been altered to say 1922. This latter date cannot be correct, however, as the certificate states that he left this school upon committee approval in order to take a job.
28. Hermann Simon, *Die Neue Synagoge Berlin: Geschichte, Gegenwart, Zukunft*. Edition Hentrich, third edition, Berlin, 1997, 2.
29. Gilya G. Schmidt, translator, and with an introduction. *Friedrich Schleiermacher, Letters on the Occasion of the Political Theological Task and the Sendschreiben (Open Letter) of Jewish Heads of Household*. The Edwin Mellen Press, Lewiston/Queenston/Lampeter, 2001, 45.
30. Hermann Simon, *Die Neue Synagoge Berlin*, 8–10.
31. Hermann Simon, *Die Neue Synagoge Berlin*, 12.

32. Amos Elon, *The Pity of It All: A Portrait of Jews in Germany 1743–1933*. Metropolitan Books, New York, 2002, 342–43.
33. David Clay Large, *Berlin*. Basic Books, New York, 2000, 158.
34. Eisenberg & Struck letter. Stein Collection.
35. For information on Hermann Struck, see Gilya Gerda Schmidt, *The Art and Artists of the Fifth Zionist Congress, 1901: Heralds of a New Age*, 85–119.
36. Hermann Struck letter, dated March 31, 1933. Stein Collection.
37. *Bestätigung*, Kultusverwaltung, Jüdische Gemeinde Berlin, dated January 17, 1929. Stein Collection.
38. *B'nai Israel Golden Anniversary Book*, 1954, 25.
39. Stern Conservatory in Wikipedia.org, online. Accessed 2/14/23.
40. See Felix Asch, Internet Archive: Digital Library of Free & Borrowable Books, Movies, and Music, archive.org. Also Kolnidre/Lewandowski online: Felix Asch Kol nidre provided to YouTube by NAXOS of America. My First Opera Recordings (1895–1902). The information available on these sites is minimal.
41. For Lewandowski biography, see Aron Friedmann, ed., *Lebensbilder berühmter Kantoren*. Volume II. C. Boas Nachf. Berlin, 1918. For Friedmann interaction with Lewandowski, see also *50 Jahre in Berlin (1878–1928)*. C. Boas Nachf. Berlin, 1929. Also *Der Synagogale Gesang. Eine Studie*. C. Boas Nachf. Berlin, 1908, for brief biographies on Sulzer and Lewandowski.
42. Michael Brenner, *After the Holocaust: Rebuilding Jewish Lives in Postwar Germany*. Princeton University Press, Princeton, N.J., 1997, 102–106.
43. Brenner, *After the Holocaust*, 1997, 104.
44. Brenner, *After the Holocaust*, 1997, 105; CD cover, Oberkantor Estrongo Nachama, "Es tönt von der Erde zum Himmel empor," by Louis Lewandowski, RIAS-Kammerchor, Uwe Gronostay, direction, RIAS Berlin, GEMA CD 66.211 87, 1995; CD cover, Oberkantor Estrongo Nachama, "Jom Kipur, Gebetsgesänge zum Versöhnungstag," RIAS-Kammerchor, Uwe Gronostay, direction, RIAS Berlin, GEMA CD 66.219 80, no date.
45. *Bestätigung II*, Kultusverwaltung, Jüdische Gemeinde Berlin, dated January 17, 1929. Stein Collection.
46. Simon Neisser letter, dated November 1, 1938. Stein Collection. Simon Neisser was the chairman of the board of the Israelitische Religionsgemeinde Berlin-Lichterfelde-Lankwitz from 1912 until his emigration to Eretz Israel; he died in Tel Aviv in 1950. In 1955, probably in connection with reparations, his widow, Dora Neisser, wrote an affidavit for Gustav Heiser, affirming that he was employed as cantor by this congregation

from 1925 until 1937 [discrepancy with letter from congregation which says 1938]. His salary had been 300 marks a month. Dora Neisser letter, Tel Aviv-Jaffa, dated May 15, 1955. Stein Collection.
47. John Rayner letter, June 21, 1990. Stein Collection.
48. Card announcing *Probevortrag* is extant. Stein Collection.
49. Elly Hochmann *Geburtsurkunde*. Stein Collection.
50. Elly Hochmann *Geburtsurkunde*. Addendum. Stein Collection.
51. Judith Heiser Stein Notes. Stein Collection.
52. Judith Heiser Stein Notes. Stein Collection. The Koblenz Memor Book says that Betti Hochmann Lieberson was born on September 30, 1906. Volume III, 2071.
53. Judith Heiser Stein Notes. Stein Collection. The Koblenz Memor Book says that Adela was born May 20, 1877, in Grzymalow. She was deported from Berlin to Riga on November 27, 1941, her death date is listed as November 30, 1941. Volume II, 1395.
54. Berlin Weissensee Cemetery. Visit in 1999. The Jewish community put up a pauper's tombstone in 1931.
55. There is a Leiser (Leo) Hochmann in the Koblenz Memor Book, Vol. II, 1395, but neither birth date nor birthplace correspond to the available information.
56. Judith Heiser Stein Notes. Stein Collection.
57. *Jüdische Rundschau* announcement, September 7, 1934. Stein Collection.
58. Heiser *Aufgebot*. Stein Collection.
59. Heiser *Aufgebot*. Stein Collection.
60. Receipt for Jewish wedding extant. Stein Collection.
61. Receipt for *Brautstrauss* extant. Stein Collection.
62. Heiser *Staatsangehörigkeitsausweis*. Stein Collection.
63. Judith Heiser *Geburtsurkunde*. Stein Collection.
64. Telegram. Stein Collection.
65. Heiser *Zwischenprüfung*. Stein Collection.
66. Postcard from Onkel Emil and Tante Mäuschen. Stein Collection.
67. *Anmeldung* and *Abmeldung*. Stein Collection.
68. Elly Heiser letter. Stein collection. It could have been Sophie Weiss née Birnbaum in Pittsburgh.
69. Israelitische Religionsgemeinde letter (I), dated November 1, 1938. Stein Collection.
70. Israelitische Religionsgemeinde letter (II), dated November 1, 1938. Stein Collection.
71. Letter dated November 1, 1938. Stein Collection.

72. *Hochschule für die Wissenschaft des Judentums. Encyclopedia Judaica*, Vol. 8, He-Ir. Macmillan, New York and Jerusalem, 1972, 799–801.
73. Emil Fackenheim, *What is Judaism?* Syracuse University Press, Syracuse, N.Y., 1987, 153.
74. Gershom Scholem, *From Berlin to Jerusalem: Memories of my Youth*. Paul Dry Books, Philadelphia, 2012, 36 and 68. See also *Encyclopedia Judaica*, Vol. 8, He-Ir, Macmillan, New York and Jerusalem, 1972, 799–801.
75. Fackenheim, *What Is Judaism?*, 14.
76. Emil Fackenheim, *An Epitaph for German Judaism: From Halle to Jerusalem*. The University of Wisconsin Press, Madison, Wisc., 2007, 44.
77. Fackenheim, *What Is Judaism?*, 14.
78. Heiser Farewell Speech to Friendship Club, on tape. Stein Collection.
79. Fackenheim, *What Is Judaism?*, 198.
80. Fackenheim, *Epitaph*, 43. See also "Leo Baeck," in *Encyclopedia Judaica*, Vol. 4, B, Macmillan, New York and Jerusalem, 1972, 77–78.
81. Fackenheim, *What Is Judaism?*, 107.
82. "Max Wiener," in *Encyclopedia Judaica*, Vol. 16, Ur-Z, Macmillan, New York and Jerusalem, 1972, 500.
83. "Max Wiener," in *Wikipedia, Die freie Enzyklopädie*. Bearbeitungsstand: 1. February 2016, 16:47 UTC; also *Encyclopedia Judaica*, Vol. 16, Ur-Z, Macmillan, New York, and Jerusalem, 1972, 499.
84. Brenner, *After the Holocaust*, 183.
85. Fackenheim, *Epitaph*, 56.
86. Brenner, *After the Holocaust*, 107.
87. 'Leo Baeck,' Jewish Virtual Library, accessed 2/3/16, https://www.jewishvirtuallibrary.org/jsource/biography/baeck.html; see also "Eugen Täubler," Sm-Un, *Encyclopedia Judaica*, Volume 15, Macmillan, New York and Jerusalem, 1972, 699; Brenner, *After the Holocaust*, 107.
88. Fackenheim, *What Is Judaism?*, 107.
89. 'Ismar Elbogen,' Jewish Virtual Library, accessed 2/3/16, https://www.jewishvirtuallibrary.org/jsource/judaica/ejud_0002_0006_0_05730.html; see also *Encyclopedia Judaica*, Volume 6, Di-Fo, Macmillan, New York and Jerusalem, 1972, 573.
90. 1938 picture of class in Fackenheim, *Epitaph*, 120.
91. 'Alexander Guttmann', American Jewish Archives, online, accessed 4/6/16, http://americanjewisharchives.org.
92. Harry Torczyner, born in Lemberg, Galicia, took on the Hebrew name Naftali Herz Tur-Sinai upon making Aliyah. He had already spent time in Eretz Israel before World War I, and later became a professor of Semitic

languages at the Hebrew University of Jerusalem and a member of the Israel Academy of Sciences and Humanities. In 1959, he finished the 50-year 17-volume Hebrew dictionary project begun by Eliezer Ben-Yehuda, whose fame as one of Israel's most respected philologists he shares. *Wikipedia*, accessed 6/30/17.

93. Fackenheim, *What Is Judaism?*, 81 and 107.
94. Fackenheim, *Epitaph*, 49.
95. Fackenheim, *What Is Judaism?*, 81.
96. Fackenheim, *Epitaph*, 50–54.
97. See Gustav Heiser letters to Elly from Amsterdam, dated March 27, April 18, June 16, and June 21 of 1934, and two envelopes, one from July 23. Stein Collection.
98. Fackenheim, *Epitaph*, 70.
99. Fackenheim, *Epitaph*, 43 and 51–52.
100. Fackenheim, *Epitaph*, 120.
101. Heiser *Hochschule Bescheinigung für Zwischenprüfung*. Stein Collection.
102. See appendix in Fackenheim, *Epitaph*, for certificate as rabbi, 272–73.
103. By accident, I came across a *Wikipedia* entry that sheds additional light on Hans's life. Born in Berlin, he left on one of the last Kindertransports to England. Sadly, both of his parents, Ferdinand Rahmer and Charlotte Landshut, were murdered in the Holocaust. Hans changed his name to John Desmond Rayner and served in the British Army from 1943 until 1947. Upon returning to private life, he continued his studies by claiming an open scholarship in modern languages that he had previously won at Cambridge. He switched to Moral Science, which included philosophy, logic, ethics, and psychology, and in 1950 he received his degree with First Class Honors. During this time he studied Hebrew, Aramaic, Syriac, and Semitic Epigraphy, writing a thesis about Maimonides. In 1953, he was ordained as a Rabbi in the Liberal tradition and served a number of congregations in London. He made one trip to the United States, in 1963, when Hebrew Union College offered him a graduate fellowship. From a later letter we learn that he did visit with the Heisers in Pittsburgh during this time, the only time that they met again after leaving Berlin. Rabbi Rayner was an active participant in interfaith work and a prolific author. In 1993, he was honored with the appointment as a Commander of the Order of the British Empire. "John Rayner," *Wikipedia: The Free Encyclopedia*, https://en.wikipedia.org/w/index.php?title=John_Rayner&oldid=701577462 (accessed April 6, 2016).
104. Gustav Heiser letter, dated October 2, 1938. Stein Collection.

105. See Michael Berenbaum, *The World Must Know*, The History of the Holocaust as Told in the USHMM. Little, Brown & Co., Boston/Toronto/London, 1993, 54.
106. Heiser Farewell Speech to Friendship Club 1979, on tape. Stein Collection.
107. Gustav Heiser letter, dated May 30, 1939, Richborough, England. Stein Collection.
108. Documents re: Gustav Heiser release from internment in Sachsenhausen. Courtesy of Agnes Ohm, Director, Archive, Library, and Holdings as well as Media Holdings, Gedenkstätte und Museum Sachsenhausen, January 5, 2023. Many thanks to Frau Ohm!
109. Emil L. Fackenheim, "Sachsenhausen 1938: Groundwork for Auschwitz," in *The Jewish Return into History*. Schocken Books, New York, N.Y., 1978.
110. Fackenheim, *Epitaph*, 64.
111. Fackenheim, *Epitaph*, 258. Fackenheim also tells about this experience in *What Is Judaism?*, 45.
112. Klinkerwerke is a tile factory; see Emil Fackenheim, "Sachsenhausen 1938: Groundwork for Auschwitz," 59.
113. Fackenheim, *Epitaph*, 65.
114. Fackenheim, "Sachsenhausen 1938: Groundwork for Auschwitz," 59–60.
115. Fackenheim, *Epitaph*, 70.
116. Letter to Gustav Heiser from Hebrew University. Stein Collection.
117. Fackenheim, *Epitaph*, 266.
118. In a typed translation it says Liebestück, but a Hans Liebeschütz is listed in the Ismar Elbogen Collection, 1842–1974, AR 64/MF515 of the BETA Europeana Collections in the Leo Baeck Institute, New York, and in *Wikipedia*. Liebeschütz was born in Hamburg and began university studies at the University of Berlin in 1912, the year that Leo Baeck and Max Wiener moved to Berlin. He served in World War I, and, after being wounded, continued his studies in medieval history in Heidelberg. Starting in 1920, he taught at many different schools and colleges, including the *Hochschule*. In 1938 his family left Germany, while he remained. He was subsequently arrested during Kristallnacht and spent four weeks in Sachsenhausen along with Emil Fackenheim and Gustav Heiser and others. Like Heiser and Fackenheim, Liebeschütz fled Germany for England in March 1939, where he was interned on the Isle of Man as an enemy alien for six months. From 1942 on, he taught Latin in England, became a British citizen, and eventually principal lecturer at the University of Liverpool. He and his family remained in England, where he died in 1978. Online. Both accessed 6/21/17.

119. Gustav Heiser *Zeugnis*. Stein Collection.
120. I was not able to learn more about Dr. Kahane.
121. Gustav Heiser *Hochschule* Certificate as Prediger and Religionslehrer. Stein Collection.
122. Franz Grosse Receipt. Stein Collection.
123. Gustav Heiser letters to Elly from Amsterdam. Stein Collection. See Note 97.
124. Gustav Heiser letter from Amsterdam. Stein Collection.
125. Gustav Heiser letter to Elly Hochmann, dated March 27, 1934, Amsterdam.
126. Gustav Heiser Passport. Stein Collection.
127. Arthur Spanier studied Classical Philology at the *Hochschule* as well as the University of Berlin from 1908 to 1913. He served in World War I from 1915 to 1918, after which time he joined the *Akademie für die Wissenschaft des Judentums* as a Fellow. After completing his dissertation at the University of Freiburg, he worked in the Section for Judaica and Hebraica at the Prussian State Library until his dismissal in 1935. He, too, was arrested during Kristallnacht and spent time in Sachsenhausen. In 1939 he left for Holland on his way to the United States, but was arrested by the Nazis, who incarcerated him in Bergen-Belsen, where he perished. "Arthur Spanier," in *Wikipedia, Die freie Enzyklopädie*. Bearbeitungsstand: 18. März 2016, 21:00 UTC.
128. Heiser *Hochschule* Certificate from Leo Baeck. Stein Collection.
129. Gustav Heiser *Abmeldung*. Stein Collection.
130. Hilfsverein letter re: Gustav Heiser leaving on a *Sammel-Transport*. Stein Collection.
131. Heiser letter to Hans, May 30, 1939. Stein Collection.
132. Jüdische Gemeinde letter, dated May 2, 1939. Stein Collection.
133. Judith Heiser *Abmeldung*. Stein Collection.
134. Judith Heiser *Anmeldung*. Stein Collection.
135. Dr. W. Israel Leszczynski letter. Stein Collection.
136. Permission from Foreign Currency Office to take property into emigration. Stein Collection.
137. Permission from Foreign Currency Office to take property into emigration. Stein Collection.
138. Document from Feldkommandantur 520 to Emile Meerberger, S.A., dated June 22, 1942. Stein Collection.
139. Document from Emile Meerberger S. A. about lift. Stein Collection.
140. Elly Heiser Passport. Stein Collection.

141. Information Booklet for Foreigners in Great Britain. Stein Collection.
142. *Abmeldung* for Elly and Judith Heiser. Stein Collection.
143. Elly Heiser, "A Holocaust Remembrance," in *The Jewish Chronicle of Pittsburgh*, February 2, 1989, 14. Stein Collection.
144. Heiser letter to Hans, dated May 30, 1939. Stein Collection.
145. Receipts from American Consulate. Stein Collection.
146. Stein Collection. For confirmation of London as the location, see postcard to Elly Heiser.
147. Kitchener Camp letter, dated January 25, 1940. Stein Collection.
148. Permit for Gustav Heiser to leave Kitchener Refugee Camp, January 24, 1940. Stein Collection.
149. Hans's brother helped; see 1938 letter from Mordecai to Hans, and Elly's request. Stein Collection.
150. Manifest of M.V. "Georgie" from Liverpool to New York. Stein Collection.

Chapter 2

1. Letter from Monte Daniels, dated March 15, 1940. Stein Collection.
2. Envelope addressed to Heisers c/o Weiss. Stein Collection.
3. MSS #470, B'nai Israel Congregation Records, Rauh Jewish Archive, Detre Library and Archives Division, Heinz History Center, Pittsburgh, PA.
4. See letter before June 8, 1940, from Elli and Julius Zellner. Stein Collection.
5. See letter from Rabbi Hailperin in 1944. Stein Collection.
6. See Cantors Assembly Convention Proceedings Internet Archive, starting in 1949.
7. See Cantors Assembly Convention Proceedings Internet Archive, and various letters and envelopes.
8. Dr. George Feldstein, a physician, who resided at 1122 Mellon Street in Pittsburgh, provided an affidavit for Elly Heiser's sister, Betty, and her husband, Leo Lieberson. In the affidavit he says he is a friend. The affidavit attests that: He is a native-born citizen of the United States, who was born in Pittsburgh, Pennsylvania. At the time he was 58 years old, having lived continuously in the U.S. since March 27, 1883 [his birth date]. It is his intention and desire to have his friends whose names appear on the affidavit come to the U.S. for permanent residence. They currently live at No. 214 Linienstrasse, Berlin N 54, Germany. Leiser Lieberson, male, born March 14, 1904, country of birth Russia, occupation tobacco manufacturer. Relationship to deponent is that of friend. Berta [Betty] Lieberson

(née Hochmann, crossed out), female, born September 30, 1906, country of birth Berlin, occupation housewife. Relationship to deponent is that of friend. His regular occupation is that of physician. His average earnings amount to $250 weekly. He possesses the financial assets listed on the affidavit as well as proof thereof:

>Assets valued at $50,000
>Life insurance $59,000
>Cash surrender value about $20,000
>Stocks and Bonds $30,000. . . .
>[more, but doesn't make sense].

9. There is a second affidavit for three people by the name of Kanozuka, also from Dr. George Feldstein. Who they are and whether they made it is not known. Dr. George Feldstein, residing at 1122 Mellon Street, Pittsburgh, Pennsylvania, being duly sworn depose and say: That I am a native-born citizen of the United States having been born in the City of Pittsburgh, State of Pennsylvania. That it is my intention and desire to have my relatives whose names appear below, at present residing at Camp Devens, Italy: Abraham Kanozuker, Viale Abruzzi 11, Milano, Italy; Feige Kanozuker (wife) and Blanka Kanozuker (daughter) come to the United States for permanent residence.

>Abraham Kanozuker, male, October 27, 1900 (date of birth), Poland
>Feige Kanozuker (wife), female, November 12, 1901 (date of birth), Poland
>Blanka Kanozuker (daughter), female, April 3, 1933 (date of birth), Austria

That my regular occupation is Physician (Office: 3401 Fifth Avenue), and my average earnings amount to $250.00 weekly. That I possess the following financial assets of which corroborative evidence is herewith attached:

>1st Lieut. U.S.A. Medical Corps—Camp Denus Base Hospital, 1918–19.
>War Risk Insurance No. K 476723. Present value about $7,000.00.
>In addition I have other assets valued at $50,000.00.
>That my dependents consist of one sister (partly).
>December 1950, George Feldstein

10. Undated 1941 letter from Leo Lieberson and Betty with postscript from Meta to Gustav and Elly. Stein Collection. What happened to Julius Zellner and son, Joel, is uncertain. Cantor Heiser did not list them in the prayer book where the murdered family members are recorded, although Eleonore (Elke) is there, and they are not in the Koblenz Memor Book; neither is Eleonore Heiser Zellner.

11. Undated Elli [Eleonore] Heiser Zellner letter to Gustav and Elly Heiser. Stein Collection.
12. Gustav Heiser letter, June 8, 1940. Stein Collection.
13. Letter from Julius Zellner to Gustav and Elly Heiser, July 15, 1940. Stein Collection.
14. Undated Betty and Leo Lieberson letter indicating Elli Zellner's pregnancy. Stein Collection.
15. Letter from Elli Heiser Zellner, married to Julius Zellner, dated Aachen, September 27, 1940. Stein Collection.
16. Louis Younger letter dated February 21, 1941. Stein Collection.
17. See Fackenheim 1938 class picture in his book *Epitaph*, in center section of book; see about Rautenberg, 62.
18. Letter from Mordecai to Charles, dated September 21, 1941. Stein Collection. The Koblenz Memor Book lists a Betty Rautenberg née Marcuse, born November 5, 1874, in Falkenburg, Pommern, living in Berlin, and deported from Berlin to Warsaw on April 2, 1942. Volume III, 2736. So his brother was not able to do anything for Betty; she was deported in 1942.
19. Michael W. Grunberger, ed., *From Haven to Home: 350 Years of Jewish Life in America*. Library of Congress in association with George Braziller Inc., 2004.
20. Emma Lazarus, "The New Collossus," in Ellen M. Umansky and Dianne Ashton. *Four Centuries of Jewish Women's Spirituality. A Source Book*. Revised edition. Brandeis University Press, Waltham, Mass., and University Press of New England, Lebanon, NH, 2009, 137.
21. See Michael Berenbaum, *The World Must Know*, 49–50.
22. Rabbi Herman Hailperin, Ph.D., letter dated June 14, 1944. Stein Collection.
23. Mordecai Gustav Heiser Naturalization document. Stein Collection.
24. Edelman, Marsha Bryan. *Discovering Jewish Music*, 125–147. Also all of Slobin, *Chosen Voices*.
25. Slobin, *Chosen Voices*, 3; Edelman, *Discovering Jewish Music*, 125; and Grunberger, ed., *From Haven to Home*, 23–26.
26. Slobin, *Chosen Voices*, 44. Slobin quotes Wise, who calls the *hazzan* a *kol-bo*. Slobin translates this as "jack of all trades."
27. For an interesting account of the early American cantor, see Mark Slobin and Jacob Rader Marcus in Slobin, *Chosen Voices*, 31–32.
28. See Edelman, *Discovering Jewish* Music, 125.
29. Edelman, *Discovering Jewish Music*, 127–130, and Slobin, *Chosen Voices*, 59.
30. See Slobin, *Chosen Voices*, 64–65. This organization still exists. It now

calls itself the Jewish Ministers Cantors Association of the United States and Canada and has a website, http://www.thejmca.org. See also Charles Davidson, *From Szatmar to the New World: Max Wohlberg. American Cantor.* Jewish Theological Seminary, New York, 2001, on a running dispute between the *Chazzanim Farband* and another group, the Cantors Ministers Cultural Organization,125–143.
31. Grunberger, ed., *From Haven to Home*, 77.
32. Barbara S. Burstin, *Steel City Jews: A History of Pittsburgh and Its Jewish Community 1840–1915*, self-published in 2008, 51. She likewise produced a film, "A Jewish Legacy: Pittsburgh," which was nominated for a regional Emmy Award.
33. *Wikipedia online*, "Jewish Pittsburgh," accessed 9/12/22.
34. Burstin, *Steel City Jews*, 10–17.
35. Burstin, *Steel City Jews*, 19 and 23.
36. Grunberger, ed., *From Haven to Home*, 75 and 88.
37. Burstin, *Steel City Jews*, 30.
38. "Jewish Pittsburgh" in *Wikipedia*. I would like to acknowledge here that I owe much gratitude to Rabbi Jacob for his kindness to me when I was a graduate student at the University of Pittsburgh, writing my Prelims on Abraham Geiger, the father of Reform Judaism in Germany. Rabbi Jacob owned a complete set of the journal that Geiger edited. He invited me to use it and to work in his office library whenever needed, which was an invaluable resource for my project.
39. Burstin, *Steel City Jews*, 273–274. See Chapter 7, "Hill Street Jews," 269–314 for a very troubling and depressing account of these poor immigrants.
40. Jewishwebsite.com, "Pittsburgh Jewish Population." Accessed 9/12/22.
41. There is some discrepancy in the records of the Rauh Jewish Archive in the Senator John Heinz History Center in Pittsburgh, PA, concerning B'nai Israel's origins. According to the congregation, the congregation was very clearly founded in 1904 and celebrated milestones accordingly. However, the Heinz Archive files, MSS #470, B'nai Israel Congregational Records, have no founding date, but a charter date of 1911. There is a picture of a "Congregation B'nai Israel 50th Anniversary Dance Committee," dated to 1962 (but it should be 1953 or 1954). See MSP #470 B'nai Israel Congregational Records, 2013053-hpichswp-0084, Rauh Jewish Archive, Detre Library and Archives Division, Heinz History Center, Pittsburgh, PA. The *B'nai Israel Golden Anniversary Book* clearly has the dates of 1904–1954/5664–5714.
42. *B'nai Israel Golden Anniversary Book*, 17.

43. *B'nai Israel Golden Anniversary Book*, 17 and 19.
44. Groundbreaking picture in Heinz History Center Archives, Pittsburg, PA. MSP #470, B'nai Israel Congregational Records. Box 1, Folder 5, Rauh Jewish Archive, Detre Library and Archives Division, Senator John Heinz History Center, Pittsburgh, PA.
45. *B'nai Israel Golden Anniversary Book*, 20.
46. Patricia Lowry, "Looking for an angel," *Pittsburgh Post-Gazette*, December 9, 1997, D-1 and D-12. Stein Collection. I owe thanks to Kelseigh at Hodges Library, University of Tennessee, for an electronic copy of this article.
47. *B'nai Israel Golden Anniversary Book*, 21.
48. *B'nai Israel Golden Anniversary Book*, 21–22.
49. Assistants to Rabbi Lichter. MSS #470, B'nai Israel Congregational Records, Board Meeting Minutes, November 7, 1950. Box 24, Folder 20, Rauh Jewish Archive, Detre Library and Archives Division, Heinz History Center, Pittsburgh, PA, 3.
50. Robert Schwartz, Religion Editor, "His Ministry Is More Than Music. Cantor Interprets The Prayers Of Jewish People In Worship. Hazzan's Responsibility Carries A Sacred Trust For Tenor Here," in *The Pittsburgh Press*, April 22, 1967, 6. Digital copy thanks to Carnegie Mellon University Libraries staff.
51. *B'nai Israel 75th Anniversary* booklet, 16.
52. MSS 470, B'nai Israel Congregational Records, Executive Committee Minutes, June 23, 1953. Box 25, Folder 5, Rauh Jewish Archive, Detre Library and Archives Division, Heinz History Center, Pittsburgh, PA, front page.
53. MSS #470, B'nai Israel Congregational Records, Board Meeting Minutes, November 15, 1960. Box 24, Folder 22, Rauh Jewish Archive, Detre Library and Archives Division, Heinz History Center, Pittsburgh, PA, 3.
54. MSS #470, B'nai Israel Congregational Records, Board Meeting Minutes, July 10, 1962. Box 24, Folder 23, Rauh Jewish Archive, Detre Library and Archives Division, Heinz History Center, Pittsburgh, PA, 2.
55. MSS #470, B'nai Israel Congregational Records, Board Meeting Minutes, March 1, 1966. Box 24, Folder 25, Rauh Jewish Archive, Detre Library and Archives Division, Heinz History Center, Pittsburgh, PA, 2.
56. MSS #470, B'nai Israel Congregational Records, Board Meeting Minutes, June 3, 1969. Box 24, Folder 26, Rauh Jewish Archive, Detre Library and Archives Division, Heinz History Center, Pittsburgh, PA.
57. *B'nai Israel 75th Anniversary* booklet, 16.
58. *B'nai Israel Golden Anniversary Book*, 23.

NOTES TO PAGES 61–63

59. MSS #470, B'nai Israel Congregational Records, Board Meeting Minutes, May 1, 1951. Box 24, Folder 20, Rauh Jewish Archive, Detre Library and Archives Division, Heinz History Center, Pittsburgh, PA.
60. MSS #470, B'nai Israel Congregational Records, Board Meeting Minutes, October 7, 1952. Box 24, Folder 21, Rauh Jewish Archive, Detre Library and Archives Division, Heinz History Center, Pittsburgh, PA.
61. *B'nai Israel Golden Anniversary Book*, 26.
62. *B'nai Israel Golden Anniversary Book*, 26–32.
63. *Congregation B'nai Israel 75th Anniversary 1904–1979/5664–5739* booklet, 16.
64. "Jean-Jacques Duval." *Wikipedia.org*. Accessed 1/23/23.
65. *Congregation B'nai Israel 75th Anniversary 1904–1979/5664–5739* booklet, 16.
66. *Congregation B'nai Israel 75th Anniversary 1904–1979/5664–5739* booklet, 17.
67. "Business and Professional Division of Hadassah," *Jewish Criterion*, Vol. 97, No. 5, Dec. 6, 1940, 16. Cantor Heiser still uses Gustav Heiser. Online in http://digitalcollections.library.cmu.edu/portal/collections/pin/index/jsp, updated to http://digitalcollections.library.cmu.edu/pjn. Accessed 2/16/16. Future references will be to "Jewish Newspaper Project." I would like to thank Ryan Splenda, Carnegie-Mellon Business and Economic Librarian; Charlotte Kiger Price, Liaison Librarian to History and Modern Foreign Languages; and Julia Corrin, University Archivist, Carnegie-Mellon University Libraries, for their considerable help in accessing and obtaining digital copies of the Pittsburgh Jewish Newspapers. Future acknowledgements will be to Carnegie-Mellon University Libraries Digital Collection (CMU Libraries Digital Collection). Accessed 11/22/22 and many other times. All newspaper references were originally researched in 2016 and earlier.
68. "B'nai Israel Chevra Tehillim to Give Annual Dinner," *Jewish Criterion*, Vol. 97, No. 18, March 7, 1941, 16, "Jewish Newspaper Project" and CMU Libraries Digital Collection.
69. "Congregation B'nai Israel," *Jewish Criterion*, Vol. 99, No. 17, February 27, 1942, 17. "Jewish Newspaper Project" and CMU Libraries Digital Collection.
70. "Congregational News," Obituary for Cantor Bloom, *Jewish Criterion*, Vol. 99, No. 19, March 13, 1942, 21. "Jewish Newspaper Project" and CMU Libraries Digital Collection.
71. MSS #470, B'nai Israel Congregational Records, Executive Committee Meeting Minutes, April 6, 1942. Box 24, Folder 18, Rauh Jewish Archive, Detre Library and Archives Division, Heinz History Center, Pittsburgh, PA.
72. M. G. Heiser letter to Charles Rautenberg, dated September 21, 1941. Stein Collection.

73. MSS #470, B'nai Israel Congregational Records, Board Meeting Minutes, April 6, 1942. Box 23, Folder 6, Rauh Jewish Archive, Detre Library and Archives Division, Heinz History Center, Pittsburgh, PA.
74. MSS #470, B'nai Israel Congregational Records, Board Meeting Minutes, April 6, 1942. Box 23, Folder 6, Rauh Jewish Archive, Detre Library and Archives Division, Heinz History Center, Pittsburgh, PA.
75. MSS #470, B'nai Israel Congregational Records, Board Meeting Minutes, April 6, 1942. Box 23, Folder 6, 2 and 3, Rauh Jewish Archive, Detre Library and Archives Division, Heinz History Center, Pittsburgh, PA.
76. MSS #470, B'nai Israel Congregational Records, Board Meeting Minutes, August 3, 1943. Box 24, Folder 18, 1 and 2, Rauh Jewish Archive, Detre Library and Archives Division, Heinz History Center, Pittsburgh, PA.
77. MSS #470, B'nai Israel Congregational Records, Board Meeting Minutes, August 3, 1943. Box 24, Folder 18, 1 and 2, Rauh Jewish Archive, Detre Library and Archives Division, Heinz History Center, Pittsburgh, PA.
78. MSS #470, B'nai Israel Congregational Records, Board Meeting Minutes, May 1, 1945. Box 24, Folder 19, 3, Rauh Jewish Archive, Detre Library and Archives Division, Heinz History Center, Pittsburgh, PA.
79. "Hebrew School to Give Concert," *Jewish Criterion*, Vol. 100, No. 3, May 22, 1942, 18. "Jewish Newspaper Project."
80. "B'nai B'rith of Pittsburgh to Celebrate 100th Year Anniversary Lists Week of Special Events," *Jewish Criterion*, Vol. 100, No. 23, October 9, 1942, 9. "Jewish Newspaper Project" and CMU Libraries Digital Collection.
81. "B'nai B'rith Presents Armistice Day Program Sunday," *Jewish Criterion*, Vol. 103, No. 1, Nov. 5, 1943, 17. "Jewish Newspaper Project" and CMU Libraries Digital Collection.
82. "Tri-State U.J.F. Conference Noteworthy," *Jewish Criterion*, Vol. 103, No. 22, March 31, 1944, 16. "Jewish Newspaper Project" and CMU Libraries Digital Collection.
83. "In Memory of Our Departed Soldiers," *Jewish Criterion*, Vol. 107, No. 6, Dec. 7, 1945, 4. "Jewish Newspaper Project" and CMU Libraries Digital Collection. During this time, it was customary to address clergy of different faiths with "Reverend," a designation that alternates throughout the years with "Cantor" and with "Hazzan," depending on who is writing and to whom.
84. "Veterans' Plots To Be Dedicated at B'nai Israel Cemetery," *Jewish Criterion*, Vol. 108, No. 21, September 20, 1946, 289.
85. "Cantors Association Elects Officers," *Jewish Criterion*, Vol. 102, No. 3, May 21, 1943, 21. "Jewish Newspaper Project" and CMU Libraries Digital Collection.

86. Death notice for Rev. Elias Zaludkowsky, as well as large announcement signed by Cantor Heiser, *Jewish Criterion*, Vol. 102, No. 9, July 2, 1943, 7. "Jewish Newspaper Project" and CMU Libraries Digital Collection.
87. "Slobodka Yeshiva Holds Party," *Jewish Criterion*, Vol. 105, No. 26, April 27, 1945, 12. "Jewish Newspaper Project" and CMU Libraries Digital Collection. "Palestinian" here means the songs of the *chalutzim* in pre-state Israel.
88. "Pliskovers Schedule Israel Night," *Jewish Criterion*, Vol. 112, No. 24, October 8, 1948, 12. "Jewish Newspaper Project" and CMU Libraries Digital Collection.
89. "Capt. Wayland to Speak at Local Israel Celebration," *American Jewish Outlook*, Vol. 29, No. 24, May 6, 1949, 14. "Jewish Newspaper Project" and CMU Libraries Digital Collection.
90. "Labor Zionists Meet Sunday," *Y.M.&W.H.A. Weekly*, Nov. 4, 1949, 4. "Jewish Newspaper Project."
91. "Third Seder Opens UJF Campaign," *Y.M.&W.H.A. Weekly*, April 23, 1948, front page and 2. "Jewish Newspaper Project."
92. "UJF Solicitation Begins Monday," *Y.M.&W.H.A. Weekly*, April 15, 1949, front page and 3; "'After the Seder' Touches Off Huge Workers' Rally at Mosque Sunday Night," *Jewish Criterion*, Vol. 113, No. 26, April 22, 1949, 7; "'After the Seder' to launch UJF Campaign," *Y.M.&W.H.A. Weekly*, April 8, 1949, front page; *Y.M.&W.H.A. Weekly*, April 15, 1949, 3; advertisement for 'After the Seder' Rally in *American Jewish Outlook*, Vol. 29, No. 19, April 1, 1949, 9; "April 24 'After the Seder' Program Will Open U.J.F. Drive," *American Jewish Outlook*, Vol. 29, No. 20, April 8, 1949, 14; "Campaign Commentary," *American Jewish Outlook*, Vol. 29, No. 22, April 22, 1949, 7 and entire front page; "Jewish Newspaper Project" and CMU Libraries Digital Collection.
93. "Program Sunday Is Free to Y Members," *Y.M.&W.H.A. Weekly*, December 16, 1949, front page; "Special Program Sunday Night for 'Y' Chanukah Celebration," *Jewish Criterion*, Vol. 115, No. 8, December 16, 1949, 82. "Jewish Newspaper Project" and CMU Libraries Digital Collection.
94. "Hebrew Institute Schedules Music Festival," *Jewish Criterion*, Vol. 113, No. 17, February 18, 1949, 17; also "B'nai Israel YPL," *Jewish Criterion*, Vol. 113, No. 18, February 25, 1949, 20; "Star-Studded Program at Hebrew Institute Music Festival," *Jewish Criterion*, Vol. 113, No. 20, March 11, 1949, 10; "Jewish Music Fete Saturday," *Y.M.&W.H.A. Weekly*, March 25, 1949, 2; "Lorin Maazel Among Talent at Institute Music Festival," *Jewish Criterion*, Vol. 113, No. 22, March 4, 1949, 20; and "Talented Singer Directs Institute 'Purim Spiel,'" *Jewish Criterion*, Vol. 113, No. 21, March 18, 1949, 8. "Jewish Newspaper Project" and CMU Libraries Digital Collection.

95. "Opera Members to Be Featured at Hebrew Institute Festival," *American Jewish Outlook*, Vol. 29, No. 16, March 11, 1949, 12. "Jewish Newspaper Project" and CMU Libraries Digital Collection.
96. "National and Local Leaders Participate in Seminary Dinner," *Jewish Criterion*, Vol. 115, No. 6, December 2, 1949, 5. "Jewish Newspaper Project" and CMU Libraries Digital Collection.
97. "Capacity Crowd Expected at Seminary Dinner December 4," *Jewish Criterion*, Vol. 115, No. 6, December 2, 1949, 6. "Jewish Newspaper Project" and CMU Libraries Digital Collection.
98. "Talent and Committee Ready for Annual Seminary Dinner," *American Jewish Outlook*, Vol. 31, No. 4, December 2, 1949, 7. "Jewish Newspaper Project" and CMU Libraries Digital Collection. For Eternal Light series, see also *Wikipedia*, accessed June 30, 2017. There is an intriguing website, https://www.oldtimeradiodownloads.com that has 581 of the Eternal Light episodes for sale, for $5 each. One sample episode from October 15, 1944 is quite enlightening, and does not mince words in its dramatic presentation of the dangerous political situation for European Jews. Cantor Putterman and choir sing "V'Shamru" and "Shomer Israel."
99. Pittsburgh Concert Society printed announcement extant. Stein Collection.
100. "Cantor Heiser in Recital Sponsored By Pittsburgh Concert Society," *Jewish Criterion*, Vol. 113, No. 10, December 31, 1948, 9; also *Y.M.&W.H.A. Weekly*, December 31, 1948, 3; "Cantor Heiser in Concert Recital Today," *Jewish Criterion*, January 7, 1949, 24; "Cantor Heiser Gives Concert," *Y.M.&W.H.A. Weekly*, December 31, 1948, 3; "Cantor Heiser to Appear In Concert and Recital," *American Jewish Outlook*, Vol. 29, No. 7, January 7, 1949, 25; "Jewish Newspaper Project" and CMU Libraries Digital Collection.
101. Pittsburgh Concert Society printed program announcement. Stein Collection.
102. "Cantor to Give Recital," *American Jewish Outlook*, Vol. 29, No. 15, March 4, 1949, 19. "Jewish Newspaper Project" and CMU Libraries Digital Collection.
103. "Be strong and have courage," Joshua 1:6, a Zionist watchword made famous by HaShomer Hatzair (the Young Watchman), a socialist-Zionist secular Jewish youth movement founded in 1913 in Galicia, also a political party in the Yishuv.
104. Original Carnegie Recital Hall program extant. Stein Collection.
105. "Mordecai Heiser, Tenor, Bows," by R.P., *New York Times*, March 23, 1949, 35; also "Music Notes," *New York Times*, March 22, 1949, 30. "Jewish Newspaper Project."

106. Edelman, *Discovering Jewish Music*, 135. Also Slobin, *Chosen Voices*, 95. For an excellent history of Cantor Max Wohlberg, who was a member of the *Hazzanim Farband* and participated in a short-lived competing organization, the Cantors Ministers Cultural Organization, see Charles Davidson, *From Szatmar to the New World: Max Wohlberg. American Cantor*. Jewish Theological Seminary, New York, 2001. For minutes from the Cantors Ministers Cultural Organization 1938–1940, see Davidson, 125–145. Wohlberg later had a hand in the creation of the Cantors Assembly at JTS.
107. For two excellent extensive histories of the American Cantorate, see Slobin, *Chosen Voices*, 29–132; Edelman, *Discovering Jewish Music*, 125–147.
108. Cantors Assembly Convention Proceedings Internet Archive, 1947, 3, https://archive.org/details/CantorsAssemblyConventionProceedings. This URL is no longer needed. Simply entering Cantors Assembly Convention Proceedings Internet Archive leads to a very accessible website. Thank you!
109. Cantors Assembly Convention Proceedings Internet Archive, 1947, 9.
110. Cantors Assembly Convention Proceedings Internet Archive, 1947, 9.
111. Cantors Assembly Convention Proceedings Internet Archive, 1947, 14–15.
112. Cantors Assembly Convention Proceedings Internet Archive, 1947, 14–15.
113. "Society," under "Personals," *Jewish Criterion*, Vol. 109, No. 18, February 28, 1947, 12. "Jewish Newspaper Project" and CMU Libraries Digital Collection.
114. Cantors Assembly Convention Proceedings Digital Archive, 1947, 15.
115. Cantors Assembly Convention Proceedings Digital Archive, 1950, 23.
116. MSS #470, B'nai Israel Congregational Records, Board Meeting Minutes, May 1, 1951, Box 24, Folder 20, Rauh Jewish Archive, Detre Library and Archives Division, Heinz History Center, Pittsburgh, PA.
117. Routtenberg letter, dated August 21, 1952. Stein Collection.
118. Routtenberg letter, dated October 21, 1952. Stein Collection.
119. MSS #470, B'nai Israel Congregational Records, Board Meeting Minutes, August 5, 1952, Box 24, Folder 21, Rauh Jewish Archive, Detre Library and Archives Division, Heinz History Center, Pittsburgh, PA.
120. Cantors Assembly Convention Proceedings Digital Archive, 1953. Inside cover for picture, second from right, and 13.
121. Cantors Assembly Convention Proceedings Digital Archive, 1953, 14.
122. Cantors Assembly Heiser Certificate. Stein Collection.
123. *B'nai Israel Golden Anniversary Book*, 25.
124. *Congregation B'nai Israel Bulletin*, January 22, 1954.
125. "Cantors to Present Concert," *Jewish Criterion*, Vol. 123, No. 17, February 5, 1954, 5; "Cantors in Jewish Music Festival," *Jewish Criterion*, Vol. 123,

No. 19, February 19, 1954, 8; "Cantors Benefit Concert March 9," *Jewish Criterion*, Vol. 123, No. 20, February 26, 1954, 3; "Cantors Concert Tuesday, March 9," *Jewish Criterion*, Vol. 123, No. 21, March 5, 1954, 3; "Jewish Newspaper Project," also CMU Libraries Digital Collection.

126. Cantors Concert Committee letter, dated January 20, 1954. Stein Collection.
127. Heiser letter, dated January 19, 1954. Stein Collection.
128. Cantors Concert Committee and Lichter letter dated February 23, 1954. Stein Collection.
129. March 9, 1954, Concert Ticket. Stein Collection.
130. March 9, 1954, Concert Program. Stein Collection.
131. Cantors Assembly Convention Proceedings Internet Archive, 1954, 16. Cantor Heiser signs with *Hazzan* for the first time after receiving his certificate.
132. See *Journal of Jewish Identities* (2017), 10(1), 1–6. "Introduction: Jewish Music and Jewish Identity in the Rust Belt," by Randall Goldberg, Francesco Spagnolo, and Judah M. Cohen, Johns Hopkins University Press. Conference on Jewish Music and Jewish Identity, organized by Professor Helene Sinnreich, then Youngstown State University, now University of Tennessee.
133. Cantors Assembly Convention Proceedings Internet Archive, 1955, 10.
134. Picture of Five Pittsburgh Cantors in *Jewish Criterion*, Vol. 128, No. 1, April 13, 1956, 6. Stein Collection and CMU Libraries Digital Collection.
135. Cantors Assembly Convention Proceedings Internet Archive, 1956, 6.
136. "B'nai Israel Marks Jewish Music Month with Cantata," *Jewish Criterion*, Vol. 119, No. 20, March 7, 1952, 19. "Jewish Newspaper Project" and CMU Libraries Digital Project.
137. Picture and article, "Special Music Service at B'nai Israel Next Friday Night," *Jewish Criterion*, Vol. 121, No. 22, March 13, 1953, 18; "B'nai Israel to Hold Special Music Service," *American Jewish Outlook*, Vol. 37, No. 21, March 13, 1953, 13. "Jewish Newspaper Project" and CMU Libraries Digital Collection.
138. "B'nai Israel Sets Annual Music Service March 25," *American Jewish Outlook*, Vol. 41, No. 20, March 18, 1955, 19; "B'nai Israel to Hear New Sabbath Cantata," *Jewish Criterion*, Vol. 133, No. 26, April 3, 1959, 16. "Jewish Newspaper Project" and CMU Libraries Digital Collection.
139. "New Cantata By Rabbi, Cantor Honors Jewish Music Month," *Jewish Criterion*, Vol. 127, No. 21, March 2, 1956, 27. "Jewish Newspaper Project" and CMU Libraries Digital Collection.

140. "New Cantata to Be Premiered Here," *American Jewish Outlook*, Vol. 45, No. 22, March 29, 1957, 5; "Cantata Premiere at B'nai Israel," *Jewish Criterion*, Vol. 129, No. 25, March 29, 1957, 8; also *The Pittsburgh Press*, April 4, 1957, 3; all "Jewish Newspaper Project," *American Jewish Outlook*, and *Jewish Criterion*, also CMU Libraries Digital Collection.
141. "Synagogues Will Hold Services in Honor of Israel," *American Jewish Outlook*, Vol. 47, No. 25, April 18, 1958, front page; "Synagogue Performing Cantata," *American Jewish Outlook*, Vol. 48, No. 4, May 23, 1958, 16. "Jewish Newspaper Project" and CMU Libraries Digital Collection.
142. "Congregation to Hear Cantata at B'nai Israel on April 10," *American Jewish Outlook*, Vol. 49, No. 23, April 3, 1959, 20; also "United Synagogue Area Women Plan Two-Day Confab," *American Jewish Outlook*, Vol. 51, No. 25, April 15, 1960, 20; "Jewish Newspaper Project" and CMU Libraries Digital Collection.
143. "The Living Word" cantata, performed Friday, March 25, 1966, at 8:15 p.m. at B'nai Israel's annual Music Shabbat. MSS #470, B'nai Israel Congregational Records, Box 9, Folder 13, Rauh Jewish Archive, Detre Library and Archives Division, Heinz History Center, Pittsburgh, PA.
144. My thanks to Mr. Alvin Stein, who helped both with the engagement date and with the names of his fraternities. He stated in an email of July 2016 that he belonged to Kappa Kappa Psi, a band fraternity, and Tau Beta Sigma, the National Honor Band Society.
145. "Honored at Tea," *Pittsburgh Post-Gazette*, May 4, 1957, 3; also "To Be Honored," *Squirrel Hill News*, April 25, 1957, 8; in Stein Collection and "Jewish Newspaper Project." Electronic copies courtesy of Kelseigh, UT Hodges Library.
146. "Engagements and Weddings," in *Squirrel Hill News*, June 6, 1957, 5. Stein Collection. Date and page number courtesy of Carnegie Library, Pittsburgh, PA. In-person visit.
147. Picture and article, "Weddings," *Jewish Criterion*, Vol. 130, No. 9, June 7, 1957, 10. "Jewish Newspaper Project."
148. Cantors Assembly Convention Proceedings Internet Archive, 1958, 6.
149. Cantors Assembly Convention Proceedings Internet Archive, 1958, 19.
150. Cantors Assembly Convention Proceedings Internet Archive, 1960, 39.
151. "Hazzan Heiser Becomes 'Honorary Fellow'," *Jewish Criterion*, Vol. 136, No. 8, May 27, 1960, 3. "Jewish Newspaper Project" and CMU Libraries Digital Collection.
152. See Critendda of "Society," by Barnetta Davis Lange, *Jewish Criterion*, Vol.

135, No. 19, February 12, 1960, 10. "Jewish Newspaper Project" and CMU Libraries Digital Collection.
153. MSS #470, B'nai Israel Congregational Records, Board Meeting Minutes, January 12, 1960. Box 9, Folder 11, Rauh Jewish Archive, Detre Library and Archives Division, Heinz History Center, Pittsburgh, PA.
154. MSS #470, B'nai Israel Congregational Records, Samuel Rosenbaum letter, dated March 20, 1961. Box 24, Folder 22, Rauh Jewish Archive, Detre Library and Archives Division, Heinz History Center, Pittsburgh, PA.
155. MSS #470, B'nai Israel Congregational Records, Festival of Music Invitation and Program, March 24, 1961. Box 9, Folder 11, Rauh Jewish Archive, Detre Library and Archives Division, Heinz History Center, Pittsburgh, PA.
156. MSS #470, B'nai Israel Congregational Records, Cantor Heiser thank you letter, dated April 6, 1961. Box 9, Folder 11, Rauh Jewish Archive, Detre Library and Archives Division, Heinz History Center, Pittsburgh, PA.
157. About Cantor Heiser officiating at *ma'ariv* service of fourteenth annual convention on Wednesday, April 19, 6:30 p.m. Cantors Assembly Convention Proceedings Digital Archive, 1961, 6.
158. MSS #470, B'nai Israel Congregational Records, "A Grand Concert of Jewish Music" Invitation and Program, April 1, 1962. Box 9, Folder 12, Rauh Jewish Archive, Detre Library and Archives Division, Heinz History Center, Pittsburgh, PA.
159. Cantors Assembly Convention Proceedings Internet Archive, 1962, 8 and 75. The paragraph reads, "Our God and God of our fathers, accept our rest. Sanctify us through Your commandments and grant our portion in Your Torah." Adapted from Rabbi Morris Silverman, ed., *Sabbath and Festival Prayer Book*, 1966, 98.
160. Picture of ZOA leadership team in *Jewish Criterion*, Vol. 137, No. 6, November 11, 1960, 15. "Jewish Newspaper Project" and CMU Libraries Digital Collection.
161. Probably modeled on "Sing Along with Mitch (Miller)," who was popular then; "Daily Magazine," by Charles F. Danver, *Pittsburgh Post-Gazette*, May 22, 1961, 35, www.newspapers.com, accessed 8/3/17. Also, sing-alongs were popular on *kibbutzim* in Israel, and Cantor Heiser invited Rakhel Hadass, the founder of the Haifa Oranim Folk Group to Pittsburgh for a concert.
162. A series, "Songs of Israel," was published by Metro Music in 1949–50.
163. Heiser anonymous lecture, 10. Stein Collection.
164. "ZOA Membership Campaign Starts Off with Rally," *The Jewish Chronicle*, Vol. 1, No. 37, November 16, 1962, 24. "Jewish Newspaper Project" and CMU Libraries Digital Collection.

165. Publicity flyer for event. Stein Collection. Also "Bonds Chanukah Show," *The Jewish Chronicle*, Vol. 1, No. 41, December 14, 1962, 2. "Jewish Newspaper Project" and CMU Libraries Digital Collection.
166. MSP #470, B'nai Israel, Picture of 1968 or 1969? Congregational trip to Israel. Box 3, Folder 10, Rauh Jewish Archive, Detre Library and Archives Division, Heinz History Center, Pittsburgh, PA. According to Executive Committee Minutes of December 9, 1969, "Another Israel trip is being planned for the spring [1970] at the same price as last year [1968 or 1969?]."
167. Elly Heiser, "Will Edmundson Died for the Israel He Loved," *The Jewish Chronicle*, Vol. 4, No. 25, August 20, 1965, 8; also *Jewish Exponent*, November 19, 1965. Stein Collection, "Jewish Newspaper Project," and CMU Libraries Digital Collection.
168. Picture of Cantor Heiser, coordinator of 1965–66 ZOA membership campaign. No source; no date. Stein Collection.
169. MSS #470, B'nai Israel Congregational Records, Board Meeting Minutes, January 6, 1970. Box 25, Folder 1, 4, Rauh Jewish Archive, Detre Library and Archives Division, Heinz History Center, Pittsburgh, PA.
170. MSS #470, B'nai Israel Congregational Records, Board Meeting Minutes, February 3, 1970. Box 25, Folder 1, 4, Rauh Jewish Archive, Detre Library and Archives Division, Heinz History Center, Pittsburgh, PA.
171. Thirtieth Anniversary Concert in *The Jewish Chronicle*, Vol. 9, No. 5, March 26, 1970, 2. "Jewish Newspaper Project" and CMU Libraries Digital Collection.
172. *Congregation B'nai Israel Bulletin*, March 27, 1970. Stein Collection.
173. Thirtieth Anniversary Concert Ticket extant. Stein Collection.
174. Letter from Morton Siegel, dated April 1, 1970. Stein Collection.
175. Glatstein letter dated May 13, 1970. Stein Collection.
176. B'nai Israel Young Adult Congregation Telegram. Stein Collection.
177. Presidents of B'nai Israel Young Adult Congregation in *Congregation B'nai Israel Bulletin*, May 30, 1969, 5. Stein Collection.
178. Milton K. Susman, "As I See It," *The Jewish Chronicle*, Vol. 9, No. 8, April 16, 1970, 7. "Jewish Newspaper Project" and CMU Libraries Digital Collection.
179. Cantor Heiser Thanks for Thirty Years Celebration. *Congregation B'nai Israel Bulletin*, May 8, 1970, Vol. XIV, No. 16, 4. Stein Collection.
180. Cantor Moshe Taube (1927–2020) was also a Holocaust survivor and one of Schindler's Jews. He graduated from the Juilliard School of Music and came to Pittsburgh in 1965. From then on he shared in communal events.
181. Large ad for Israel's Twenty-third Anniversary Celebration in *The Jewish*

Chronicle, Vol. 10, No. 9, April 22, 1971, 12. "Jewish Newspaper Project" and CMU Libraries Digital Collection.
182. B'nai B'rith was established in New York City in 1843. The organization advocates for Jewish rights, engages in social service activities, disaster relief, language classes, and today advocates for Social Security and fights hate crimes. See Wikipedia.org, accessed 11/2/22.
183. Musical program in honor of B'nai B'rith centennial celebration, October 25, 1972. Stein Collection.
184. Picture titled "Ready for Tribute," *The Jewish Chronicle*, Vol. 11, No. 37, November 2, 1972, 9. "Jewish Newspaper Project" and CMU Libraries Digital Collection.
185. Invitation to Israel's Twenty-fifth Anniversary Tribute Dinner, October 29, 1972. Stein Collection.
186. Program honoring Cantor Heiser at Israel Bonds dinner is extant. Stein Collection.
187. Picture of Israel Bonds participants in *The Jewish Chronicle*, Vol. 11, No. 39, November 16, 1972, 22; "Cantor Heiser of B'nai Israel Set for Honors," *The Jewish Chronicle*, Vol. 11, No. 33, October 5, 1972, 26; "Ex-Moscow News Chief to Speak at Dinner October 29," *The Jewish Chronicle*, Vol. 11, No. 35, October 19, 1972, 8. "Jewish Newspaper Project" and CMU Libraries Digital Collection.
188. See *Congregation B'nai Israel Bulletin*, Volume XIX, No. 14, May 25, 1976, 3.
189. "Proclamation for B'nai Israel's 75th Anniversary," *The Jewish Chronicle*, Vol. 17, No. 41, November 16, 1978, 18. "Jewish Newspaper Project" and CMU Libraries Digital Collection.
190. "B'nai Israel to Observe Its 75th Anniversary," *The Jewish Chronicle*, Vol. 17, No. 31, September 7, 1978, 9. "Jewish Newspaper Project" and CMU Libraries Digital Collection.
191. *Aufbau*, December 27, 1944. "Jewish Newspaper Project."
192. Marga Silbermann Randall, *How Beautiful We Once Were: A Remembrance of the Holocaust and Beyond*. Cathedral Publications, Pittsburgh, PA, 1998, 30.
193. Heiser speech to Friendship Club, November 11, 1979, on tape. Stein Collection.
194. Milton K. Susman, "As I See It," *The Jewish Chronicle*, Vol. 19, No. 4, March 13, 1980, 6. "Jewish Newspaper Project" and CMU Libraries Digital Collection.
195. Milton K. Susman, "As I See It," *The Jewish Chronicle*, Vol. 19, No. 6,

March 27, 1980, 6. "Jewish Newspaper Project" and CMU Libraries Digital Collection. The University of Pittsburgh Archives hold the records of the Friendship Club: Friendship Club Records, 1935–1976. AIS.1976.31, Archives Service Center, University of Pittsburgh.

196. "Cantor Heiser slated for JTS honor December 14," *The Jewish Chronicle*, Vol. 19, No. 40, November 20, 1980, 18. "Jewish Newspaper Project" and CMU Digital Collection.

197. Rabbi Sanford D. Shanblatt speech and fortieth anniversary program. Stein Collection.

198. "Rabbi Shanblatt keys Cantor Heiser salute," *The Jewish Chronicle*, Vol. 19, No. 42, December 4, 1980, 14; picture "Milestone Event" in *The Jewish Chronicle*, Vol. 19, No. 43, December 11, 1980, 10. "Jewish Newspaper Project."

199. Unidentified breakfast speech. Stein Collection. I later identified the author as Rabbi Sanford D. Shanblatt, who had grown up at B'nai Israel. See also program for breakfast, which is extant.

200. Advertisement for May 23, 1982, concert, *The Jewish Chronicle*, Vol. 21, No. 13, May 13, 1982, 28. "Jewish Newspaper Project" and CMU Libraries Digital Collection.

201. Picture of Yom HaShoah Observance in *The Jewish Chronicle*, Vol. 22, No. 10, April 21, 1983, 24. "Jewish Newspaper Project" and CMU Libraries Digital Collection.

202. "B'nai Israel to Honor Cantor Heiser," *The Jewish Chronicle*, Vol. 22, No. 18, June 16, 1983, 2; also "PZD to hold Bonds evening on June 29," *The Jewish Chronicle*, Vol. 22, No. 17, June 9, 1983, 3. "Jewish Newspaper Project" and CMU Libraries Digital Collection.

203. "Organizations," *The Jewish Chronicle*, Vol. 22, No. 42, December 1, 1983, 16. "Jewish Newspaper Project" and CMU Libraries Digital Collection. See also program.

204. "Tiny Israeli soldier leads Masada torch relay," *The Jewish Chronicle*, Vol. 22, No. 44, December 15, 1983, 25. "Jewish Newspaper Project" and CMU Libraries Digital Collection.

205. "Mayor to join ZOA Hanuka ceremony," *The Jewish Chronicle*, Vol. 23, No. 43, December 6, 1984, 6; ad for 1984 Chanukka Concert, *The Jewish Chronicle*, Vol. 23, No. 43, December 6, 1984, 2; picture of Mayor Richard Caliguiri lighting the Hanuka menorah, *The Jewish Chronicle*, Vol. 23, No. 45, December 27, 1984, 26. "Jewish Newspaper Project" and CMU Libraries Digital Collection.

206. See ad for concert to benefit Camp Ramah Scholarship Fund in *The*

Jewish Chronicle, Vol. 23, No. 42, November 29, 1984, 26; see also ad on page 2 and on page 26. See Milton K. Susman, "As I See It," in *The Jewish Chronicle*, Vol. 23, No. 43, December 13, 1984, 6; see ad with Cantor Heiser picture in *The Jewish Chronicle*, Vol. 23, No. 43, December 6, 1984, 2. "Jewish Newspaper Project" and CMU Libraries Digital Collection. See also program.
207. Osborn letter, dated January 28, 1985. Stein Collection.
208. Kimel letter, dated January 3, 1985. Stein Collection.
209. Heisers' Fiftieth Wedding Anniversary, in *Congregation B'nai Israel Bulletin*, January 1985.
210. Letter about leaf on Simcha Tree, dated January 7, 1985. Stein Collection.
211. Singer letter, no date. Stein Collection. My thanks to Patti Boring of Adat Shalom, Fox Chapel, PA, who sent me a photo of the two leaves on the Mitzvah Tree.
212. *Congregation B'nai Israel Bulletin*, April 1985.
213. MSS #470, B'nai Israel Congregational Records, Board Meeting Minutes, January 7, 1964. Box 24, Folder 24, 4, Rauh Jewish Archive, Detre Library and Archives Division, Heinz History Center, Pittsburgh, PA.
214. MSS #470, B'nai Israel Congregational Records, Board Meeting Minutes, September 9, 1969. Box 24, Folder 26, Rauh Jewish Archive, Detre Library and Archives Division, Heinz History Center, Pittsburgh, PA.
215. MSS #470, B'nai Israel Congregational Records, Board Meeting Minutes, November 4, 1969. Box 24, Folder 26, Rauh Jewish Archive, Detre Library and Archives Division, Heinz History Center, Pittsburgh, PA.
216. MSS #470, B'nai Israel Congregational Records, Board Meeting Minutes, November 2, 1971. Box 21, Folder 1, Rauh Jewish Archive, Detre Library and Archives Division, Heinz History Center, Pittsburgh, PA.
217. MSS #470, B'nai Israel Congregational Records, Board Meeting Minutes, January 7, 1969. Box 24, Folder 26, 2, Rauh Jewish Archive, Detre Library and Archives Division, Heinz History Center, Pittsburgh, PA.
218. MSS #470, B'nai Israel Congregational Records, Board Meeting Minutes, February 4, 1969. Box 24, Folder 26, Rauh Jewish Archive, Detre Library and Archives Division, Heinz History Center, Pittsburgh, PA.
219. Elly Heiser poem for Charlotte Finkelstein. Stein Collection.
220. Elly Heiser poem for Adele and Warren's wedding, June 21, 1987. Stein Collection.
221. Stein-Sufrin Aufruf, in *Beth El Bulletin*, July 4, 1987. Stein Collection.
222. "Simchas & Such," Stein-Sufrin wedding announcement, in *The Jewish Chronicle*, Vol. 26, No. 23, July 23, 1987, 19. Stein Collection.

223. See also letter from Louis Zeiden to Cantor and Mrs. Heiser inviting them to the event, dated July 15, 1987. Stein Collection.
224. "Cantor honored," *The Pittsburgh Press*, June 24, 1987, A2; "Tri-State ZOA meets Sunday," *The Jewish Chronicle*, Vol. 26, No. 22, July 16, 1987, 3; "Sov.-Jewry tops ZOA agenda," *The Jewish Chronicle*, Vol. 26, No. 23, July 23, 1987, 6; see picture of Cantor Heiser receiving first annual Classical Zionist Award in *The Jewish Chronicle*, Vol. 26, No. 26, August 13, 1987, 7. "Jewish Newspaper Project" and CMU Libraries Digital Collection. Special thanks for digital copy of *Pittsburgh Press* article to Jill Chisnell, Arts and Design Librarian, CMU Libraries.
225. Kimel letter dated July 21, 1987. Stein Collection.
226. "Kfar Silver Scholarship," *The Jewish Chronicle*, Vol. 26, No. 24, July 30, 1987, 14; also "Cantor Heiser to receive ZOA honors," *The Jewish Chronicle*, Vol. 26, No. 19, June 25, 1987, 6. "Jewish Newspaper Project" and CMU Libraries Digital Collection.
227. "Tri-State ZOA elects Goldberg to 4th term," *The Jewish Chronicle*, Vol. 27, No. 29, September 1, 1988, 13. "Jewish Newspaper Project" and CMU Libraries Digital Collection.
228. "Goldberg leads ZOA again," *The Jewish Chronicle*, Vol. 28, No. 26, August 10, 1989, 4. "Jewish Newspaper Project" and CMU Libraries Digital Collection.
229. Cilly Ebner, P.O. Box 1073, Haifa/Palestine. See envelope to Elly Heiser at 1114 N. Euclid Avenue, dated November 25, 1940. Stein Collection. Rena Sufrin Kennedy informed me that she is another first cousin to Judy. Rena learned in 2014 that Cilly Ebner in Israel had died in the meantime.
230. Letter to M. Gustav Heiser from Cilly Brauer Haar, January 18, 1988, Stein Collection. Both Cilly Haar and her brother, Albert, are Judy's cousins; they are the children of Cantor Heiser's mother Selma Brauer Heiser's brother Simon (Cantor Heiser's uncle), who was murdered in the Holocaust. (Thank you, Rena!) According to the Koblenz Memor Buch, Volume 1, 389, Simon, who was born in Kovno on January 21, 1881, and lived in Berlin, was deported from Berlin to Auschwitz on December 14, 1942. On August 4, 2023, in a phone conversation, Adele Stein Sufrin told me that she and her husband just visited Cilly Brauer Haar in London. Cilly, who now goes by Tilly, is 101 years old and doing well.
231. "US sweeps medals at Maccabiah Games," *The Jewish Chronicle*, Vol. 24, No. 25, August 1, 1985, front page and 36. Stein Collection.
232. "Joy and Ambivalence," *Near East Report*, July 29, 1985, 122. Stein Collection.

233. "Weddings," *Pittsburgh Post-Gazette*, Saturday, July 30, 1988, 10; also "Simchas & Such," *The Jewish Chronicle*, Vol. 27, No. 26, August 11, 1988, 15; "Jewish Newspaper Project" and CMU Libraries Digital Collection.
234. Elly Heiser poem in honor of Shari and Mark's wedding. Stein Collection.
235. Original Feidman poster by Larry Reznick in Schmidt possession.
236. Giora Feidman. "Klezmer Trio to begin anniversary events," *The Jewish Chronicle*, Vol. 28, No. 14, May 18, 1989, 6. "Jewish Newspaper Project" and CMU Libraries Digital Collection.
237. "Klezmer Trio to begin anniversary events," *The Jewish Chronicle*, Vol. 28, No. 16, June 1, 1989, 17. "Jewish Newspaper Project."
238. Picture and article, "Giora Feidman concert for B'nai Israel event," *The Jewish Chronicle*, Vol. 28, No. 15, May 25, 1989, 7. "Jewish Newspaper Project" and CMU Libraries Digital Collection. Program is extant.
239. Florence Rosner, "Singing team at B'nai Israel," *The Jewish Chronicle*, Vol. 28, No. 23, July 20, 1989, 26. Stein Collection.
240. Mordecai Gustav Heiser Obituary, in *Pittsburgh Post-Gazette*, Thursday, October 26, 1989, 9; also "Community Mourns Loss of Mordecai Heiser," *The Jewish Chronicle*, Vol. 28, No. 37, October 26, 1989, 33. "Jewish Newspaper Project."
241. Schmidt, "Remembering Cantor Heiser," Letters to the Editor, *The Jewish Chronicle*, Vol. 28, No. 40, November 16, 1989, 9. "Jewish Newspaper Project" and CMU Libraries Digital Collection.
242. Letter from Rabbi John D. Rayner, formerly Hans S. Rahmer, dated June 21, 1990, to Elly Heiser; see also Heiser letters to Hans in 1938 and 1939. Stein Collection.
243. Cantor Heiser picture dedication, *Congregation B'nai Israel Bulletin*, May 19, 1990.
244. Article "A Final Shalom at B'nai Israel," in *Pittsburgh Post-Gazette*, April 8, 1996, C-3. In Louik File 2010.0076, Rauh Jewish Archive, Detre Library and Archives Division, Heinz History Center, Pittsburgh, PA. Digital copy courtesy of Kelseigh, UT Hodges Library.
245. Article, "A Jewish beacon goes out," in *Pittsburgh Post-Gazette*, June 24, 1996, Section C, front page, and C-2. Stein Collection. Digital copy courtesy of Kelseigh, UT Hodges Library.
246. "Looking for an Angel," in *Pittsburgh Post-Gazette*, December 9, 1997, front page and D-12, Stein Collection. Digital copy courtesy of Kelseigh, UT Hodges Library.
247. Toby Tabachnick, "On the block again, former synagogue building might disappear," in *The Jewish Chronicle*, Vol. 59, No. 27, July 7, 2016, 1, 2 and 4. Courtesy of Heinz Archives and Stein Family.

Chapter 3

1. Edelman, *Discovering Jewish Music*, 145.
2. Kalib, *The Musical Tradition of the Eastern European Synagogue*. Volume One. Introduction: History and Definition. Part One. Text, 198.
3. MSS #470, B'nai Israel Congregational Records, Board Meeting Minutes, June 1, 1948. Box 24, Folder 20, Rauh Jewish Archive, Detre Library and Archives Division, Heinz History Center, Pittsburgh, PA, 2.
4. MSS #470, B'nai Israel Congregational Records, Board Meeting Minutes, June 6, 1950. Box 24, Folder 20, Rauh Jewish Archive, Detre Library and Archives Division, Heinz History Center, Pittsburgh, PA, 2.
5. MSS #470, B'nai Israel Congregational Records, Board Meeting Minutes, June 5, 1951. Box 24, Folder 20, Rauh Jewish Archive, Detre Library and Archives Division, Heinz History Center, Pittsburgh, PA, 2.
6. MSS #470, B'nai Israel Congregational Records, Board Meeting Minutes, June 5, 1951. Box 24, Folder 20, Rauh Jewish Archive, Detre Library and Archives Division, Heinz History Center, Pittsburgh, PA, 2.
7. MSS #470, B'nai Israel Congregational Records, Board Meeting Minutes, January 8, 1963. Box 23, Folder 23, Rauh Jewish Archive, Detre Library and Archives Division, Heinz History Center, Pittsburgh, PA, 5–6.
8. MSS #470, B'nai Israel Congregational Records, Board Meeting Minutes, April 7, 1970. Box 25, Folder 1, Rauh Jewish Archive, Detre Library and Archives Division, Heinz History Center, Pittsburgh, PA, 1.
9. MSS #470, B'nai Israel Congregational Records, Board Meeting Minutes, April 7, 1970. Box 25, Folder 1, Rauh Jewish Archive, Detre Library and Archives Division, Heinz History Center, Pittsburgh, PA, 1–2.
10. *Congregation B'nai Israel Golden Anniversary Book*, 27.
11. MSS #470, B'nai Israel Congregational Records, Board Meeting Minutes, January 4, 1949. Box 24, Folder 20, Rauh Jewish Archive, Detre Library and Archives Division, Heinz History Center, Pittsburgh, PA, 3.
12. *Congregation B'nai Israel Golden Anniversary Book*, 27.
13. MSS #470, B'nai Israel Congregational Records, Board Meeting Minutes, January 3, 1950. Box 24, Folder 20, Rauh Jewish Archive, Detre Library and Archives Division, Heinz History Center, Pittsburgh, PA, 2.
14. MSS #470, B'nai Israel Congregational Records, Board Meeting Minutes, May 1, 1951. Box 24, Folder 20, Rauh Jewish Archive, Detre Library and Archives Division, Heinz History Center, Pittsburgh, PA, 2.
15. MSS #470, B'nai Israel Congregational Records, Board Meeting Minutes, October 7, 1952. Box 24, Folder 21, Rauh Jewish Archive, Detre Library and Archives Division, Heinz History Center, Pittsburgh, PA, 2.

16. Betty Sue Stein Bat Mitzvah speech, 1981 Shabbat service recording. Stein Collection.
17. MSS #470, B'nai Israel Congregational Records, Board Meeting Minutes, April 7, 1970. Box 25, Folder 1, Rauh Jewish Archive, Detre Library and Archives Division, Heinz History Center, Pittsburgh, PA, 1–2.
18. MSS #470, B'nai Israel Congregational Records, Board Meeting Minutes, November 2, 1971. Box 21, Folder 1, Rauh Jewish Archive, Detre Library and Archives Division, Heinz History Center, Pittsburgh, PA, 2.
19. MSS #470, B'nai Israel Congregational Records, Board Meeting Minutes, December 7, 1971. Box 25, Folder 1, Rauh Jewish Archive, Detre Library and Archives Division, Heinz History Center, Pittsburgh, PA, front page.
20. MSS #470, B'nai Israel Congregational Records, Board Meeting Minutes, October 10, 1972. Box 25, Folder 1, Rauh Jewish Archive, Detre Library and Archives Division, Heinz History Center, Pittsburgh, PA, 3.
21. MSS #470, B'nai Israel Congregational Records, Board Meeting Minutes, July 10, 1973. Box 25, Folder 2, Rauh Jewish Archive, Detre Library and Archives Division, Heinz History Center, Pittsburgh, PA, 3.
22. The title of Richard Mark Berlin's M.A. thesis was "A Methodology for the Study of a Partitur." A Master's Thesis Submitted in Partial Fulfillment of the Requirements for the Master of Sacred Music Degree from the H. L. Miller Cantorial School and School of Sacred Music. Jewish Theological Seminary, New York, May 1, 2000.
23. The Recorded Sound Archives at Florida Atlantic University Libraries are located in Wimberly Library on FAU's Boca Raton campus.
24. Hilary Daninhirsch, "Pittsburgh Music Preserved," in *Pittsburgh Jewish Chronicle*, November 14, 2013, online. Accessed 11/8/22. On November 11, 2022, I contacted the Recorded Sound Archives at FAU by email. They responded that they "do not have any recordings by this cantor." They also confirmed that they have "two donations made by a Judith Stein from Pittsburgh, PA, on 7/5/2011, where forty-nine recordings were donated (thirty-two LPs, one other, sixteen cassettes), and on 1/13/2012 where four recordings were donated (two LPs and two CDs)." Unfortunately, they "were unable to identify which recordings they were." Email dated 11/15/2022. This means that the three clips Rena received back from FAU are not in the Archive's system.
25. Judith Vander. *Songprints*, xi.
26. Mordecai G. Heiser, "Jewish Music Month," in *Congregation B'nai Israel Bulletin*, Volume XXIX, No 5, March 1985, 2.
27. *The Complete Artscroll Siddur*. Nusach Ashkenaz. Weekday/Sabbath/Fes-

tival. A new translation and anthologized commentary by Rabbi Nosson Scherman, co-edited by Rabbi Meir Zlotowitz. Mesorah Publications, Ltd., Brooklyn, N.Y., 1999/1984, 714.
28. Robert Schwartz, "His Ministry Is More Than Music. Cantor Interprets the Prayers of Jewish People in Worship," in *The Pittsburgh Press*, April 22, 1967, 6.
29. Heiser autobiography, 2. Stein Collection.
30. Abraham Joshua Heschel, "The Vocation of the Cantor," online, 2. Also in Slobin Bibliography, "The Vocation of the Cantor," in *The Insecurity of Freedom*. New York: Noonday Press, 1967, 242–253.
31. Frigyesi, *Writing on Water*, 210–211.
32. Heschel, "The Vocation of the Cantor," online, 2–3.
33. Heiser anonymous lecture, no date, 4. Stein Collection.
34. "The Music of the Synagogue," by Mordecai G. Heiser, Hazzan, in the *Congregation B'nai Israel Bulletin 1973/5734*, High Holy Days, September 1973, New Year edition, 9. Stein Collection.
35. Robert Schwartz, "His Ministry Is More Than Music. Cantor Interprets the Prayers of Jewish People in Worship," in *The Pittsburg Press*, April 22, 1967, 6. Stein Collection.
36. Robert Schwartz, "His Ministry Is More Than Music. Cantor Interprets the Prayers of Jewish People in Worship," in *The Pittsburgh Press*, April 22, 1967, 6. Stein Collection.
37. I do not know where Schlagory is located. Not even the USHMM was able to help.
38. See Förderverein Jüdischer Friedhof Berlin-Weissensee online. Accessed 6/30/17. Natalie Baeck, Rabbi Leo Baeck's wife, is buried next to Cantor Gollanin.
39. Steven Spielberg Film and Video Archive, United States Holocaust Memorial Museum, Washington, D.C. In September 1932, the night before Kol Nidre, Cantor Gollanin sings "Kol Nidre" during choir practice in the New Synagogue with a mixed choir. The footage contains two extremely brief shots, one of the women in the choir, the other of Cantor Gollanin singing "Kol Nidre" (3 seconds!), mixed in among very nasty Nazi propaganda shots. My thanks to Bruce Levy of the USHMM for giving me access to this video, FV0055-RG601049 dv50.mov.
40. Artur Holde, *Jews in Music, From the Age of Enlightenment to the Mid-Twentieth Century*. New edition. Prepared by Irene Heskes, Bloch Publishing Co., New York, 1974, 33 and 204 in Holde, *Jews in Music*. Aron Friedmann published *50 Jahre in Berlin (1878–1928)*, 1929; *Synagogaler Gesang* [1908];

Lebensbilder berühmter Kantoren [1918], and *Schir li Schelomo*; Holde says that Friedman became known through this work, published in 1901, 33.

41. Cantor Felix Asch. Symposium Records Catalogue website. *The First Opera Recordings (1895–1902), a Survey.* Accessed 6/21/17. In Appendix 3, "Leib Glantz's Recording History," in Jerry Glantz, ed., *Leib Glantz—The Man Who Spoke to God,* we read, "The first cantors who are known to have been recorded were Cantor Felix Asch from Berlin, who immortalized a verse of the prayer Kol Nid'rei in 1902 . . . ," 484.

42. Heiser autobiography. Stein Collection.

43. Louis (Eliezer) Lewandowski was born into a merchant family in Wreschen in Poznan, Prussia, in 1821. Exposed to synagogue liturgy by his father, who was a volunteer cantor on the High Holy Days, he left home at age twelve upon the death of his mother and traveled to Berlin. Artur Holde explains Lewandowski's development under Cantor Ascher Lion and the transformation of synagogal music by Lewandowski under Rabbi Jacob Lichtenstein. Lion "took an interest in the boy who had an exceptionally beautiful soprano voice, and placed him in the synagogue choir as a 'singer'." Lewandowski "became the first Jew to be accepted by the Prussian Academy of Arts." In 1844, Lewandowski took the position of conductor at the old synagogue in Heidereutergasse. The service was "still conducted by the chazzan with his meshorerim (sopranos and basses)." But "a young musician of his standing was expected to reorganize thoroughly the musical service which was viewed as no longer in keeping with the spirit of the time." This became possible when Cantor Lion retired and was succeeded by Rabbi Jacob Lichtenstein, "a fellow artist receptive to his plans." A new prayer book for the new synagogue at Oranienburger Strasse [1866] "was a further aid to the musical reforms envisaged by Lewandowski." Holde, *Jews in Music,* 21–22. See Lewandowski, *Kol Rinnah u'T'fillah,* published in 1870, reprinted in Out-of-Print Classics Series No. 9, Sacred Music Press, New York, no year; *Todah v'Zimrah, Volume I: Shabbat,* 1876, reprinted in Out-of-Print Classics Series No. 10 Sacred Music Press, New York, no year; and *Todah v'Zimrah Volume II: Festgesänge,* 1883, reprinted in Out-of-Print Classics Series No. 11 and No. 12, Sacred Music Press, New York, no year.

44. Salomon Sulzer, born in Hohenems, Vorarlberg, in 1804, was something of a Wunderkind whom "the congregation of his native town entrusted . . . with the office of cantor on account of his clear, pure soprano voice" at age thirteen. Holde, *Jews in Music,* 18. Between ages thirteen and sixteen, Sulzer studied music in Endigen, Switzerland, and then in Karlsruhe, Germany. He returned to Hohenems and, during the next six years, affected the nature of the musical service at his synagogue considerably, so much

so that he came to the attention of the Seitenstettengasse Synagogue in Vienna. There he began his tenure as their first cantor at age twenty-two in 1826. In Holde's estimation, "The great merits of Sulzer in behalf of the artistic advance of European synagogue music remain undiminished. He cleansed it of much impurity and helped to preserve many melodies by their restoration to a more impeccable form." Holde, *Jews in Music*, 19. See Sulzer, *Schir Zion I: Shabbat*, 1840, reprinted in Out-of-Print Classics Series No. 6, Sacred Music Press, New York, 1953, and *Schir Zion II: Festivals*, 1867, reprinted in Out-of-Print Classics Series No. 7, Sacred Music Press, New York, 1953. See also Friedmann on Sulzer in *Der Synagogale Gesang*, 121–136.

45. Samuel Naumbourg was born in 1815 in Donaulohe, Bavaria, Germany. His father was a cantor. He joined the synagogue choir in Munich as a young man, served as conductor in Strasbourg, and officiated as a cantor in Besano, Italy. In 1845 he was chosen as the chief cantor at the Great Synagogue in Paris, where he remained until his death in 1880. Holde, *Jews in Music*, 20. Also Eliyahu Schleifer, ed., Jewish Miniatures, Vol. 136A, *Louis Lewandowski Festival: Samuel Naumbourg: The Cantor of French Jewish Emancipation*, Centrum Judaicum, Hentrich & Hentrich, Berlin, 2015. See Naumbourg, *Zemiroth Israel: Chants Religieux des Israelites*, published in 1847, reprinted in Out-of-Print Classics Series of Synagogue Music No. 14, Sacred Music Press, New York, 1954.

46. Irene Heskes, *Passport to Jewish Music. Its History, Traditions, and Culture*, Tara Publications, Greenwood Press, New York/Maryland/Israel, 1994, 188. See also Edelman, *Discovering Jewish Music*, "Emancipation, Enlightenment, and Evolution," 53–70.

47. See Abraham Z. Idelsohn, *Jewish Liturgy and Its Development*, 33, Footnote 11, "A. Berliner, Randbemerkungen I, 1909, 19."

48. For an excellent essay on service building, see Mark Slobin, "Annotated Accounts of Service Building," in *Chosen Voices*, 287–297.

49. Gershon Ephros, ed., *Cantorial Anthology of Traditional and Modern Synagogue Music*. Volume I. Rosh Hashonoh. Bloch Publishing Company, New York, 1972/1961, xi. Idelsohn, in his introduction to Vol. I of Gershon Ephros' Anthology, heaps praise upon Ephros for his "commendable impulse" to compile "an anthology of liturgical compositions for cantor and choir, with organ accompaniment, arranged according to the Ashkenazic ritual." Ephros, Vol. I, ix.

50. Edelman, *Discovering Jewish Music*, 15.

51. Debbie Friedman (2/23/1951 Utica, NY—1/9/2011 Mission Viejo, CA) was a singer and songwriter whose music became very popular in certain circles of Judaism. A posthumous collection of her music, *Sing Unto*

God: The Debbie Friedman Anthology, was published in 2014. It is said to contain "every song she ever wrote and recorded in lead sheet format, with complete lyrics, melody line, guitar chords, Hebrew, transliteration, and English translation." In 2011, the Reform Movement's HUC-JIR New York branch renamed their School of Sacred Music in her memory. See https://Wikipedia.org/wiki/Debbie_Friedman.

52. Cohen, "Introduction: Jewish Music and Jewish Identity in the Rust Belt," in *Journal of Jewish Identities* (2017), 10(1), 2. For an excellent essay on Friedman's music, see Cohen, "Higher Education: Debbie Friedman in Chicago," in same *JoJI*, 7–26.

53. See Eliyahu Schleifer, "Jewish Liturgical Music from the Bible to Hasidism," in Hoffman and Walton, eds., *Sacred Sound and Social Change*, 38–41.

54. Heiser anonymous lecture, no date, 4.

55. Jerry Glantz, ed., *Leib Glantz—The Man Who Spoke to God*, 330–331.

56. Frigyesi, *Writing on Water*, 119.

57. For a definition of modal and tonal, see https://orchestramagcom/difference-between-modal-and-tonal-music/; also https://en.wikipedia.org/wiki/Renaissance_music.

58. Professor Schleifer writes, "A *shtayger* is a musical corpus of melodic patterns that are related to a scale and are associated with particular prayers, functions, and services." Hoffman and Walton, eds., "Jewish Liturgical Music from the Bible to Hasidism," in *Sacred Sound and Social Change*, 41. The verb "steigen" in German means "to climb," as in to climb a ladder. Aron Friedmann uses both Leiter (ladder and leader), 45, and Steiger (which can be a person, as in a mining foreman), 53, in *Der synagogale Gesang* (1908). See also *Encyclopedia Judaica*, 609 and 610.

59. On Modes, see Jerry Glantz, ed., *Leib Glantz—The Man Who Spoke to God*, Part III. "The Musical Basis of Nus'ach Ha'Te'fi'la," 329–355; "Nu'sach A'ha'va Ra'bbah," Fourth Kol Yisrael Radio Lecture, by Leib Glantz, 403–412; "Nu'sach A'do'nai Ma'lach and the Jewish Major," Fifth Kol Yisrael Radio Lecture by Leib Glantz, 413–425. See also *Encyclopedia Judaica*, Volume 12, Min-O. Macmillan, New York and Jerusalem, 1972, 586 and 608ff. See Aron Friedmann, *Shir Lisch'laumau*. Chasonus für das ganze liturgische Jahr. Published by "Deutsch-New York: The Jewish Theological Seminary Posen, Leipzig, Hannover, München, des liberalen Vereins zu Breslau und des schlesischen Provinzialverbandes," 1901. Friedmann illustrates the *shtaygers*: "Ahava Rabah," 46; "Magen Avot," 115; "Adonai Malach" is different, 53. See Eliyahu Schleifer, "Jewish Liturgical Music from the Bible to Hasidism," in Hoffman and Walton, eds., *Sacred Sound and Social Change*, 41.

60. *Encyclopedia Judaica, Volume 12,* Min-O. Macmillan, New York and Jerusalem, 1972, 586.
61. Heiser anonymous lecture, no date, 2–4.
62. See Kalib, *The Musical Tradition of the Eastern European Synagogue,* Volume I. Introduction. History and Definition, Part One. Text, 70.
63. See *Encyclopedia Judaica,* Volume 12, Min-O. Macmillan, New York and Jerusalem, 1972, 627, and My Jewish Learning, "What Is a Cantor," online; also Kalib, *The Musical Tradition of the Eastern European Synagogue,* Vol. One. Introduction. History and Definition, Part 1. Text, 112.
64. *Encyclopedia Judaica,* Volume 12, Min-O. Macmillan, New York, and Jerusalem, 1972, 611. See also Kalib, *The Musical Tradition of the Eastern European Synagogue,* Volume One. Introduction. History and Definition, Part One. Text, 66.
65. Heiser anonymous lecture, no date, 2–3.
66. Frigyesi, *Writing on Water,* 69.
67. Slobin, *Chosen Voices,* 79.
68. *Encyclopedia Judaica,* Vol. 12 Min-O, "Music." Macmillan, New York, and Jerusalem, 1972, 598.
69. Frigyesi, *Writing on Water,* 73.
70. Operatic Nostalgia, online, accessed 10/31/2022.
71. Eliyahu Schleifer, introductory remarks for session honoring him for his compositions by World Congress for Jewish Studies in Jerusalem, August 10, 2022. Link provided by Professor Schleifer.
72. Glantz on *mi Sinai nusach,* in Jerry Glantz, ed., *Leib Glantz—The Man Who Spoke to God,* 331.
73. Kalib, *The Musical Tradition of the Eastern European Synagogue,* Vol. One. Introduction. History and Definition, Part One. Text, 105.
74. Idelsohn, *Jewish Liturgy and Its Development,* 31.
75. For a wonderful discussion of the *piyyut,* see Idelsohn, *Jewish Liturgy and Its Development,* 35–46.
76. Some of the Heiser compositions that we are aware of are "V'chol Ma'aminim," No. 1 in Moshe Nathanson, ed., *Zamru Lo III,* 151; "Kad'shenu," in Nathanson, ed., *Zamru Lo II,* 40; and "Hu Elohenu," notated by Mordecai G. Heiser, also in Nathanson, ed., *Zamru Lo II,* 110.
77. Neil W. Levin, "Israel Alter 1901–1979," Milken Archive of Jewish Music, online. Accessed 12/26/22. See also Kalib, *The Musical Tradition of the Eastern European Synagogue,* Vol. I. Introduction. History and Definition, Part 1. Text, 113.
78. "R'tze Vimnuchosenu" (Recitative) by Sholom Secunda, with Lazar Weiner

at the piano. See page 8 in the 1962 Cantors Assembly Convention Proceedings Page of Contents, and page 76 in program. Cantors Assembly Convention Proceedings Internet Archive, 1962.

79. See Eliyahu Schleifer, "Jewish Liturgical Music from the Bible to Hasidism," in Hoffman and Walton, eds., *Sacred Sound and Social Change: Liturgical Music in Jewish and Christian Experience*, 29–32.

80. Rabbi Morris Silverman, ed., *Sabbath and Festival Prayer Book*. The Rabbinic Assembly of America and The United Synagogue of America. New York, 1966/1946, 100.

81. My deepest gratitude to Rabbi Shoshana Carson for her effort to trace one journey of this melody in her own life, and to her friend, Rabbi Jonathan Slater, and to his friend, Cantor Richard Cohn, for their quick help, and to Rabbi Elisheva Salamo for explaining the connection. What a wonderful gift!

82. In his chapter, "Jewish Liturgical Music from the Bible to Hasidism," in Hoffman and Walton, eds., *Sacred Sound and Social Change*, Professor Schleifer discusses four layers of *hazzanut*, 38–42. I only discuss three, not the cantillation of Scripture, which is really the foundation of *nusach* and the oldest of the *trops*.

83. Jakob Beimel (Yakov Baymel) was an American cantor, composer, and musicologist. Born in Russia, he came to the U.S. in 1915, where he settled in New York and Philadelphia. He founded the journal *Jewish Music*, which celebrated its fiftieth anniversary in 2017. See Jewish Music Research Center, National Library, Hebrew University of Jerusalem, online. Accessed 6/21/17.

84. Abraham Dunajewsky was a Russian cantor in Odessa. See *Israelische Tempel Compositionen für den Sabbath*, published in Moscow in 1893 and in Odessa in two volumes in 1898. There is a third volume, *Liturgische feierliche Synagogen-Kompositionen für Cantor und gemueschten [sic!] Chor*, published in Odessa in 1898. Holde, *Jews in Music*, 25, 287.

85. Baruch Schorr was born in Lemberg (Lvov) into a Hasidic family. As a child he sang with the choirs in his hometown; he then served a number of congregations in Podolia, Rumania, and Bessarabia, after which time he was chosen as first cantor at the Great Synagogue in Lemberg. In his music he was influenced by Sulzer and Lewandowski. With the exception of five years in New York (from 1890 through 1895), where he served the Attorney Street Synagogue, he spent his entire later life in Lemberg. Marsha Edelman writes that "The Lemberg community eventually missed his improvisations and the innovative choral compositions that had so stirred

their emotions," so they asked him to come back, and he did. Edelman, 65. Also Holde notes that "The name of Baruch Schorr has retained its luster," 31. As to his style, "Schorr largely depends on traditional melodies, and presents them in plain four-part harmony." Holde, *Jews in Music*, 24. *Neginoth Baruch Schorr* was published by his son, Israel Schorr.

86. Israel Schorr is the son of Baruch Schorr. He was cantor in Brooklyn, N.Y., and added several compositions of his own to his father's work. Holde, *Jews in Music*, 24.

87. From Irene Heskes we learn that "Nowakowsky . . . succeeded his mentor [Nissan] Blumenthal at the . . . Odesser Broder Shul, and in 1900 in Odessa, published [both of their repertoires in] a combined collection of their melodic chants, *Gebete und Gesänge zum des [sic] Sabbath (Prayers and Songs for the Sabbath)*." Heskes, *Passport to Jewish Music*, 50, 51. Holde points out that David Nowakowsky . . . "attempted to blend the Eastern Jewish chazzanuth with the musical style of his time . . . his specific art greatly stimulated a temple music that followed in the steps of Sulzer and Lewandowski." Holde, *Jews in Music*, 32. Holde informs us that the "only works available in print" during his lifetime "were a Friday-evening service and the Neila services for Yom Kippur." Holde, *Jews in Music*, 286. See also Edelman, *Discovering Jewish Music*, 67.

88. Cantor Wolf Velvele Schestopol of Odessa had studied in Vienna with Cantor Salomon Sulzer. Irene Heskes notes that "He was a prolific composer of hymn melodies, often based upon folk themes or reminiscent of popular Italian operatic arias. Schestopol's music was widely known, though never published." Heskes, *Passport to Jewish Music*, 142.

89. Cantor Heiser pasted Yossele Rosenblatt's "Chassidic Kaddish" written in his own hand into the back of his personal *siddur* [not his *machzor* for the holidays when he used the prayer].

90. Josef Yossele Rosenblatt was an unlikely figure to become a popular star in America, yet that is exactly what happened. Born into a Chassidic family with nine sisters, Yossele began his career "by the age of four . . . singing with his father, an itinerant cantor. . . . (H)e studied music industriously and showed particular talent in composition." Heskes, *Passport to Jewish Music*, 65. Holde writes that Rosenblatt had a meteoric rise as a cantor, officiating "at the age of 17 . . . as cantor at Munkacsi." Married at 18, "he became chief cantor at Pressburg (now Bratislava); and five years later, he was in Hamburg." From there he journeyed to New York, where he officiated at "the largest orthodox congregation in New York City, Ohab Zedek." Holde, *Jews in Music*, 33–34. This was in 1912. Heskes concludes that

"Rosenblatt [who also sang at Carnegie Hall] brought the sounds of traditional Jewish liturgical music to the general American public." Heskes, *Passport to Jewish Music*, 65, 193.

91. Abraham Zvi Idelsohn was a giant in Jewish music scholarship. He was of a modest background without much formal schooling. Born to a cantor and ritual slaughterer, he went to *cheder* and sang in the local choir as a "singerl." In the district city of Libau he "studied with an itinerant cantor named Abraham Mordechai Rabinowitz and sang in his choir." Heskes, *Passport to Jewish Music*, 13. From there he traveled to Königsberg, Berlin, Leipzig, and Regensburg, Germany, before leaving Europe forever. His travels to Johannesburg, South Africa, in 1904 were only the beginning of his life journey to Jerusalem, where he began the great work that led to a ten-volume collection of oriental melodies, published under the title *Hebräisch-Orientalischer Melodienschatz*. Idelsohn immigrated to the United States in 1922, and lived out his life at HUC in Cincinnati, OH. See Holde, *Jews in Music*, 204, and again Heskes, 13.

92. Julius Freudenthal was an "organist and a court musician" as well as "a leader of the rising Jewish reformist movement in Germany" at the time of Abraham Geiger. "Eyn Keloheynu" was published in an 1844 collection of hymns for soloist, choir, and congregation, to be sung as a concluding hymn on Shabbat and festivals. Heskes, *Passport to Jewish Music*, 82 and 183.

93. Artur Holde writes that "Hugo Adler shows an intimate knowledge of chazzanuth in *Nachlat Israel* for Friday evening and in *Shirah Chadashah*." Holde, *Jews in Music*, 42.

94. Max Janowski, raised in Germany, came to the United States via Japan in 1937 and was choir director in Chicago for the next fifty years. He introduced Eastern European nusach into the Reform service with compositions like "L'chu N'ran'nah lAdonai." Source is study session with Professor Schleifer in Jerusalem. According to an online article by Neil W. Levin, "Max Janowski 1912–1991," Janowski had a particular gift for transcription. Writes Levin, "When, for example, Cantor Maurice Levy needed a complete musical notation of a traditional s'lihot service for cantor and choir, with all its modal complexities, traditional melodies, turns of phrases, and characteristic improvisations—which he was accustomed to singing on his own without benefit of notated music—he turned to Janowski for the task. Naturally adept at musical transcription by dictation (a skill that is often called 'take-down' in the commercial music world), Janowski was able to notate the entire service upon hearing Levy sing it for him. He then made

simple four-part arrangements (as requested) for those sections requiring choral responses, interludes, introductions, and set pieces." Levin in Milken Archive of Jewish Music, online. Accessed 5/18/16.

95. Neil W. Levin, "Max Janowski 1912–1991," in Milken Archive of Jewish Music, online. Accessed 5/18/16.

96. Irene Heskes writes, "The rapid growth in America of organized Jewish education resulted in the publication of numerous songsters and folk song collections with Hebrew, Yiddish, Ladino, and English texts. (N. 37)." Beginning "in the second decade of the twentieth century ... Rabbi Israel Goldfarb and his brother Samuel Goldfarb (1884–1967) ... early leaders in Jewish education, collaborated upon a series of music pamphlets that were later published as children's songsters. They consisted of traditional Sabbath hymns in single vocal lines or simple choral arrangements, with easy piano accompaniments. All the materials were intended for practical pedagogical purposes." Heskes, *Passport to Jewish Music*, 211.

97. Israel Alter (1901–1979) was born in Lemberg, Galicia. After serving for some years as cantor in Vienna, he became the chief cantor of the Orthodox synagogue in Hannover, Germany. When the Nazis came to power in 1935, he left for Johannesburg, South Africa, and eventually found his way to New York. There he was a teacher to many future cantors at HUC-JIR's School of Sacred Music. Milken Archive of Jewish Music online. Accessed 12/26/22. Also study session with Professor Schleifer in Jerusalem.

98. Sholom Secunda already sang with a synagogue choir at age seven. After immigration to the United States, he studied at Juilliard in New York. Mentored by Ernest Bloch in composition, he was involved in the Yiddish theater all of his life. In 1945, Secunda became the musical director of the Concord Hotel in Kiamesha Lake, New York, where some of the early Cantors Assembly Conventions took place. There he organized concerts for twenty-eight years, also with Cantor Richard Tucker. Milken Archive of Jewish Music; also *Wikipedia*, accessed 6/21/17. Secunda was one of Cantor Heiser's favorite contemporary composers.

99. *Pa'amey Hahechal*, Compositions for Cantor and Choir as sung at Hechal Shlomo, Jerusalem, by Dr. Zvi Talmon (Monsohn), choir master of Hechal Shlomo, Jerusalem, 1992, 86. Courtesy of Professor Schleifer. See also *T'ruot HaHekhl*, Jerusalem. Another collection by Zvi Talmon, *Rinat ha-Heikhal* anthology, was published by the Cantors Assembly in 1965. See also item on Kedem Auction House Ltd. Website for Zvi Talmon (Monsohn), accessed 6/21/17. My thanks to HUC-JIR librarian Laurel Wolfson, Klau Library Cincinnati, and Yoram Bitton, Director of Libraries, HUC-JIR

New York, for sending me a Hebrew version of cover and contents page of *Pa'amey Hahechal* and *T'ruot HaHekhl*.

100. For a reference on Jewish religious life in Youngstown, OH, see Conference on Jewish Music and Jewish Identities 2014 in *Journal of Jewish Identities* (2017), 10(1), 1–6.
101. Heskes, *Passport to Jewish Music*, 212.
102. Frigyesi, *Writing on Water*, 117.
103. Heskes, *Passport to Jewish Music*, 212. Judit Frigyesi sheds additional light on the importance of Idelsohn and her difficulty in obtaining a copy of his world-famous book on the history of Jewish liturgy, in Hungary, 117, as well as the importance of Hasidic *nigunim* for the Eastern European cantorial repertoire, 69.
104. Frigyesi, *Writing on Water*, 190.
105. See Nachama in Brenner, *After the Holocaust*, 105.
106. *Encyclopedia Judaica*, Volume 12, Min-O. Macmillan, New York and Jerusalem, 598.
107. Abraham Joshua Heschel, "The Vocation of the Cantor," Hebrew College, online, 1.
108. Cantor Heiser used the tape recorder to make practice tapes for students. Some of the tapes were reused, so that a service piece may be interrupted at any point.
109. Slobin, *Chosen Voices*, xxi.
110. Slobin, *Chosen Voices*, 261.
111. Slobin, *Chosen Voices*, Example No. 32, "Ashrei," 262.
112. Kalib, *The Musical Tradition of the Eastern European Synagogue*. Volume I. Introduction. History and Definition, Part One. Text. Example 89, 58; and Volume One, Part Two. Music. Example 89, 66.
113. According to Professor Schleifer, "Asher b'yado" was not usually set to music, only in the London synagogue. Is it possible that Cantor Heiser heard this melody there during his time in England, even though travel for German refugees would have been heavily restricted? It is possible, as he was allowed to meet Elly and Judy in Dover when they arrived in England from Germany. He may have been able to visit them in London while living in the Kitchener Camp; perhaps he even went to synagogue in London. Or perhaps Cantor Heiser became aware of Max Janowski's composition in the U.S. Discussed in study session with Professor Schleifer in Jerusalem.
114. Study session with Professor Schleifer in Jerusalem.
115. Chemjo Vinaver, ed., *Anthology of Jewish Music*. Edward B. Marks Music Corporation, MCMLV, New York, 1953, 153–154.
116. Study session with Professor Schleifer in Jerusalem.

117. Sheet music for Yossele Rosenblatt's "Shomer Israel" courtesy of Hebrew Union College, Klau Music Library, Cincinnati.
118. Kalib, *The Musical Tradition of the Eastern European Synagogue*. Volume One. Introduction. History and Definition. Part One. Text. Example 128f, 127; Volume I, Part Two. Music. Example 128f, 130.
119. Kalib, *The Musical Tradition of the Eastern European Synagogue*. Volume One. Introduction: History and Definition. Part One. Text. Example 99c, 71; Volume I, Part Two. Music. Example 99c, 80.
120. In his book, *Chosen Voices*, Mark Slobin explains that no matter the peregrinations of the cantor during an improvisation, they must always return to the beginning at the end. "Uniformity in the ninety-three variants is clear enough: all end on what is transcribed here as 'g'. This supports one of our original quotes: it is at the endings where one looks for nusach in the strictly musical sense." Page 261. A few pages later he again explains, "Yet twenty-three of our ninety-three examples take the path shown by example 35, which is to shift the sense of tonal orientation by temporarily introducing a radically different sound . . . , then returning to the familiar for the necessary conclusion." Page 264.
121. Study session with Professor Schleifer in Jerusalem.
122. Study session with Professor Schleifer in Jerusalem.
123. Study session with Professor Schleifer in Jerusalem.
124. Study session with Professor Schleifer in Jerusalem.
125. Psalm 97:11 in *Machzor Chadash* for Rosh HaShanah and Yom Kippur. Compiled and edited by Rabbi Sidney Greenberg and Rabbi Jonathan D. Levine. The Prayer Book Press, Hartford, CT, 1955, 397.
126. Translation from *High Holiday Prayer Book*, compiled and arranged by Rabbi Morris Silverman. Prayer Book Press, Hartford, CT, 1939, 207.
127. Kalib, *The Musical Tradition of the Eastern European Synagogue*. Volume One. Introduction: History and Definition, Part One. Text. Example 39, 25, and Example 91, 59; also Volume One. Part Two. Music. Example 39, 28, and Example 91, 67.
128. John Rayner letter to Mrs. Heiser, dated June 21, 1990, 2.
129. Leo Gollanin. Choir Practice in the New Synagogue in Berlin on the Night Before Yom Kippur, 1932. Story RG-60.4817, Film ID 2854. Online. Accessed 6/21/17.
130. *High Holiday Prayer book*, compiled and arranged by Rabbi Morris Silverman, 1939, 207.
131. "Ki Hineh Kachomer" is a medieval *piyyut* by an unknown author, perhaps from the twelfth century. The ideas in the poem, namely that we are clay and God is the potter who shapes us, are well-grounded in the Hebrew

Bible, both in Isaiah (64:7–8) and Jeremiah (18:6). See "Parasha Poems: Weekly Poems Drawn from a Theme in the Parasha." Post by Elizabeth Topper. Accessed 7/18/17.

132. I did find a recording of Louis Lewandowski's "Tavo L'Fanecha" [Ana Tavo] on YouTube, posted two years ago by Ben Mandresh. Accessed 10/7/22. It is worth listening to.

133. Translation from *Machzor Chadash*. Compiled and edited by Rabbi Sidney Greenberg and Rabbi Jonathan D. Levine. The Prayer Book Press, Hartford, CT, 5755/1995, 784.

134. Kalib, *The Musical Tradition of the Eastern European Synagogue*. Volume One. Introduction: History and Definition. Part One. Text. Examples 119 g and h, 117; and Volume One. Part Two. Music. Examples 119 g and h, 117.

135. Study session with Professor Schleifer in Jerusalem.

136. Study session with Professor Schleifer in Jerusalem.

137. Zvi Talmon (Monsohn), *Pa'amey Hahechal*, Compositions for Cantor and Choir as sung at Hechal Shlomo, Jerusalem, 1992, 86. Courtesy of Eli Schleifer.

138. Kalib, *The Musical Tradition of the Eastern European Synagogue*. Volume One. Introduction: History and Definition. Part One. Text. Example 164c, 118; and Volume One, Part Two. Music. Example 146c, 194.

139. Professor Schleifer notes that it is rare to hear this rendition of "Av Harachamim."

140. Louis Lewandowski, *Todah W'simrah Volume II: Festgesänge*, Part 1. Sacred Music Press, New York, no year, 25.

141. The medieval *piyyut* "Akdamut," authored by Rabbi Meir of Orleans, also known as Meir, the son of Rabbi Yitzchak, who was a cantor in Worms, Germany, serves as an introduction to the Torah reading on Shavuot. Hence, the poem is chanted after the first person has been called up to the Torah and before he/she recites the blessings. The poem is extremely long; it has ninety verses and is written in Aramaic. The *Artscroll Siddur* tells us that forty-four verses consist of a double acrostic of the Hebrew alphabet; the remaining verses begin with the author's name and a blessing which translates into "Meir, the son of Rabbi Yitzchak, may he grow in Torah and in good deeds. Amen. Be strong and of good courage." *Artscroll Siddur*, 714. As if this was not complicated enough, we learn from *Artscroll* that each line which constitutes a verse ends in the letters Taph and Aleph, which are the last and first letters of the Hebrew alphabet, "to signify that the cycle of Torah study is endless, and that as soon as one completes the Torah, he should begin anew." *Artscroll Siddur*, 714. This we actually do on Simchat Torah, when we conclude the Five Books of Moses and

begin again with Genesis. See also Isaac Klein, *A Guide to Jewish Religious Practice*, Volume VI in the Moreshet Series, Studies in Jewish History, Literature and Thought. The Jewish Theological Seminary of America, New York, 1979, 149.

142. Kalib, *The Musical Tradition of the Eastern European Synagogue*. Volume One. Introduction: History and Definition, Part One. Text. Examples 144c and d, 142; and Volume One, Part Two. Music. Examples 144c and d, 151.

143. Translation from *Artscroll Siddur*, 715. Judit Niran Frigyesi discusses "Akdamut" in her study *Writing on Water*, 63. She seems to think that she is reading the *Machzor*, but the text is actually in the *Siddur*, where Shabbat and festival services can be found.

144. Kalib, *The Musical Tradition of the Eastern European Synagogue*. Volume One. Introduction: History and Definition. Part One. Text. Example 99f, 72; and Volume One. Part Two. Music. Example 99f, 81.

145. Kalib, *The Musical Tradition of the Eastern European Synagogue*. Volume One. Introduction: History and Definition, Part One. Text. Example 100, 76–77; also Volume One, Part Two. Music. Example 100, 82.

146. Translation from *Artscroll Siddur*, 815.

147. Adapted from Rabbi Morris Silverman, ed., *Sabbath and Festival Prayer Book*, 1966, 148.

148. See Shabbat tape, May 2, 1981, 24:49ff, Stein Collection.

149. Adapted from Rabbi Morris Silverman, ed., *Sabbath and Festival Prayer Book*, 1966, 129.

150. Adapted from Rabbi Morris Silverman, ed., *Sabbath and Festival Prayer Book*, 1966, 129.

151. Translation from Rabbi Morris Silverman, ed., *Sabbath and Festival Prayer Book*, 1966, 129.

152. Formula for new month, Rabbi Morris Silverman, ed., *Sabbath and Festival Prayer Book*, 1966, 129.

153. Adaptation from Rabbi Morris Silverman, ed., *Sabbath and Festival Prayer Book*, 1966, 129.

154. See Shabbat tape, May 2, 1981, 29:07ff.

155. Betty Sue Stein remarks at her Bat Mitzvah, May 2, 1981, 29:07–31:24, amateur family recording. Stein Collection.

156. Rabbi Richard M. E. Marcovitz remarks. See Shabbat tape, May 2, 1981, 31:48ff. Stein Collection.

Conclusion

1. Slobin, *Chosen Voices*, 32.

BIBLIOGRAPHY

Publications

Adler, Hugo Chaim. "Eyl Moleh Rachamim," for Cantor, Mixed Choir, and Organ. New York: Transcontinental Music Publications, 1965.

Alter, Israel. "Yihi ratzon Milfanecha for Birchas Hachodesh," Choral and organ arrangement by Morris Barash, in *Shirei Israel*. Recitatives for the Hazzan with piano or organ accompaniment. New York: Cantors Assembly of America, Inc., 1968.

——. *The Study of Jewish Music: A Bibliographical Guide*. Yuval Monograph Series X. Jerusalem: The Magnes Press, The Hebrew University, 1995.

Aschheim, Steven E. *Brothers and Strangers*. Madison: University of Wisconsin Press, 1982.

Berenbaum, Michael. *The World Must Know: The History of the Holocaust as Told in the United States Holocaust Memorial Museum*. Boston/Toronto/London: Little, Brown and Co., 1993.

Berlin, Richard Mark. "A Methodology for the Study of a Partitur." A Master's Thesis submitted in Partial Fulfillment of the Requirement for the Master of Sacred Music Degree from the H. L. Miller Cantorial School and School of Sacred Music. New York: Jewish Theological Seminary, May 1, 2000.

B'nai Israel Golden Anniversary Book, 1962. Pittsburgh, PA: Congregation B'nai Israel, 1962.

Brenner, Michael. *After the Holocaust: Rebuilding Jewish Lives in Postwar Germany*. Princeton, N.J.: Princeton University Press, 1997.

Burstin, Barbara S. *Steel City Jews: A History of Pittsburgh and Its Jewish Community 1840–1915*. Pittsburgh: Barbara S. Burstin, 2008.

Cohen, Judah M. *The Making of a Reform Jewish Cantor: Musical Authority, Cultural Investment*. Bloomington: Indiana University Press, 2009.

——. "Higher Education: Debbie Friedman in Chicago." In JoJL (2017), 10(1), 7–26.

Congregation B'nai Israel 75th Anniversary 1904–1979/5664–5739 Booklet. Pittsburgh, PA: Congregation B'nai Israel, 1979.

Congregation B'nai Israel Bulletin, January 22, 1954. Pittsburgh, PA: Congregation B'nai Israel, 1954.
Congregation B'nai Israel Bulletin, Volume XIII, No. 17, May 30, 1969. Pittsburgh, PA: Congregation B'nai Israel, 1969.
Congregation B'nai Israel Bulletin, Volume XIV, No. 16, May 8, 1970. Pittsburgh, PA: Congregation B'nai Israel, 1970.
Congregation B'nai Israel Bulletin, March 27, 1970. Pittsburgh, PA: Congregation B'nai Israel, 1970.
Congregation B'nai Israel Bulletin, September 1973/5734, New Year's edition. Pittsburgh, PA: Congregation B'nai Israel, 1973.
Congregation B'nai Israel Bulletin, Volume XIX, No. 14, May 25, 1976. Pittsburgh, PA: Congregation B'nai Israel, 1976.
Congregation B'nai Israel Bulletin, Volume XXIX, No. 3, January 1985. Pittsburgh, PA: Congregation B'nai Israel, 1985.
Congregation B'nai Israel Bulletin, Vol. XXIX, No. 5, March 1985. Pittsburgh, PA: Congregation B'nai Israel, 1985.
Congregation B'nai Israel Bulletin, Volume XXIX, No. 6, April 1985. Pittsburgh, PA: Congregation B'nai Israel, 1985.
Congregation B'nai Israel Bulletin, May 19, 1990. Pittsburgh, PA: Congregation B'nai Israel, 1990.
Davidson, Charles. *From Szatmar to the New World: Max Wohlberg. American Cantor*. New York: Jewish Theological Seminary, 2001.
Edelman, Marsha Bryan. *Discovering Jewish Music*. Philadelphia: The Jewish Publication Society, 2003/5763.
Edelstein, Leopold. "Sim Sholom: A Prayer for Peace," for Mixed Chorus and Organ or Piano. New York: Metro Music, 1958.
Elbogen, Ismar. *Jewish Liturgy: A Comprehensive History*. Translated by Raymond P. Scheindlin. New York and Philadelphia: Jewish Publication Society, 1993.
Elon, Amos. *The Pity of It All: A Portrait of the German-Jewish Epoch 1743–1933*. New York: A Metropolitan Book, Henry Holt and Co., 2002.
Ephros, Gershon, ed. *Cantorial Anthology of Traditional and Modern Synagogue Music*. Volume I Rosh Hashonoh. New York: Bloch Publishing Company, 1972/1961.
———, ed. *Cantorial Anthology of Traditional and Modern Synagogue Music*, Volume II Yom Kippur. Arranged for Cantor and Choir with Organ Accompaniment. New York: Bloch Publishing Company, 1977/1953.
———, ed. *Cantorial Anthology of Traditional and Modern Synagogue Music*. Volume III Sholosh R'golim. New York: Bloch Publishing Company, no year.

———, ed. *Cantorial Anthology of Traditional and Modern Synagogue Music*. Volume IV Shabbat. New York: Bloch Publishing Company, 1953.

———, ed. *Cantorial Anthology of Traditional and Modern Synagogue Music*. Volume V Y'mot HaChol. New York: Bloch Publishing Company, 1957.

Fackenheim, Emil. *An Epitaph for German Judaism: From Halle to Jerusalem*. Madison, Wisconsin: The University of Wisconsin Press, 2007.

———. *What Is Judaism? An Interpretation for the Present Age*. Syracuse, New York: Syracuse University Press, 1987.

———. "Sachsenhausen 1938: Groundwork for Auschwitz," in *The Jewish Return into History: Reflections in the Age of Auschwitz and a New Jerusalem*. New York: Schocken Books, 1978.

Friedmann, Aron. *50 Jahre in Berlin (1878–1928)*. Berlin: C. Boas Nachf., 1929.

———. *Der synagogale Gesang*. Leipzig: Edition Peters, 1978. Original print 1904/1908.

———. *Schir Lisch'laumau: Chasonus für das ganze liturgische Jahr*. Published by "Deutsch-New York: The Jewish Theological Seminary Posen, Leipzig, Hannover, München, des liberalen Vereins zu Breslau und des schlesischen Provinzialverbandes," 1901.

———. *Lebensbilder berühmter Kantoren*. Three Volumes. Berlin: C. Boas Nachf., 1918.

Frigyesi, Judit Niran. *Writing on Water: The Sounds of Jewish Prayer*. Budapest-New York: Central European University Press, 2018.

Gedenkbuch: Opfer der Verfolgung der Juden unter der nationalsozialistischen Gewaltherrschaft in Deutschland 1933–1945. Herausgegeben vom Bundesarchiv. Zweite, wesentlich erweiterte Auflage. Koblenz: Bundesarchiv, 2006. Further mention to Koblenz Memor Book.

Glantz, Jerry, ed. *Leib Glantz—The Man Who Spoke to God*. Tel Aviv: Tel Aviv Institute for Jewish Liturgical Music, 2008.

Goldberg, Randall, Francesco Spagnolo, and Judah M. Cohen. "Introduction: Jewish Music and Jewish Identity in the Rust Belt." *Journal of Jewish Identities* (2017), 10(1). Johns Hopkins University Press.

Goldfarb, Israel and Samuel Eliezer Goldfarb. *Jewish Songster, Friday Evening Melodies*. Brooklyn, New York: Publishing Committee, 1964.

Goldfarb, Israel and Israel Herbert Levinthal. *Song and Praise for Sabbath Eve*. Eighth revised edition. Brooklyn, New York: Published by Levinthal and Goldfarb, 1941.

Greenberg, Rabbi Sidney, and Rabbi Jonathan D. Levine, compiled and edited by. *Machzor Chadash*, for Rosh Hashanah and Yom Kippur. Hartford, CT: The Prayer Book Press, 1995.

Grunberger, Michael W., ed. *From Haven to Home: 350 Years of Jewish Life in America*. Library of Congress in association with George Braziller Inc., 2004.

Heilman, Samuel C. *Synagogue Life: A Study in Symbolic Interaction*. New Brunswick and London: Transaction Publications, 1998.

Hertz, Dr. J. H., ed. *The Pentateuch and Haftorahs*, Hebrew Text, English Translation, and Commentary. Second Edition. London: Soncino Press, 1979/5739.

Heskes, Irene. *Passport to Jewish Music: Its History, Traditions, and Culture*. New York/Maryland/Israel: Tara Publications Greenwood Press, 1994.

Hoffman, Lawrence A., and Walton, Janet R. eds. *Sacred Sound and Social Change: Liturgical Music in Jewish and Christian Experience*. Notre Dame/London: University of Notre Dame Press, 1992.

Holde, Artur. *Jews in Music. From the Age of Enlightenment to the Mid-Twentieth Century*. New edition. Prepared by Irene Heskes. New York: Bloch Publishing Company, 1974.

Idelsohn, A. Z. *Jewish Song Book for Synagogue, School and Home*. A. Z. Idelsohn, Cincinnati, OH: Publications for Judaism, 1951.

———. *Jewish Liturgy and Its Development*. New York: Dover Publications, Inc., 1995/1932.

Janowski, Max. "L'Chu N'ran'nah," Slichot. Chicago, IL: Friends of Jewish Music, 1973.

Jüdische Frontsoldaten aus Württemberg und Hohenzollern. Württembergischer Landesverband des Zentralvereins deutscher Staatsbürger jüdischen Glaubens. Stuttgart: J. Fink, 1926.

Kalib, Sholom. *The Musical Tradition of the Eastern European Synagogue*. Volume One. Introduction: History and Definition, Part One. Text. Syracuse, NY: Syracuse University Press, 2002.

———. *The Musical Tradition of the Eastern European Synagogue*. Volume One. Introduction: History and Definition, Part Two. Music. Syracuse, NY: Syracuse University Press, 2002.

Kimmelman, Mira Ryczke. *Life Beyond the Holocaust. Memories and Realities*. Edited by Gilya Gerda Schmidt. Knoxville: UT Press, 2005.

Klein, Amit, in collaboration with Professor Eliyahu Schleifer and Professor Edwin Seroussi, Jewish Music Research Centre, Hebrew University, Jerusalem, "Harmonizing Theory with Creativity: Cantor Leib Glantz's Musical Agenda," in Jerry Glantz, ed. *Leib Glantz—The Man Who Spoke to God*. Tel Aviv: Tel Aviv Institute for Jewish Liturgical Music, 2008.

Klein, Isaac. *A Guide to Jewish Religious Practice*. Volume VI in the Moreshet

Series, Studies in Jewish History, Literature and Thought. New York: The Jewish Theological Seminary of America, 1979.

Koblenz Memor Book. See *Gedenkbuch: Opfer der Verfolgung der Juden unter der nationalsozialistischen Gewaltherrschaft in Deutschland 1933–1945.*

Large, David Clay. *Berlin.* New York: Basic Books, 2000.

Lewandowski, Louis. *Kol Rinnah UT'fillah.* Out-of-Print Classics Series No. 9. New York: Sacred Music Press, no year. Originally published in 1870.

———. *Todah W'simrah, Volume I: Shabbat.* Out-of-Print Classics Series No. 10. New York: Sacred Music Press, no year.

———. *Todah W'simrah, Volume II. Part 1: Festivals.* Out-of-Print Classics Series No. 11. New York: Sacred Music Press, no year.

———. *Todah W'simrah, Volume II. Part 2: Festivals.* 11th edition. Out-of-Print Classics Series No. 12. New York: Sacred Music Press, no year.

Liturgisches Liederbuch für den Gebrauch der Religionsschulen. Vorstand der jüdischen Gemeinde zu Berlin. Berlin: Verlag v. M. Poppelauer, 1912.

Mann, Vivian B., ed., with commentary. *Jewish Texts on the Visual Arts.* The Jewish Museum, New York; The Jewish Theological Seminary. Cambridge, U.K. and New York: Cambridge University Press, 2000.

Nachama, Oberkantor Estrongo. CD cover: Lewandowski, Louis, "Es tönt von der Erde zum Himmel empor." RIAS-Kammerchor, Uwe Gronostay, direction. RIAS Berlin, GEMA CD 66.211 87, 1995.

Nachama, Oberkantor Estrongo. CD cover: "Jom Kipur, Gebetsgesänge zum Versöhnungstag." RIAS-Kammerchor, Uwe Gronostay, direction. RIAS Berlin, GEMA CD 66.219 80, no date.

Narkiss, Bezalel. *Hebrew Illuminated Manuscripts.* Foreword by Cecil Roth. Encyclopedia Judaica Jerusalem; The Macmillan Company. Jerusalem: Keter Publishing House Ltd, and New York: Macmillan, 1969.

Nathanson, Moshe, ed. *Zamru Lo I, Congregational Melodies and Z'mirot for the Friday Evening Service.* New York: Cantors Assembly, 1974.

———, ed. *Zamru Lo II, Congregational Melodies and Z'mirot for the Entire Sabbath Day.* New York: Cantors Assembly, 1974.

———, ed. *Zamru Lo III, Congregational Melodies for the Shalosh R'galim and the High Holidays.* New York: Cantors Assembly, 1974.

Naumbourg, Samuel. *Zemiroth Israel: Chants Religieux des Israelites*, Out-of-Print Classics Series of Synagogue Music No. 14. Sacred Music Press, 1954. Originally published in 1847.

Nowakowsky, David. *Schlußgebet für Jom-Kippur*, für Cantor, Solo und gemischten Chor. Out-of-Print Classics Series No. 23. Sacred Music Press, New York, no year.

Randall, Marga Silbermann. *How Beautiful We Once Were: A Remembrance of the Holocaust and Beyond.* Pittsburgh, PA: Cathedral Publications, 1998.

Rosenblatt, Josef. "Shomer Israel," The Joint Distribution Committee of the American Friends for Jewish War Sufferers, NCMXXI.

Rosenblatt, The Music of Yossele. "The Chassidic Kaddish at the Conclusion of the N'iloh Service." Arrangements by Henry Rosenblatt. New York, NY: Tara Publications, no year.

Scherman, Rabbi Nosson, co-edited by Rabbi Meir Zlotowitz. *The Complete Artscroll Siddur.* Nusach Ashkenaz. Weekday/Sabbath/Festival. A new translation and anthologized commentary. The Artscroll Mesorah Series. Brooklyn, New York: Mesorah Publications, Ltd., 1990/1984.

Schleifer, Eliyahu. ed. *Samuel Naumbourg: The Cantor of French Jewish Emancipation.* Jewish Miniatures, Vol. 136A, Louis Lewandowski Festival. Berlin: Centrum Judaicum, Hentrich & Hentrich, 2015.

———. "Jewish Liturgical Music From the Bible to Hasidism," in Lawrence A. Hoffman and Janet R. Walton, eds., *Sacred Sound and Social Change: Liturgical Music in Jewish and Christian Experience.* Notre Dame/London: University of Notre Dame Press, 1992, 13–58.

———. "Jewish Musical Culture—Past and Present," in *The World of Music,* Volume 37, No. 1, 1995.

Schmidt, Gilya Gerda, translator, with an introduction. *Friedrich Schleiermacher, Letters on the Occasion of the Political Theological Task and the Sendschreiben (Open Letter) of Jewish Heads of Household.* Schleiermacher Studies and Translations, Volume 21. Lewiston/Queenston/Lampeter: The Edwin Mellen Press, 2001.

———. *The Art and Artists of the Fifth Zionist Congress, 1901. Heralds of a New Age.* Syracuse, N.Y.: Syracuse University Press, 2003.

———. *Süssen Is Now Free of Jews.* New York: Fordham University Press, 2012.

Scholem, Gershom. *From Berlin to Jerusalem: Memories of My Youth.* Philadelphia: Paul Dry Books, 2012.

Secunda, Sholom. Pis'chu li" for Mixed Voices. New York: Mills Music Inc., 1951.

Shir U'Tefillah. Songs and Prayers for Jewish Youth. New York: Central Conference of American Rabbis (CCAR), 1960.

Silverman, Rabbi Morris, compiled and arranged by. *Machzor: High Holiday Prayer Book*, Rosh Hashanah – Yom Kippur. With a new translation and explanatory notes, together with supplementary prayers, meditations, and readings in prose and verse. Hartford, CT: Prayer Book Press, 1949/1939.

———, ed., prepared by the Joint Prayer Book Commission of the Rabbinical Assembly of America and the United Synagogue of America. *Sabbath and*

Festival Prayer Book, with a new translation, supplementary readings and notes. New York: 1946/1966.

Simon, Hermann. *Die Neue Synagoge Berlin: Geschichte, Gegenwart, Zukunft*. Dritte ergänzte Auflage. Berlin: Edition Hentrich, 1997.

Slichot. New York: The Rabbinical Assembly, 1964.

Slobin, Mark. *Chosen Voices: The Story of the American Cantorate*. Urbana and Chicago: University of Illinois Press, 2002/1998.

Songs of Israel. New York: Metro Music, 1949–50.

Sulzer, Salomon. *Schir Zion I, Gesänge für den israelitischen Gottesdienst*, Out-of-Print Classics Series No. 6, 150th Jubilee Issue, Joseph Sulzer, ed. New York, NY: Sacred Music Press, 1953. Originally published in 1840.

———. *Schir Zion II, Gesänge für den israelitischen Gottesdienst*, Out-of-Print Classics Series No. 7, Joseph Sulzer, ed. New York, NY: Sacred Music Press, 1953. Originally published in 1876.

Talmon (Monsohn), Zvi. "Nedarai LAdonai" in *Pa'amey Hahechal: Compositions for Cantor and Choir as sung at Hechal Shlomo, Jerusalem*. Jerusalem: Hechal Shlomo, 1992.

———. *Truot HaHekhl*. Jerusalem: Hechal Shlomo, no date.

———. *Rinat ha-Heikhal Anthology*. New York: Cantors Assembly, 1965.

Umansky, Ellen M. and Dianne Ashton, eds., *Four Centuries of Jewish Women's Spirituality: A Sourcebook*. Revised edition. Waltham, MS: Brandeis University Press, and Hanover and London: University of New England, 2009.

Union Hymnal, *Songs and Prayers for Worship*. Cincinnati: Central Committee of American Rabbis (CCAR), 1949.

Vander, Judith. *Songprints: The Musical Experience of Five Shoshone Women*. Urbana and Chicago: University of Illinois Press, 1988.

Vinaver, Chemjo, ed. *Anthology of Jewish Music: Sacred Chant and Religious Folk Song of the Eastern European Jews*. New York, NY: Edward B. Marks Music Corporation, MCMLV.

Werner, Eric. *A Voice Still Heard…The Sacred Songs of the Ashkenazic Jews*. University Park and London: The Pennsylvania State University Press, 1976.

Online

American Jewish Archives. "Alexander Guttmann." http://americanjewish archives.org/. Accessed April 6, 2016.

Asch, Cantor Felix. Symposium Records Catalogue Website. *The First Opera Recordings (1895–1902), a Survey*. Accessed June 21, 2017.

———. Internet Archive. Digital Library of Free and Borrowable Books, Movies, and Music: archive.org.
Cantors Assembly, New York. Cantors Assembly Convention Proceedings Internet Archive 1949–present (website). https://archive.org/details/CantorsAssemblyConventionProceedings. Accessed various times.
Carnegie Mellon University. "Jewish Newspaper Project." http://digitalcollections.library.cmu.edu/portal/collections/pjn/index.jsp. Updated to http://digitalcollections.library.cmu.edu/pjn. Accessed from February 2, 2016, to February 2023. CMU Libraries Digital Collection.
Eternal Light, The. https://www.oldtimeradiodownloads.com.
Förderverein Jüdischer Friedhof Berlin-Weissensee. Accessed June 30, 2017.
Gollanin, Leo. Choir Practice in the New Synagogue in Berlin on the Night Before Yom Kippur, 1932. Story RG-60.4817, Film ID 2854. Steven Spielberg Film and Video Archive. "Leo Gollanin," FV0055-rg60104 9 dv50.mov. United States Holocaust Memorial Museum, Washington, D. C. Accessed June 21, 1917.
Heschel, Abrahahm Joshua. "The Vocation of the Cantor," online. Accessed November 20, 2022. See also in Slobin Bibliography for *Chosen Voices*, "The Vocation of the Cantor," in *The Insecurity of Freedom*. New York: Noonday Press, 1967.
Jewish Music Research Center, National Library, Hebrew University of Jerusalem. "Jakob Beimel." Accessed June 21, 2017.
Jewish Virtual Library. "Leo Baeck." https://www.jewishvirtuallibrary.org/jsource/biography/baeck.html. Accessed February 3, 2016.
Jewish Virtual Library. "Elbogen, Ismar." https://www.jewishvirtuallibrary.org/jsource/judaica/ejud_0002_0006_0_05730.html. Accessed February 3, 2016.
Jewish Virtual Library. "Virtual Jewish World: Berlin, Germany." Accessed 12/11/22.
Jewishwebsite.com. "Pittsburgh Jewish Population." Accessed 9/12/22.
Leo Baeck Institute, New York. Hans Liebeschütz, in "Ismar Elbogen Collection, 1842–1974," AR 64/MF515 BETA Europeana Collections online. Accessed June 21, 2017.
McKerrel, Alex. "Scheunenviertel: History, Architecture, and Sights." Accessed 12/6/22.
Milken Archive of Jewish Music. Neil W. Levin, "Max Janowski 1912–1991." Accessed May 18, 2016.
Milken Archive of Jewish Music. Neil W. Levin, "Israel Alter (1901–1979)." Accessed 12/26/22.
Milken Archive of Jewish Music. Neil W. Levin, "Sholom Secunda." Accessed June 21, 2017.

Topper, Elizabeth, "Parasha Poems: Weekly Poems Drawn from a Theme in the Parasha." Accessed 7/18/17.
Wikipedia, Die Freie Enzyklopädie. "Arthur Spanier."
Wikipedia, Die Freie Enzyklopädia. "Max Wiener."
Wikipedia.org. "John Rayner."
Wikipedia.org. "Stern Conservatory."
Wikipedia.org. "Harry Torczyner."
Wikipedia.org. "Jewish Pittsburgh."
Wikipedia.org. "B'nai B'rith."
Wikipedia.org. "Debbie Friedman."
Wikipedia.org. "Renaissance Music."

Archival

Friendship Club Records, 1935–1976, AIS.1976.31, University of Pittsburgh, Pittsburgh, PA.
Leo Baeck Institute, New York. Ismar Elbogen Collection, 1842–1974, AR 64/MF515. BETA Europeana Collections re Hans Liebeschütz.
MSP #470, B'nai Israel Congregational Records. Rauh Jewish Archive, Detre Library and Archives Division, Senator John Heinz History Center, Pittsburgh, PA.
MSS #470, B'nai lsrael Congregational Records. Rauh Jewish Archive, Detre Library and Archives Division, Senator John Heinz History Center, Pittsburgh, PA.
Sachsenhausen Gedenkstätte und Museum. Heiser documents re release from concentration camp.
Stein Collection. Judith Heiser Stein and Stein Family, Pittsburgh, PA.

INDEX

Page numbers in **boldface** *refer to illustrations*

Adler, Hugo Chaim (1894–1955), 155, 205, 224, 286n93
Affidavit for visa, 23, 24
"Akdamut," 222
Alter, Israel (1901–1979), 156, 225, 230, 231, 287n97
American Jewish life changed when German Reform Jews arrived, 53; Eastern European Jews 1880s, 54
Antisemitism, 8
Asch, Oberkantor Felix (1853–1929), 16, 141, 184, 252n40, 280n41
Aufgebotsverzeichnis for Gustav and Elly Heiser, 1935, 20

Baal Shem Tov (1700–1760), 145
Baeck, Rabbi Leo (1873–1956), 27; Head of *Reichsvertretung*, 27; member of 1937 Heiser exam committee, 30; Heiser examination 1939, **118**; imprisoned in Theresienstadt, 27; liberated in 1945, 27, member of *Centralverein*, 27; President of B'nai B'rith Lodge, 27; teacher at *Hochschule*, 27
Baer Collection, 199
Baerwald, Max, Berlin architect, 15
Barash, Morris, 225, 231
Beautification of the Torah (*hiddur mitzvah*), 10

Beimel, Jakob (1875–1944), 154, 197, 203, 284n83
Berenbaum, Michael, 96, 256n105
Berlin: aspiring Weltstadt, 14; map, Bavarian Quarter, 21, 22; capital of Second German Empire 1871, 12; center of German Jewish culture and religion, 12; difficult years following World War I, 14; Jewish population in 1847, 13; magnet for Jews from provinces, 13; map, Introduction, N. 3, 248; map, Bavarian Quarter, 21, 22; map, Winsviertel, 19; Scheunenviertel, 12; Zionism, 15; Berlin-Lichterfelde-Lankwitz congregation, 22, 134, 142, recommendation November 1, 1938, **114**
Berlin, Cantor Richard Mark, 137, 278n22
Bimah (podium), 136
Binstock, Doris D. 94
Birkat HaChodesh (Prayer for the New Month), 134, 158, 225–27
Birnbaum, Max, 20
Birnbaum, Sophie, 20
Black Death of 1348, 9
Bloom, Chazen Julius, 61, 62, 63, 79, 156; death April 6, 1942, 62, 63

B'nai B'rith centennial celebration 1972, 89, 272n183
B'nai Israel Day 1978, 90
B'nai Israel Golden Anniversary Book, 1954, 16, 252n38
B'nai Israel Summer Camp Scholarship Fund, 86; ticket, 86
B'nai Israel's 75th Anniversary booklet, 61, 262n51
B'nai Israel Cemetery in Penn Township, 65, 239
Brauer, Albert (died 1972), 103
Brauer, Selma (died 1931), origin, 11, 251n14
Brauer, Simon (1881-deported 1942), 49, 103
Brenner, Michael, *After the Holocaust: Rebuilding Jewish Lives in Postwar Germany*, 1997, 17, 252n42; Cantor Estrongo Nechama, 17
Buchenwald Concentration Camp, 8
Burstin, Barbara S., 55; *Steel City Jews: A History of Pittsburgh and Its Jewish Community, 1840–1915*, 55, 261n32

Cantatas for the Nation, 74, 79–81; Cantor Heiser and Rabbi Seymour Cohen, 79
Cantor, role not well defined early on, 53; "Jack of all trades," in Slobin, 53, 260n26; origin of term, 249n4
Cantorate, 15; American, 53–54, 70; as a sacred calling, 15; European style, 54; expansion after 1945, 70; Golden Age of Cantors 1890–1940, 54; *Hazzanim Farband*, early professional organization 1897, also called Jewish Ministers Cantors Association, 54; recordings are new in 1900, 54
Cantors institutes: Reform 1947, 70, 72; Conservative 1951, 70; Orthodox 1954, 70
Cantors Assembly, 70–74, 84, 149, 239, 240, 242; Cantors Convention Proceedings Internet Archive website, 71, 258n6; Officers: Corresponding Secretary is David J. Putterman, 71, 73; President is Abraham J. Rose, 71; Recording Secretary is Morris Shore, 71; Treasurer is Gershon Ephros, 71; Vice-President is Martin Adolf, 71
Cantors Assembly annual conference, second, 1949, 71; annual conference, third, 1950, 71; annual conference, fourth, 1951, 72; annual conference, fifth, 1952, 72; annual conference, seventh, 1954, 77; annual conference, eighth, 1955, 78; annual conference, ninth, 1956, 78; annual conference-convention, 1960, at Grossinger's, 82; Cantor Heiser on Convention meeting committee 1960, 82; designated Honorary Fellow 1960, 82; annual convention, fourteenth, 1961, 84; Cantor Heiser on Convention meeting committee, 84; Cantor Heiser on program, 84; annual convention, fifteenth, 1962, 84; Cantor Heiser participates in program, 84; annual convention, thirty-sixth, 1983, 96; Cantor Heiser receives Yuval award, 96; Cantors Institute established 1952, 72, 78, 79; Cantor Max J.

Routtenberg, director, 72; Cantor Heiser attends 1947 conference, 70; Conference on Jewish music in synagogue 1947, 70; National Council, 82; Retirement and Insurance Plan established 1949, 72; Tri-State Regional Branch, 72–73, 77, 78, 79, 82; Cantor Heiser is chairman, 72

Carnegie Recital Hall, New York; Cantor Heiser recital, March 22, 1949, 66, 68, 71, 240; Program, 68, **122**, 266n104; Performance review, 69

Carson, Rabbi Shoshana, 150, 284n81

Catalogue of Cantor Heiser worship services, 4

Catalogue of Cantor Heiser music, 151–157

Chalutzim (pioneers), 85, 148, 239

Chevra Chas (Talmud Study Group), 59

Chertoff, Rabbi Mordecai S., assistant rabbi 1961–66, 59

Chmielnicki massacres 1648, 8

Choral synagogue (*Khorshul*), 133, 145

Chorister, singer, *meshorer*, 146

Cohen, Rabbi Seymour J., assistant rabbi 1951–1956, 61; Rabbi 1957–1961, 59, 74, 79

Compositions by Cantor Heiser, 148

Congregation Adat Shalom, 110

Congregation B'nai Israel, 1, 57–62; Bat Mitzvah for girls 1955 and 1972, 62; B'nai Israel Day, October 22, 1978, 90; Camp Ramah Scholarship Fund, 96, 273n206; Cantor location in synagogue, 136; changes in Shabbat service, 62; change from Ashkenazi Hebrew to Sephardic 1966, 62; choir location in synagogue, 136; closes its doors in 1996, 110; *Congregation B'nai Israel Bulletin*, 86; congregational trip to Israel, 1969, 85; confirmation picture 1950, **120**; dedication of additional structure, 61, 62; description of outside of building by Patricia Lowry, 58, **120**; East End Jews formed *minyanim* in 1904, 57; eighty-fifth anniversary of congregation 1989, 105, 106; establishment of Sisterhood, 57; family pews, 59; *Golden Anniversary Book*, 74; groundbreaking for additional construction 1951, 61; Hebrew School graduation class 1943, **121**; hired Rabbi Benjamin A. Lichter in 1920, 57; late Friday night service, 57; LaTovah society, 58; *minyanim* in people's homes, 57; mixed choir, 57; new *machzorim* for High Holy Days, 59; purchase of site for new building 1921, 58; rededication of sanctuary in memory of Rabbi Lichter, 62; responsive readings by rabbi and congregation, 59; B'nai Israel sanctuary, **132**; seventy-fifth anniversary 1979, 62, 90, 205, 212, 214; Silver Jubilee 1929, 58; singing of Sabbath hymns in English, 57; Sisterhood presents service flag honoring 135 men in service 1942, 61; Sisterhood Shabbat, 62; site for future synagogue building, 58; stained-glass windows by Jean-Jacques Duvall, 62; women receive *aliyot* in 1979, 62

Dachau Concentration Camp, 8
Daniels, Anna, cousin to Elly Heiser, 43, 48
Daniels, Monte, Wertheimer & Co.; letter 1940 to Heisers, 43, 258n1
Dedication of memorial plaques, 209
Dominican Republic: invites 100,000 European Jews in 1938, 52
Dubrow, Samuel, 156, 165, 170, 176, 181, 194, 202
Dutch governor of New Amsterdam, Peter Stuyvesant (1592–1672), 53
Dunajewski, Avraham (1843–1911), 154, 206, 214, 284n84
Duvall, Jean-Jacques (1930–2021), 62

Eastern European composers and arrangers, 154–55
Ebner, Cilly, 103, 275n229
Edelman, Marsha Bryan, 4, 133, 260n24
Edelstein, Cantor Leopold (1909–1985), 89, 157, 158, 233, 234, 236
Edmundson, William, 85
Ehrenreich, Elieser, *Kultusverwaltung*, 17
Eisenberg & Struck; Gustav Heiser's employer, 14, 15, 18, 36, 252n34
"El Male Rachamim," 242
Elbogen, Ismar (1874–1943), 4, 28, 157, 254n89; *Der jüdische Gottesdienst in seiner Entwicklung*, 1913, 28; *A Century of Jewish Life*, 1944, 28; on Cantor Heiser 1937 examination committee, 30
Elly and Mordecai Heiser Music Fund, 96
Elon, Amos, *The Pity of It All*, 14, 252n32

Emancipation, 8, 13
Embellishment, 145, 186
Ephros, Gershon, 70, 195. 199
Erev Rosh Hashanah service, 172; Guide, 172; Worksheet 177–181
"Eternal Light" radio program, 67; from 1952 also television program, 67
Evian Conference in France, 1938, 52

Fackenheim, Professor Rabbi Emil (1917–2003), 26, 241; *An Epitaph for German Judaism: From Halle to Jerusalem*, 2007, 26; arrested and incarcerated in Sachsenhausen 1938, 26, 33; classmate of Cantor Heiser's, 26, 240; diploma as *Rabbiner, Prediger*, und *Religionslehrer*, 30; Fackenheim and Heiser in 1938 *Hochschule* class picture, 28, **117**, 254n90; Fackenheim ordained by Alexander Guttmann, 29; Rabbi Max Wiener in "What is Judaism?" 27; "Sachsenhausen 1938: Groundwork for Auschwitz", 1987, 33; arrival in Sachsenhausen, 34; conditions in camp, 33; daily routine, 34; Kapo, 34; transportation to Sachsenhausen, 33
Falsetto, 170, 180, 190, 203
Feidman, Giora, 105, 106; B'nai Israel concert 1989, 105, 276nn235, 236; program, 106, **130**
Feldkommandantur 520; 39, 257n138
Finkelstein, Charlotte, 100
Finkelstein, Dr. Louis, JTS, 82
Folk music, Jewish, 2, 145, 146, 148, 163, 239

Freed, Cantor Isadore, 70
Freehof, Rabbi Solomon (1892–1990), 56
Fried, Henry, 73
Friedman, Debbie (1951–2011), 144, 281n51
Friedmann, Cantor Aron (1855–1936), 16, 141, 155, 233; *Schir Lisch'laumau* cover, 113, 252n41; Friedmann and Lewandowski, 16; Student of Lewandowski, 141
Freudenthal, Julius, 154, 234, 236, 286n92
Friendship Club (1936–79), 91, 242; dissolution of club, 93; Hanukkah celebration 1944, 91; Heiser speech, 32, 254n78, 256n106, 272n193
Frigyesi, Judit Niran, 4, 11,157, 248n1, 250n10, 288n103; *Writing on Water: The Sounds of Jewish Prayer* (2018), 248n1

Gays, 241
Geshem (Prayer for Rain), 148
German Reform Jews, 53
Gisser, Meyer, 95, 182; President of B'nai Israel, 1977–80, 90, 182
Glantz, Cantor Leib, 4, 250n7, 282n59; *Mi Sinai nusach*, 283n72; on *hazzanut* (Jewish prayer modes), 10, 148; on *nusach* and biblical cantillation modes, 10
Glatstein, Rabbi Mordecai, 271n175
Goebbels, Josef, Propaganda Minister, 22
Göttingen *Synagogengemeinde*, 18
Goldfarb, Cantor Israel (1879–1967), 70, 71, 196, 200, 211, 220, 233, 234, 235, 236, 237, 287n96

Gollanin, *Oberkantor* Leo (1872–1948), 16, 17, 141, 184, 289n129
"Good Yom Tov" (holiday greeting), 209
Graumann, Max (1871–1933), 187
Gregorian chant, 144, 145
Grosse, Franz, receipt, 36, 257n122
Guttmann, Julius, 28
Guttmann, Alexander (1904–1994), 28, 30, 35, 254n91; on Cantor Heiser 1937 examination committee, 30

Haalman, Rev. Mordechai Max, 60, 61, 223, 225, 229; Holocaust survivor, 60
Haar, Cilly Brauer, 103, 275n230
Hachscharah (agricultural training program), 36
Haggim (major festivals), 143, 205, 227
"Hag Sameach" (Hebrew greeting), 209
Hailperin, Rabbi Hermann, Ph.D.; letter of support for citizenship, 52, 260n22
Hanukkah concert 1983, 96, **127**
Hanukkah concert 1984, 96
Hasidism, 145
Hatzi Kaddish prayer, 164, 169, 175, 180, 186, 192, 193, 210, 219, 225, 229, 233, 235
"Hazak, hazak, v'nithazek," 242
Hazkarah (memorial service), 208
Hazzan, term, 9, 250n4
Hazzan fulfills important role, 10
Hazzanim Farband, 54, 70, 267n106
Hazzanut, 155, 158, 239, 242, 248n5
Hebrew language: Ashkenazi, 165, 172, 176; Sephardic, 165, 172, 176

Hebrew Immigrant Aid Society (HIAS), 42
Hecha kedushah (Amidah chanted out loud through *Kedushah*), 233
Heiser, Eleonore (Elke) (1903- deported), 12, 103
Heiser, Elly Hochmann (1911–1992), 1, 18, 37, 48, 50, 74, 225, 229, 239; "A Holocaust Remembrance," 1989 article, 40, 258n143; about valuables, 38, 39; application to Foreign Currency office, 38, 39; birth certificate, 18, **115**, 253nn49, 50; emigration to England in 1939, 39; Emile Meerberger, S.A. shipping company, 39; items to take into emigration, 38, 39, 257nn136, 137; letter from *Feldkommandantur* 520 in Antwerp, 39, 257nn138, 139, 257n138; letter to unnamed cousin regarding refuge, 23; Naturalization document, 1945, 53; nickname "Pucci", 20, 104; notification of emigration to authorities, 39–40; passport issued to Elly 1939, 39, 257n140; poem for Charlotte Finkelstein, 100; poem for Adele and Warren's wedding, 101; poem for Shari and Mark's wedding, 104, 276n234; preparations for emigration, 38; visit to Dr. med. W. Leszczynski, 38, 257n135; William Edmundson in Israel, 85
Heiser, *Hazzan* (Cantor) Mordecai Gustav Heiser (1905–1989), 1, 4, 11, 61, 78, 160, 239; appraisal of valuables by Franz Grosse, 36; Armistice Day Program 1943, 64; arrest and incarceration in Sachsenhausen 1938, in letter to Hans Rayner 1939, 33, 240; arrival in Pittsburgh, 240; *Aufgebotsverzeichnis* 1935, 253nn58, 59; birthplace Singhofen, district Unterlahn, 11; Cantor Heiser chanting prayer, **129**; Certificate of Admission from Hebrew University in Jerusalem 1939, 34, 256n116; certificate of graduation 1939, 36; certificate as *Prediger* and *Religionslehrer*, 35, 257n121; certification as *Hazzan* and *Sheliach Tsibbur* 1954, 73, **123**; choir is great strength, 134; classes at Cantors Institute New York, 72; grades received, 72; compositions, 149, 283n76; concert to inaugurate Mordecai and Elly Heiser Music Fund, May 23, 1982 (with Hazzan Lissek, Mimi Lerner, Hazzan Heiser), 95; debut at Carnegie Hall 1949, 71; elected by Kultus-Gemeinde to serve Berlin-Lichterfelde-Lankwitz congregation, 142; emigration to England, 37; employment with Eisenberg & Struck, 14; engagement to Elly, *Jüdische Rundschau*, 1934, 20, 36; fear of God (*yirat shamayim*), 147; First Cantor 1925–1938, 17, 24; Five Cantors concert 1956, **124**, five Israel visits, 65, 242; Fragment of Heiser family letter, **132**; Friendship Club, 91; Fortieth anniversary breakfast by JTS 1980, 94, **126**; guest speaker Rabbi Sanford D.

Shanblatt, 94; *Geburtsschein*, 12, 251n17; *Geburtsurkunde*, **112**; Golden Wedding anniversary 1985, 97; two leaves dedicated on *Simcha* Tree, 98; Gustav and Elly civil marriage 1935, 20–21; Gustav and Elly Jewish wedding 1935, 21; receipt for ceremony, 21, **115**, 253n60; *Brautstrauss*, 21, 253n61; Hanukkah concert to support Heiser music fund, December 4, 1983, 96, **128**; *Hazzan* (precentor), 9, 10, *Hazzanut*, 2, 3, 69, 110, 137, 138, 239, appreciation for, 140, 147, 160, 164; *hazzanut* is sacred task, 140; Hebrew Institute Parent-Teachers Association, 66; Heiser accident Spring 1989, 106; Heiser death October 24, 1989, 106, obituary, 107, 276n240; Heiser certificate attesting to competency in general subjects, 35; Heiser compositions, 149, 283n76; Heiser receives one of first certificates as *Hazzan* and *Sheliach Tsibbur* 1954, 73, **123**; Heiser exam on April 14, 1939, 36, **118**; Heiser letters to Elly from Amsterdam 1934, 36, 255n97, 257nn123, 124, 125; Heiser becomes cantor on March 1, 1942, 63–64; Heiser grave, **131**, Heiser portrait with *siddur*, **127**; Heiser portrait in B'nai Israel sanctuary, **128**; Heiser version of "Y'varech'cha,"notation by Schmidt, **130**; Heiser/Stein family picture, **127**; *Hochschule* class picture, 28, 30, **117**; Hoch-*schulreife* (*Abitur*) certificate, 35; Holocaust survivor, 3, 12; Holocaust victims, 4; Importance of music in Jewish life, 140; Interim exam (*Zwischenprüfung*) 1937, 22, 26, 30; **116**, 253n65, 255n101; *Israelitische Religionsverein* Berlin-Lichterfelde-Lankwitz, 17, **114**; letter of good conduct (*Führungszeugnis*) 1939, 36, 251n26; letter to Hans re affidavit business, 31, 40, 258n144; letter to Hans re Kitchener Camp, 37; letter to Rabbi Charles Rautenberg, 49–50, 260n18, 263n72; letter to Hans re Sachsenhausen, 33; melodist, 148; member of Pittsburgh Opera Company, 66; *mohel* 1972, **125**; Mordecai and Elly Heiser photo 1960, **129**; Mordecai and Elly Heiser Music Fund of B'nai Israel Congregation 1982, 95; Mordecai and Elly Heiser ZOA Masada Scholarship Fund created in 1987, 102; music memorial for European Jews, 4; music as affirmation of Jewish life, 4; Naturalization document 1945, 53, **121**, 260n23, also name change to Mordecai Gustav Heiser on document, 53, **121**; passage on M.V. "Georgie" January 30, 1940 from Liverpool to New York, 42; passport issued in 1939, 36, **118**, 257n126; philosophy of Liturgy, 137; Pittsburgh speech in 1979 mentioning Fackenheim, 27; police permit, 22; prayer book entry of murdered relatives, 49;

Heiser, *Hazzan* (Cantor) Mordecai Gustav Heiser (1905–1989) (*cont.*), *Probevortrag* at Synagogengemeinde Göttingen, 18, 253n48; Ramah Hanukkah concert December 16, 1984, 96, with Wilkinsburg Symphony, 96; Shannon Osborn letter, 97; receipts from American Consulate for fee to transfer Gustav Heiser's affidavit, 41; repertoire, 151; serious about studies in *hazzanut*, 142; *Shaliach Tzibur*, 147; Songprint, 4, 158; Soundscape of Jewish music, 239, of Eastern European composers, 11; sweet singer of B'nai Israel, 11, 133; Thirtieth anniversary with B'nai Israel 1970, 86, **125**, 271n173, benefit of B'nai Israel Summer Camp Scholarship Fund, 86; congratulatory telegram from B'nai Israel Young Adult Congregation, 87, 271n176; letter from Rabbi Mordecai L. Glatstein, 87, 271n175, letter from Samuel Rosenbaum, 87; letter from Morton Siegel, 87, 271n174, letter from Cantor Raymond Smolover, 87, ticket, 86; thirty-two years of service to B'nai Israel 1972 , 89; thirty-fifth wedding anniversary 1970, 86; twentieth anniversary with B'nai Israel 1960, 82; twenty-fifth wedding anniversary 1960, 82, **129**; twenty-fifth anniversary tribute dinner honoring Israel 1972, 89; winner of Pittsburgh Concert Society auditions, 85

Heiser, Hugo (1907-deported 1941), 12, 18, 19, 36, 44, 49, 103

Heiser, Isaac (1872-deported 1942), 12, 44, 49; Prussian civil servant, 12; witness for Heiser wedding, 20, 21, 44

Heiser, Judith (1936–2021), birth certificate 1936, 22, **116**, 253n63; confiscation of valuables by War Office, 39; emigration to England, 39; engagement to Alvin Stein 1995, 81; move to Baby and Toddler Home, 38, 257nn133, 134; Zamler, 137

Heiser, Meta nee Hochmann (2905-deported 1941), 12, 18, 19, 36, 44, 49, 103

Heiser, Selma nee Brauer, 12, died 1931, buried in Weissensee Cemetery, 12

Heiser, Sylvia[e] (1934 Amsterdam-deported 1941), 12, 19, 36, 44, 49

Heschel, Professor Rabbi Joshua, 4, 29, 139, 159, 279n30; ordained by Alexander Guttmann, 29

Heuser, Beyer nee Reuter, 12

Heuser, Emma nee Katz, 12

Heuser, Gumbert, 12

Heuser, Tobias (Tovia) (1847–1913), 12

High Holy Days (Rosh Hashanah and Yom Kippur), 9

Hiddur mitzvah (beautification of the Torah), 10, 249n6

Hilfsverein der Juden in Deutschland, e.V., 37, **119**

Hindenburg, President Paul von; death 1934, 22

Hochmann, Adele Eidel nee Birnbaum (1877-deported 1941), 18, 20, 44, 49

Hochmann, Berta (Betti or Bayla) (1906-deported 1942), 19
Hochmann, Elly (1911–1992), 18; birth certificate 1911, 18, 19, 20, **115**
Hochmann, Juda Samson (1877–1922), 18, 19
Hochmann, Leo Leiser (1900–deported), 20, 44
Hochmann, Meta (1905–deported 1941), 18, 19
Hochmann, Salomon (1910–1928), 18, 20
Hochschule für die Wissenschaft des Judentums, 2, 21, 25, 26–31, 157, 242, 254n72; founded in 1872, 26; *Hochschule* demoted to *Lehranstalt* in 1934, 26, 34
Holocaust experiences, 2, 12, 233
Holocaust Memorial Day, 242
Horn, Maxine, 106

Idelsohn, Abraham Zvi (1882–1938), 4, 155, 157, 225, 281n47, 281n49, 283n74, 283n75, 286n91
Improvisations, cantorial, 145, 147, 185, 186, 190
Israel, state of, 78, 84, 102, 242
Israel Bonds, 85, 90, 96, 1972 event, **125**, 272n187
Israeli tunes, 2, 163
Israel's Eighth Anniversary Celebration concert 1956, 78–79; Five Pittsburgh cantors, 78
Israel's twenty-fifth anniversary tribute dinner 1972, 89
Israelitische Religionsverein in Berlin-Lichterfelde-Lankwitz, 17; recommendation for Cantor Heiser, 17, 24, 253n69; second letter states objective circumstances for dismissal, 25, **114** 253n70; subjective circumstances for dismissal, 24, 253n69

Jacob, Walter (1930–), 2, 56, 261n38
Janowski, Max (1912–1991), 155, 156, 164, 169, 170, 186, 193, 286n94
Jehovah's Witnesses, 241
Jewish Music Month, *B'nai Israel Bulletin* 1985, 137; Heiser article on music, 137–138; Festival of Music, March 24, 1961, 82, 83; Grand Concert of Jewish Music, April 1, 1962, 84 (Cantors Meisels, Secunda, Heiser), 84; Jewish Music Festival March 9, 1954, 74, 75, ticket, 75, program (Cantors Lipson, Meisels, Heiser), 74, 75, 76
Jewish Theological Seminary, New York, 67, 70, breakfast honoring Cantor Heiser for 40 years of service, December 14, 1980, 70, 94
Jewish War Orphans' Fund, 167, 171
Jews, American, 53; first from Recife, Brazil 1654, 53; Sephardim, 53; deportation of Jews from Berlin 1941, 51; early enclaves in Europe, 7; Eastern European, 3, 54; excluded from German economy, 22; in Poland, 7; *Kehillot*, 9; music and Jewish life, 9; persecution, 7; no freedom of movement 1934, 22; police permit for travel, 22; Polish Jews' expulsion 1938, 24; synagogue as communal center, 9
Jonas, Hans, Pittsburgh photographer, 110

Judaica Sound Archives at Florida Atlantic University, 137
Jüdische Gemeinde Berlin, *Bestätigung* II, 25, 252n45; final recommendation for Cantor Heiser, 37

Kabbalah (Jewish mysticism), 145
Kaddish Shalem, 168, 171, 180, 206, 211, 220, 234, 236
Kahane, Dr., 35
Kalib, Sholom, 4, 10, 145, 169, 177, 183, 203, 207, 214, 215, 217, 218, 234, 249n1, 250n7, 277n2, 283nn62, 63, 64, 283n73, 283n77, 288n112, 289nn118, 119, 289n127, 290n134, 290n138, 291n142, 291n144, 291n145
Karsh, Claryne Bernstein, 134, 135, 167, 171, 205, 210, 219
Kaufmann, Jakob, 56
Kavanah (intent, concentration), 11, 139, 140, 143, 159
Kehilot, 9
Kennedy, Rena Anna Sufrin, 3, 137, 248n4, 251n14
Kimel, Rev. Benjamin M., 65
Kitchener Refugee Camp, Richborough, Kent, 37, 134, 258nn147, 148; Cantor Heiser served as precentor, 42; permit to leave camp, 42, **119**
Klafter, Mark, 104, Maccabiah Games Silver medalist 1985, 104
Klezmer, 145
Klinkerwerke (tile factory), 34, 256n112
Königstädtische Oberrealschule, Berlin; Heiser final report card, 13
"Kol Nidre," 148, 182, 183, 189; *mi Sinai* tune, 183, 184; Cantor Leo Gollanin, 184; Cantor Felix Asch, 184

Kristallnacht November 9–10, 1938, 8, 18, 30, 31–35, Heiser as witness in 1979 speech, 32
Kultusverwaltung der jüdischen Gemeinde zu Berlin, 16, 17; Heiser report card for cantorial school, 1929, 16, 17, 113, 252n37

Labor Zionist Movement of Pittsburgh, 65, 66
Large, David Clay, *Berlin*, 2000, 14, 252n33
Lazarus, Emma, "The New Colossus," 1883, 51, 260n20
Levinson, Nathan Peter, 28
Levinthal, Israel Herbert (1888–1982), 156
Leszczynski, Dr. W. Israel, 38, 257n135
Levites in Temple, 9
Lewandowski, Louis (1821–1894), 2, 3, 13, 17, 142, 150, 155, 163, 165, 173, 174, 177, 178, 179, 180, 182, 183, 184 , 185, 186, 189, 190, 191, 192, 196, 200, 206, 207, 208, 210, 213, 214, 215, 216, 218, 219, 227, 231, 232, 233, 235, 280n43; concert master of Neue Synagogue, 13; Lewandowski revival, 2; "Tavo L'Fanecha," 290n132
Lichter, Rabbi Benjamin A. (1886–1963), 44, 57; B'nai Israel rabbi from 1920–1957, 59, 74
Lieberson, Berta (Betti or Bayla) Hochmann (1906-deported 1942), 19, 44, 49
Lieberson, Leiser (Leo) (1904- deported 1942), 20, 44, 49; witness at Heiser wedding, 20, 21

Liebeschütz, Hans (1893–1978), 35, 256n118; teacher at *Hochschule*, 35
Lippman, Hyman, sexton or *shamash*, 60
"Living Word, The," radio and TV program on NBC, 67, 242, 266n98

Meisels, Cantor Saul, 84
Marcovitz, Rabbi Richard M. E., 69, 94; B'nai Israel rabbi from 1976–1996, 60; speech for Betty Sue's bat mitzvah, 232, 291n156
Maazel, Lorin, violinist for Pittsburgh Symphony Orchestra, 1949, 66
Meerberger, Emile, S.A., 39, 257nn138, 139
Melave malke (fourth meal at end of Shabbat), 59
Mentally and physically challenged persons, 241
Memorial service (*Yizkor*), 208, 242
Mi Sinai nusach, 169, 196, 207, 283n72
Minyan (quorum), 9
Misheberach (prayer for the sick), 229
Mizrachi, religious Zionist organization (1902), 14
Modes, also *Shtayger*, scales, 144, 282n58; Ahavah Rabah, 144; Magen Avot, 144; Adonai Malach, 144
Mohel (circumciser), 96
Music important in Jewish life, 9
Musikdirektor Aron Friedmann, 16
M. V. "Georgie" manifest, 42, 258n150

Nachama, Cantor Estrongo (1918–2000), 17, 69, 159, 288n105; Holocaust survivor, 17; and *hazzanut*, 17
Nathanson, Moshe (1899–1981), 73, 157, 210
Naumbourg, Cantor Samuel (1817–1880), 142, 150, 163, 206, 208, 215, 217, 281n45
Nazis, ascent to power 1933, 8, 240; Reichstag fire 1933, 8; boycott of Jewish businesses, 8
Ne'ilah service, 195
Neisser, Simon, 1938 letter, 17, **114**, 252n46
Neue Synagoge Berlin, dedicated 1866, 13
Niggun (tune), 173, 234
Niggunim, Hasidic, 2, 145, 146, 148, 163, 166, 239
Nowakowsky, David (1848–1921), 154, 197, 198, 202, 203, 285n87
Nuremberg Laws 1935, 8, 22, Law of German Blood and Honor, 22; Reich Citizenship Law, 22
Nusach (prayer mode), 143, 145, 147, 148, 149, 211; Ashkenazi, 17; High Holy Day *nusach*, 169, 172, 173, 177, 178, 179, 180, 190, 191, 192; Mi Sinai *nusach*, 169, 196, 207; Western European, 176; Eastern European, 145, 146, 155, 163, 176, 195; Shabbat *nusach*, 168, 175, 210, 211, 213, 220, 233, 235; Peregrinations of cantor, 289n120

Oberkantor Leo Gollanin, 16
Oberkantor Professor Felix Asch, 16
Olympics in Berlin 1936, 22
Organ, 133, 135
Osborn, Shannon, 96, 274n207

Palästina-Amt, Berlin, 15, immigration certificate, 15
Payyetan (poet), 148
Penitential season, 164
Perlmutter, Rev. Hyman, 60
Pesach (Passover), festival of, 9
Pestalozzi Street Synagogue, 17
Piyyut, 148, 207, 283Ch. 3n75; "Ki Hineh Kachomer," 187, 289n131; "Akdamut," 222, 290n141
Pittsburgh, PA, Jewish, 54–55, early Jewish settlers mid-nineteenth century, 55; East Liberty, 56; Fifty to sixty Jewish families 1860s, 56; Jewish population, 54–57; Lower Hill District, 56; Pittsburgh Platform 1885, 56; Squirrel Hill, 56; Stanton Heights Neighborhood 1950s, 61
Pittsburgh Cantors Association, 65, leadership of Rev. Zaludkowski, 65; Cantor Heiser secretary 1943, 65
Pittsburgh Concert Society concert 1949, 66, 67, 266n99, 266n101
Pittsburgh Friends of the Jewish Theological Seminary of America, Third annual dinner 1949, 67
Pittsburgh Opera Company, 66
Pogroms, 8, 51
Poland, period of kingship, 7
Polish intellectuals, 241
Polish Jews, 29, deported from Germany 1938, 24, 29; Moshe Sister, 29
Prinzregentenstrasse Synagogue, 32
Putterman, Cantor David J., 70, 73

Randall, Marga Silbermann, 54, 92, 272n192; *How Beautiful We Once Were*, 1998, 92

Randall, Jordan, 92
Rautenberg, Rabbi Charles, 49, 260n18
Rayner, Rabbi John D., also Hans Sigismund Rahmer (1924–2005), 18, 31, 184, 255n103, 258n144, 253n47; Heiser letter to Hans re visa 1938, 31; Letter to Elly Heiser 1990, 18, 109, 276n242, 289n128
Recorded Sound Archives, Florida Atlantic University Libraries, 137, 278n23
Recitative, 149, 166, 171, 180, 198, 225
Ritual Committee, also Religious Service Committee, 134, 135
Rodef Shalom Congregation founded in 1853, 56, National convention of rabbis in 1885, 56; Pittsburgh Platform 1885, 56
Roitman, Cantor David (1884–1943), 147
Rosenbaum, Hazzan Samuel, 73, 87, Letter on occasion of Cantor Heiser's twentieth anniversary with B'nai Israel, 83
Rosenblatt, Cantor Yossele, 69, 146, 147, 154, 159, 167, 171, 184, 240, "Chassidic Kaddish" in Cantor Heiser's *siddur*, 285n89, 285n90
Rosh Hashanah, 9
Routtenberg, Rabbi Max J., 72 267nn117, 118
Ruach (spirit), 143
Russian POWs, 241

Sabel, Sigmund (1849–1924), 156, 234, 236, 237
Sachsenhausen Concentration Camp, 4, 8, 22, 30, 31–35, 240
Sammel-Transport, 37, **119**, 257n130

Schechter, Rabbi Jack, 1966–1976, 59
Schestapol, Wolf (1832–1872), 154, 193, 285n88
Schleifer, Professor Cantor Eliyahu, xiii, 2, 4, 10, 147, 149, 165, 175, 176, 198, 205, 247n1, 249n5, 282n53, 282n58, 283n71, 284n79, 284n82, 287n99, 288nn113–14, 288n116, 289nn121–24, 290nn135–36, 290n139
Schmidt, Gilya Gerda, University of Pittsburgh, 1; letter to editor of *Jewish Chronicle* 1989, 108, 276n241
Scholem, Gershom, 26, 254n74
Schorr, Baruch (1823–1904), 154, 195, 199, 211, 220, 284n85
Schorr, Israel (1886–1935), 154, 196, 201, 202, 285n86
Second German Empire in 1871, 13
Secunda, Sholom (1894–1974), 83, 84, 149, 156, 175, 205, 206, 213, 287n98
Seder (Passover), 9
Service building, 147
Shabbat Musaf Service November 5, 1988, 233, 235, Guide, 233; Worksheet, 235–37
Shabbat Service May 2, 1981/28 Nisan 5741, 225–228, 227, 229, 231, Guide, 225; Worksheet, 229–232; Betty Sue Stein Bat Mitzvah, 229–239; *Birkat HaChodesh*, 225–7; Return of the Torah Service, 227, 232
Shalosh Regalim (Three Pilgrim Festivals), 154
Shanblatt, Sanford D, 94, 95, 273nn197, 198, 199

Shavuot (pilgrim festival), 205, Guide, 205; Worksheet, 212–24; Hallel service 1979, 205, 212; Musaf service 1980, 205, 210, 219, Musaf Kedushah, 210–211; Return of Torah service 1979, 207, 214, 217, 223, 232, Torah service 1979, 205, 206, 214; Yizkor service (*hazkarah*) 1983, 205, 224; 7 Sivan, second day of Shavuot, 209
Shtayger (ladder), 163, 169, 170, 171, 179, 282n58
Shtetl (Jewish village), 146
Siddur (prayer book), 143
Siegel, Morton, Director of United Synagogue of America, Department of Education, 87, 271n174
Silverman, Rabbi Morris, ed., Shabbat and Festival Prayer Book (*siddur*), 214, 227, 229, 231, 235, 284n80
Silverman High Holy Day Prayer Book (*machzor*), 177, 182, 189
Silverman, Wolf, JTS, 90
Simcha (celebration, happy occasion), 134, 159
Simcha Tree, two leaves from family and congregation, 98, 274nn210, 211
Simon, Hermann, on Neue Synagoge, 31, 251n28
Sinti and Roma, 241
Sister, Moshe, teacher at *Hochschule*, 29, 35; on 1937 examination committee for Cantor Heiser, 30
Slichot, 160, 163–71, Guide 163; Worksheet, 169–71; "Slichot" booklet, The Rabbinical Assembly, 1964, 163, 169
Slobin, Mark, 4, 146, 163, 169, 239, 260nn25, 26, 27, 288nn109, 110,

Slobin, Mark, (*cont.*)
111, 289n120, 291n1, *Chosen Voices: the Story of the American Cantorate*, 2002/1998, 169

Smolover, Cantor Raymond, 87

Soundscape, 239

Spanier, Dr. Arthur Israel (1889–1944), Lecturer at *Hochschule*, 36, 257n127

Stained-glass windows by Jean-Jacques Duval, 62, 263n64

Stein, Adele, 2, 102, 104, 227, 231, bat mitzvah 1976, 90, 104; marriage to Warren Sufrin, 102

Stein, Alvin, 88, 239, 269n144

Stein, Betty Sue, 2, 95, 96, 97, 106, 136, 158, 164, 165, 170, 172, 174, 176, 181, 185, 186, 187, 188, 190, 192, 193, 205, 208, 210, 211, 213, 218, 220, 223, 225, 226, 229, 230 231, 232; bat mitzvah 1981, 95, 159, 225; Bat mitzvah speech, 136, 227, 228, 232, 278n16, 291n155; Betty Sue and grandfather Cantor Mordecai G. Heiser, **126**

Stein, Judith Heiser, xi, 2, 22, 225, 229, 239, 240; Judith and Alvin Stein wedding June 2, 1957, 81, **124**

Stein Shari, 225, Confirmation 1980, 93, 159, 205, 210, 223, 230; marriage to Mark Klafter in 1988, 104

Stern Conservatory, founded in 1850, 16, 252n39

Struck, Hermann (1876–1944), 14, 252n35; emigrated to Eretz Israel in 1920, 14; German war artist, 14; house in Haifa built by Max Baerwald, Berlin, 15; Jewish etcher and engraver, 14; letter to Gustav Heiser 1933, 15

Sudock, Charles, 73

Sufrin, Warren J., 102, marriage to Adele Stein 1987, 104

Sukkah (hut), 9

Sukkot (Tabernacles), festival of, 9

Sulzer, Salomon (1804–1890), 2, 3, 17, 133, 142, 145, 152, 155, 163, 165, 173, 174, 177, 178, 179, 180, 185, 186, 190, 191, 196, 200, 201, 206, 207, 208, 209, 210, 211, 217, 219, 220, 224, 232, 233, 234, 235, 236, 280n44

Synagogue as communal center, 9

Tabachnick, Toby, *The Jewish Chronicle*, Pittsburgh, PA, 111

Tachanun (supplications), 167

Talmon, Zvi (Monsohn) (1922–2012), Hechal Shlomo, 156, 187, 194, 205, 212, 287n99, 290n137

Taube, Cantor Moshe (1927–2020), 89, 96, 271n180

Täubler, Eugen (1879–1953), 28, 35, 36, Founder of *Gesamtarchiv der deutschen Juden* in 1906, 28 Teacher at *Hochschule*, 28

Tefillah (prayer), 164

Teshuvah (repentance), 164

Third Seder Committee of United Jewish Fund, 66

Torczyner, Harry (1886–1973), 28, 254n92; emigrated to Palestine, 29; teacher at *Hochschule*, 28

Trop (chant for Torah reading), 173, 178

United States, citizenship, 52; Nation of immigrants until 1924, 51; re-

strictions to immigration starting in 1924, 51
University of Pittsburgh, Nationality Rooms, 57; Israel Heritage Room, 57

Vander, Judith, 4, *Songprints: The Musical Experience of Five Shoshone Women*, 1988; 4, 137, 249n6
Viddui (confession), 188
Vigoda, Cantor Samuel (1892–1990), 146
Vinaver, Chemjo (1895–1973), 166; *Anthology of Jewish Music*, 166, 171

Weiss, Josef, 20
Weiss, Sophie Birnbaum, 20, 103
Weissensee Jewish Cemetery, 2, 141, 131, 251n16, 253n54
Wiener, Rabbi Max (1882–1950), 27, 35, 36, 254n83; on Cantor Heiser's 1937 examination committee, 30
Wilkinsburg Civic Symphony, 96
Winsviertel map, Berlin, 19
Wohlberg, Cantor Max, 70
Word repetition, 180
World War II begins on September 1, 1939, 51; United States enters World War II on December 7, 1941, 51

Yiddish Songs, 239
Yizkor Service (*hazkarah*), 208; dedication of memorial plaques, 209; Memorial Service, 208; Yizkor prayers, 209
Yom HaShoah (Holocaust Remembrance Day, 242

Yom Kippur, 9, 185; Special for Yom Kippur: High Priest enters Holy of Holies, 185; On this day, atonement shall be made, 186; Kol Nidre, 182, 189, Guide, 182; Worksheet, 189–194; *Ne'ilah*, 195, 196, 199; Guide, 195; Worksheet, 199–204
Younger, Louis, The Working Man's Store, Bakersfield, CA, 48, 260n16
YouTube, 5, 162; YouTube.com, M. G. Heiser, 162: No. 1 "L'chu N'ran'nah LAdonai," 164; No. 2 "Han'shamah lach," 165; No. 3 "Ta'azin shav'atenu," 165; No. 4 "Lishmoa el harinah," 165; No. 5 "Ashamnu," 166; No. 6 "Shomer Israel, 167; No. 7 "Entire Erev Rosh Hashanah Service," 172; No. 8 "Kol Nidre," 182; No. 9 "V'nislach," 184; No. 10 "Ya'ale," 186; No. 11 Amidah," 195; No. 12 "P'sach lonu" and "Hayom yifneh," 196; No. 13 Four Piyyutim, 197; No. 14 Torah Service, 206; No. 15 "Akdamut," 207; No. 16 Return of the Torah Service, 207; No. 17 "El Male Rachamim," 209; No. 18 Musaf Service 1980, 210; No. 19 *Birchat HaChodesh*, 225; No. 20 "Sim Shalom," 233

Zedakah (charity), 164
Zellner, Elli (1903–deported?), 44, 47, 49, 103
Zellner, Julius (1917–deported?), 44, 46, 48, 103
Zellner, Joel (1940?–deported?), 44, 47

Zionist Organization of America (ZOA), 84–86, 240, 242; Cantor Heiser becomes chairman of local membership campaign 1961, 85; First Annual Classical Zionist Award 1987, 102; Israel Bonds Chanukkah concert 1962, 85, **125**; Kimel, Hyman H., director of ZOA, 102, Member of Board of Directors of Tri-State region, 102; Mordecai and Elly Heiser ZOA Masada Foundation Fund, 1987, 102; Music of *chalutzim*, 85; "Sing along with Cantor Heiser" starting in 1961, 85; Twenty-third Annual Anniversary Celebration (for Israel) 1971, 88, (Cantors Gold, Heiser, Silversmith, Taube), 89; **128**

Zohar (Kabbalistic publication), 145

www.ingramcontent.com/pod-product-compliance
Lightning Source LLC
Chambersburg PA
CBHW060513080526
44586CB00012B/469